Why Do You Need This New Edition?

If you're wondering why you should buy this new edition of *A Short Guide to Writing about Literature*, here are six good reasons!

1. **A new chapter on graphic novels (Chapter 11)** offers guidance for writing about a fast-emerging genre.

2. **A new chapter on writing about poems and pictures (Chapter 14)** explores the challenges of assignments that ask for comparisons of these two genres.

3. **New literary selections** for analysis and interpretation, including poems by Gwendolyn Brooks and William Blake, as well as the Parable of the Prodigal Son (see **Chapters 4 and 7**).

4. **A new appendix on plagiarism**—including a quick self-review quiz—enables you to test yourself on your use of sources.

5. **Expanded coverage of Internet resources** provides a wider range of sources for your literary assignments in explication, analysis, and comparison.

6. **A new section on synthesis (Chapter 17)** encourages students to understand and practice this critical skill.

PEARSON

D1250413

THE SHORT GUIDE SERIES
FROM PEARSON LONGMAN

■   ■   ■

Series Editors
SYLVAN BARNET AND MARCIA STUBBS

A Short Guide to Writing about Art
SYLVAN BARNET

A Short Guide to Writing about Biology
JAN PECHENIK

A Short Guide to Writing about Chemistry
HOLLY DAVIS, JULIAN TYSON, AND JAN PECHENIK

A Short Guide to Writing about Film
TIMOTHY CORRIGAN

A Short Guide to Writing about History
RICHARD MARIUS AND MELVIN PAGE

A Short Guide to Writing about Law
KATIE ROSE GUEST PRYAL

A Short Guide to Writing about Literature
SYLVAN BARNET AND WILLIAM E. CAIN

A Short Guide to Writing about Music
JONATHAN BELLMAN

A Short Guide to Writing about Psychology
DANA S. DUNN

A Short Guide to Writing about the Social Sciences
LEE J. CUBA

A Short Guide to Writing about Theater
MARCIA L. FERGUSON

A Short Guide to Writing about Literature

TWELFTH EDITION

SYLVAN BARNET
Tufts University

WILLIAM E. CAIN
Wellesley College

Boston   Columbus   Indianapolis   New York   San Francisco   Upper Saddle River
Amsterdam   Cape Town   Dubai   London   Madrid   Milan   Munich   Paris   Montreal   Toronto
Delhi   Mexico City   São Paulo   Sydney   Hong Kong   Seoul   Singapore   Taipei   Tokyo

Publisher: Joseph Opiela
Senior Media Producer: Stefanie Liebman
Senior Marketing Manager: Sandra McGuire
Production Manager: Eric Jorgensen
Project Coordination, Text Design, and Electronic Page Makeup:
   Nesbitt Graphics, Inc.
Cover Design Manager: John Callahan
Cover Image: © Kimmet/Dreamtime.com
Visual Researcher: Rona Tuccillo
Senior Manufacturing Buyer: Roy L. Pickering, Jr.
Printer and Binder: Edwards Brothers
Cover Printer: Lehigh Phoenix

Credits and acknowledgments borrowed from other sources and reproduced, with permission, in this textbook appear on pages 373–374.

Library of Congress Cataloging-in-Publication Data

Barnet, Sylvan.
   A short guide to writing about literature / Sylvan Barnet, William E. Cain.—12th ed.
      p. cm.—(The short guide series)
   Includes bibliographical references and indexes.
   ISBN-13: 978-0-205-11845-8
   ISBN-10: 0-205-11845-3
   1. English language–Rhetoric–Handbooks, manuals, etc. 2. Literature–History
and criticism–Theory, etc.–Handbooks, manuals, etc. 3. Criticism–Authorship–
Handbooks, manuals, etc. 4. Exposition (Rhetoric)–Handbooks, manuals, etc.
5. Report writing–Handbooks, manuals, etc. I. Cain, William E., 1952- II. Title.
   PE1479.C7B3 2011
   808'.0668--dc23

                                                                      2011020175

1 2 3 4 5 6 7 8 9 10—EB—14 13 12 11

www.pearsonhighered.com
ISBN-13: 978-0-205-11845-8
ISBN-10: 0-205-11845-3

CONTENTS

Preface xvi
Letter to Students xix

PART 1
Jumping In

1—WRITING ABOUT LITERATURE: A CRASH COURSE 2

The Pleasures of Reading—and of Writing about Literature 2
The Open Secret of Good Writing 3
The Writing Process 4
✔ *Checklist: The Basics* 7

2—THE WRITER AS READER: READING AND RESPONDING 8

Kate Chopin, "Ripe Figs" 8
The Act of Reading 9
Reading with a Pen in Hand 11
Recording Your First Responses 12
Audience and Purpose 13
A Writing Assignment on "Ripe Figs" 14
The Assignment 14
A Sample Essay: "Images of Ripening in Kate Chopin's 'Ripe Figs'" 14
The Student's Analysis Analyzed 16
Critical Thinking and the Study of Literature 17

3—THE READER AS WRITER: DRAFTING AND WRITING 19

Pre-writing: Getting Ideas 19

Annotating a Text   19

More about Getting Ideas: A Second Story by Kate Chopin, "The Story of an Hour"   20

Kate Chopin, "The Story of an Hour"   20

Brainstorming for Ideas for Writing   22

Focused Free Writing   23

Listing   24

Asking Questions   25

Keeping a Journal   26

Critical Thinking: Arguing with Yourself   27

Arriving at a Thesis and Arguing It   29

Writing a Draft   31

A Sample Draft: "Ironies in an Hour"   31

Revising a Draft   33

✔ *Checklist: Revising for Clarity   34*

Two Ways of Outlining a Draft   35

✔ *Checklist: Reviewing a Revised Draft   36*

Peer Review   37

The Final Version   39

Sample Essay: "Ironies of Life in Kate Chopin's 'The Story of an Hour'"   39

The Students Analysis Analyzed   41

Quick Review

From First Response to Final Version: Writing an Essay about a Literary Work   42

4—TWO FORMS OF CRITICISM: EXPLICATION AND ANALYSIS   43

Explication   43

A Sample Explication: Langston Hughes's "Harlem"   43

Working toward an Explication of "Harlem"   44

Some Journal Entries   46

The Final Draft: "Langston Hughes's 'Harlem'"   48

The Explication Analyzed 49
✔ *Checklist: Drafting an Explication 50*
Analysis: The Judgment of Solomon 51
   Thinking about Form 52
   Thinking about Character 53
   Thoughts about Other Possible Topics 53
For Further Study and Analysis 55
   The Parable of the Prodigal Son 55
   Comparison: An Analytic Tool 56
✔ *Checklist: Revising a Comparison 59*
For Further Reading and Comparing 60
   Gwendolyn Brooks's "We Real Cool" 60
Finding a Topic 60
Considering the Evidence 61
Organizing the Material 61
Communicating Judgments 62
Review: How to Write an Effective Essay 63
   1. Pre-writing 63
   2. Drafting 64
   3. Revising 65
   4. Editing 66
✔ *Editing Checklist: Questions to Ask Yourself
      When Editing 67*
For Further Reading, Explication, and Comparison 68
   William Blake's "The Tyger" 68

5—OTHER KINDS OF WRITING ABOUT LITERATURE 70

A Summary 70
A Paraphrase 72
A Review 73
   A Review of a Dramatic Production 74
   A Sample Review: "An Effective Macbeth" 75*

PART 2
Standing Back:
Thinking Critically about Literature

6—LITERATURE, FORM, AND MEANING   80

Literature and Form   80
   Literature and Meaning   83
   Arguing about Meaning   84
Form and Meaning   85
   Robert Frost, "The Span of Life"   85
Literature, Texts, Discourses, and Cultural Studies   86
   Suggestions for Further Reading   87

7—WHAT IS INTERPRETATION?   89

Interpretation and Meaning   89
Is the Author's Intention a Guide to Meaning?   90
Features of a Good Interpretation   91
An Example: Interpreting Pat Mora's "Immigrants"   92
Thinking Critically about Literature   94
A Student Interpretation of Robert Frost's "Stopping by Woods on a Snowy Evening"   95
   A Sample Essay: "Stopping by Woods and Going On"   96
   ✔ *Checklist: Writing an Interpretation   99*
For Further Interpretation, Comparison, and Writing   100
   Suggestions for Further Reading   100

8—WHAT IS EVALUATION?   101

Criticism and Evaluation   101
Are There Critical Standards?   102
   Morality and Truth as Standards   103
   Other Ways to Think about Truth and Realism   104
   Suggestions for Further Reading   106

9—WRITING ABOUT LITERATURE: AN OVERVIEW   108

    The Nature of Critical Writing   108

    Some Critical Approaches   109

      Formalist Criticism (New Criticism)   110

      Deconstruction   112

      Reader-Response Criticism   113

      Archetypal (or Myth) Criticism   115

      Historical Criticism   116

      Marxist Criticism   117

      New Historicism   117

      Biographical Criticism   118

      Psychological (or Psychoanalytic) Criticism   119

      Gender (Feminist, and Lesbian and Gay) Criticism   119

 Suggestions for Further Reading   123

PART 3

Up Close: Thinking Critically about Literary Forms

10—WRITING ABOUT FICTION: THE WORLD OF THE STORY   130

    Plot and Character   130

      Writing about a Character   132

      A Sample Essay on a Character: "Holden's Kid Sister"   135

      The Student's Analysis Analyzed   137

    Foreshadowing   137

      Organizing an Essay on Foreshadowing   140

    Setting and Atmosphere   140

    Symbolism   141

      A Sample Essay on Setting as Symbol: "Spring Comes to Mrs. Mallard"   143

      "Spring Comes to Mrs. Mallard"   144

Point of View   147

   Third-Person Narrators   147

   First-Person Narrators   149

Notes and a Sample Essay on Narrative Point of View in James Joyce's "Araby"   151

   A Sample Essay: "The Three First-Person Narrators of Joyce's 'Araby' "   152

   The Student's Analysis Analyzed   154

Theme: Vision or Argument?   155

   Determining and Discussing the Theme   156

Preliminary Notes and a Sample Essay on the Theme of Eudora Welty's "A Worn Path"   156

   Preliminary Notes   157

   "Rising into Love" (on Welty's "A Worn Path")   160

   A Brief Overview of the Essay   163

   ✔ *Checklist: Writing about Theme   163*

   Basing the Paper on Your Own Responses   164

   A Note on Secondary Sources   164

A Second Essay about Theme: Notes and the Final Version of an Essay on Shirley Jackson's "The Lottery"   167

   "We All Participate in 'The Lottery' "   169

   The Student's Analysis Analyzed   171

 Suggestions for Further Reading   171

   ✔ *Checklist: Getting Ideas for Writing about Fiction   172*

   ✔ *Checklist: Getting Ideas for Writing about a Film Based on a Work of Literature   176*

11—GRAPHIC FICTION   179

Letters and Pictures   179

   Grant Wood's Death on the Ridge Road *(painting)   181*

Topic for Writing   183

Reading an Image: A Short Story Told in One Panel   183

   Tony Carrillo's F Minus   183

12—WRITING ABOUT DRAMA   187

A Sample Essay   187
Preliminary Notes   188
A Sample Essay: "The Solid Structure of The Glass Menagerie"   *189*
Types of Plays   193
Tragedy   193
✔ *Checklist: Writing about Tragedy   197*
Comedy   197
✔ *Checklist: Writing about Comedy   199*
Aspects of Drama   199
Theme   199
Plot   201
✔ *Checklist: Writing about Plot   204*
Characterization and Motivation   206
Conventions   207
Costumes, Gestures, and Settings   208
A Sample Essay on Setting in Drama: "What the Kitchen in *Trifles* Tells Us"   210
"What the Kitchen in Trifles *Tells Us   211*
The Student's Analysis Analyzed   213
Suggestions for Further Reading   213
✔ *Checklist: Getting Ideas for Writing about Drama   214*
✔ *Checklist: Getting Ideas for Writing about a Film Based on a Play   216*
A Student's Essay on a Filmed Version of a Play: "Branagh's Film of *Hamlet*"   217
✔ *Checklist: Topics for Critical Thinking and Writing   220*

13—WRITING ABOUT POETRY   221

The Speaker and the Poet   221
Emily Dickinson, "Wild Nights–Wild Nights!"   222
The Language of Poetry: Diction and Tone   223

Edna St. Vincent Millay, "I, being born a woman and distressed"   224

Writing about the Speaker: Robert Frost's "The Telephone"   227

Robert Frost, "The Telephone"   227

Journal Entries   228

Figurative Language   231

John Keats, "On First Looking into Chapman's Homer"   232

Preparing to Write about Figurative Language   235

William Blake, "The Sick Rose"   236

Structure   237

Annotating and Thinking about a Poem   237

Robert Herrick, "Upon Julia's Clothes"   238

The Student's Finished Essay: "Herrick's Julia, Julia's Herrick"   239

Some Kinds of Structure   241

William Wordsworth, "A Slumber Did My Spirit Seal"   241

John Donne, "The Flea"   242

Verbal Irony   244

Paradox   244

Explication   244

A Sample Explication of Yeats's "The Balloon of the Mind"   245

William Butler Yeats, "The Balloon of the Mind"   245

Rhythm and Versification: A Glossary for Reference   248

Rhythm   248

Meter   250

Patterns of Sound   253

Stanzaic Patterns   255

Blank Verse and Free Verse   255

Walt Whitman, "When I Heard the Learn'd Astronomer"   256

Preparing to Write about Prosody   258

Sample Essay on Metrics: "Sound and Sense in A. E. Housman's 'Eight O'Clock'"   259

The Student's Analysis Analyzed   262

Suggestions for Further Reading   263

✔ *Checklist: Getting Ideas for Writing about Poetry   264*

14—POEMS AND PICTURES   267

A Poem and a Sample Student Essay   269

Vincent van Gogh, The Starry Night (painting)   269

Anne Sexton, "The Starry Night"   270

A Sample Essay: "Two Ways of Looking at a Starry Night"   270

Topics for Critical Thinking and Writing   271

The Language of Pictures   272

Writing about Pictures   273

Comparing and Contrasting   274

William Notman, Foes in '76, Friends in '85 (photograph)   275

Analyzing and Evaluating Evidence   276

Thinking Critically: Arguing with Oneself, Asking Questions, and Comparing—E. E. Cummings's "Buffalo Bill 's"   277

A Writing Assignment: Connecting a Picture with a Work of Literature   278

A Sample Essay: "Two Views of Buffalo Bill"   279

Topic for Writing   280

15—WRITING ABOUT AN AUTHOR IN DEPTH   281

A Case Study: Writing about Langston Hughes   282

Langston Hughes, "The South"   283

Langston Hughes, "Ruby Brown"   285
Langston Hughes, "Ballad of the Landlord"   286
A Sample Essay: "A National Problem: Race and Racism in the Poetry of Langston Hughes"   287
A Brief Overview of the Essay   290

PART 4
Inside: Style, Format, and Special Assignments

16—STYLE AND FORMAT   292

Principles of Style   292
Get the Right Word   293
Write Effective Sentences   297
✔ *Checklist: Revising for Conciseness   299*
Write Unified and Coherent Paragraphs   301
✔ *Checklist: Revising Paragraphs   307*
Write Emphatically   308
Notes on the Dash and the Hyphen   309
Remarks about Manuscript Form   309
Basic Manuscript Form   309
Quotations and Quotation Marks   310

17—WRITING A RESEARCH PAPER   315

What Research Is Not, and What Research Is   315
Primary and Secondary Materials   316
Locating Material: First Steps   316
Other Bibliographic Aids   318
The Basics   318
Moving Ahead: Finding Sources for Research Work   319

What Does Your Own Institution Offer? 319

Taking Notes 320

Incorporating Your Reading into Your Thinking: How to Use and Synthesize Sources 322

Drafting Your Paper 325

Focus on Primary Sources 326

Documentation 327

   What to Document: Avoiding Plagiarism 327

✔ *Checklist: Avoiding Plagiarism* 328

   How to Document: Internal Parenthetical Citations and a List of Works Cited (MLA Format) 329

Sample Essay with Documentation: "The Women in *Death of a Salesman"* 340

✔ *Checklist: Reading the Draft of a Research Paper* 347

Electronic Sources 348

   Encyclopedias: Print and Electronic Versions 348

The Internet and the Web 348

Evaluating Sources Internet Web sites 349

✔ *Checklist: Using Web sites on the Internet* 349

   Wikipedia 350

Documentation: Citing a Web Source 350

✔ *Checklist: Citing Internet Sources* 350

APPENDIX A: TWO STORIES 353

   James Joyce, "Araby" 353

   Eudora Welty, "A Worn Path" 357

APPENDIX B: HOW MUCH DO YOU KNOW ABOUT CITING SOURCES? A QUIZ WITH ANSWERS 364

Credits 373

Index of Authors, Titles, and First Lines of Poems 375

Index of Terms 379

Preface

We have been pleased to learn that *A Short Guide to Writing about Literature*, which seeks to help students to write analytically about fiction, poetry, drama, and film, has been used in a wide range of literature courses. It is perhaps most suitable for courses that combine intensive work in composition with an introduction to literature; introductory courses in literature, or in a major literary genre; and required courses—in research, writing, or both—designed for English majors. Instructors have also found it appropriate for courses taken during the first year of graduate school in which skills in literary analysis, effective writing, and research are given special attention.

For the twelfth edition, we have revised the text throughout, making changes and adjustments in word choice and phrase, revising and updating chapters, and including new chapters. The most evident changes are:

- **A new chapter on graphic fiction (Chapter 11)** offers guidance for writing about a fast-emerging genre.
- **A new chapter on writing about poems and pictures (Chapter 14)** explores the challenges of assignments that ask for comparisons of these two genres.
- **New literary selections** for analysis and interpretation, including poems by Gwendolyn Brooks, William Blake, Robert Frost, and Anne Sexton, as well as the Parable of the Prodigal Son.
- **Expanded coverage of Internet resources** provides a wider range of sources for your literary assignments in explication, analysis, and comparison.
- **A new section on synthesis (Chapter 17)** encourages students to understand and practice this critical skill.
- **New checklists** on writing an interpretation and writing about theme.
- **Updated bibliographies and suggestions for further reading**.
- **Updated MLA instructions concerning style and format.**
- **A new appendix on plagiarism**—including a quick self-review quiz—enables you to test yourself on your use of sources.

Even as we revised *A Short Guide*, we preserved much that our colleagues and our students have told us is valuable, such as:

- Examples of preliminary notes, drafts, and revisions of drafts
- Lists of questions that one can ask about a literary work
- Checklists that one can use as a way of evaluating a draft.

Why does anyone write about literature? The answer, we think, is that the act of writing helps a reader to understand and to enjoy literature. Listen to Ralph Waldo Emerson on the connection between reading and writing:

> The best of all ways to make one's reading valuable is to write about it.

To this comment we can append one by Ernest Gaines:

> The six Golden Rules of writing: Read, read, read, and Write, write, write.

Why? Because, as John Updike says,

> You always find things you didn't know you were going to say, and that is the adventure of writing.

We will now survey the contents of *A Short Guide to Writing about Literature*, 12th Edition.

Part 1 (five chapters emphasizing the close connection between reading and writing) assumes that we cannot write well unless we can read well. If nothing else, we must be able to read *our own* prose thoughtfully. Reading, after all, is a way of getting ideas for writing. These early chapters emphasize the importance in the writing process of such activities as annotating a text, brainstorming, keeping a journal, and (especially) asking oneself questions in order to generate ideas. (Although these activities are often called "pre-writing," they are in fact part of the process of writing.) Explication and analysis are discussed and illustrated with examples.

Part 2 (four chapters on thinking critically about literature) looks at some definitions of literature; considers the relationships among interpretation, meaning, and evaluation; gives advice about writing persuasive arguments; and then offers a survey of some of the chief critical approaches.

Part 3 (six chapters on writing about fiction, drama, and poetry) introduces the reader to the elements of each genre, and looks back to Part 1 and provides drafts and essays by students on representative works. In accordance with the assumption in Part 1 that asking questions is an invaluable way of getting ideas, each chapter on writing about a genre concludes with a checklist of questions that readers may ask themselves as they read, reread, and think about a work. The essays by students are accompanied either by marginal annotations or by analytic overviews following the essays.

Part 4 contains three chapters. The first of these, **"Style and Format,"** is a short and direct approach to the elements of clear writing. It treats such matters as denotation, connotation, subordination, and paragraphing. The latter part of the chapter, devoted to manuscript form, is concerned chiefly with mechanical matters, ranging from the form of the title of an essay to advice on how to introduce quotations. The second chapter in this section, **"Writing a Research Paper,"** includes material on discovering a topic and thesis, on finding materials, on using the MLA system of documentation, and on working with electronic resources.

Two appendixes follow: Appendix A includes **two stories** ("Araby" and "A Worn Path") that are the subjects of student essays, printed in the book; Appendix B, a quiz about using sources, allows you to test your understanding of what constitutes plagiarism.

We hope that the preceding remarks adequately describe the scope of the book, but some further words must be added. The eighteenth-century critic and essayist Samuel Johnson said:

> There is not so poor a book in the world that would not be a prodigious effort were it wrought out entirely by a single mind, without the aid of previous investigators.

We cannot name all of the previous investigators who have helped shape our ideas about literature, and about teaching and writing, but we want to acknowledge our indebtedness to Morton Berman, William Burto, and Marcia Stubbs, who never tire of improving our pages. One of us, William E. Cain, would like to thank his wife Barbara, and his daughters, Julia and Isabel, for their love and support. At Pearson, we are grateful for invaluable help to Virginia Blanford, Rebecca Gilpin, and Eric Jorgenen. We are also grateful to Vernon Nahrgang for copyediting, Charles Gandy for proofreading, and Lois Lombardo for supervising the production of the book. The findings of their eagle-eyes daily reminded us that every author needs editorial help. We urge all students to submit their writing to a fellow-student, for editorial suggestions, before submitting it to the instructor.

We are grateful for the comments of the following reviewers: Diane Susan Beckman, North Carolina State University; Ian Ferris Roberts, Missouri Western State University; Peter J. Fields, Midwestern State University; and A. G. (Jerry) Wemple, Bloomsburg University.

SYLVAN BARNET
WILLIAM E. CAIN

Letter to Students

We do not need to define "literature" here because you probably already have a pretty good idea of what it is—things like *Hamlet* and "Stopping by Woods on a Snowy Evening" and *The Color Purple*—and because you will be refining and deepening this idea throughout the course in which you are using this book. Still, a very brief comment may be useful. Robert Frost said that literature is "A performance in words," a point that we discuss at some length on page 102, and to some degree all of us, from time to time, engage in such a performance. When we sing a song, whether "The Farmer in the Dell" in kindergarten or "Auld Lang Syne" at a party on New Year's Eve, we are engaging in a performance in words. We are not creating literature but we are at least re-creating it, and providing entertainment—recreation—for ourselves. Similarly, when we tell a joke to a friend we are giving a performance in words: Like a short-story writer or a novelist, we are narrating an invented story, an episode that never really happened, and we are telling it as skillfully as we can. Or if in a friendly discussion we say, "Well, let's assume for the sake of argument that Professor Jones assigns her students . . . ," we are again constructing a make-believe world. Further, if we make a pun, or engage in any sort of wordplay, or call someone "Mr. Knowitall," we are using language metaphorically, and thereby we are engaging in a performance in words. Or think for a moment about the nonstandard language we use in the act of texting, for instance, the use of *b* for *be*.

Consider the following performance in words by Julia Bird. Bird entered a poetry contest sponsored by a British publication, *The Guardian*. The ground rules: Write a poem limited to the 160 characters of the mobile phone screen. Bird's poem won a Special Prize of £250 (something like $400) for what *The Guardian* called "the most creative use of SMS 'shorthand' in a poem."

> 14: a txt msg pom.
> his is r bunsn brnr bl%,
> his hair lyk fe filings
> W/ac/dc going thru.
> I sit by him in kemistry,

it splits my @oms
wen he :-)s @ me.

Translation:

14: a text message poem.
his eyes are bunsen burner blue,
his hair like iron filings
with ac/dc going through.
I sit by him in chemistry,
it splits my atoms
when he smiles at me.

Joining the Conversation: Critical Thinking and Writing

1. Do you agree that Bird's work is a "performance"? Why, or why not?
   The use of *r* for *are* in line 1 is certainly not original, but do you find
   some things in this piece that strike you as highly imaginative and especially entertaining?

2. Do you think that the translation itself is something of a performance
   in words? If you think it is, which performance do you prefer? Why?

3. Imagine that you are the person about whom Julia Bird wrote her
   poem. Are you pleased, or not? Write a txt pom in response.

As you can tell from a glance at the Contents, *A Short Guide to
Writing about Literature* includes practical advice about reading and responding to literature and writing analytical papers, advice that comes
directly from our experience not only as readers and writers but also as
teachers. This experience derives from classrooms, from conferences
with students, and from assignments we have given, read, responded to,
and graded. We have learned from our experiences and have done our
best to give you the tools that will help you make yourself a more perceptive reader and a more careful, cogent writer.

We cannot claim to equip you for the rest of your life—though some
of these works of literature surely will remain in your mind for years—
but we do claim that, with your instructor, we are helping you to develop
skills that are important for your mental progress. We have in mind skills
that are useful not merely in the course in which you are now enrolled,
or other literature courses, or even courses in the humanities in general
that you may take. We go further. We think that these skills in reading

and writing are important for your development as an educated adult. Becoming an alert reader and an effective writer should be among the central goals of your education, and they are goals that *A Short Guide to Writing about Literature* is designed to help you to reach.

The skills we stress in *A Short Guide to Writing about Literature* will enable you to gain confidence as a reader of literary works so that you will increase your understanding of what literature offers. You need not enjoy all authors equally. You will have your favorites—and also some authors whom you do not much like. There is nothing wrong with that; reading literature is very much a personal encounter. But at the same time, the skills we highlight in *A Short Guide to Writing about Literature* can help you to know and explain why one author means much to you and another does not. In this respect, reading and studying literature is more than personal; as we share our responses and try to express them effectively in writing, the work that we perform becomes cooperative and communal, a conversation among fellow students, teachers, and friends.

As you proceed through *A Short Guide to Writing about Literature* and gain further experience as a reader and writer, you will start to see features of poems, stories, and plays that you had not noticed before, or that you had noticed but not really understood, or that you had understood but not fully experienced. You may even find yourself enjoying an author you thought you disliked and would never be able to understand. The study of literature calls for concentration, commitment, and discipline. It is work—sometimes hard, challenging work. But it is rewarding work, and we believe that it will lead you to find literature more engaging and more pleasurable.

We hope that *A Short Guide to Writing about Literature* will have this effect for you. Feel free to contact us with your comments and suggestions. We are eager to know what in this book has served you well, and what we might do better.

SYLVAN BARNET
WILLIAM E. CAIN

PART 1

Jumping In

1

WRITING ABOUT LITERATURE: A CRASH COURSE

Literary criticism [is] . . . a reasoned account of the feeling pro-
duced upon the critic by the book he is criticizing.
— D. H. Lawrence

THE PLEASURES OF READING—AND OF WRITING ABOUT LITERATURE

"The pleasures of reading," some may say, are obvious, "but when it comes to talking about the 'pleasures' of writing, surely you must be kidding." Students who make this reply have on their side the authority of a good many distinguished writers. Ernest Hemingway is reported to have said, "There is nothing to writing. All you do is sit down at a typewriter and bleed"; and in our own day the novelist William Styron said, "Let's face it, writing is hell."

Every student and every professor understands what these writers are talking about. The bad news is that they are talking about the challenging job that you will be doing—getting on to paper some coherent thoughts that are good enough to share with a reader. (You will be writing not only in this course but also in other courses and probably in whatever jobs you hold after leaving college.) But there is good news too: All writers know that the very act of writing will stimulate *better* thoughts than those they begin with. Writers—professionals as well as students—put words on paper with the understanding that the *process of writing* is a way of getting better ideas, a way of improving the nearly incoherent stuff that at first drifts through our minds.

- *A Common Misapprehension:* Students often think they are writing "for the teacher." Such an assumption leads to (a) attempts to guess what this mysterious figure has in mind, and (b) writing that satisfies neither the student nor the instructor.
- *The Facts:* You are, first of all, writing *for yourself*: you are trying to clarify something. The instructor may have set the problem— let us say (to take a famous example), "Is Hamlet mad or only pretending to be?"—or the problem may be one of your own choosing, possibly even so broad and so basic as "Why don't I care for this work?" In any event, you start looking again at the text, thoughts and ideas come to mind, and you make notes of them. Then perhaps you comment on these notes, amplifying them, almost immediately seeing that even though you wrote them only a few seconds ago you no longer agree with them. Again, you are writing in order to explain something *to yourself*.
- Finally, of course, you will revise your thoughts and offer them to the instructor and perhaps to your classmates, *in an effort to persuade readers to see things your way.* You have listened to yourself, quarreled with yourself, taught yourself something, arrived at a place where you think you at last have some clear and coherent ideas, and now you want to teach your readers.

The Open Secret of Good Writing

We have just said that in drafting your essay you have "quarreled with yourself." One of the great open secrets of effective writing is this: Good writers are good critics *of their own writing.* They know that "writing is rewriting." When writers reread their own writing, they read in a skeptical spirit, arguing with themselves

- "Have I adequately supported this point?"
- "Have I considered all of the possible counter-evidence?"
- "Do I really want to say . . . ? Ought I to have said . . . ?"
- "Come to think of it, there aren't two reasons but three reasons why I think such-and-such," and so forth.

Your pleasure in writing will come chiefly from your awareness that you are *improving* your writing, getting better ideas than those that you had at the beginning. You will feel pleasure, too, knowing that you are using words well—a pleasure of the sort we all experience when we read any work that we enjoy and admire, a work by an author who uses words skillfully. By the time you finish, you ought to think that although you began with some ideas that were only half-formulated, you now have some ideas that are pretty good, and they are worth sharing.

It is helpful to remember that writing an essay is a *process*. True, there are a few writers who are able, as if by magic, to produce a first draft that is nearly perfect: Their first draft is more or less the final draft. But most of us do not have such skill. We make use of an outline and try to make the first draft a good one, but we realize that we will have to revise this draft, moving through the pages carefully and seeking to make both large and small changes for the better. It takes time, yet it is also satisfying—there is pleasure in the process, the craft, of writing a draft and revising it, and revising it again, and again.

The poet W. B. Yeats remarked that he did not write poems but, rather, that he revised poems: He delighted in the process of revising drafts and, stage-by-stage, seeing his work take shape.

THE WRITING PROCESS

Later chapters give extensive advice concerning particular assignments (for instance, writing a comparison, or writing a review of a play), but here, for the moment, is a brief overview. No process works for all writers, but the following advice may help you get started.

1.   **Consider the writing situation.**

- Is the specific topic assigned, or do you choose your own? If the choice is yours, choose a work you like—but allow plenty of time because you may find, once you get to work, that you want to change your topic.
- How long will the essay be? (Allow an appropriate amount of time.)
- What kinds of sources are you expected to use? (Only your own insights, supplemented by conversations with friends, and perhaps familiarity with your textbooks? Secondary sources? How many?) Again, allow the appropriate amount of time.
- Who is the audience? Awareness of the audience will help you to determine the amount of detail you need to provide. (More about the audience below, under items 5 and 7.)
- When is the essay due? (Allow time to type, proofread, and check any sources.)

2.   **Get at least a few ideas *before* you write a first draft.** You can immediately generate some ideas by thinking about the impact the

work makes on you—*why* does it please or displease or even anger you? Did some words puzzle you? Look them up, and think about why the writer may have used unusual words. You may also get some starting ideas by thinking about classroom discussions, for instance, concerning litera- ture and truth, or symbolism, or the depiction of women, or the use of dialect. (In your final version, be sure to give credit for any ideas that you borrow.) Jot down whatever comes to mind—key phrases will do—and you will find that these jottings engender further ideas.

3.   **Rearrange these jottings into an outline, that is, a tenta- tive plan for a draft.** A list of a few phrases indicating the topics you plan to address (for instance, "historical context"), and the sequence, will help you to get going. Such an outline will probably indicate that the first para- graph will name the writers or the works of literature and will specify the general approach or scope of the paper. Additional jottings, in sequence, indicate the focus of each paragraph.

4.   **Start writing.** Yes, you have been putting down words, but these activities are what composition instructors call "pre-writing." Now you are in a position to write. If you have made an outline, begin by following it, but remember, the outline is a helpful guide to get you going, not a road map that must be followed. Write freely, get your ideas down on paper or on the computer screen. At this stage, you are still wrestling with ideas, trying things out, clarifying things for yourself, engaging in a search-and- discovery operation.

These pages are not a first draft; rather, they are what teachers of writ- ing call a "rough draft," so do not worry about mechanical matters such as spelling and punctuation and stylistic elegance. Such things will be impor- tant when you revise and edit, but at the moment you are trying to find out what your ideas are and how much sense they make. Do not be afraid to set forth your hunches. As the twentieth-century English novelist E. M. Forster put it, "How do I know what I think until I see what I say?" Write in a spirit of confidence, and if you are using a computer, be sure to save your material.

Later, of course, you will reread with a critical (skeptical) mind what you have said—you will want to make sure that assertions are supported by evidence—but for now, follow your instincts.

5.   **Reread and revise the material,** preferably after an interval of a few hours or even a day.

You are now prepared to write a serious draft. Your tentative or work- ing thesis has evolved into a point that you have confidence in. *Do not try to revise by merely reading your work on the computer screen.* You need to see the essay as your reader will see it, on paper. Only a hard copy will let you see if a paragraph is much too long, or if quotations are too long and too frequent. Revise the hard copy with a pen or pencil, and then keyboard your revisions into the computer.

Revisions will be of two sorts, *global* (large scale, such as reorganization) and *local* (the substitution of a precise word for an imprecise one, or a spelling correction). Generally speaking, try to begin by making the necessary global revisions. You may, for instance, decide that introductory background material is or is not needed, or that background material should be distributed throughout the essay rather than given all at once at the start, or that additional evidence is needed to support some assertion, or that some material in your final paragraph ought to appear earlier. But if you spot a spelling error, or realize that a particular word is not the best word, there is no harm in pausing to make such a correction when you first see the need.

Now is the time to keep asking yourself, "What will my audience—my readers—make of this word, this sentence, this paragraph? Does this word need to be defined? Do I support this generalization? Is my point clear, and is it expressed effectively?" Put yourself in your reader's shoes; ask yourself if readers will be aware of where they are going. You are inventing a skeptical reader who in fact will be your helpful collaborator.

6. Reread and revise the draft again, asking yourself what your reader will make out of each sentence.

Read your prose carefully, and try to hear it. You might even read the draft aloud to yourself, or to a friend. Writing an essay is not the same thing as having a conversation, but you'll want to write the essay in a voice that is natural to you.

7. Make certain that the mechanics are according to specifications. Here you are acting not so much as an author but as an editor. It is appropriate for an author, in the heat of drafting material, to be indifferent to mechanical details, but it is appropriate for an editor to be cool, detached, finicky—in short, for the editor to tell the author to come down to earth and to present the essay correctly.

Margins, spacing, page numbering, and labeling of illustrations should follow the instructor's requirements. Documentation should be according to the *MLA Handbook for Writers of Research Papers,* 7th ed. (2009).

8. If possible, get a classmate or a friend to read your essay and to make suggestions. This representative of your audience should not rewrite the essay for you, but he or she can call your attention to paragraphs that need development, to unclear organization, to unconvincing arguments, to awkward sentences, and even to errors in punctuation and spelling.

9. **Consider the reader's suggestions, and revise where you think necessary.** If your reader finds some terms obscure, or an argument unsubstantiated, you will want to revise, clarifying the terms and providing evidence for the argument. As before, in the process of revising, try to imagine yourself as your hypothetical reader.

10. **Print out a copy of the revised draft, read it, and revise again**—and again—as needed.

✍ A RULE FOR WRITERS

You are not knocking off an assignment; you are writing an *essay,* engaging in a process that, first, will teach you and, second, will engage the interest of your readers and will teach them.

✔ Checklist: The Basics

- ❑ Is my title engaging?
- ❑ Does the introduction provide essential information (author, work, topic, or approach of the essay)?
- ❑ Does the paper have a thesis, a point?
- ❑ Do I support my argument with evidence from the text?
- ❑ Have I kept the needs of my audience in mind—for instance, have I defined unfamiliar terms?
- ❑ Is the paper organized, and is the organization clear to the reader?
- ❑ Have I done what the assignment asked me to do?

2

THE WRITER AS READER: READING AND RESPONDING

Interviewer: *Did you know as a child you wanted to be a writer?*
Toni Morrison: *No. I wanted to be a reader.*

Learning to write is in large measure learning to read. The text you must read most carefully is the one you write, an essay you will ask someone else to read. It may start as a jotting in the margin of a book you are reading or as a brief note in a journal, and it will go through several drafts before it becomes an essay.

To produce something that another person will find worth reading, you yourself must read each draft with care, trying to imagine the effect your words are likely to have on your reader. In writing about literature, you will apply some of the same critical skills to your reading; that is, you will examine your responses to what you are reading and will try to account for them.

Let us begin by looking at a very short story by Kate Chopin (1851–1904). (The name is pronounced in the French way, something like "show pan.") Kate O'Flaherty, born into a prosperous family in St. Louis, in 1870 married Oscar Chopin, a French-Creole businessman from Louisiana. They lived in New Orleans, where they had six children. Oscar died of malaria in 1882, and in 1884 Kate returned to St. Louis, where, living with her mother and children, she began to write fiction.

Kate Chopin

RIPE FIGS

Maman-Nainaine said that when the figs were ripe Babette might go to visit her cousins down on the Bayou-Lafourche where the sugar cane

8

grows. Not that the ripening of figs had the least thing to do with it, but that is the way Maman-Nainaine was.

It seemed to Babette a very long time to wait; for the leaves upon the trees were tender yet, and the figs were like little hard, green marbles.

But warm rains came along and plenty of strong sunshine, and though Maman-Nainaine was as patient as the statue of la Madone, and Babette as restless as a humming-bird, the first thing they both knew it was hot summertime. Every day Babette danced out to where the fig-trees were in a long line against the fence. She walked slowly beneath them, carefully peering between the gnarled, spreading branches. But each time she came disconsolate away again. What she saw there finally was something that made her sing and dance the whole long day.

When Maman-Nainaine sat down in her stately way to breakfast, the following morning, her muslin cap standing like an aureole about her white, placid face, Babette approached. She bore a dainty porcelain platter, which she set down before her godmother. It contained a dozen purple figs, fringed around with their rich, green leaves.

"Ah," said Maman-Nainaine arching her eyebrows, "how early the figs have ripened this year!"

"Oh," said Babette, "I think they have ripened very late."

"Babette," continued Maman-Nainaine, as she peeled the very plumpest figs with her pointed silver fruit-knife, "you will carry my love to them all down on Bayou-Lafourche. And tell your Tante Frosine I shall look for her at Toussaint—when the chrysanthemums are in bloom."

THE ACT OF READING

If we had been Chopin's contemporaries, we might have read this sketch in *Vogue* in 1893 or in an early collection of her works, *A Night in Acadie* (1897). But we are not Chopin's original readers, and, because we live more than a century later, we inevitably read "Ripe Figs" in a somewhat different way.

This difference gets us to an important point about writing and reading. A writer writes, sets forth his or her meaning, and attempts to guide the reader's responses, as we all do when we write an e-mail home saying that we are thinking of dropping a course or asking for news or money. To this extent, the writer creates the written work and puts a meaning in it.

As readers, we can and should make an effort to understand what the author seems to be getting at; that is, we should make an effort to understand the words in their context. Perhaps we need not look up every word we do not know, at least on the first reading, but if certain unfamiliar words are repeated and thus seem especially important, we will probably want to look them up.

It happens that in "Ripe Figs" three French words are used: *maman, madone,* and *tante. Maman* is "Mother," and *Tante,* in "Tante Frosine," is simple enough: It means "Aunt Frosine." Fortunately, the words are not crucial, and the context probably makes clear that Frosine is an adult, which is all that we really need to know about her. *Madone* is more interesting. It means "madonna," which is Italian for "my lady" or "madam," and which is commonly used to refer to Mary, the mother of Jesus. (You may know Raphael's painting *The Alba Madonna* or Dürer's *The Madonna and Child.*) It is unlikely that Chopin is saying that Maman-Nainaine *is* Mary: Good writers are rarely as heavy-handed as that. But the reference is there for a reason: Chopin wants us to notice it, and, no doubt, to see how it is connected later to the word *aureole,* which is the radiant light around the head or body of a sacred figure in a work of art.

The point is this: A reader who does not know—or who does not look up—the meanings of these words, or who does not know that chrysanthemums bloom in the late summer or early autumn, for instance, will miss part of Chopin's meaning.

Although writers tell us a good deal, they do not tell us everything. We know that Maman-Nainaine is Babette's godmother, but we do not know exactly how old Maman-Nainaine and Babette are. Further, Chopin tells us nothing of Babette's parents. It *sounds* as though Babette and her godmother live alone, but readers may differ. One reader may argue that Babette's parents must be dead or ill; another may say that the status of her parents is irrelevant and that what counts is that Babette is supervised by only one person, a mature woman.

In short, a text includes **indeterminacies** (passages that careful readers agree are open to various interpretations) and **gaps** (things left unsaid in the story, such as why a godmother rather than a mother takes care of Babette). As we work our way through a text, we keep reevaluating what we have read, pulling the details together to make sense of them in a process called **consistency building.**

Whatever the gaps, careful readers are able to draw many reasonable inferences about Maman-Nainaine. We can list some of them:

She is older than Babette.
She has a "stately way," and she is "patient as the statue of la Madone."
She has an odd way (is it exasperating or engaging or a little of
    each?) of connecting actions with the seasons.
Given this last point, she seems to act slowly, to be very patient.
She apparently is used to being obeyed.

You may at this point want to go back and reread "Ripe Figs" to see
what else you can say about Maman-Nainaine.

And now, what of Babette?
She is young.
She is active and impatient ("restless as a humming-bird").
She is obedient.

Is there more you could add to this list?

READING WITH A PEN IN HAND

Perhaps the best way to read attentively is to mark the text, underlining
or highlighting passages that interest you, and to jot notes or queries in
the margins. Here is the work once more, this time with the marks that a
student made after a second reading.

Kate Chopin

RIPE FIGS

Maman-Nainaine said that when the (figs) were ripe
Babette might go to visit her cousins down on the Bayou-   *Where is*
Lafourche where the sugar cane grows. Not that the ripen-   *this place?*
odd ing of figs had the least thing to do with it, but that is the
way Maman-Nainaine was.

    It seemed to Babette a very long time to wait; for the
leaves upon the trees were tender yet, and the figs were
like little hard (green marbles.)

    But warm rains came along and plenty of strong sun-   *contrast*
shine, and though Maman-Nainaine was as patient as the   *between*
statue of la Madone, and Babette as restless as a humming-   *M–N and*
bird, the first thing they both knew it was hot summer-   *B*
time. Every day Babette danced out to where the fig-trees

were in a long line against the fence. She walked slowly beneath them, carefully peering between the gnarled, spreading branches. But each time she came disconsolate away again. What she saw there finally was something that made her sing and dance the whole long day.

another contrast

When Maman-Nainaine sat down in her stately way to breakfast the following morning, her muslin cap standing like an aureole about her white, placid face, Babette

check this?

approached. She bore a dainty porcelain platter, which she *ceremonious?* set down before her godmother. It contained a dozen purple figs, fringed around with their rich, green leaves.

"Ah," said Maman-Nainaine arching her eyebrows, *time passes* "how early the figs have ripened this year!" *——fast for M-N*

nice echo; contrast; like a song

"Oh," said Babette, "I think they have ripened very *slowly for B* late."

"Babette," continued Maman-Nainaine as she peeled *is M-N* the very plumpest figs with her pointed silver fruit-knife, *herself like* "you will carry my love to them all down on Bayou- *a plump fig?* Lafourche. And tell your Tante Frosine I shall look for her at Toussaint—when the chrysanthemums are in bloom."

B entrusted with a message of love

opens with figs; ends with chrys. (autumn)   *fulfillment?*
Equivalent to figs ripening

RECORDING YOUR FIRST RESPONSES

After you annotate your text, another useful way of getting at meanings is to write down your initial responses to the story, jotting down your impressions as they come to you in any order—almost as though you are talking to yourself. Because no one else is going to read your notes, you can be entirely free and at ease. You can write in sentences or not; it is up to you. Write whatever comes into your mind, whatever the story triggers in your own imagination, whatever rings true or reminds you of your own experiences. Here is the response of the student who annotated the text.

I like the way the "green marbles" turn into "purple figs." And I like the way Babette and M-N are sort of opposite. B sings and dances and is restless. On the other hand, M-N is "patient" and like a statue and she sits "in a stately way." A young girl and a mature woman. But, come to think of it, B can also be dignified—she serves M-N the figs in a fancy dish. I feel I can see these people, I almost know them. And I'd like to see Aunt Frosine in the fall, in chrysanthemum time. She's probably a mature woman, like M-N, with lots of dignity.

Here is another student's first response to "Ripe Figs."

This is a very short story. I didn't know stories were this short, but I like it because you can get it all quickly and it's no trouble to reread it carefully. The shortness, though, leaves a lot of gaps for the reader to fill in. So much is *not* said. Your imagination is put to work.

But I can see Maman-N sitting at her table—pleasantly powerful—no one you would want to argue with. She's formal and distant—and definitely has quirks. She wants to postpone Babette's trip, but we don't know why. And you can sense B's frustration. But maybe she's *teaching* her that something really good is worth waiting for and that anticipation is as much fun as the trip. Maybe I can develop this idea.

Another thing. I can tell they are not poor—from two things. The pointed silver fruit knife and the porcelain platter, and the fact that Maman sits down to breakfast in a "stately" way. They are the leisure class. But I don't know enough about life on the bayous to go into this. Their life is different from mine; no one I know has that kind of peaceful rural life.

AUDIENCE AND PURPOSE

Suppose you are beginning the process of writing about "Ripe Figs" for someone else, not for yourself. The first question to ask yourself is:

For whom am I writing? In other words, Who is my *audience?*

Of course, you probably are writing because an instructor has asked you to do so, but you still must imagine an audience. Your instructor may tell you, for instance, to write for your classmates. If you are writing for people who are familiar with some of Chopin's work, you will not have to say much about the author. If you are writing for an audience that perhaps has never heard of Chopin, you may want to include a brief biographical note of the sort given on page 8. If you are writing for an audience that (you have reason to believe) has read several works by Chopin, you may want to make some comparisons, explaining how "Ripe Figs" resembles or differs from Chopin's other work.

In a sense, the audience is your collaborator; it helps you decide what you will say. You are helped also by your sense of *purpose:* If your aim is to introduce readers to Chopin, you will make certain points; if your aim is to tell people what you think "Ripe Figs" says about human relationships or about time, you will say some different things; if your aim is to have a little fun and to entertain an audience that is familiar with "Ripe Figs," you might write a parody (a humorous imitation).

✍ A RULE FOR WRITERS

You may think you are writing for the teacher, but this view is a misconception. When you write, *you* are the teacher.

A WRITING ASSIGNMENT ON "RIPE FIGS"

The Assignment

Let us assume that you are trying to describe "Ripe Figs" to someone who has not read it. You will briefly summarize the action, such as it is, will mention where it takes place and who the characters are (including their relationship), and what, if anything, happens to them. Beyond that, you will explain as honestly as you can what makes "Ripe Figs" appealing or interesting or trifling or boring.

Here is an essay that a student, Antonia Tenori, wrote for this assignment. Because this story is only one page long, the instructor told students that they need not cite page references, but for a sample paper with the kind of documentation normally required, including a list of Works Cited, see pages 39–41.

A Sample Essay

Antonia Tenori
Professor Cargill
College Writing 101A
1 October 2010

Images of Ripening in Kate Chopin's "Ripe Figs"

Very little happens in Kate Chopin's one-page story, "Ripe Figs." Maman-Nainaine tells her goddaughter Babette that she may "visit her cousins down on the Bayou-Lafourche" "when the figs were ripe"; the figs ripen, and Babette is given permission to go. So little happens in "Ripe Figs" that the story at first appears merely to be a character sketch that illustrates, through Babette and her godmother, the contrast between youth and age. But by means of the natural imagery of the tale, Chopin suggests more than this: she asks her readers to see the relationship of human time to nature's seasons, and she suggests that, try as we may to push the process of maturity, growth, or "ripening," happens in its own time.

The story clearly contrasts the impatience of youth with the patience and dignity that come with age. Babette, whose name suggests she is still a "little baby," is "restless as a humming-bird." Each day when she eagerly goes to see if the figs have ripened, she doesn't simply walk but she dances. By contrast, Maman-Nainaine has a "stately way," she is "patient as the statue of la Madone," and there is an "aureole"—radiance—"about her white, placid face." The brief dialogue near the end of the story also emphasizes the difference between the two characters. When the figs finally ripen, Maman-Nainaine is surprised (she arches her eyebrows), and she exclaims, "how early the figs have ripened this year!" Babette replies, "I think they have ripened very late."

Chopin is not simply remarking here that time passes slowly for young people and quickly for old people. She suggests that nature moves at its own pace regardless of human wishes. Babette, young and "tender" as the fig leaves, can't wait to "ripen." Her visit to Bayou-Lafourche is not a mere pleasure trip, but represents her coming into her own season of maturity. Babette's desire to rush this process is tempered by a condition that her godmother sets: Babette must wait until the figs ripen, since everything comes in its own season. Maman-Nainaine recognizes the patterns of the natural world, the rhythms of life. By asking Babette to await the ripening, the young girl is asked to pay attention to the patterns as well.

Chopin further suggests that if we pay attention and wait with patience, the fruits of our own growth will be sweet, plump, and beautiful, like the "dozen purple figs, fringed around with their rich, green leaves," that Babette finally offers her godmother. Chopin uses natural imagery effectively, interweaving the young girl's growth with the rhythms of the seasons. In this way, the reader is connected with both processes in an intimate and inviting way.

The Student's Analysis Analyzed

- The title of the essay is informative; it clearly indicates the focus of the analysis. Notice, too, that it is much more interesting than "An Analysis of a Story" or "An Analysis of Kate Chopin's 'Ripe Figs'" or "'Ripe Figs': A Study" or "An Analysis of Imagery." In your own essays, construct titles that inform and interest the reader.

- The first sentence names the author and title. Strictly speaking, this information is redundant (it appears in the title), but it is customary to give the author's full name and the title of the work early in the essay, and it is essential to give such information if it is not in the title.

- The second sentence offers enough plot summary to enable the reader to follow the discussion. But notice that the essay as a whole is much more than a summary of the plot. Summary here is offered early, merely to make the analysis intelligible. The opening paragraph presents one view (the view that the essayist believes is inadequate); then, after a transitional "but," it offers a second view and presents a thesis—the point that she will argue. Perhaps the most common error students make in writing about literature is to confuse a summary of the plot with a thoughtful analysis of the work. A little plot telling is acceptable, to remind your reader of what happens, but normally your essay will be devoted to setting forth a thesis about a work, and supporting the thesis with evidence. Your readers do not want to know what happens in the work; they want to know what you make of the work—how you interpret it, or why you like or dislike it.

- In the second paragraph, the writer supports her thesis by providing brief quotations. These quotations are not padding; rather, they are evidence supporting her assertion that Chopin "contrasts the impatience of youth with the patience and dignity that comes with age."

- In the third paragraph, the writer develops her thesis ("Chopin is not simply. . . . She is . . . ").

- The final paragraph begins with a helpful transition ("Chopin *further* suggests"), offers additional evidence, and ends with a new idea (about the reader's response to the story) that takes the discussion a step further. The essay avoids the deadliest kind of conclusion, a mere summary of the essay ("Thus we have seen," or some such words). The writer's effective final sentence nicely draws the reader into the essay. (Effective final sentences are hard to write, but we give advice about them on pages 66–67.)

Antonia Tenori wrote this paper for an assignment early in the semester, and it's worth noting that students were told to write "a page or two (about 250–500 words)." If

- the first question to ask is "To whom am I writing?"
- then the second question to ask is, "What is the length of the assignment?"

The answer to this second question will provide two sorts of guidance: It will give you some sense of how much time you should devote to preparing the paper—obviously an instructor expects you to spend more time on a ten-page paper than on a one-page paper—and, second, it will give you a sense of how much detail you can include.

For a short paper—say, one or two pages—you will need to make your main point with a special kind of directness; you will not have space for lots of details, but just for those that support the main point.

For a longer paper, three to five pages, or one that is longer still, you can examine the characters, setting, and central themes in greater depth, and you can focus on more details in the text to strengthen your analysis.

✍🏻 A RULE FOR WRITERS

Support your thesis—your point—with evidence. (Brief quotations are often the best evidence.) Assume that your readers are skeptical and show them the details that support your interpretations.

CRITICAL THINKING AND THE STUDY OF LITERATURE

Sometimes we may feel that analyzing a literary work takes away from the pleasure that it offers. But that is not really the case. Through our analysis of a short story by Kate Chopin, for example, we can understand more clearly why we have enjoyed it. Close and careful study helps us to get "inside" the story: We are trying to find out how it works and to learn what—in its style, structure, characterization, and exploration of theme—makes it interesting. As we do so, the story becomes even more interesting.

In this way, the analysis of literature is a special form of critical thinking. We are thinking critically about Chopin's story, and, furthermore, we are thinking carefully and critically about our *own* thinking—about the nature of our response to the literary work. We focus on specific details and put into words our general responses. Then we test these responses once again against the evidence of the text itself. The process continues until we are satisfied that we have given the work a sensitive and full interpretation.

Part of our activity as critical thinkers is to ask ourselves: Is my interpretation of this story as perceptive and as accurate as I can make it? What have I taken account of? Is there anything that I may have overlooked, or that I need to reconsider? Is there another way, another point of view, according to which this literary work might be examined and understood? (Chapters 6 and 7 will go into detail about "meaning" and "interpretation.")

Reading literature on our own gives pleasure and stimulates our minds. When we study literature in the classroom or in a writing assignment, usually we find not that our pleasure diminishes, but, rather, that it increases: We gain insight into how something that is well-made operates, how it is put together. Our appreciation of the work is deepened, and our thinking is made sharper, and more complex.

3

THE READER AS WRITER: DRAFTING AND WRITING

All there is to writing is having ideas. To learn to write is to learn to have ideas.

—Robert Frost

PRE-WRITING: GETTING IDEAS

How does one "learn to have ideas"? Among the methods are the following: reading with a pen or pencil in hand so that (as we have already seen) one can annotate the text; keeping a journal in which one jots down reflections about one's reading; and talking with others about the reading. Let us take another look at the first method, annotating.

Annotating a Text

In reading, if you own the book do not hesitate to mark it up, indicating (by highlighting or underlining, or by marginal notes) what puzzles you, what pleases or interests you, and what displeases or bores you. Later you will want to think further about these responses, asking yourself if, on rereading, you still feel this way, and if not, why not, but these first responses will get you started.

Annotations of the sort given on pages 11–12, which chiefly call attention to contrasts, indicate that the student is thinking about writing an analysis of the story, an essay in which the parts are examined to see how they relate to each other or in which a part is examined to see how it relates to the whole.

More about Getting Ideas: A Second Story by Kate Chopin, "The Story of an Hour"

Now we will consider a story that is a little longer than "Ripe Figs," and then we will discuss how, in addition to annotating, one might get ideas for writing about it.

Kate Chopin

THE STORY OF AN HOUR

Knowing that Mrs. Mallard was afflicted with a heart trouble, great care was taken to break to her as gently as possible the news of her husband's death.

It was her sister Josephine who told her, in broken sentences, veiled hints that revealed in half concealing. Her husband's friend Richards was there, too, near her. It was he who had been in the newspaper office when intelligence of the railroad disaster was received, with Brently Mallard's name leading the list of "killed." He had only taken the time to assure himself of its truth by a second telegram, and had hastened to forestall any less careful, less tender friend in bearing the sad message.

She did not hear the story as many women have heard the same, with a paralyzed inability to accept its significance. She wept at once with sudden, wild abandonment, in her sister's arms. When the storm of grief had spent itself she went away to her room alone. She would have no one follow her.

There stood, facing the open window, a comfortable, roomy armchair. Into this she sank, pressed down by a physical exhaustion that haunted her body and seemed to reach into her soul.

She could see in the open square before her house the tops of trees that were all aquiver with the new spring life. The delicious breath of rain was in the air. In the street below a peddler was crying his wares. The notes of a distant song which some one was singing reached her faintly, and countless sparrows were twittering in the eaves.

There were patches of blue sky showing here and there through the clouds that had met and piled above the other in the west facing her window.

She sat with her head thrown back upon the cushion of the chair quite motionless, except when a sob came up into her throat and shook her, as a child who has cried itself to sleep continues to sob in its dreams.

She was young, with a fair, calm face, whose lines bespoke repression and even a certain strength. But now there was a dull stare in her eyes, whose gaze was fixed away off yonder on one of those patches of blue sky. It was not a glance of reflection, but rather indicated a suspension of intelligent thought.

There was something coming to her and she was waiting for it, fearfully. What was it? She did not know; it was too subtle and elusive to name. But she felt it creeping out of the sky, reaching toward her through the sounds, the scents, the color that filled the air.

Now her bosom rose and fell tumultuously. She was beginning to recognize this thing that was approaching to possess her, and she was striving to beat it back with her will—as powerless as her two white slender hands would have been.

When she abandoned herself a little whispered word escaped her slightly parted lips. She said it over and over under her breath: "Free, free, free!" The vacant stare and the look of terror that had followed it went from her eyes. They stayed keen and bright. Her pulses beat fast, and the coursing blood warmed and relaxed every inch of her body.

She did not stop to ask if it were not a monstrous joy that held her. A clear and exalted perception enabled her to dismiss the suggestion as trivial.

She knew that she would weep again when she saw the kind, tender hands folded in death; the face that had never looked save with love upon her, fixed and gray and dead. But she saw beyond that bitter moment a long procession of years to come that would belong to her absolutely. And she opened and spread her arms out to them in welcome.

There would be no one to live for her during those coming years; she would live for herself. There would be no powerful will bending her in the blind persistence with which men and women believe they have a right to impose a private will upon a fellow creature. A kind intention or a cruel intention made the act seem no less a crime as she looked upon it in that brief moment of illumination.

And yet she had loved him—sometimes. Often she had not. What did it matter! What could love, the unsolved mystery, count for in face of this possession of self-assertion which she suddenly recognized as the strongest impulse of her being.

"Free! Body and soul free!" she kept whispering.

Josephine was kneeling before the closed door with her lips to the keyhole, imploring for admission. "Louise, open the door! I beg; open the door—you will make yourself ill. What are you doing, Louise? For heaven's sake open the door."

"Go away. I am not making myself ill." No; she was drinking in the very elixir of life through that open window.

Her fancy was running riot along those days ahead of her. Spring days, and summer days, and all sorts of days that would be her own. She breathed a quick prayer that life might be long. It was only yesterday she had thought with a shudder that life might be long.

She arose at length and opened the door to her sister's importunities. There was a feverish triumph in her eyes, and she carried herself unwittingly like a goddess of Victory. She clasped her sister's waist and together they descended the stairs. Richards stood waiting for them at the bottom.

Some one was opening the front door with a latchkey. It was Brently Mallard who entered, a little travel-stained, composedly carrying his grip-sack and umbrella. He had been far from the scene of accident, and did not even know there had been one. He stood amazed at Josephine's piercing cry; at Richards' quick motion to screen him from the view of his wife.

But Richards was too late.

When the doctors came they said she had died of heart disease—of joy that kills.

Brainstorming for Ideas for Writing

Unlike annotating, which consists of making brief notes and small marks on the printed page, *brainstorming*—the free jotting down of ideas—invites you to jot down whatever comes to mind, without inhibition. Do not worry about spelling, about writing complete sentences, or about unifying your thoughts; just let one thought lead to another.

Later, you will review your jottings, deleting some, connecting others that are related, amplifying still others. For now, you want to get going, and so there is no reason to look back. Thus, you might jot down something about the title:

> Title speaks of an hour, and story covers an hour, but maybe takes five minutes to read.

And then, perhaps prompted by "an hour," you might add something to this effect:

> Doubt that a woman who got news of the death of her husband
> could move from grief to joy within an hour.

Your next jotting might have little or nothing to do with this issue; it might simply say:

> Enjoyed "Hour" more than "Ripe Figs" partly because "Hour" is so
> shocking.

And then you might ask yourself:

> By shocking, do I mean "improbable," or what? Come to think of it,
> maybe it's not so improbable. A lot depends on what the marriage
> was like.

Focused Free Writing

Focused free writing, or directed free writing, is a related method that some writers use to uncover ideas they want to write about. Concentrating on one issue, such as a question that strikes them as worth puzzling over (What kind of person is Mrs. Mallard?), they write at length, nonstop, for perhaps five or ten minutes.

Writers who find free writing helpful put down everything that bears on the one issue or question they are examining. They do not stop at this stage to evaluate the results, and they do not worry about niceties of sentence structure or of spelling. They explore ideas in a steady stream of writing, using whatever associations come to mind. If they pause in their writing, it is only to refer to the text, to search for more detail—perhaps a quotation—that will help them to answer their question.

After the free-writing session, these writers go back and reread what they have written, highlighting or underlining what seems to be of value. They may find much that is of little or no use, but they also usually find that some strong ideas have surfaced and have received some development. At this point the writers are often able to make an outline and then begin a draft.

Here is an example of one student's focused free writing:

> What do I know about Mrs. Mallard? Let me put everything down
> here I know about her or can figure out from what Kate Chopin tells
> me. When she finds herself alone after the death of her husband,
> she says, "Free. Body and soul free" and before that she said "Free,

free, free." Three times. So she has suddenly perceived that she has not been free; she has been under the influence of a "powerful will." In this case it has been her husband, but she says no one, man nor woman, should impose their will on anyone else. So it's not a feminist issue—it's a power issue. No one should push anyone else around is what I guess Chopin means, force someone to do what the other person wants. I used to have a friend that did that to me all the time; he had to run everything. They say that fathers— before the women's movement—used to run things, with the father in charge of all the decisions, so maybe this is an honest reaction to having been pushed around by a husband. I think Mrs. Mallard is a believable character, even if the plot is not all that believable—all those things happening in such quick succession.

Listing

In your preliminary thinking you may find it useful to make lists. In the previous chapter we saw that listing the traits of characters was helpful in thinking about Chopin's "Ripe Figs":

Maman-Nainaine
  older than Babette
  "stately way"
  "patient as the statue of la Madone"
  expects to be obeyed
  connects actions with seasons
Babette
  young
  active
  obedient

For "The Story of an Hour" you might list Mrs. Mallard's traits, or you might list the stages in her development. Such a list is not the same as a summary of the plot. The list helps the writer to see the sequence of psychological changes.

  weeps (when she gets the news)
  goes to room, alone

"pressed down by a physical exhaustion"

"dull stare"

"something coming to her"

strives to beat back "this thing"

"Free, free, free!" The "vacant stare went from her eyes"

"A clear and exalted perception"

Rejects Josephine

"She was drinking in the very elixir of life"

Gets up, opens door, "A feverish triumph in her eyes"

Sees B, and dies

Unlike brainstorming and annotating, which let you go in all directions, listing requires that you first make a decision about what you will be listing—traits of character, images, puns, or whatever. Once you make the decision you can then construct the list, and, with a list in front of you, you will see patterns that you were not fully conscious of earlier.

Some students prefer to approach listing a bit differently. They like to list everything that occurs to them, almost as if they were doing a free-writing exercise. Then, once they have a list, they separate the items on it, clustering them into smaller, more specific groups. Which items, for example, concern or refer to Mrs. Mallard's thoughts? Her feelings? Her appearance? Her relationship to other people?

A list is a handy organizational device; by working with it, you can begin to see how your comments and questions, and the details you have noted in the text, fit together. By constructing a list, and using it as a tool for thinking, you can start to sense the shape of the paper as a whole.

Asking Questions

If you feel stuck, ask yourself questions. If you are thinking about a work of fiction, ask yourself questions about the plot and the characters: Are they believable? Are they interesting? What does it all add up to? What does the story mean to *you*? (The chapters in this book on fiction, drama, and poetry include questions on each form.) One student found it helpful to jot down the following questions:

Plot

Ending false? Unconvincing? Or prepared for?

Character

    Mrs. M. unfeeling? Immoral?

    Mrs. M. unbelievable character?

    What might her marriage have been like? Many gaps.

    (Can we tell what her husband was like?)

    "And yet she loved him—sometimes." Fickle? Realistic?

    What is "this thing that was approaching to possess her"?

Symbolism

    Set on spring day = symbolic of new life?

You do not have to be as tidy as this student. You may begin by jotting down notes and queries about what you like or dislike and about what puzzles or amuses you.

What follows are the jottings of another student. They are, obviously, in no particular order—the student is brainstorming, putting down whatever occurs to her—though it is equally obvious that one note sometimes led to the next:

    Title nothing special. What might be a better title?

    Could a woman who loved her husband be so heartless?

    Is she heartless? *Did* she love him?

    What are (were) Louise's feelings about her husband?

    Did she want too much? *What* did she want?

    Could this story happen today? Feminist interpretation?

    Sister (Josephine)—a busybody?

    Tricky ending—but maybe it could be true

    "And yet she had loved him—sometimes. Often she had not." Why
        does one love someone "sometimes"?

    Irony: plot has reversal. Are characters ironic too?

Such jottings will help the reader-write to think about the story, find a special point of interest, and develop a thoughtful argument about it.

Keeping a Journal

A journal is not a diary, a record of what the writer did during the day ("Today I read Chopin's 'Hour'"). Rather, a journal is a place to store some of the thoughts you may have inscribed on a scrap of paper or in the margin of the text, such as your initial response to the title of a work or to the ending. It is also a place to jot down further reflections, such as thoughts about what the work means to you, and what was said in the classroom about writing in general or specific works.

You will get something out of your journal if you write an entry at least once a week, but you will get much more if you write entries after reading each assignment and after each class meeting. You may want to reflect on why your opinion is so different from that of another student, or you may want to apply a concept such as "character" or "irony" or "plausibility" to a story that later you may write about in an essay. Comparisons are especially helpful: How does this work (or this character, or this use of symbolism) differ from last week's reading?

You might even make an entry in the form of a letter to the author or from one character to another. You might write a dialogue between characters in two works or between two authors, or you might record an experience of your own that is comparable to something in the work.

Another student who wrote about "The Story of an Hour" began with the following entry in his journal. In reading this entry, notice that one idea stimulates another. The student was, quite rightly, concerned with getting and exploring ideas, not with writing a unified paragraph.

> Apparently a "well-made" story, but seems clever rather than moving or real. Doesn't seem plausible. Mrs. M's change comes out of the blue—maybe *some* women might respond like this, but probably not most.
>
> Does literature deal with unusual people, or with usual (typical?) people? Shouldn't it deal with typical? Maybe not. (Anyway, how can I know?) Is "typical" same as "plausible"? Come to think of it, prob. not.
>
> Anyway, whether Mrs. M is typical or not, is her change plausible, believable? Think more about this.
>
> Why did she change? Her husband dominated her life and controlled her actions; he did "impose a private will upon a fellow creature." She calls this a crime, even if well-intentioned. Is it a crime?

CRITICAL THINKING: ARGUING WITH YOURSELF

In our discussion of annotating, brainstorming, free writing, listing, asking questions, and writing entries in a journal, the emphasis has been on responding freely rather than in any highly systematic or disciplined way.

Something strikes us (perhaps an idea, perhaps an uncertainty), and we jot it down. Maybe even before we finish jotting it down we go on to question it, but probably not; at this early stage it is enough to put onto paper some thoughts, rooted in our first responses, and to keep going.

The almost random play of mind that is evident in brainstorming and in the other activities discussed is a kind of thinking, but the term **critical thinking** (which we addressed briefly in Chapter 2) is reserved for something different. When we think critically, we skeptically scrutinize our own ideas—for example, by searching out our underlying assumptions, or by evaluating what we have quickly jotted down as evidence. We have already seen some examples of this sort of analysis of one's own thinking in the journal entries, where a student wrote that literature should probably deal with "typical" people, then wondered if "typical" and "plausible" were the same, and then added "probably not."

Critical thinking is rational, logical thinking. In thinking critically,

- one scrutinizes one's assumptions;
- one tests the evidence one has collected, even to the extent of looking for counterevidence; and
- one revises one's thesis when necessary, in order to make the argument as complete and convincing as possible.

Let us start with assumptions. If I say that a story is weak because it is improbable, I ought to think about my assumption that improbability is a fault. I can begin by asking myself if all good stories—or all the stories that I value highly—are probable. I may recall that among my favorites is *Alice in Wonderland* (or *Gulliver's Travels* or *Animal Farm*)—so I probably have to withdraw my assumption that improbability in itself makes a story less than good. I may go on to refine the idea and decide that improbability is not a fault in satiric stories but is a fault in other kinds, but that is not the same as saying bluntly that improbability is a fault.

The second aspect of critical thinking that we have isolated—searching for counterevidence within the literary work—especially involves rereading the work to see if we have overlooked something significant or have taken a particular detail out of context. If, for instance, we say that in "The Story of an Hour" Josephine is a busybody, we should reexamine the work to make sure that she indeed is meddling needlessly and is not offering welcome or necessary assistance. Perhaps the original observation will stand up, but perhaps on rereading the story we may come to feel, as we examine each of Josephine's actions, that she cannot reasonably be characterized as a busybody.

Different readers may come to different conclusions; the important thing is that all readers should subject their initial responses to critical thinking, testing their responses against all of the evidence. Remember, your instructor expects you to hand in an essay that is essentially an **argument,** a paper that advances a thesis of your own, and therefore you will revise your drafts if you find counterevidence. The **thesis** might be that

- the story is improbable,
- the story is typical of Chopin,
- the story is anti-woman,
- the story is a remarkable anticipation of contemporary feminist thinking.

Whatever your thesis, it should be able to withstand scrutiny. You may not convince every reader that you are right, but you should make every reader feel that your argument is thoughtful. If you read your notes and then your drafts critically, you will write a paper that meets this standard.

One last point, or maybe it is two: Just as your first jottings probably will not be the products of critical thinking, your first reading of the literary work probably *will not* be a critical reading. It is entirely appropriate to begin by reading simply for enjoyment. After all, the reason we read literature (or listen to music, or go to an art museum, or watch dancers) is to derive pleasure. It happens, however, that in this course you are trying to deepen your understanding of literature, and therefore you are *studying* literature. On subsequent readings, therefore, you will read the work critically, taking careful note of the writer's view of human nature and the writer's ways of achieving certain effects.

This business of critical thinking is important, and we will discuss it again, on pages 94–95, in talking about interpretations of literature.

Arriving at a Thesis and Arguing It

If you think critically about your early jottings and about the literary work itself, you may find that some of your jottings lead to dead ends, but some will lead to further ideas that hold up under scrutiny. What the thesis of the essay will be—the idea that will be asserted and argued (supported with evidence)—is still in doubt, but there is no doubt about one thing: A good essay will have a thesis, a point, an argument. You ought to be able to state your point in a **thesis sentence.**

Consider these candidates as possible thesis sentences:

1. Mrs. Mallard dies soon after hearing that her husband has died.

True, but scarcely a point that can be argued or even developed. About the most the essayist can do with this sentence is amplify it by summarizing the plot of the story, a task not worth doing unless the plot is unusually obscure. An essay may include a sentence or two of summary to give readers their bearings, but a summary is not an essay.

2. The story is a libel on women.

In contrast to the first statement, this one can be developed into an argument. Probably the writer will try to demonstrate that Mrs. Mallard's behavior is despicable. Whether this point can be convincingly argued is another matter; the thesis may be untenable, but it is a thesis. A second problem, however, is this: Even if the writer demonstrates that Mrs. Mallard's behavior is despicable, he or she will have to go on to demonstrate that the presentation of one despicable woman constitutes a libel on women in general. That is a pretty big order.

3. The story is clever but superficial because it is based on an unreal character.

Here, too, is a thesis, a point of view that can be argued. Whether this thesis is true is another matter. The writer's job will be to support it by presenting evidence. Probably the writer will have no difficulty in finding evidence that the story is "clever"; the difficulty will be in establishing a case that the characterization of Mrs. Mallard is "unreal." The writer will have to set forth some ideas about what makes a character real and then will have to show that Mrs. Mallard is an "unreal" (unbelievable) figure.

4. The irony of the ending is believable partly because it is consistent with earlier ironies in the story.

It happens that the student who wrote the essay printed on pages 39–41 began by drafting an essay based on the third of these thesis topics, but as she worked on a draft she found that she could not support her assertion that the character was unconvincing. In fact, she came to believe that although Mrs. Mallard's joy was the reverse of what a reader might expect, several early reversals in the story helped to make Mrs. Mallard's shift from grief to joy acceptable.

Remember: It is not likely that you will quickly find a thesis. Annotating, making entries in a journal, and writing a first draft are ways of finding a thesis.

WRITING A DRAFT

After jotting down notes, and further notes stimulated by rereading and further thinking, you will be able to formulate a tentative thesis. At this point most writers find it useful to glance over their preliminary notes and to jot down the thesis and highlight a few especially promising notes— brief statements of what they think their key points may be, such as key quotations that may support the thesis.

Here are the selected notes (not the original brainstorming notes, but a later selection from them, with additions) and a draft that makes use of them:

title? Ironies in an Hour (?) An Hour of Irony (?) Kate Chopin's Irony (?)

thesis: irony at end is prepared for by earlier ironies

chief irony: Mrs. M. dies just as she is beginning to enjoy life

smaller ironies:

1. "sad message" brings her joy
2. Richards is "too late" at end;
3. Richards is too early at start

These notes are in effect a brief **outline.** Some writers at this point like to develop a fuller outline, but probably most writers begin with only a brief outline, knowing that in the process of developing a draft from these few notes additional ideas will arise. For these writers, the time to jot down a detailed outline is *after* they have written a first or second draft. The outline of the written draft will help them to make sure that their draft has an adequate organization, and that main points are developed.

A Sample Draft: "Ironies in an Hour"

Now for the student's draft—not the first version, but a revised draft with some of the irrelevancies of the first draft omitted and some evidence added.

The digits within the parentheses refer to the page numbers from which the quotations are drawn, though with so short a work as "The Story of an Hour," page references may not be necessary. (Here the references are *not* to the book you are now reading, but to the anthology that the student used.) Check with your instructor to find out if you must always give citations. (Detailed information about how to document a paper is given on pages 327–40, 347–52.)

Ironies in an Hour

After we know how the story turns out, if we reread it we find irony at the very start, as is true of many other stories. Mrs. Mallard's friends assume, mistakenly, that Mrs. Mallard is deeply in love with her husband, Brently Mallard. They take great care to tell her gently of his death. The friends mean well, and in fact they *do* well. They bring her an hour of life, an hour of freedom. They think their news is sad. Mrs. Mallard at first expresses grief when she hears the news, but soon she finds joy in it. So Richards's "sad message" (67), though sad in Richards's eyes, is in fact a happy message.

Among the ironic details is the statement that when Mallard entered the house, Richards tried to conceal him from Mrs. Mallard, but "Richards was too late" (68). This is ironic because earlier Richards "hastened" (67) to bring his sad message; if he had at the start been "too late" (68), Brently Mallard would have arrived at home first, and Mrs. Mallard's life would not have ended an hour later but would simply have gone on as it had been. Yet another irony at the end of the story is the diagnosis of the doctors. The doctors say she died of "heart disease—of joy that kills" (68). In one sense the doctors are right: Mrs. Mallard has experienced a great joy. But of course the doctors totally misunderstand the joy that kills her.

The central irony resides not in the well-intentioned but ironic actions of Richards, or in the unconsciously ironic words of the doctors, but in her own life. In a way she has been dead. She "sometimes" (68) loved her husband, but in a way she has been dead. Now, his apparent death brings her new life. This new life comes to her at the season of the year when "the tops of trees . . . were all aquiver with the new spring life" (67). But, ironically, her new life will last only an hour. She looks forward to "summer days" (68) but she will not see even the end of this spring day. Her years of marriage were ironic. They brought her a sort of living death instead of joy. Her new life is ironic too. It grows out of her moment of grief for her supposedly dead husband, and her vision of a new life is cut short.

[New page]

Work Cited

Chopin, Kate. "The Story of an Hour." *An Introduction to Literature*. Ed. Sylvan Barnet, William Burto, and William E. Cain. 16th ed. New York: Longman, 2011. 67-68. Print.

Revising a Draft

The draft, though excellent, is not yet a finished essay. The student went on to improve it in many small but important ways.

First, the draft needs a good opening that will let the **audience**—the readers—know where the writer will be taking them. (Pages 65–66 discuss introductory paragraphs.) Doubtless you know, from your own experience as a reader, that readers can follow an argument more easily and with more pleasure if early in the discussion the writer alerts them to the basic argument. (The title, too, can strongly suggest the thesis.) Second, some of the paragraphs could be clearer.

In revising paragraphs—or, for that matter, in revising an entire draft—writers unify, organize, clarify, and polish. Writers who revise well imagine that they are readers. They try to put themselves into the mind of the imagined audience, asking themselves, "Is this clear?" "Will a reader need another example?" Or, on the other hand, "Will a reader feel that I am talking down, giving more examples than are needed?"

1. **Unity** is achieved partly by eliminating irrelevancies. Notice that in the final version, printed on pages 39–41, the writer has deleted "as is true of many other stories."
2. **Organization** is a matter of arranging material into a sequence that will help the reader grasp the point.
3. **Clarity** is achieved by providing concrete details and quotations to support generalizations and by providing helpful transitions ("for instance," "furthermore," "on the other hand," "however").

4. **Small-scale revision** is cutting, adding, and combining. So for instance, one deletes unnecessary repetitions. (In the second paragraph of the draft the phrase "the doctors" appears three times, but it appears only once in the final version of the paragraph.) Similarly, in polishing, a writer combines choppy sentences into longer sentences and breaks overly long sentences into shorter sentences.

Later, after producing a draft that seems close to a finished essay, writers engage in yet another activity: They edit.

5. **Editing** is concerned with such matters as checking the accuracy of quotations by comparing them with the originals, checking a dictionary for the spelling of doubtful words, and checking a handbook for doubtful punctuation—for instance, whether a comma or a semicolon is needed in a particular sentence.

✍ A RULE FOR WRITERS

In re-reading your draft, imagine you are not the writer, but a reader. If you imagine a classmate as the reader of the draft, you may find that you need to add transitions, clarify definitions, and provide additional supporting evidence.

✔ Checklist: Revising for Clarity

❏ Is word choice precise and specific? While writing the draft, did you feel that a particular word was close to what you meant, but not quite right? If so, replace that word with the *right* word.

❏ Do you offer concrete examples where necessary?

❏ Are technical terms used appropriately and helpfully? Can any jargon be replaced with plain English?

❏ Does your prose include any dead or mixed metaphors, or clichés?

❏ Have you put together what belongs together? Do modifiers appear close to, and refer clearly to, the words they modify?

❏ Have you eliminated sexist language? Have you replaced such words as "mankind" and "poetess" with gender-neutral terms, and eliminated the generic "he," "him," and "his"? (Usually you can change such an expression as "The novelist . . . he" to "Novelists . . . they.")

❏ Have you replaced passive verbs with active verbs where appropriate? A verb is in *active voice* when the subject is doing the action: "Anne Sexton wrote a sonnet." A verb is in *passive voice* when you make the object of an action into the subject of a sentence: "The sonnet was written by Anne Sexton."

❏ Do pronouns have clear references, and do they agree in number with the nouns to which they refer?

❏ Does the structure of your sentence reflect the structure of your thought? Are parallel ideas in parallel constructions?

Two Ways of Outlining a Draft

Whether or not you draw up an outline as a preliminary guide to writing a draft, you will be able to improve your draft if you prepare an outline of what you have written. If you write on a computer it is especially important that you make an outline of your written draft. Writing on a computer is—or seems—so easy, so effortless, that we can all too easily fill screen after screen with loosely structured writing.

1. Outline what each paragraph says. For each paragraph in your draft, jot down the topic sentence or topic idea, and under each of these sentences, indented, jot down key words for the idea(s) developed in the paragraph. Thus, in an outline of the draft we have just looked at, for the first two paragraphs the writer might make these jottings:

story ironic from start
    friends think news is sad
    Ms. M. finds joy
some ironic details
    Richards hastened, but "too late"
    doctors right and also wrong

An outline of what you have written will help you to see if your draft is good in three important ways. The outline will show you

1. the sequence of major topics,
2. the degree of development of these topics, and
3. the argument, the thesis.

By studying your outline you may see that your first major point (probably after an introductory paragraph) would be more effective as your third point, and that your second point needs to be developed further. An outline of this sort, perhaps even using some phrases from the draft, is essentially a brief version of your draft.

2. Outline what each paragraph does. Consider making yet another sort of outline, an outline indicating not what each paragraph says but what each paragraph *does*. A first attempt at such an outline of the three-paragraph draft of the essay on "The Story of an Hour" might look something like this:

1. Action of the friends is ironic
2. Gives some specific (minor) details about ironies
3. Explains "central irony"

One ought to see something wrong here. The jotting for the first paragraph does *not* tell us what the paragraph *does;* rather, it more or less summarizes the content of the paragraph. It does not clearly introduce the thesis, or define a crucial term, or set the story in the context of Chopin's other work. An outline indicating the *function* of each paragraph will force you to see if your essay has an effective structure. We will see that the student later wrote a new opening paragraph for the essay on "The Story of an Hour."

✍ A RULE FOR WRITERS

You may or may not want to sketch a rough outline before drafting your essay, but you certainly should outline what you hope is your final draft, to see (a) if it is organized, and (b) if the organization will be evident to the reader. (If you imagine a classmate as the reader, you may find that you need to add transitions, clarify definitions, and provide additional supporting evidence.)

✔ Checklist: Reviewing a Revised Draft

❏ Does the draft fulfill the specifications (e.g., length, scope) of the assignment?

❏ Does the draft have a point, a focus?

❏ Is the title interesting and informative? Does it create a favorable first impression?

❏ Are the early paragraphs engaging, and do they give the reader a good idea of what the thesis is and how the paper will be organized?

❑ Are assertions supported with evidence?
❑ Do you keep your readers in mind, for instance, by defining terms that they may be unfamiliar with?
❑ If any quotations are included, are they introduced with signal phrases (for instance, "One critic argues"), rather than just dumped into the essay? Are quotations as brief as possible? Might summaries (properly credited to the sources) be more effective than long quotations?
❑ Are quotations adequately commented on, not simply left to speak for themselves?
❑ Are *all* sources cited—not only words, but also ideas—including Internet material?
❑ Is the organization clear, reasonable, and effective? (Check by making a brief outline. Remember not only that the paper must be organized, but also that the organization must be clear to the reader. Check to see that helpful transitions ("A second example," "On the other hand") guide the reader.)
❑ Does the final paragraph nicely round off the paper, or does it merely restate—unnecessarily—what is by now obvious?
❑ Is the documentation in correct form?

Peer Review

Your instructor may encourage (or even require) you to discuss your draft with another student or with a small group of students; that is, you may be asked to get a review from your peers. Such a procedure is helpful in several ways. First, it gives the writer a real audience, readers who can point to what pleases or puzzles them, who make suggestions, who may disagree (with the writer or with each other), and who frequently, though not intentionally, *misread.*

While it is true that writers don't necessarily like everything they hear (they seldom hear "This is perfect. Don't change a word!"), reading and discussing their work with others almost always gives them a fresh perspective on their work, and a fresh perspective may stimulate thoughtful revision. (Having your intentions *misread* because your writing isn't clear enough can be particularly stimulating.)

The writer whose work is being reviewed is not the sole beneficiary. When students regularly serve as readers for each other, they become better readers of their own work and consequently better revisers. As we said in Chapter 2, learning to write is also learning to read.

If peer review is a part of the writing process in your course, the instructor may distribute a sheet with some suggestions and questions. An example of such a sheet follows.

QUESTIONS FOR PEER REVIEW   ENGLISH 125a

Read each draft once, quickly. Then read it again, with the following questions in mind.

1. What is the essay's topic? Is it one of the assigned topics, or a variation from it? Does the draft show promise of fulfilling the assignment?
2. Looking at the essay as a whole, what thesis (main idea) is stated or implied? If implied, try to state it in your own words.
3. Is the thesis reasonable? How might it be strengthened?
4. Looking at each paragraph separately:
   a. What is the basic point? (If it isn't clear to you, ask for clarification.)
   b. How does the paragraph relate to the essay's main idea or to the previous paragraph?
   c. Should some paragraphs be deleted? Be divided into two or more paragraphs? Be combined? Be put elsewhere? (If you outline the essay by jotting down the main point of each paragraph, you will get help in answering these questions.)
   d. Is each sentence clearly related to the sentence that precedes and to the sentence that follows?
   e. Is each paragraph developed well?
   f. Are there sufficient details, such as brief supporting quotations from the text?
5. What are the paper's chief strengths?
6. Make at least two specific suggestions that you think will assist the author to improve the paper.

✍ A RULE FOR WRITERS

Good writing is rewriting.

—Truman Capote

THE FINAL VERSION

Two Important Notes:

1. Reminder: Page references are not to the present book, but to the anthology that the student refers.
2. The essay that the student submitted to the instructor was entirely keyboarded, but here, so that you can see how the draft has been revised, we print the keyboarded draft but with the final revisions written in by hand..

Julia Pearl
Professor Cain
English 200B
9 May 2011

Ironies of Life in Kate Chopin's
"The Story of an Hour"
~~Ironies in an Hour~~

Kate Chopin's "The Story of an Hour"—which takes only a few minutes to read—turns out to have an ironic ending. On rereading it, however, one sees that the irony is not concentrated only in the outcome of the plot—Mrs. Mallard dies just when she is beginning to live—but is also present in many details.

After we know how the story turns out, if we reread it we find irony at the very start. ~~as is true of many other stories.~~ *Because* Mrs. Mallard's friends *and her sister* assume, mistakenly, that ~~Mrs. Mallard~~ *she* is deeply in love with her husband, Brently Mallard. *They* ~~They~~ take great care to tell her gently of his death. ~~The friends~~ *They* mean well, and in fact they do well. ~~They~~ bring*ing* her an hour of life, an hour of *joyous* freedom. *but it is ironic that* ~~They~~ *They* think their news is sad.

True, Mrs. Mallard at first expresses grief when she hears the news, but *(unknown to her friends)* soon she finds joy in it. So Richards's "sad message" (67), though sad in Richards's eyes, is in fact a happy message.

Among the small but significant ironic details is the statement near the end of the story that when Mallard entered the house, Richards tried to conceal him from Mrs. Mallard, but "Richards was too late" (68). This is ironic because almost at the start of the story, in the second paragraph Richards "hastened" (67) to bring his sad message; if he had at the start been "too late" (68), Brently Mallard would have arrived at home first, and Mrs. Mallard's life would not have ended an hour later but would simply have gone on as it has been. Yet another irony at the end of the story is the diagnosis of the doctors. They say she died of "heart disease--of joy that kills" (68). In one sense they are right: Mrs. Mallard has for the last hour experienced a great joy. But of course the doctors totally misunderstand the joy that kills her. It is not joy at seeing her husband alive, but her realization that the great joy she experienced during the last hour is over.

All of these ironic details add richness to the story, but the central irony resides not in the well-intentioned but ironic actions of Richards, or in the unconsciously ironic words of the doctors, but in Mrs. Mallard's own life. She "sometimes" (68) loved her husband, but in a way she has been dead, a body subjected to her husband's will. Now, his apparent death brings her new life. Appropriately, this new life comes to her at the season of the year when "the tops of trees . . . were all aquiver with the new spring life" (67). But, ironically, her new life will last only an hour. She is free, free, free-but only until her husband walks through the doorway. She looks forward to "summer days" (68) but she will not see even the end of this spring day. If her years of marriage were ironic, bringing her a sort of living death instead of joy, her new life is ironic too, not only because it grows out of her moment of grief for her supposedly dead husband, but also because her vision of "a long procession of years" (68) within an hour on a spring day, is cut short.

[New page]

Work Cited

Chopin, Kate. "The Story of an Hour." *An Introduction to Literature.* Ed. Sylvan Barnet, William Burto, and William E. Cain. 16th ed. New York: Longman, 2011. 67–68. Print.

The Student's Analysis Analyzed

Finally, as a quick review, we will highlight several principles illustrated by this essay.

- The **title of the essay** is not merely the title of the work discussed; rather, it gives the reader a clue, an idea of the essayist's topic. Because your title will create a crucial first impression, make sure that it is interesting.
- The **opening or introductory paragraph** does not begin by saying "In this story. . . ." Rather, by naming the author and the title it lets the reader know exactly what story is being discussed. It also develops the writer's thesis a bit so that readers know where they will be going.
- The **organization** is effective. The smaller ironies are discussed in the second and third paragraphs, the central (chief) irony in the last paragraph; that is, the essay does not dwindle or become anticlimactic—rather, it builds up. (Again, if you outline your draft you will see if it has an effective organization.)
- Some **brief quotations** are used, both to provide evidence and to let the reader experience Kate Chopin's writing.
- The essay is chiefly **devoted to analysis, not to summary.** The writer, properly assuming that the reader has read the work, does not tell the plot in detail. But, aware that the reader has not memorized the story, the writer gives helpful reminders.
- The **present tense** is customarily used in narrating the action: "Mrs. Mallard dies"; "Mrs. Mallard's friends and relatives all assume."
- Although a **concluding paragraph** is often useful, it is not essential in a short analysis. In this essay, the last sentence explains the chief irony and, therefore, makes an acceptable ending.
- **Documentation** is given according to the form set forth in Chapter 17.

- There are no typographical errors. The author has **proofread** the paper carefully.

QUICK REVIEW

From First Response to Final Version: Writing an Essay about a Literary Work

- Read the text, then reread it, circling or underlining key words and jotting down questions and comments in the margins.
- If a specific topic has been assigned, reread the text with an eye toward finding evidence relevant to the topic.
- If you are to develop your own topic, follow your interests—for instance, about a particular character or theme.
- Develop your thoughts through free writing and note taking.
- Organize your thoughts—the computer can help you with this— by connecting related points, ideas, and questions.
- Refer to the text for quotations to use as evidence.
- Prepare a tentative outline.
- Write your first draft, focusing on presenting your thesis effectively.
- Review the literary work to make sure it fully supports your thesis. Quote from it—but use quotations as evidence, not as padding.
- Reread and revise the draft for content.
- Polish the draft for style.
- Check all quotations for accuracy, and check your spelling and punctuation.

📖 SUGGESTIONS FOR FURTHER READING

If you have enjoyed the two stories by Kate Chopin we have discussed, you might be interested in reading more of her work and in learning more about her life and era. The Kate Chopin International Society maintains a very good Internet site: <http://www.katechopin.org/>. It includes commentaries on Chopin's fiction, photographs and other visual materials, and links to the full texts of her novels *At Fault* (1890) and *The Awakening* (1899) and her short stories. We especially recommend the stories "The Storm" and "Désirée's Baby."

4

TWO FORMS OF CRITICISM: EXPLICATION AND ANALYSIS

Unexplained beauty arouses an irritation in me, a sense that this would be a good place to scratch.

—William Empson

EXPLICATION

A line-by-line or episode-by-episode commentary on what is going on in a text is an **explication** (literally, unfolding or spreading out). An explication does not deal with the writer's life or times, and it is not a paraphrase, a rewording—although it may include paraphrase. An explication is a commentary revealing your sense of the meaning of the work. To this end it calls attention, as it proceeds, to the implications of words, the function of rhymes, the shifts in point of view, the development of contrasts, and any other contributions to the meaning.

A Sample Explication: Langston Hughes's "Harlem"

The following short poem is by Langston Hughes (1902–67), an African-American writer who was born in Joplin, Missouri; lived part of his youth in Mexico; spent a year at Columbia University; served as a merchant seaman; and worked in a Paris nightclub. Later, when he returned to the United States, he showed some of his poems to Alain Locke, an influential critic, educator, and advocate of African-American literature. Hughes went on to publish fiction, plays, essays, and biographies; he also founded theaters, gave public readings, and was, in short, an important force.

43

HARLEM[1]

What happens to a dream deferred?

> Does it dry up
> like a raisin in the sun?
> Or fester like a sore—
> And then run?
> Does it stink like rotten meat?
> Or crust and sugar over—
> like a syrupy sweet?
>
> Maybe it just sags
> like a heavy load.
>
> *Or does it explode?*

Different readers will respond at least somewhat differently to any work. On the other hand, because writers want to communicate, they try to guide their readers' responses, and they count on their readers to understand the denotations of words as they understand them. Hughes assumed that his readers knew that Harlem was the site of a large African-American community in New York City. Explication is based on the assumption that the poem contains a meaning and that by studying the work thoughtfully we can unfold the meaning or meanings.

We will assume that the reader understands that Hughes is talking about Harlem, New York, and that the "dream deferred" refers to the unfulfilled hopes of African-Americans who live in a dominant white society. But Hughes does not say "hopes," he says "dream," and he does not say "unfulfilled," he says "deferred." You might ask yourself exactly what differences there are between these words. Next, after you have read the poem several times, you might think about which expression is better in the context, "unfulfilled hopes" or "dream deferred," and why.

Working toward an Explication of "Harlem"

In preparing to write an explication,

- Write on a computer or handwrite the complete text of the work—usually a poem but sometimes a short passage of prose—

---

[1] Langston Hughes, "Harlem (2)" [A Dream Deferred] from *The Collected Poems of Langston Hughes* by Langston Hughes, edited by Arnold Rampersad with David Roessel, Associate Editor, copyright © 1994 by the Estate of Langston Hughes. Used by permission of Alfred A. Knopf, a division of Random House, Inc. (print), and by permission of Harold Ober Associates Incorporated (electronic).

that you will explicate. The act of typing or writing it will help you to get into the piece, word by word, comma by comma.

- Type or write it *double-spaced,* so that you will have plenty of room for annotations as you study the piece.
- Make a few copies (or print a few copies, if you are using a word processor) before you start annotating, so that if one page gets too cluttered you can continue working on a clean copy. Or you may want to use one copy for certain kinds of annotations—let us say those concerning imagery—and other copies for other kinds of notes—let us say those concerning meter, or wordplay.
- If you are writing on a computer, you can highlight words, bold-face them, put them in capitals (for instance, to indicate accented syllables), and so forth.

Here is an explication of the poem, a detailed examination of the whole, and preliminary jottings.

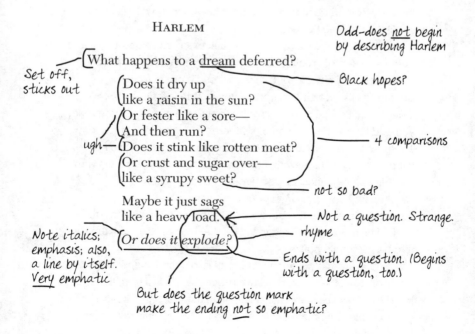

HARLEM

Odd-does not begin by describing Harlem

What happens to a <u>dream</u> deferred?

Set off, sticks out

Does it dry up
like a raisin in the sun?
Or fester like a sore—
And then run?
Does it stink like rotten meat?
Or crust and sugar over—
like a syrupy sweet?

Black hopes?

ugh—

4 comparisons

not so bad?

Maybe it just sags
like a heavy load.

Not a question. Strange.

Or does it explode?

rhyme

Note italics; emphasis; also, a line by itself. Very emphatic

Ends with a question. (Begins with a question, too.)

But does the question mark make the ending not so emphatic?

These annotations get at the structure of the poem, the relationship of the parts. The student notices that the poem begins with a line set off by itself and ends with a line set off by itself, and he also notices that each of these lines is a question. Further, he indicates that each of these two lines is emphasized in other ways: The first begins farther to the left than any of the other lines—as though the other lines are subheadings or are in some way subordinate—and the last is italicized.

Some Journal Entries

Tim Clark, the student who made these annotations, later wrote an entry in his journal:

> Feb. 18. Since the title is "Harlem," it's obvious that the "dream" is by African-American people. Also, obvious that Hughes thinks that if the "dream" doesn't become real there may be riots ("explode"). I like "raisin in the sun" (maybe because I like the play), and I like the business about "a syrupy sweet"— much more pleasant than the festering sore and the rotten meat. But if the dream becomes "sweet," what's wrong with that? Why should something "sweet" explode?
>
> Feb. 21. Prof. McCabe said to think of structure or form of a poem as a sort of architecture, a building with a foundation, floors, etc., topped by a roof—but since we read a poem from top to bottom, it's like a building upside down. Title is foundation (even though it's at top); last line is roof, capping the whole. As you read, you add layers. Foundation of "Harlem" is a question (first line). Then, set back a bit from foundation, or built on it by white space, a tall room (7 lines high, with 4 questions); then, on top of this room, another room (2 lines, one statement, not a question).
>
> Funny; I thought that in poems all stanzas are the same number of lines. Then—more white space, so another unit—the roof. Man, this roof is going to fall in—"explodes." Not just the roof, maybe the whole house.
>
> Feb. 21, pm. I get it; one line at start, one line at end; both are questions, but the last sort of says (because it is *in italics*) that it is the *most likely* answer to the question of the first line. The last line is also a question, but it's still an answer. The big stanza (7 lines) has 4 questions: 2 lines, 2 lines, 1 line, 2 lines. Maybe the switch to

1 line is to give some variety, so as not to be dull? It's exactly in the middle of the poem. I get the progress from raisin in the sun (dried, but not so terrible), to festering sore and to stinking meat, but I still don't see what's so bad about "a syrupy sweet." Is Hughes saying that after things are very bad they will get better? But why, then, the explosion at the end?

Feb 23. "Heavy load" and "sags" in next-to-last stanza seem to me to suggest slaves with bales of cotton, or maybe poor cotton pickers dragging big sacks of cotton. Or maybe people doing heavy labor in Harlem. Anyway, very tired. Different from running sore and stinking meat earlier; not disgusting, but pressing down, deadening. Maybe *worse* than a sore or rotten meat—a hard, hopeless life.

And then the last line. Just one line, no fancy (and disgusting) simile. Boom! Not just pressed down and tired, like maybe some racist whites think (hope?) blacks will be? Bang! Will there be survivors?

Drawing on these notes, Tim Clark jotted down some key ideas to lead him through a draft of an explication of the poem. The organization of the draft posed no problem; for this explication, he simply followed the organization of the poem.

11 lines; short, but powerful; explosive
Question (first line)
Answers (set off by space and also indented)
"raisin in the sun": shrinking ⎤
"sore"   ⎬ disgusting
"rotten meat"   ⎦
"syrupy sweet": relief from disgusting comparisons
final question (last line): explosion?
  explosive (powerful) because:
    short, condensed, packed
    in italics
    stands by self—like first line
    no fancy comparison; very direct
    metaphor, not simile

The Final Draft

Here is Tim Clark's final essay (see following page).

Barry Brown
Professor Gregorian
English 10A
3 October 2010

Langston Hughes's "Harlem"

"Harlem" is a poem that is only 11 lines long, but it is charged with power. It explodes. Hughes sets the stage, so to speak, by telling us in the title that he is talking about Harlem, and then he begins by asking, "What happens to a dream deferred?" The rest of the poem is set off by being indented, as though it is the answer to his question. This answer is in three parts (three stanzas, of different lengths).

In a way, it's wrong to speak of the answer, since the rest of the poem consists of questions, but I think Hughes means that each question (for instance, does a "deferred" hope "dry up / like a raisin in the sun?") really is an answer, something that really has happened and that will happen again. The first question, "Does it dry up / like a raisin in the sun?" is a famous line. To compare hope to a raisin dried in the sun is to suggest a terrible shrinking. The next two comparisons are to a "sore" and to "rotten meat." These comparisons are less clever, but they are very effective because they are disgusting. Then, maybe because of the disgusting comparisons, he gives a comparison that is not at all disgusting. In this comparison he says that maybe the "dream deferred" will "crust over—/ like a syrupy sweet."

The seven lines with four comparisons are followed by a stanza of two lines with just one comparison:

> Maybe it just sags
> like a heavy load.

So if we thought that this postponed dream might finally turn into something "sweet," we were kidding ourselves. Hughes comes down to earth, in a short stanza, with an image of a heavy load, which probably also calls to mind images of people bent under heavy loads, maybe of cotton, or maybe just any sort of heavy load carried by African-Americans in Harlem and elsewhere.

The opening question ("What happens to a dream deferred?") was followed by four questions in seven lines, but now, with "Maybe it just sags / like a heavy load" we get a statement, as though the poet at last has found an answer. But at the end we get one more question, set off by itself and in italics: *"Or does it explode?"* This line itself is explosive for four reasons: It is short, it is italicized, it is a metaphor rather than a simile, and it is a stanza in itself. It's also interesting that this line, unlike the earlier lines, does *not* use a simile. It's almost as though Hughes is saying, "OK, we've had enough fancy ways of talking about this terrible situation; here it is, straight."

The Explication Analyzed

- The **title of the essay** merely names the author and the work. Normally, an essay ought to have a more interesting title, something created by the essayist and something that at least hints at the essayist's thesis, but in this instance, where the assignment was simply to write an explication of the work, Tim Clark's title is acceptable.
- The **opening paragraph** provides a helpful overview. An explication begins at the beginning and continues to the end of the work or the part of the work that is being examined, but an introductory paragraph usually is welcome. Notice, too, that although explication is chiefly concerned with explaining (unpacking, unfolding) the meanings of words, because it is essentially concerned with the meaning of a literary work it can and should take account of anything that contributes to the meaning. The writer astutely points out that the appearance on the page (the indentation of certain lines) is a part of the meaning.
- The **organization** of an explication is almost never a problem because the essayist usually proceeds through the work, from start to finish. But notice that the writer does not just say, "In the next line . . . ," and "In the following line. . . ." When appropriate, he summarizes and he contrasts: "The seven lines with four comparisons are followed by a stanza of two lines with just one comparison."
- The **concluding paragraph** wraps things up nicely. It begins by referring to the beginning ("The opening question"), moves to the last line of the poem (*"Or does it explode?"*), and comments effectively on this last line. Notice that the comment is **an argument, not merely an unsupported assertion.** It indeed begins with an assertion ("This line itself is explosive") but, and this is important, it offers **evidence** for the assertion that the line is explosive: "It is short, it is italicized, it is a metaphor

rather than a simile, and it is a stanza in itself." That is, the writer gives reasons, a sure sign of an argument. If he had said something like "This line seems very powerful to me," we could reply that he is giving a personal opinion but not saying anything that can help us to see things his way.

Note: Another explication (of William Butler Yeats's "The Balloon of the Mind") appears in Chapter.13

✔ Checklist: Drafting an Explication

Overall Considerations

❏ Does the poem imply a story of some sort, for instance, the speaker's report of a love affair, or of a response to nature? If so, what is its beginning, middle, and end?

❏ If you detect a story in the speaker's mind, a change of mood—for instance, a shift from bitterness that a love affair has ended to hope for its renewal—is this change communicated by the connotations of certain words? By syntax? By metrical shifts?

Detailed Considerations

❏ If the poem has a title other than the first line, what are the implications of the title?

❏ Are there clusters or patterns of imagery—for instance, religious or economic images, or images drawn from nature? If so, how do they contribute to the meaning of the poem?

❏ Is irony (understatement or overstatement) used? To what effect?

❏ How do the connotations of certain words (for example, "dad" rather than "father") help to establish the meaning?

❏ What are the implications of the syntax—for instance, of notably simple or notably complex sentences? What do such sentences tell us about the speaker?

❏ Do metrical variations occur, and if so, what is their significance?

❏ Do rhyming words have some meaningful connection, as in the clichés "moon" and "June," "dove" and "love"?

❏ What are the implications of the appearance of the poem on the page—for example, of an indented line or of the stanzaic pattern? (For instance, if the poem consists of two stanzas of four lines each, does the second stanza offer a reversal of the first?)

ANALYSIS: THE JUDGMENT OF SOLOMON

Explication is a method used chiefly in the study of fairly short poems or brief extracts from essays, stories, novels, and plays. Of course, if one has world enough and time one can set out to explicate all of *The Color Purple* or *Hamlet;* more likely, one will explicate only a paragraph or at most a page of the novel and a speech or two of the play. In writing about works longer than a page or two, a more common approach than explicating is **analyzing** (literally, separating into parts in order better to understand the whole). An analysis of, say, *The Color Purple* may consider the functions of the setting or the uses that certain minor characters serve; an analysis of *Hamlet* may consider the comic passages or the reasons for Hamlet's delay; an analysis of *Death of a Salesman* may consider the depiction of women or the causes of Willy Loman's failure.

Analysis is not a process used only in talking about literature. It is commonly applied in thinking about almost any complex matter: Venus Williams plays a brilliant game of tennis. What does her serve do to her opponent? How does her backhand contribute? And so it makes sense, if you are writing about literature, to examine one or more of the components of the work, to see how they contribute to the whole, either as part of a stylistic pattern or as part of the meaning. In Chapter 6 we will see, for example, how the meter of Frost's "The Span of Life" contributes to the meaning—heavy stresses for the line about the tired old dog, fewer and lighter stresses for the line about the puppy.

Although other chapters of this book include specimens of analytic criticism—for instance, of a proverb ("A rolling stone gathers no moss") and of short poems by Robert Frost and Pat Mora—a brief analysis of a very short story about King Solomon may be useful here. Because the story is short, the analysis can consider most of the story's parts, and therefore the analysis can seem relatively complete.

The following story about King Solomon, customarily called "The Judgment of Solomon," appears in the Hebrew Bible, in the latter part of the third chapter of the book called 1 Kings or First Kings, probably written in the mid-sixth century BCE. The translation is from the King James Version of the Bible (1611). Two expressions in the story need clarification: (1) The woman who "overlaid" her child in her sleep rolled over on the child and suffocated it; (2) it is said of the other woman that her "bowels yearned upon her son"—that is, her heart longed for her son. (Among the early Hebrews, the bowels were thought to be the seat of emotion.)

Then came there two women, that were harlots, unto the king, and stood before him. And the one woman said, "O my lord, I and this woman dwell in one house, and I was delivered of a child with her in the house. And it came to pass the third day after that I was delivered, that this woman was delivered also, and we were together; there was no stranger in the house, save we two in the house. And this woman's child died in the night, because she overlaid it. And she rose at midnight, and took my son from beside me, while thine handmaid slept, and laid it in her bosom, and laid her dead child in my bosom. And when I rose in the morning to give my child suck, behold, it was dead; but when I considered it in the morning, behold, it was not my son, which I did bear."

And the other woman said, "Nay, but the living son is my son, and the dead is thy son." And this said, "No, but the dead is thy son, and the living is my son." Thus they spoke before the king.

Then said the king, "The one said, 'This is my son that liveth, and thy son is dead.' And the other said, 'Nay, but thy son is the dead, and my son is the living.'" And the king said, "Bring me a sword." And they brought a sword before the king. And the king said, "Divide the living child in two and give half to the one, and half to the other."

Then spake the woman whose the living child was unto the king, for her bowels yearned upon her son, and she said, "O my lord, give her the living child, and in no wise slay it." But the other said, "Let it be neither mine nor thine, but divide it."

Then the king answered and said, "Give her the living child, and in no wise slay it. She is the mother thereof."

And all Israel heard of the judgment which the king had judged, and they feared the king, for they saw that the wisdom of God was in him, to do judgment.

Thinking about Form

Let us begin by analyzing the *form,* or the shape, of the story. One form or shape that we notice is this: The story moves from a problem to a solution. We can also say, still speaking of the overall form, that the story moves from quarreling and talk of death to unity and talk of life. In short, it has a happy ending, a form that (because it provides an optimistic view of life and also a sense of completeness) gives pleasure to most people.

In thinking about a work of literature, it is always useful to take notice of the basic form of the whole, the overall structural pattern. Doubtless you are already familiar with many basic patterns, for example, tragedy (joy yielding to sorrow) and romantic comedy (angry conflict yielding to joyful union). If you think even briefly about verbal works, you will notice the structures or patterns that govern songs, episodes in soap operas, political speeches (beginning with the candidate's expression of pleasure at being in New York City, and ending with "God bless you all"), detective stories, Westerns, and so on. And just as viewers of a Western film inevitably experience one Western in the context of others, so readers inevitably experience one story in the context of similar stories, and one poem in the context of others.

Thinking about Character

Second, we can say that "The Judgment of Solomon" is a detective story:

- There is a death, followed by
- a conflict in the testimony of the witnesses, and
- a solution by a shrewd outsider.

Consider Solomon's predicament. Ordinarily in literature characters are sharply defined and individualized, yet the essence of a detective story is that the culprit should not be easily recognized as wicked, and here nothing seems to distinguish the two petitioners. Solomon is confronted by "two women, that were harlots" (that is, immoral women, prostitutes). Until late in the story—that is, up to the time Solomon suggests dividing the child—they are described only as "the one woman," "the other woman," "the one," "the other."

Does the story suffer from weak characterization? If we think analytically about this issue, we realize that the point surely is to make the women as alike as possible, so that we cannot tell which of the two is speaking the truth. Like Solomon, we have nothing to go on; neither witness is known to be more honest than the other, and there are no other witnesses to support or refute either woman.

Thoughts about Other Possible Topics

Analysis is concerned with

- seeing the relationships between the parts of a work, but
- analysis also may take note of what is *not* in the work.

An additional witness would destroy the story or at least turn it into an utterly different story. Another thing missing from this story is an explicit editorial comment or interpretation, except for the remark at the end, that the people "feared the king." If we had read the story in the Geneva

Bible (1560), which is the translation of the Bible that Shakespeare was familiar with, we would have found a marginal comment: "Her motherly affection herein appeareth that she had rather endure the rigour of the lawe, than see her child cruelly slaine." Would you agree that it is better, at least in this story, for the reader to draw conclusions than for the story-teller explicitly to point them out?

Solomon wisely contrives a situation in which these two claimants, who seem so similar, will reveal their true natures: The mother will reveal her love, and the liar will reveal her hard heart. The early symmetry (the identity of the two women) pleases a reader, and so does the device by which we can at last distinguish between the two women.

But even near the end there is a further symmetry. To save the child's life, the true mother gives up her claim, crying out, "Give her the living child, and in no wise slay it." The author (or, rather, the translator who produced this part of the King James Version) takes these very words, with no change whatsoever, and puts them into Solomon's mouth as the king's final judgment. Solomon too says, "Give her the living child, and in no wise slay it," but now the sentence takes on a new meaning. In the first sentence, "her" refers to the liar (the true mother will give the child to "her"); in Solomon's sentence, "her" refers to the true mother: "Give her the living child. . . ." Surely we take pleasure in the fact that the very words by which the mother renounces her child (1) are the words that reveal to Solomon the truth and (2) are the words Solomon uses to restore the child to its mother.

This analysis has chiefly talked about the relations of parts, and es-pecially it has tried to explain why the two women in this story are *not* distinct, until Solomon finds a way to reveal their distinctive natures: If the story is to demonstrate Solomon's wisdom, the women must seem identical until Solomon can show that they differ. But the analysis could have gone into some other topic.

A student might begin by asking this question: "Although it is impor-tant for the women to be highly similar, why are they harlots?" (It is too simple to say that the women in the story are harlots because the author is faithfully reporting a historical episode in Solomon's career. The story is widely recognized as a folktale, found also in other ancient cultures.) One possible reason for making the women harlots is that the story de-mands that there be no witnesses; by using harlots, the author disposed of husbands, parents, and siblings who might otherwise be expected to live with the women. A second possible reason is that the author wanted to show that Solomon's justice extended to all, not only to respectable folk. Third, perhaps the author wished to reject or at least to complicate the stereotype of the harlot as a thoroughly disreputable person. He did this by introducing another (and truer?) stereotype, the mother as motivated by overwhelming maternal love.

FOR FURTHER STUDY AND ANALYSIS

Here is another passage from the Bible (King James Version), Jesus's parable of the Prodigal Son, which appears in the Gospel of Luke (15:11–32) in the New Testament. Read the parable carefully, taking good notes and jotting down key points and questions that occur to you about it. Pay close attention to the form, to the shape of the work as a whole, from beginning to middle to end. In an essay of 1–2 pages, present an analysis of this parable, keeping in mind the suggestions for effective writing and analysis that we have given.

Consider, for example,

- the characterizations of the father and the younger and elder sons. What do we learn about each of them as the story unfolds?
- Does the ending surprise you? Should the story have given us the responses of the sons to the father's words, or is the conclusion just right the way it is?
- What is the lesson that this parable aims to teach us?

THE PARABLE OF THE PRODIGAL SON

And [Jesus] said, A certain man had two sons: And the younger of them said to his father, Father, give me the portion of goods that falleth to me. And he divided unto them his living. And not many days after the younger son gathered all together, and took his journey into a far country, and there wasted his substance with riotous living. And when he had spent all, there arose a mighty famine in that land; and he began to be in want. And he went and joined himself to a citizen of that country; and he sent him into his fields to feed swine.

And he would fain have filled his belly with the husks that the swine did eat: and no man gave unto him. And when he came to himself, he said, How many hired servants of my father's have bread enough and to spare, and I perish with hunger! I will arise and go to my father, and will say unto him, Father, I have sinned against heaven, and before thee, And am no more worthy to be called thy son: make me as one of thy hired servants.

And he arose, and came to his father. But when he was yet a great way off, his father saw him, and had compassion, and ran, and fell on his neck, and kissed him. And the son said unto him, Father, I have sinned against heaven, and in thy sight, and am no more worthy to be called thy son.

But the father said to his servants, Bring forth the best robe, and put it on him; and put a ring on his hand, and shoes on his feet: And bring hither the fatted calf, and kill it; and let us eat, and be merry: For this my son was dead, and is alive again; he was lost, and is found. And they began to be merry.

Now his elder son was in the field: and as he came and drew nigh to the house, he heard musick and dancing. And he called one of the servants, and asked what these things meant. And he said unto him, Thy brother is come; and thy father hath killed the fatted calf, because he hath received him safe and sound.

And he was angry, and would not go in: therefore came his father out, and intreated him. And he answering said to his father, Lo, these many years do I serve thee, neither transgressed I at any time thy commandment: and yet thou never gavest me a kid, that I might make merry with my friends: But as soon as this thy son was come, which hath devoured thy living with harlots, thou hast killed for him the fatted calf.

And he said unto him, Son, thou art ever with me, and all that I have is thine. It was meet that we should make merry, and be glad: for this thy brother was dead, and is alive again; and was lost, and is found.

Comparison: An Analytic Tool

If you really want to see something, look at something else.

—Howard Nemerov

Analysis frequently involves comparing: Things are examined for their resemblances to and differences from other things. Strictly speaking, if one emphasizes the differences rather than the similarities, one is contrasting rather than comparing, but we need not preserve this distinction; we can call both processes *comparing*.

Although your instructor may ask you to write a comparison of two works of literature, the *subject* of the essay is the works; comparison is simply an effective analytic technique to show some of the qualities in the works. You might compare Chopin's use of nature in "The Story of an Hour" (page 20) with the use of nature in another story, to reveal the subtle differences between the stories, but a comparison of works utterly unlike can hardly tell the reader or the writer anything.

How does one organize a comparison, say between the settings in two stories, between two characters in a novel (or even between a character at the end of a novel and the same character at the beginning), or between the symbolism of two poems? Probably, a student's first thought after making some jottings is to discuss one half of the comparison and then go on to the second half. Instructors and textbooks (though not this one) usually condemn such an organization, arguing that the essay breaks into two parts and that the second part involves a good deal of repetition of categories set up in the first part. Usually, they recommend that the students organize their thoughts differently, somewhat along these lines:

1. First similarity
   a. first work (or character, or characteristic)
   b. second work
2. Second similarity
   a. first work
   b. second work
3. First difference
   a. first work
   b. second work
4. Second difference
   a. first work
   b. second work

and so on, for as many additional differences as seem relevant. If one wishes to compare *Adventures of Huckleberry Finn* with *The Catcher in the Rye,* one may organize the material thus:

1. First similarity: the narrator and his quest
   a. Huck
   b. Holden
2. Second similarity: the corrupt world surrounding the narrator
   a. society in *Huck*
   b. society in *Catcher*
3. First difference: degree to which the narrator fulfills his quest and escapes from society
   a. Huck's plan to "light out" to the frontier
   b. Holden's breakdown

Another way of organizing a comparison and contrast:

1. First point: the narrator and his quest
   a. similarities between Huck and Holden
   b. differences between Huck and Holden
2. Second point: the corrupt world
   a. similarities between the worlds in *Huck* and *Catcher*
   b. differences between the worlds in *Huck* and *Catcher*
3. Third point: degree of success
   a. similarities between Huck and Holden
   b. differences between Huck and Holden

A comparison need not employ either of these structures. There is even the danger that an essay employing either of them may not come into focus until the essayist stands back from the seven-layer cake and announces in the concluding paragraph that the odd layers taste better. In one's preparatory thinking, one may want to make comparisons in pairs (good-natured humor: the clown in *Othello,* the clownish grave digger in *Hamlet;* social satire: the clown in *Othello,* the grave digger in *Hamlet;* relevance to main theme: . . . ; length of role: . . . ; comments by other characters: . . .), but one must come to some conclusions about what these add up to before writing the final version.

This final version should not duplicate the thought processes; rather, it should be organized so as to make the point—the thesis—clearly and effectively. After reflection, one may believe that although there are superficial similarities between the clown in *Othello* and the clownish grave digger in *Hamlet,* there are essential differences; then in the finished essay one probably will not wish to obscure the main point by jumping back and forth from play to play, working through a series of similarities and differences. It may be better to discuss the clown in *Othello* and then to point out that, although the grave digger in *Hamlet* resembles him in A, B, and C, the grave digger also has other functions (D, E, and F) and is of greater consequence to *Hamlet* than the clown is to *Othello.* Some repetition in the second half of the essay ("The grave digger's puns come even faster than the clown's. . . . ") will bind the two halves into a meaningful whole, making clear the degree of similarity or difference. The point of the essay presumably is not to list pairs of similarities or differences but to illuminate a work or works by making thoughtful comparisons.

Although in a long essay one cannot postpone until halfway through a discussion of the second half of the comparison, in an essay of fewer than ten pages nothing is wrong with setting forth one half of the comparison and then, in light of it, the second half. The essay will break into two unrelated parts if the second half makes no use of the first or if it fails to modify the first half, but not if the second half looks back to the first half and calls attention to differences that the new material reveals.

Finally, a reminder: The purpose of a comparison is to call attention to the unique features of something by holding it up against something similar but significantly different. You can compare Macbeth with Banquo (two men who hear a prophecy but who respond differently), or Macbeth with Lady Macbeth (a husband and wife, both eager to be monarchs but differing in their sense of the consequences), or Hamlet and Holden Caulfield (two people who see themselves as surrounded by a corrupt world), but you can hardly compare Holden with Macbeth or with Lady Macbeth—there simply are not enough points of resemblance to make it worth your effort to call attention to subtle differences.

✐ A RULE FOR WRITERS

In making a comparison, do not simply make a list of similarities or of differences; make a *point*. In fact, consider introducing your comparison with a thesis sentence indicating your argument.

✔ Checklist: Revising a Comparison

❑ Does it make sense to compare these things? What question will the comparison help to answer? What do you hope your reader will learn?

❑ Is the point of the comparison—the reason for making it—clear?

❑ Does the comparison cover all significant similarities and differences?

❑ Is the comparison readable; that is, is it clear and yet not tediously mechanical?

❑ Is the organization that is used—perhaps treating one text first and then the other, or perhaps shifting back and forth between texts—the best way to make this comparison?

❑ If the essay offers a value judgment, is the judgment fair? Does the essay offer enough evidence to bring a reader into at least partial agreement?

FOR FURTHER READING AND COMPARING

Take a moment to reread Langston Hughes's poem "Harlem," on page 44. Then, for comparison, read the poem below, "We Real Cool," published in 1960 by the acclaimed African-American poet and fiction writer Gwendolyn Brooks (1917–2000). In your notebook or journal, explicate Brooks's poem so that you understand it well. Then set the two poems side by side—you might want to type out your own copies and literally place the pages side by side.

- In its style, theme, and perspective on African-American experience, what makes each poem special?
- What, furthermore, makes the poems similar to one another?

Be as clear and as specific as you can, and refer to details in the poems to support the points of similarity and difference that you see. Present your comparison in an essay of two pages.

WE REAL COOL

The Pool Players.
Seven at the Golden Shovel.

We real cool. We
Left school. We

Lurk late. We
Strike straight. We

Sing sin. We
Thin gin. We

Jazz June. We
Die soon.

FINDING A TOPIC

All literary works suggest their own topics for analysis, and all essayists must set forth their own theses, but a few useful generalizations may be made. You can often find a thesis by asking one of two questions:

1. **What is this doing?** That is, why is this scene in the novel or play? Why is Beckett's *Waiting for Godot* in two acts, rather than one or three? Why the biblical allusions in *Waiting for Godot*? Why does Hamlet delay?

Why are these lines unrhymed? Why is this stanza form used? What is the significance of the parts of the work?

If you do not know where to begin, think about the title. Titles are often highly significant parts of the work: Ibsen explained that he called his play *Hedda Gabler* rather than *Hedda Tesman* because "She is to be regarded as her father's daughter rather than as her husband's wife." But there are other ways of beginning. If the work is a poem, you may be able to get a start by considering the stanza form or the main images. If the work is a story or play, you might consider the relation between the chief character and the second most important character.

2. **Why do I have this response?** Why do I find this poem clever or moving or puzzling? How did the author make this character funny or dignified or pathetic? How did he or she communicate the idea that this character is a bore without boring me? Why am I troubled by the representation of women in this story? Why do I regard as sexist this lover's expression of his love?

The first of these questions, "What is this doing?" requires that you identify yourself with the author, wondering, for example, whether this opening scene is the best possible for this story.

The second question, "Why do I have this response?" requires that you trust your feelings. If you are amused or bored or puzzled or annoyed, assume that these responses are appropriate and follow them up, at least until a rereading of the work provides other responses.

CONSIDERING THE EVIDENCE

Once your responses have led you to a topic ("The Clown in *Othello*") and then to a thesis ("The clown is relevant because . . . "), be certain that you have all the evidence. Usually this means that you should study the entire text carefully. For example, if you are writing about *The Catcher in the Rye,* before you argue that because Holden distrusts the adult world, "old" is his ultimate word of condemnation, remember that he speaks of "old Phoebe" and of "old Thomas Hardy," both of whom he values greatly.

ORGANIZING THE MATERIAL

"Begin at the beginning," the King of Hearts in *Alice in Wonderland* said very gravely, "and go on till you come to the end: then stop." This is how your paper should seem to the reader, but it need not have been drafted thus.

After locating a topic, converting it into a thesis, and weighing the evidence, a writer has the job of organizing the material into a coherent whole, a sequence of paragraphs that holds the reader's interest (partly because it sets forth material clearly) and that steadily builds up an effective argument. Notice that in the essay on irony in Kate Chopin's "The Story of an Hour" (pages 39–41) the student wisely moves from the lesser ironies to the chief irony. To begin with the chief irony and end with the lesser ironies would almost surely be anticlimactic.

The organization of an essay will depend on the nature of the essay: An essay on foreshadowing in *Macbeth* probably will be organized chronologically (material in the first act will be discussed before material in the second act), but an essay on the character of Macbeth may begin with the end of the play, discussing Macbeth as he is in the fifth act, and then work backward through the play, arriving at last at the original Macbeth of the beginning of the play.

The important point is not that there is only one way to organize an essay, but that you find the way that is best for the particular topic and argument. Once you think you know more or less what you want to say, you will usually, after trial and error, find what seems the best way of communicating it to a reader. An outline will help you find your way, but don't assume that once you have settled on an outline the organization of your essay finally is established. After you read the draft, you may realize that a more effective organization will be more helpful to your reader—which means that you must move paragraphs around, revise your transitions, and, in short, produce another draft.

If you look at your draft and outline it, as suggested on pages 35–36, you will quickly see whether the draft needs to be reorganized.

✍ A RULE FOR WRITERS

Organize your essay so that your readers can easily follow the argument you use—the reasons you give—to support your thesis.

COMMUNICATING JUDGMENTS

Because a critical essay is a judicious attempt to help a reader see what is going on in a work or in a part of a work, the voice of the critic usually sounds, on first hearing, impartial; but good criticism includes—at least implicitly—evaluation. The critic may say not only that the setting changes (a neutral expression) but also that "the novelist aptly shifts the setting" or "unconvincingly describes . . ." or "effectively juxtaposes. . . ." These evaluations are supported with evidence. The critic has feelings about the work under discussion and reveals them, not by continually saying "I feel" and "This moves me," but by calling attention to the degree of success or failure perceived.

Nothing is wrong with occasionally using *I*, and noticeable avoidances of it—"it is seen that," "this writer," "the present writer," "we," and the like—suggest sham modesty; but too much talk of "I" makes a writer sound self-absorbed, as if he or she were writing to himself or herself, not to a reader.

Consider this sentence from the opening paragraph in a review of George Orwell's *1984*.

> I do not think I have ever read a novel more frightening and depressing; and yet, such are the originality, the suspense, the speed of writing and withering indignation that it is impossible to put the book down.

Fine—provided that the reviewer goes on to offer evidence that enables readers to share his or her evaluation of *1984*.

One final remark on communicating judgments: Write sincerely. Any attempt to neglect your own thoughtful responses and replace them with fabrications designed to please an instructor will surely fail. It is hard enough to find the words that clearly communicate your responses; it is almost impossible to find the words that express your guess about what your instructor expects your responses to be.

✍ A RULE FOR WRITERS

When you use such terms as *forceful, moving, stirring,* and *vivid*, you probably are talking not about the work but about your response to it. If you hope to persuade your readers to share your response, you need to point to the evidence—the features in the work that cause you to respond in such a way.

REVIEW: HOW TO WRITE AN EFFECTIVE ESSAY

1. Pre-writing

Read the work carefully. You may, on this first reading, want to highlight or annotate certain things, such as passages that please or that puzzle, or you may prefer simply to read it through. In any case, on a second reading you will certainly want to annotate the text and jot down notes either in the margins or in a journal. You probably are not focusing on a specific topic but rather are taking account of your early responses to the work.

If you have a feeling or an idea, jot it down; do not assume that you will remember it when you get around to drafting your essay. Write it down so that you will be sure to remember it and so that in the act of writing it down you can improve it.

2. Drafting

After reviewing your notes and sorting them out, you will find that you have not only a topic (a subject to write about) but a thesis (a point to be made, an argument). Get it down on paper. Perhaps begin by jotting down your thesis and under it a tentative outline.

If you are writing an explication, the order is essentially the order of the lines or of the episodes. If you are writing an analysis, you may wish to organize your essay from the lesser material to the greater (to avoid anticlimax) or from the simple to the complex (to ensure intelligibility). If you are discussing the roles of three characters in a story, it may be best to build up to the one of the three that you think the most important. If you are comparing two characters, it may be best to move from the most obvious contrasts to the least obvious.

At this stage, however, do not worry about whether the organization is unquestionably the best possible organization for your topic. A page of paper with some ideas in some sort of sequence, however rough, will encourage you that you do have something to say. If you have doubts, by all means record them. By writing down your uncertainties, you will begin to feel your way toward tentative explanations of them.

Almost any organization will help you get going on your draft; that is, it will help you start writing an essay. The process of writing will itself clarify and improve your preliminary ideas. If you are like most people, you can't do much precise thinking until you have committed to paper at least a rough sketch of your initial ideas. Later, you can push and polish your ideas into shape, perhaps even deleting all of them and starting over, but it is a lot easier to improve your ideas once you see them in front of you than it is to do the job in your head. On paper, one word leads to another; in your head, one word often blocks another.

Although we have been talking about drafting, most teachers rightly regard this first effort at organizing one's notes and turning them into an essay not as a first draft but as a zero draft, really a part of pre-writing. When you reread it, you will doubtless find passages that need further support, passages that seem out of place, and passages that need clarification. You will also find passages that are better than you thought at the outset you could produce. In any case, on rereading the rough draft you will find things that will require you to go back and check the work of literature and to think further about what you have said about it. After rereading the literary work and your draft, you are in a position to write something that can rightly be called a first draft.

3. Revising

Try to allow at least a day to elapse before you start to revise your rough draft and another day before you revise your first draft. If you come to the material with a relatively fresh eye, you may see that the thesis needs to be announced earlier or more clearly or that certain points need to be supported by concrete references—perhaps by brief quotations from the literary work. A review by your peers will give you a good sense of which things need clarification and of whether your discussion is adequately organized.

At this stage, pay special attention to the following matters.

The Title If you have not already jotted down a tentative title for your essay, now is the time to do so. Make sure that the title is interesting and informative. There is nothing interesting and there is very little that is informative in a title such as "On a Play by Arthur Miller," or even in "On *Death of a Salesman*." Such titles are adequate to get you going, but as you think about your draft, come up with something more focused, such as "The Women in *Death of a Salesman*" (this title announces the topic) or "A Feminist Reading of *Death of a Salesman*" (this title announces the approach). Thinking about the title will help you to write an essay that is focused.

The Opening Your introductory sentences or paragraphs should engage the reader's interest. It is usually desirable also to give the reader the necessary information concerning which work you are writing about, to indicate your thesis (this information itself may get the reader's interest), and to indicate what your organization will be. Here is a sample that does all of these things:

> Arthur Miller's *Death of a Salesman* is so much a play about a sales*man* that one hardly thinks about the other characters, except perhaps for his wife, Linda. But there are other women in the play, too, and this essay will examine Miller's depiction of them, beginning with the briefest sketches and going to Miller's fullest picture of a woman, Linda Loman. Given that the play is chiefly about Willy Loman, and given that Miller wrote it about fifty years ago, we might not expect the representation of women to be as insightful as in fact it is.

Again, this opening paragraph

- identifies the author and the work (Miller's *Death of a Salesman*), and it
- indicates the topic (women), the thesis (Miller's depiction is surprisingly insightful), and the structure (from minor characters to a major character).

Notice, by the way, the writer says "this essay will examine." That's perfectly all right, but the use of the first person, "I," would be entirely acceptable here, provided that the writer does not use it so often that he or she sounds like an egomaniac. (For further discussion of introductory paragraphs, see pages 304–05.)

The Thesis and the Organization   In addition to announcing your thesis early—perhaps in the title or in the opening paragraph—be sure to keep the thesis in view throughout the essay. For instance, if you are arguing that Miller's depiction of women is surprisingly sympathetic, you will say so, and you will reaffirm the point during the essay, when you present supporting evidence.

Similarly, even if you have announced the organization, you will keep the reader posted by occasionally saying such things as "One other minor character must be looked at," and "The last minor character that we will look at," and "With Linda Loman, the most important woman in the play." And you will make the organization clear to your readers by using the appropriate lead-ins and transitions, such as "Furthermore," "On the other hand," "The final example . . . ."

The Closing   Say something more interesting than "Thus we see," followed by a repetition of the thesis sentence. Among the tested and effective ways of ending effectively are these: (1) Glance back to something from the opening paragraph, thus giving your essay a sense of closure;

(2) offer a new bit of evidence, thus driving the point home; or (3) indicate that the thesis, now established, can be used in other investigations of comparable material, for instance, in a discussion of Miller's later plays. (For further discussion of concluding paragraphs, see pages 305–07.)

4. Editing

Small-scale revision, such as checking the spelling, punctuation, and accuracy of quotations, is usually called *editing*. Even when you get to this stage, you may find that you must make larger revisions. In checking a quotation, you may conclude that it does not really support the point you are making, so you may have to do some substantial revising.

Print a clean copy, following the principles concerning margins, pagination, and documentation set forth in Chapters 16 and 17 of this book. If you have borrowed any ideas, be sure to give credit to your sources. Finally, proofread, make corrections, and print the final copy.

✍ A RULE FOR WRITERS

The words that you put on the page will convey an image of you to the reader; make sure that the image is favorable.

✔ Editing Checklist: Questions to Ask Yourself When Editing

❑   Is the title of my essay informative and interesting?

❑   Do I identify the subject of my essay (author and title) early?

❑   What is my thesis? Do I state it soon enough (perhaps even in the title) and keep it in view?

❑   Is the organization reasonable? Does each point lead into the next without irrelevancies and without anticlimaxes?

❑   Is each paragraph unified by a topic sentence or a topic idea? Are there helpful transitions from one paragraph to the next?

❑   Are generalizations supported by appropriate concrete details, especially by brief quotations from the text?

❑   Is the opening paragraph interesting and, by its end, focused on the topic? Is the final paragraph conclusive without being repetitive?

❑   Is the tone appropriate? No sarcasm, no apologies, no condescension?

❑   If there is a summary, is it as brief as possible, given its purpose?

❏   Are the quotations adequately introduced, and are they accurate? Do they provide evidence, or do they merely add words to the essay?
❏   Is the present tense used to describe the author's work and the action of the work ("Shakespeare *shows*," "Hamlet *dies*")?
❏   Have I kept in mind the needs of my audience—for instance, by defining unfamiliar terms, or by briefly summarizing works or opinions that the reader may be unfamiliar with?
❏   Is documentation provided where necessary?
❏   Are the spelling and punctuation correct? Are other mechanical matters (such as margins, spacing, and citations) in correct form? Have I proofread carefully?
❏   Is the paper properly identified—author's name, instructor's name, course number, and date?

FOR FURTHER READING, EXPLICATION, AND ANALYSIS

A favorite poem among students is "The Tyger," by William Blake (1757–1827), which is included in *Songs of Experience* (1794), a companion volume to his earlier *Songs of Innocence* (1789). Read the poem for yourself and enjoy it—you will feel the beat of the rhythm and the rhyme. (We should note that modern printings of this poem vary somewhat, especially in punctuation.)

THE TYGER

Tyger! Tyger! burning bright
In the forests of the night,
What immortal hand or eye
Could frame thy fearful symmetry?

In what distant deeps or skies
Burnt the fire of thine eyes?
On what wings dare he aspire?
What the hand, dare sieze the fire?

And what shoulder, & what art,
Could twist the sinews of thy heart?
And when thy heart began to beat,
What dread hand? & what dread feet?

What the hammer? what the chain?
In what furnace was thy brain?
What the anvil? what dread grasp
Dare its deadly terrors clasp?

When the stars threw down their spears,
And water'd heaven with their tears,
Did he smile his work to see?
Did he who made the Lamb make thee?

Tyger! Tyger! burning bright
In the forests of the night,
What immortal hand or eye
Dare frame thy fearful symmetry?

After you have read the poem for pleasure several times, move through it again, jotting down notes, comments, and questions, and looking up the definitions of words. Then, in your notebook or journal, or in a computer file, make your way through the poem once more, this time explicating each line.

- Ask yourself what Blake is saying in the first line, the second line, and so on.
- When you reach the end of each stanza, step back: What is the main point about the tiger that Blake is making in this stanza?

Now, in an analysis of two pages, describe how Blake presents the tiger in this poem. Notice that this assignment is a general one, the kind of assignment you might be given in an introductory course; it is your prompt, your point of departure. You need to work with it, developing a thesis about it. That is what an analysis requires. You will not be explicating each and every line in your essay but, instead, making a statement about the poem as a whole—which you will proceed to explain and support through carefully chosen quotations from the text.

If you enjoy reading and thinking about "The Tyger," you might like to visit an outstanding Internet site devoted to Blake. Maintained by expert scholars, The William Blake Archive includes many texts, illuminated books, works of art, and related materials. You can search for "The Tyger" and see the beautiful page, with the text and a drawing of a tiger, that Blake prepared for it in his *Songs of Experience*. The William Blake Archive is at <http://www.blakearchive.org/blake/>.

5

OTHER KINDS OF WRITING ABOUT LITERATURE

The best of all ways to make one's reading valuable is to write about it.

—Ralph Waldo Emerson

A SUMMARY

The essay on "The Story of an Hour" in Chapter 3 does not include a *summary* because the writer knew that all of her readers were familiar with Chopin's story. Sometimes, however, it is advisable to summarize the work you are writing about, thus reminding a reader who has not read the work recently, or informing a reader who may never have read the work. A review of a new work of literature or of a new film usually includes a summary, on the assumption that readers are unfamiliar with it.

A summary is a brief restatement or condensation of the plot. Consider this summary of Chopin's "The Story of an Hour":

A newspaper office reports that Brently Mallard has been killed in a railroad accident. When the news is gently broken to Mrs. Mallard by her sister Josephine, Mrs. Mallard weeps wildly and then shuts herself up in her room, where she sinks into an armchair. Staring dully through the window, she sees the signs of spring, and then an unnameable sensation possesses her. She tries to reject it but finally abandons herself to it. Renewed, she exults in her freedom, in the thought that at last the days will be her own. She finally comes out of the room, embraces her sister, and descends the stairs. A moment later her husband—who in fact had not been in the accident—enters. Mrs. Mallard dies—of the joy that kills, according to the doctors' diagnosis.

Here are a few principles that govern summaries:

- A summary is much briefer than the original. It is not a paraphrase—a word-by-word translation of someone's words into your own. A paraphrase is usually at least as long as the original, whereas a summary is rarely longer than one-fourth of the original and is usually much shorter. A novel may be summarized in a few paragraphs, or even in one paragraph.

- A summary usually achieves its brevity by omitting almost all of the concrete details of the original and by omitting minor characters and episodes. Notice that the summary of "The Story of an Hour" omits the friend of the family, omits specifying the signs of spring, and omits the business of the sister imploring Mrs. Mallard to open the door.

- A summary is as accurate as possible, given the limits of space. It must not misrepresent the basic ideas of the original. It may, however, be markedly different from the original in style. For instance, if the original is verbose, the summary will nevertheless be concise. There is a contradiction here: We say that a summary must be accurate, but that it need not reproduce the style or tone of the original, yet elsewhere in this book we argue that a writer's tone is part of the meaning. Here we seem to be saying that the meaning can be separated from the tone. But the "meaning" we now are talking about is large-scale meaning (for example, the basic argument, the summary of a plot), not small-scale meaning (subtle details).

- A summary is normally written in the present tense. Thus "A newspaper office reports . . ., Mrs. Mallard weeps. . . ."

- If the summary is brief (say, fewer than 250 words), it may be given as a single paragraph. If you are summarizing a long work, you may feel that a longer summary is needed. In this case your reader will be grateful to you if you divide the summary into paragraphs. As you draft your summary, you may find natural divisions. For instance, the scene of the story may change midway, providing you with the opportunity to use two paragraphs. Or you may want to summarize a five-act play in five paragraphs.

✍ A RULE FOR WRITERS

Summaries have their place in essays, but remember that a summary is not an analysis; it is only a summary.

A PARAPHRASE

A paraphrase is a restatement—a sort of translation into the same language—of a literary work or statement that may in its original form be somewhat obscure to a reader. A native speaker of English will not need a paraphrase of "Thirty days hath September," though a nonnative speaker might be puzzled by two things, the meaning of *hath* and the inverted word order. For such a reader, "September has thirty days" would be a helpful paraphrase.

Although a paraphrase seeks to clarify the original, if the original is even a little more complex than "Thirty days hath September" the paraphrase will—in the process of clarifying something—lose something, since the substitution of one word for another will change the meaning. For instance, "Shut up" and "Be quiet" do not say exactly the same thing; the former (in addition to asking for quiet) says that the speaker is rude, or it says that the speaker feels he can treat his listener contemptuously, but the paraphrase loses all of this.

Still, a paraphrase can be helpful as a first step in helping a reader to understand a line that includes an obsolete word or phrase, or a word or phrase that is current in only one region. In a poem by Emily Dickinson (1830–86), the following line appears:

The sun engrossed the East.

Engrossed here has (perhaps among other meanings) a special commercial meaning, "to acquire most or all of a commodity; to monopolize the market," and so a paraphrase of the line might go thus:

The sun took over all of the east.

(It is worth mentioning that you should have at your elbow a good desk dictionary, such as *The American Heritage Dictionary of the English Language,* fourth edition. Writers—especially poets—expect you to pay close attention to every word. If a word puzzles you, look it up. Many dictionaries are available at no cost on the Internet as well.)

Idioms, as well as words, may puzzle a reader. The Anglo-Irish poet William Butler Yeats (1865–1939) begins one poem with

The friends that have it I do wrong . . .

Because the idiom "to have it" (meaning "to believe that," "to think that") is unfamiliar to many American readers today, a discussion of the poem might include a paraphrase—a rewording, a translation into more familiar language, such as

> The friends who think that I am doing the wrong thing . . .

Perhaps the rest of the poem is immediately clear, but in any case here is the entire poem, followed by a paraphrase:

> The friends that have it I do wrong
> When ever I remake a song,
> Should know what issue is at stake:
> It is myself that I remake.

Now for the paraphrase:

> The friends who think that I am doing the wrong thing when I revise one of my poems should be informed what the important issue is: I'm not just revising a poem; rather, I am revising myself (my thoughts, feelings).

Here, as with any paraphrase, the meaning is not translated exactly; there is some distortion. If *song* in the original is clarified by *poem* in the paraphrase, it is also altered; the paraphrase loses the sense of lyricism that is implicit in *song*. Further, "Should know what issue is at stake" (in the original) is ambiguous. Does *should* mean "ought," as in "You should know better than to speak so rudely," or does it mean "deserve to be informed," as in "You deserve to know that I am thinking about quitting"? This paraphrase deals with the entire poem, and your instructor may ask you to paraphrase a short poem, but normally one paraphrases only a few lines, or even only a phrase.

Granted that a paraphrase may miss a great deal, a paraphrase often helps you, or your reader, to understand at least the surface meaning, and the act of paraphrasing will usually help you to understand at least some of the implicit meaning. Furthermore, a paraphrase makes you see that the original writer's words are better than any words we might substitute.

A REVIEW

A review also is a response; it normally includes an evaluation of the work, but at least at first glance it may seem to be an analytic essay. We will consider a review of a production of a play, but you can easily adapt this discussion to a review of a book.

A Review of a Dramatic Production

A review requires analytic skill, but it is not identical with an analysis. First, a reviewer normally assumes that the reader is unfamiliar with the production being reviewed and also with the play if the play is not a classic. The first paragraph usually provides a helpful introduction along these lines:

> Marsha Norman's play *'night, Mother,* a tragedy with only two actors and one set, shows us a woman's preparation for suicide. Jessie has concluded that she no longer wishes to live, and so she tries to put her affairs in order, which chiefly means preparing her rather uncomprehending mother to get along without her.

Inevitably some retelling of the plot is necessary if the play is new, and a summary of a sentence or two is acceptable even for a familiar play. The review will, however, chiefly be concerned with

describing,

analyzing, and

evaluating.

If the play is new, much of the evaluation may center on the play itself, but if the play is a classic, the evaluation will chiefly be devoted to the acting, the set, and the direction. Other points:

1. **Save the program;** it will give you the names of the actors and perhaps a brief biography of the author, a synopsis of the plot, and a photograph of the set, all of which may be helpful.
2. **Draft your review as soon as possible,** while the performance is still fresh in your mind. If you cannot draft it immediately after seeing the play, at least jot down some notes about the setting and the staging, the acting, and the audience's response.
3. **If possible, read the play**—ideally, before the performance and again after it.
4. **In your first draft, don't worry about limitations of space;** write as long a review as you can, putting down everything that comes to mind. Later you can cut it to the required length, retaining only the chief points and the necessary supporting details, but in your first draft try to produce a fairly full record of the performance and your response to it, so that a day or two later, when you revise, you won't have to trust a fading memory for details.

A Sample Review: "An Effective *Macbeth*"

If you read reviews of plays in newspapers and magazines or on the Internet, you will soon develop a sense of what reviews normally do. The following example, an undergraduate's review of a production of *Macbeth,* is typical except in one respect: As has been mentioned, reviews of new plays customarily include a few sentences summarizing the plot and classifying the play (a tragedy, a farce, a rock musical), perhaps briefly putting it into the context of the author's other works, but because *Macbeth* is so widely known, the reviewer has chosen not to tell her readers that *Macbeth* is a tragedy by Shakespeare.

Preliminary Jottings During the two intermissions and immediately after the end of the performance, the reviewer made a few jottings, which the next day she rewrote:

Compare with last year's *Midsummer Night's Dream*

Set: barren;

   pipe framework at rear. Duncan exits on it.

Useful?

witches: powerful, not funny

stage: battlefield? barren land?

costume: earth-colored rags

   they seduce--even caress--Mac.

Macbeth

   ~~witches caress him ?~~

   strong; also gentle (with Lady M)

Lady Macb.

   sexy in speech about unsexing her

   too attractive? Prob. ok

Banquo's ghost: naturalistic, covered with blood

Duncan: terrible; worst actor except for Lady Macduff's boy

costumes: leather, metal; only Duncan in robes

pipe framework used for D, and murder of Lady Macduff

set

forest: branches unrealistic; stylized? or cheesy?

The Finished Version The published review follows, accompanied by some marginal notes in which we comment on its strengths.

Aaron Harrison
Professor Hearn
English 101A
18 May 2011

Title conveys information about thesis.

Opening paragraph is informative, letting the reader know the reviewer's overall attitude.

Reviewer promptly turns to a major issue.

First sentence, by means of "further," provides an effective transition.

An Effective *Macbeth*

Macbeth at the University Theater is a thoughtful and occasionally exciting production, partly because the director, Mark Urice, has trusted Shakespeare and has not imposed a gimmick on the play. The characters do not wear cowboy costumes as they did in last year's production of *A Midsummer Night's Dream*.

Probably the chief problem confronting a director of *Macbeth* is how to present the witches so that they are powerful supernatural forces and not silly things that look as though they came from a Halloween party. Urice gives us ugly but not absurdly grotesque witches, and he introduces them most effectively. The stage seems to be a bombed-out battlefield littered with rocks and great chunks of earth, but some of these begin to stir—the earth seems to come alive— and the clods move, unfold, and become the witches, dressed in brown and dark gray rags. The suggestion is that the witches are a part of nature, elemental forces that can hardly be escaped. This effect is increased by the moans and creaking noises that they make, all of which could be comic but which in this production are impressive.

The witches' power over Macbeth is further emphasized by their actions. When the witches first meet Macbeth, they encircle him, touch him, caress him, even embrace him, and he seems helpless, almost their plaything. Moreover, in the scene in which he imagines that he sees a dagger, the director has arranged for one of the witches to appear, stand near Macbeth, and guide his hand toward the invisible dagger. This is, of course, not in the text, but the interpretation is reasonable rather than intrusive. Finally, near the end of the play, just before Macduff kills Macbeth, a witch appears and laughs at Macbeth as Macduff explains that he was not "born of woman." There is no doubt that throughout the tragedy Macbeth has been a puppet of the witches.

Paragraph begins with a broad assertion and then offers supporting details.

Macbeth (Stephen Beers) and Lady Macbeth (Tina Peters) are excellent. Beers is sufficiently brawny to be convincing as a battlefield hero, but he also speaks the lines sensitively, and so the audience feels that in addition to being a hero he is a man of insight and imagination, and even a man of gentleness. One can believe Lady Macbeth when she says that she fears he is "too full of the milk of human kindness" to murder Duncan. Lady Macbeth is especially effective in the scene in which she asks the spirits to "unsex her."

Reference to a particular scene.

During this speech she is reclining on a bed and as she delivers the lines she becomes increasingly sexual in her bodily motions, deriving excitement from her own stimulating words. Her attachment to Macbeth is strongly sexual, and so, too, is his attraction to her. The scene when she persuades him to kill Duncan ends with them passionately embracing. The strong attraction of each for the other, so evident in the early part of the play, disappears after the murder, when Macbeth keeps his distance from Lady Macbeth and does not allow her to touch him. The acting of the other performers is effective, except for Duncan (John Berens), who recites the lines mechanically and seems not to take much account of their meaning.

Description, but also analysis.

The set consists of a barren plot at the rear of which stands a spidery framework of piping, of the sort used by construction companies, supporting a catwalk.

Concrete details.   This framework fits with the costumes (lots of armor, leather, heavy boots), suggesting a sort of elemental, primitive, and somewhat sadistic world. The catwalk, though effectively used when Macbeth goes off to murder Duncan (whose room is presumably upstairs and offstage) is not much used in later scenes. For the most part it is an interesting piece of scenery, but it is not otherwise helpful. For instance, there is no

Concrete details to support evaluation.   reason why the scene with Macduff's wife and children is staged on it. The costumes are not in any way Scottish—no plaids—but in several scenes the sound of a bagpipe is heard, adding another weird or primitive tone to the production.

Summary.   This *Macbeth* appeals to the eye, the ear, and the mind. The director has given us a unified production that makes sense and that is faithful to the spirit of Shakespeare's play.

[New page]

Documentation.   Work Cited

Macbeth. By William Shakespeare. Dir. Mark Urice. Perf. Stephen Beers, Tina Peters, and John Berens. University Theater, Medford, MA. 3 Mar. 2004. Performance.

The marginal notes call attention to certain qualities in the review, but three additional points should be made:

1. The reviewer's feelings and evaluations are clearly stated, not in such expressions as "furthermore I feel," and "it is also my opinion," but in such expressions as "a thoughtful and occasionally exciting production," "excellent," and "appeals to the eye, the ear, and the mind."
2. The evaluations are supported by details. For instance, the evaluation that the witches are effectively presented is supported by a brief description of their appearance.
3. The reviewer is courteous, even when (as in the discussion of the catwalk, in the next-to-last paragraph) she is talking about aspects of the production she doesn't care for.

PART 2

Standing Back: Thinking Critically about Literature

6

LITERATURE, FORM, AND MEANING

Great literature is simply language charged with meaning to the utmost possible degree.

—Ezra Pound

LITERATURE AND FORM

We know why we value a newspaper or a textbook or an atlas, but why do we value a literary work that does not give us the latest news or important information about business cycles or the names of the capitals of nations? About a thousand years ago a Japanese woman, Lady Murasaki, offered an answer in *The Tale of Genji,* a book often called the world's first novel. During a discussion about reading fiction, one of the characters offers an opinion as to why a writer tells a story:

> Again and again something in one's own life, or in the life around one, will seem so important that one cannot bear to let it pass into oblivion. There must never come a time, the writer feels, when people do not know about this.

Literature is about human experiences, but the experiences embodied in literature are not simply the shapeless experiences—the chaotic passing scene—captured by an unselective camcorder. Poets, dramatists, and storytellers find or impose a shape on scenes (for instance, the history of two lovers), giving readers things to value—written or spoken accounts that are memorable not only for their content but also for their *form*—the shape of the speeches, of the scenes, of the plots. (In a little while, we will see that form and content are inseparable, but for the moment, we can talk about them separately.)

Ezra Pound said that literature is "news that *stays* news." "John loves Mary," written on a wall, or on the front page of a newspaper, is news, but it is not news that stays news. It may be of momentary interest to the friends of John and Mary, but it's not much more than simple information, and there is no particular reason to value it.

Literature is something else. The Johns and Marys in poems, plays, and stories—even though they usually are fairly ordinary individuals, in many ways often rather like us—somehow become significant as we perceive them through the writer's eye and ear. The writer selects what is essential and makes us care about the characters. Their doings stay in our minds.

To say that their doings stay in our minds is *not* to deny that works of literature show signs of being the products of particular ages and environments. It is only to say that these works are not exclusively about those ages and environments; they speak to later readers. The love affairs that we read about in the newspaper are of little or no interest a day later, but the love of Romeo and Juliet, with its joys and sorrows, has interested people for 400 years. Those who know the play may feel, with Lady Murasaki's spokesman, that there must never come a time when these things are not known. It should be mentioned, too, that readers find, on rereading a work, that the works are still of great interest but often for new reasons. That is, when as adolescents we read *Romeo and Juliet* we may value it for certain reasons, and when in maturity we reread it we may see it differently and value it for new reasons. It is news that remains news.

As the example of *Romeo and Juliet* indicates, literature need not be rooted in historical fact. Although guides in Verona find it profitable to point out Juliet's house, the play is not based on historical characters. Literature is about life, but it may be fictional, dealing with invented characters. Almost all of the characters in literature are imaginary—although they *seem* real.

One reason that literary works endure (whether they show us what we are or what we long for) is that their *form* makes their content memorable. Because this discussion of literature is brief, we will illustrate the point by looking at one of the briefest literary forms, the proverb. (Our definition of literature is not limited to the grand forms of the novel, tragedy, and so on. It is wide enough, and democratic enough, to include brief, popular, spoken texts.) Consider this statement:

A rolling stone gathers no moss.

Now let's compare it with a **paraphrase** (a restatement, a translation into other words):

> If a stone is always moving around, vegetation won't have a chance to grow on it.

What makes the original version more powerful, more memorable? Surely much of the answer is that the original is more concrete and its form is more shapely. At the risk of being heavy-handed, we can analyze the shapeliness thus: *Stone* and *moss* (the two nouns in the sentence) each contain one syllable; *rolling* and *gathers* (the two words of motion) each contain two syllables, each with the accent on the first syllable. Notice, too, the nice contrast between stone (hard) and moss (soft).

The reader probably *feels* this shapeliness unconsciously, rather than perceives it consciously. These connections become apparent when one starts to analyze, but the literary work can make its effect on a reader even before the reader analyzes it. As T. S. Eliot said in his essay on Dante (1929), "Genuine poetry can communicate before it is understood." Indeed, our *first* reading of a work, when we are all eyes and ears (and the mind is highly receptive rather than sifting for evidence), is sometimes the most important reading. Experience proves that we can feel the effects of a work without yet understanding *how* the effects are achieved.

Most readers will agree that the words in the proverb are paired interestingly and meaningfully. Perhaps they will agree, too, that the sentence is not simply some information but is also (to quote one of Robert Frost's definitions of literature) "a performance in words." What the sentence *is*, we might say, is no less significant than what the sentence *says*. The sentence as a whole forms a memorable picture, a small but complete world, hard and soft, inorganic and organic, inert and moving. The idea set forth is simple—partly because it is highly focused and therefore it leaves out a lot—but it is also complex. By virtue of the contrasts, and, again, even by the pairing of monosyllabic nouns and of disyllabic words of motion, it is unified into a pleasing whole. For all of its specificity and its compactness—the proverb contains only six words—it expands our minds.

Refresher course: Take a minute to read (or to reread) our Letter to Students, page xix, where we mention Frost's idea of literature as performance and illustrate it with "a txt msg pom" that won a prize for "the most creative use of SMS 'shorthand' in a poem."

A brief exercise: Think about some other proverb, for instance, "Look before you leap," "Finders keepers," "Haste makes waste," "Absence makes the heart grow fonder." Paraphrase it, and then ask yourself why the original is more interesting, more memorable, than your paraphrase. If you have trouble coming up with examples of proverbs, you can do a Google search for "list of proverbs," and you will get some good results. "English Proverbs and Sayings," for instance, gives many proverbs and a brief paraphrase of their meaning: <http://www.learn-english-today.com/Proverbs/proverbs.html>.

Literature and Meaning

We have seen that the form of the proverb pleases the mind and the tongue, but what about **content** or **meaning?** We may enjoy the images and the sounds, but surely the words add up to something. Probably most people would agree that the content or the meaning of "A rolling stone gathers no moss" is something like this: "If you are always on the move— if, for instance, you don't stick to one thing but you keep switching schools or jobs—you won't accomplish much."

Now, if this statement approximates the meaning of the proverb, we can say two things:

- The proverb contains a good deal of truth, and
- it certainly is not always true.

This proverb is more or less contradicted by another proverb: "Nothing ventured, nothing gained." Many proverbs contradict other proverbs. "Too many cooks spoil the broth," yes, but "Many hands make light the work"; "Absence makes the heart grow fonder," yes, but "Out of sight, out of mind"; "He who hesitates is lost," yes, but "Look before you leap." The claim that literature offers insights, or illuminates experience, is not a claim that it offers irrefutable and unvarying truths covering the whole of our experience. Literature does not give us *the* truth; rather, it wakes us up, makes us see, helps us feel intensely some aspect of our experience and perhaps evaluate it. The novelist Franz Kafka said something to this effect, very strongly, in a letter of 1904:

> If the book we are reading does not wake us, as with a fist hammering on our skull, why then do we read it? . . . What we must have are those books which come upon us like ill-fortune, and distress us deeply, like the death of one we love better than ourselves. . . . A book must be an ice-axe to break the sea frozen inside us.

Arguing about Meaning

In Chapter 7 we will discuss at length the question of whether one interpretation—one statement of the meaning of a work—is better than another, but a word should be said about it now. Suppose that while discussing "A rolling stone gathers no moss" someone said to you,

> I don't think it means that if you are always on the move you won't accomplish anything. I think the meaning is something like the saying "There are no flies on him." First of all, what's so great about moss developing? Why do you say that the moss more or less represents worthwhile accomplishments? And why do you say that the implication is that someone should settle down? The way I see it is just the opposite: The proverb says that active people don't let stuff accumulate on them, don't get covered over. That is, active people, people who accomplish things (people who get somewhere) are always unencumbered, are people who don't stagnate.

What reply can be offered? Probably no reply will sway the person who interprets the proverb this way. Perhaps, then, we must conclude that (as the literary critic Northrop Frye said) reading is a picnic to which the writer brings the words and the reader brings the meanings. The remark is witty and is probably true. Certainly readers over the years have brought very different meanings to such works as the Bible and *Hamlet*.

However, even if readers can never absolutely prove the truth of their interpretations, all readers have the obligation to make as convincing a case as possible. When you write about literature, you will begin (in your marginal jottings and in other notes) by setting down random expressions of feeling and even unsupported opinions, but later, when you are preparing to share your material with a reader, you will have to go further. You will have to try to show your reader *why* you hold the opinion you do. You must *argue* your case. In short,

- you have to offer plausible supporting evidence, and
- you have to do so in a coherent and rhetorically effective essay.

That is, you want to win over your readers, making the readers in effect say, "Yes, I see exactly what you mean, and what you say makes a good deal of sense." You may not thoroughly convince your readers, but they will at least understand *why* you hold the views you do.

FORM AND MEANING

Let us turn now to a work not much longer than a proverb—a very short poem by Robert Frost (1874–1963):

THE SPAN OF LIFE

> The old dog barks backward without getting up.
> I can remember when he was a pup.

Read the poem aloud once or twice, physically experiencing Frost's "performance in words." Notice that the first line is harder to say than the second line, which more or less trips off the tongue. Why? Because in the first line we must pause between *old* and *dog,* between *backward* and *without,* and between *without* and *getting*—and perhaps between *back* and *ward.* Further, when we read the poem aloud, or with the mind's ear, in the first line we hear four consecutive stresses in *old dog barks back,* a noticeable contrast to the rather jingling "when he was a pup" in the second line.

No two readers will read the lines in exactly the same way, but it is safe to say that most readers will agree that in the first line they may stress fairly heavily as many as eight syllables, whereas in the second line they may stress only three or four:

> The OLD DOG BARKS BACKWARD withOUT GETTing UP.
> I can reMEMber when HE was a PUP.

The *form* (a relatively effortful, hard-to-speak line, followed by a bouncy line) shapes and indeed is part of the *content* (a description of a dog that no longer has the energy or the strength to leap up, followed by a memory of the dog as a puppy).

Thinking further about Frost's poem, we notice something else about the form. The first line is about a dog, but the second line is about a dog *and* a human being ("*I* can remember"). The speaker must be getting on, too. And although nothing is said about the dog as a *symbol* of human life, the reader, prompted by the title of the poem, makes a connection between the life span of a dog and that of a human being. Part of what makes the poem effective is that this point is *not* stated explicitly, not belabored. Readers have the pleasure of making the connection for themselves—under Frost's careful guidance.

Everyone knows that puppies are frisky and that old dogs are not—although perhaps not until we encountered this poem did we think twice about the fact that "the old dog barks backward without getting up." Other people may have noticed this canine behavior, but perhaps only Frost had the ability to put his perception into memorable words. Part of what makes this performance in words especially memorable is the *relationship* between the two lines. Neither line in itself is anything very special, but because of the counterpoint the whole is more than the sum of the parts. Skill in handling language, obviously, is indispensable if the writer is to produce literature. A person may know a great deal about dogs and may be a great lover of dogs, but knowledge and love are not enough equipment with which to write even a two-line poem about a dog (or the span of life, or both). Like other kinds of literature, poems are produced by people who know how to delight us with verbal performances.

Presumably Frost reported his observation about the dog not simply as a piece of dog lore, but because it concerns all of us. It is news that stays news. Once you have read or heard the poem, you can never again look at a puppy or an old dog in quite the way you used to—and probably the poem will keep coming to mind as you feel in your bones the effects of aging.

As we will see, there are many ways of writing about literature, but one of the most interesting is to write not simply about the author's "thoughts" (or ideas) as abstractions but about the particular *ways* in which an author makes thoughts memorable, chiefly through the manipulation of words.

LITERATURE, TEXTS, DISCOURSES, AND CULTURAL STUDIES

These pages have routinely spoken of *literature* and of literary *works*, terms often supplanted now by *text*. Some say that *literature* is a word with elitist connotations. They may say, too, that a *work* is a crafted, finished thing, whereas a *text*, in modern usage, is something that in large measure is created (i.e., given meaning) by a reader. Further, the word *text* helps to erase the line between, on the one hand, what traditionally has been called literature and, on the other hand, popular verbal forms such as science fiction, Westerns, sermons, political addresses, interviews, advertisements, comic strips, and bumper stickers—and, for that matter, nonverbal products such as sports events, architecture, fashion design, automobiles, and the offerings in a shopping mall.

Texts or *discourses* of this sort (said to be parts of what is called a *discursive practice* or a *signifying practice*) in recent years have increasingly interested many people who used to teach literature ("great books") but who now teach *cultural studies*. In these courses the emphasis is not on objects inherently valuable and taught apart from the conditions of their production. Rather, the documents—whether plays by Shakespeare or comic books—are studied in their social and political contexts, especially in view of the conditions of their production, distribution, and consumption. Thus, *Hamlet* would be related to the economic and political system of England around 1600, and *also* to the context today—the educational system, the theater industry, and so on—that produces the work.

SUGGESTIONS FOR FURTHER READING

Subsequent chapters will cite a number of recent titles relevant to this chapter, but for a start a reader might first turn to an old but readable, humane, and still useful introduction, David Daiches, *A Study of Literature* (1948). Another book of the same generation, and still a useful introduction, is a businesslike survey of theories of literature, by René Wellek and Austin Warren, *Theory of Literature*, 3rd ed. (1962). For a more recent, readable study, see Gerald Graff, *Professing Literature: An Institutional History* (1987).

Some basic reference works should be mentioned: C. Hugh Holman and William Harmon have written an introductory dictionary of movements, critical terms, literary periods, and genres—*A Handbook to Literature*, 11th ed. (2008). For fuller discussions of critical terms, see Wendell V. Harris, *Dictionary of Concepts in Literary Criticism and Theory* (1992), which devotes several pages to each concept (for instance, *author, context, evaluation, feminist literary criticism, narrative*) and gives a useful reading list for each entry. Fairly similar to Harris's book are Irene Makaryk, ed., *Encyclopedia of Contemporary Literary Theory: Approaches, Scholars, Terms* (1993); Michael Groden, Martin Kreiswirth, and Imre Szeman, eds., *The Johns Hopkins Guide to Literary Theory and Criticism*, 2nd ed. (2005); and Michael Payne, ed., *A Dictionary of Cultural and Critical Theory* (1996). *The Johns Hopkins Guide,* although it includes detailed entries on individual critics as well as on critical schools, does not have entries for *theory* or for *criticism,* nor does it have entries for such words as *canon* and *evaluation*. To pair with it, we recommend *The New Princeton Encyclopedia of Poetry and Poetics,* ed. Alex Preminger and T. V. F. Brogan (1993). Although *The New Princeton Encyclopedia* does not include terms that are unique to, say, drama or fiction, it does include generous, lucid entries (with suggestions for further reading) on such terms as *allegory, criticism, canon, irony, sincerity, theory,* and *unity,* and the long entries on *poetics; poetry;* and *poetry, theories of;* are in many respects entries on *literature.* For brief definitions of terms, as well as much helpful information about authors, periods, and works, we suggest consulting Merriam Webster's *Encyclopedia of Literature* (1995) or *The Oxford Companion to English Literature,* 7th ed., revised (2009).

For a provocative collection of essays on the canon, see *Canons,* ed. Robert von Hallberg (1984). There is also a good essay by Robert Scholes, "Canonicity and Textuality," in *Introduction to Scholarship in Modern Languages and Literatures,* ed. Joseph Gibaldi, 2nd ed. (1992), pages 138–158. Gibaldi's collection includes essays on related topics, for instance, literary theory (by Jonathan Culler) and cultural studies (by David Bathrick). Also stimulating are *Making of the Modern Canon* (1991) and *Reflections on the Cultural Revolution: Canons and Disciplinary Change* (2000), both by Jan Gorak. Other aspects of the debate over the literary canon are discussed in John Guillory, *Cultural Capital: The Problem of Literary Canon Formation* (1993); Jeffrey R. Di Leo, *On Anthologies: Politics and Pedagogy* (2004); and *Multiethnic Literature and Canon Debates,* ed. Mary Jo Bona and Irma Maini (2006). For lively commentary on the traditional literary canon, see David Denby, *Great Books: My Adventures with Homer, Rousseau, Woolf, and Other Indestructible Writers of the Western World* (1996), and Andrew Delbanco, *Required Reading: Why Our American Classics Matter Now* (1997).

For a concise account of recent trends in literary theory and criticism, see Jonathan Culler, *Literary Theory: A Very Short Introduction* (2000). The history of literary criticism is covered in depth through the many selections in *The Norton Anthology of Literary Theory and Criticism,* ed. Vincent B. Leitch et al., 2nd ed. (2010).

7

WHAT IS INTERPRETATION?

Reading a book is like re-writing it for yourself. . . . You bring to a novel, anything you read, all your experience of the world. You bring your history and you read it in your own terms.

—Angela Carter

Be sure that you go to the author to get at his meaning, not to find yours.

—John Ruskin

INTERPRETATION AND MEANING

We can define **interpretation** as a setting forth of the meaning, or, better, a setting forth of one or more of the meanings of a work of literature. Although some critics believe that a work of literature has a single meaning, the meaning it had for the author, most critics hold that a work has several meanings, for instance, the meaning it had for the author, the meaning(s) it had for its first readers (or viewers, if the work is a drama), the meaning(s) it had for later readers, and the meaning(s) it has for us today. Take *Hamlet* (1600–01), for example. Perhaps this play about a man who has lost his father had a very special meaning for Shakespeare, who had recently lost his own father. And Shakespeare had earlier lost a son named Hamnet, a variant spelling of *Hamlet*. The play, then, may have had important psychological meanings for Shakespeare—but the audience could not have shared (or even known) these meanings.

What *did* the play mean to Shakespeare's audience? Perhaps the original audience of *Hamlet*—people living in a monarchy, presided over by Queen Elizabeth I—were especially concerned with the issue (specifically raised in *Hamlet*) of whether a monarch's subjects ever have the right to overthrow the monarch. But obviously for twentieth-century

Americans the interest in the play lies elsewhere, and the play must mean something else. If we are familiar with Freud, we may see in the play a young man who subconsciously lusts after his mother and seeks to kill his father (in the form of Claudius, Hamlet's uncle). Or we may see the play as largely about an alienated young man in a bourgeois society. Or—the list of interpretations is a long one.

IS THE AUTHOR'S INTENTION A GUIDE TO MEANING?

Should we be concerned, one might ask, with the *intentions* of the author? The question is reasonable, but there are difficulties, as the members of the Supreme Court find when they try to base their decisions on the original intent of the writers of the Constitution. First, for older works we almost never know what the intention is. We have *Hamlet,* but we do not have any statement of Shakespeare's intention concerning this or any other play. One might argue that we can deduce Shakespeare's intention from the play itself, but to argue that we should study the play in the light of Shakespeare's intention, and that we can know his intention by studying the play, is to argue in a circle. We can say that Shakespeare must have intended to write a tragedy (if he intended to write a comedy he failed) but we cannot go much further in talking about his intention.

Even if an author has gone on record, expressing an intention, we may think twice before accepting the statement as decisive. The author may be speaking facetiously, deceptively, mistakenly, or unconvincingly. The German writer Thomas Mann (1875–1955) said, probably sincerely and accurately, that he wrote one of his novels merely to entertain his family—but we may nevertheless take the book seriously and find it profound.

✍ A RULE FOR WRITERS

Because most writers have not told us of their intentions, and because even those writers who have stated their intentions may not be fully reliable sources, and because we inevitably see things from our own points of view, *think twice before you attribute intention to the writer* in such statements as "Shakespeare here is trying to show us that . . ." or "Alice Walker is aiming for . . ." or "Amy Tan seeks to convey. . . ."

FEATURES OF A GOOD INTERPRETATION

Even the most vigorous advocates of the idea that meaning is indeterminate do not believe that all interpretations are equally significant. Rather, they believe that an interpretive essay is offered against a background of ideas, shared by essayist and reader, as to what constitutes a *persuasive argument*. An essay (even if it is characterized as "interpretive free play" or "creative engagement") will have to be coherent, plausible, and rhetorically effective. The *presentation* as well as the interpretation are significant. This means that you cannot merely set down random expressions of feeling or unsupported opinions. As an essayist you must, on the contrary, convincingly *argue* a thesis—must point to evidence so that the reader will not only know what you believe but will also understand why you believe it.

One important way of helping readers to see things from your point of view is to do your best to face all of the complexities of the work. Some interpretations strike a reader as better than others because they are *more inclusive,* that is, because they *account for more of the details of the work*. The less satisfactory interpretations leave a reader pointing to some aspects of the work—to some parts of the whole—and saying, "Yes, but your explanation doesn't take account of. . . ."

This does not mean that a reader must feel that a persuasive interpretation says the last word about the work. We always realize that the work—if we value it highly—is richer than the discussion, but, again, for us to value an interpretation we must find the interpretation plausible and inclusive.

Interpretation often depends

- not only on making connections among various elements of the work (for instance, among the characters in a story, or among the images in a poem), and
- between the work and other works by the author, but also on
- making connections between the particular work and a **cultural context.**

The cultural context usually includes other writers and specific works of literature, because a given literary work participates in a tradition. If a work looks toward life, it also looks toward other works. A sonnet is about human experience, but it is also part of a tradition of sonnet writing. The more works of literature you are familiar with, the better equipped you are to interpret any particular work. Here is the way Robert Frost put it, in the preface to *Aforesaid* (1954):

> A poem is best read in the light of all the other poems ever written. We read A the better to read B (we have to start somewhere; we may get very little out of A). We read B the better to read C, C the better to read D, D the better to go back and get something more out of A. Progress is not the aim, but circulation. The thing is to get among the poems where they hold each other apart in their places as the stars do.

AN EXAMPLE: INTERPRETING PAT MORA'S "IMMIGRANTS"

Below is a short poem by a contemporary poet, Pat Mora (b. 1942).

IMMIGRANTS

wrap their babies in the American flag,
feed them mashed hot dogs and apple pie,
name them Bill and Daisy,
buy them blonde dolls that blink
blue eyes or a football and tiny cleats
before the baby can even walk,
speak to them in thick English,
    hallo, babee, hallo.
whisper in Spanish or Polish
when the babies sleep, whisper
in a dark parent bed, that dark
parent fear, "Will they like
our boy, our girl, our fine american
boy, our fine american girl?"

Perhaps most readers will agree that the poem expresses or drama-tizes a desire, attributed to "immigrants," that their child grow up in an Anglo mode. (Mora is not saying that *all* immigrants have this desire; she has simply invented one speaker who says such-and-such. Of course *we* may say that Mora says all immigrants have this desire, but that is our interpretation.) For this reason the parents call their children Bill and Daisy (rather than, say, José and Juanita) and give them blond dolls and a football (rather than dark-haired dolls and a soccer ball).

Up to this point, the parents seem a bit silly in their mimicking of Anglo ways. But the second part of the poem gives the reader a more interior view of the parents, bringing out the fear and hope and worried concern that lie behind their behavior: Some unspecified "they" may not "like / our boy, our girl." Who are "they"? Most readers probably will agree that "they" refers to native-born citizens, especially the blond, blue-eyed all-American Anglo types that until recently constituted "the establishment" in the United States.

One can raise further questions about the interpretation of the poem. Exactly what does the poet mean when she says that immigrants "wrap their babies in the American flag"? Are we to take this literally? If not, how are we to take it? And why in the last two lines is the word *american* not capitalized? Is Mora imitating the nonnative speaker's uncertain grasp of English punctuation? (But if so, why does Mora capitalize *American* in the first line, and *Spanish* and *Polish* later in the poem?) Or is she perhaps implying some mild reservation about becoming 100 percent American, some suggestion that in changing from Spanish or Polish to "american" there is some sort of loss?

A reader might seek Mora out and ask her why she did not capitalize *american* in the last two lines. But Mora might not be willing to answer, or she might say that she does not really know why; it just seemed right when she wrote the poem. Most authors do in fact take this last approach. When they are working as writers, they work by a kind of instinct, a feel for the material. Later they can look critically at their writing, but that's another sort of experience.

To return to our basic question: What are the features of a good interpretation? The short answer is *evidence,* and especially evidence that seems to cover all relevant issues. In an essay it is not enough merely to assert an interpretation. Your readers do not expect you to make an airtight case, but because you are trying to help readers to understand a work—to see a work the way you do—you are obliged to

- offer reasonable supporting evidence and
- take account of what might be set forth as counterevidence to your thesis.

Your essay may originate in an intuition or an emotional response, a sense that the work is about such-and-such, but this intuition or emotion must then be examined, and it must stand a test of reasonableness. It is not enough in an essay merely to set forth your response. Your readers will expect you to *demonstrate* that the response is something that they can share. They may not be convinced that the interpretation is right or true, but they must at least feel that the interpretation is plausible and in accord with the details of the work, rather than, say, highly eccentric and irreconcilable with some details.

THINKING CRITICALLY ABOUT LITERATURE

Usually you will begin with a *response* to your reading—interest, boredom, bafflement, annoyance, shock, pleasure. Then, if you are going to think critically about the work, you will go on to *examine* your response in order to understand it, or to deepen it, or to change it.

How can you change a response? Critical thinking involves seeing an issue from all sides, to as great a degree as possible. As you know, in ordinary language to *criticize* usually means to find fault, but in literary studies it does not have a negative connotation. Rather, it means "to examine carefully." (The word *criticism* comes from a Greek verb meaning "to distinguish, to decide, to judge.") Nevertheless, in one sense the term *critical thinking* does approach the usual meaning, since critical thinking requires you to take a skeptical view of your response. You will argue with yourself, seeing if your response can stand up to doubts.

If you have found the story implausible, you might question yourself:

- Exactly what is implausible in it?
- Is implausibility always a fault?
- If so, exactly why?

Your answers may deepen your response. Usually, in fact, you will find supporting evidence for your response, but in your effort to distinguish and to decide and to judge, try also (if only as an exercise) to locate **counterevidence.** See what can be said against your position. (The best lawyers, it is said, prepare two cases—their own and the other side's.) As you consider the counterevidence, you will sometimes see that it requires you to adjust your thesis. You may even find yourself developing a different response. There is nothing wrong with that—although of course the paper that you ultimately hand in should clearly argue a thesis.

Critical thinking, in short, means examining or exploring one's own responses, by questioning and testing them. Critical thinking is not so much a skill (though it does involve the ability to understand a text) as it is a *habit of mind,* or, rather, several habits, including

- openmindedness,
- intellectual curiosity, and
- willingness to work.

It may also involve the willingness to discuss the issues with others, and to do research, a topic that will be treated separately in Chapter 17, on writing a research paper.

A STUDENT INTERPRETATION OF ROBERT FROST'S "STOPPING BY WOODS ON A SNOWY EVENING"

Read Frost's "Stopping by Woods on a Snowy Evening," and then read this interpretation, written by a first-year student. This interpretation is followed by a discussion that is devoted chiefly to two questions:

- What is the essayist's thesis?
- Does the essayist offer convincing evidence to support the thesis?

Robert Frost

STOPPING BY WOODS ON A SNOWY EVENING

Whose woods these are I think I know.
His house is in the village though;
He will not see me stopping here
To watch his woods fill up with snow.

My little horse must think it queer
To stop without a farmhouse near
Between the woods and frozen lake
The darkest evening of the year.

He gives his harness bells a shake
To ask if there is some mistake.
The only other sound's the sweep
Of easy wind and downy flake.

The woods are lovely, dark and deep.
But I have promises to keep,
And miles to go before I sleep,
And miles to go before I sleep.

Darrel MacDonald
Professor Phillips
College Writing 2G
17 March 2011

Stopping by Woods and Going On

Robert Frost's "Stopping by Woods on a Snowy Evening" is about what the title says it is. It is also about something more than the title says.

When I say it is about what the title says, I mean that the poem really does give us the thoughts of a person who pauses (that is, a person who is "stopping") by woods on a snowy evening. (This person probably is a man, since Robert Frost wrote the poem and nothing in the poem clearly indicates that the speaker is not a man. But, and this point will be important, the speaker perhaps feels that he is not a very masculine man. As we will see, the word "queer" appears in the poem, and, also, the speaker uses the word "lovely," which sounds more like the word a woman would use than a man.) In line 3 the speaker says he is "stopping here," and it is clear that "here" is by woods, since "woods" is mentioned not only in the title but also in the first line of the poem, and again in the second stanza, and still again in the last stanza. It is equally clear that, as the title says, there is snow, and that the time is evening. The speaker mentions "snow" and "downy flake," and he says this is "The darkest evening of the year."

But in what sense is the poem about *more* than the title? The title does not tell us anything about the man who is "stopping by woods," but the poem—the man's meditation—tells us a lot about him. In the first stanza he reveals that he is uneasy at the thought that the owner of the woods may see him stopping by the woods. Maybe he is uneasy because he is trespassing, but the poem does not actually say that he has illegally entered someone else's property. More likely, he feels uneasy, almost ashamed, of watching the "woods fill up with snow." That is, he would not want anyone to see that he actually is enjoying a beautiful aspect of nature and is not hurrying about whatever his real business is in thrifty Yankee style.

The second stanza gives more evidence that he feels guilty about enjoying beauty. He feels so guilty that he even thinks the horse thinks there is something odd about him. In fact, he says that the horse thinks he is "queer," which of course may just mean odd, but also (as is shown by *The American Heritage Dictionary*) it can mean "gay," "homosexual." A real man, he sort of suggests, wouldn't spend time looking at snow in the woods.

So far, then, the speaker in two ways has indicated that he feels insecure, though perhaps he does not realize that he has given himself away. First, he expresses uneasiness that someone might see him watching the woods fill up with snow. Second, he expresses uneasiness when he suggests that even the horse thinks he is strange, maybe even "queer" or unmanly, or at least unbusinesslike. And so in the last stanza, even though he finds the woods beautiful, he decides *not* to stop and to see the woods fill up with snow. And his description of the woods as "lovely"—a woman's word—sounds as though he may be something less than a he-man. He seems to feel ashamed of himself for enjoying the sight of the snowy woods and for see-ing them as "lovely," and so he tells himself that he has spent enough time looking at the woods and that he must go on about his business. In fact, he tells himself *twice* that he has business to attend to. Why? Perhaps he is insisting too much. Just as we saw that he was excessively nervous in the first stanza, afraid that someone might see him trespassing and enjoying the beauti-ful spectacle, now at the end he is again afraid that someone might see him loitering, and so he very firmly, using repetition as a form of emphasis, tries to reassure himself that he is not too much attracted by beauty and is a man of business who keeps his promises.

Frost gives us, then, a man who indeed is seen "stopping by woods on a snowy evening," but a man who, afraid of what society will think of him, is also afraid to "stop" long enough to fully enjoy the sight that attracts him, because he is driven by a sense that he may be seen to be trespassing and also may be thought to be unmanly. So after only a brief stop in the woods he forces himself to go on, a victim (though he probably doesn't know it) of the work ethic and of an oversimple idea of manliness.

The **title** is interesting. It gives the reader a good idea of which literary work will be discussed ("Stopping by Woods") *and* it arouses interest, in this case by a sort of wordplay ("Stopping . . . Going On"). A title of this sort is preferable to a title that merely announces the topic, such as "An Analysis of Frost's 'Stopping by Woods'" or "On a Poem by Robert Frost."

The **opening paragraph** helpfully names the exact topic (Robert Frost's poem) and arouses interest by asserting that the poem is about something more than its title.

The **body of the essay,** beginning with the second paragraph, begins to develop the thesis. (The **thesis** perhaps can be summarized thus: "The speaker, insecure of his masculinity, feels ashamed that he responds with pleasure to the sight of the snowy woods.") The writer's evidence in the second paragraph is that the word *queer* (a word sometimes used to mean "homosexual") appears, and that the word *lovely* is "more like the word a woman would use than a man." Readers of Darrel MacDonald's essay may at this point be unconvinced by this evidence, but at least he has offered what he considers evidence in support of his thesis.

The next paragraph dwells on what is said to be the speaker's uneasiness, and the following paragraph returns to the word *queer,* which, MacDonald correctly says, can mean "gay, homosexual." The question is whether *here,* in this poem, the word has this meaning. Do we agree with his assertion, in the last sentence of this paragraph, that Frost is suggesting that "A real man . . . wouldn't spend time looking at snow in the woods"? Clearly this is the way the writer takes the poem—but is his response to these lines reasonable? After all, what Frost says is this: "The little horse must think it queer / To stop without a farmhouse near." Is it reasonable to see a reference to homosexuality (rather than merely to oddness) in *this* use of the word *queer?* Hasn't MacDonald offered a response that is private? It is *his* response—but are we likely to share it, to agree that we see it in Frost's poem?

The next paragraph, amplifying the point that the speaker is insecure, offers as evidence the argument that *lovely* is more often a woman's word than a man's. Probably most readers will agree on this point, though many or all might deny that only a gay man would use the word *lovely.* And what do you think of the writer's assertions that the speaker of the poem "was excessively nervous in the first stanza" and is now "afraid that someone might see him loitering"? In your opinion does the text lend much support to this view?

The **concluding paragraph** effectively reasserts and clarifies the writer's thesis, saying that the speaker hesitates to stop and enjoy the woods because "he is driven by a sense that he may be seen to be trespassing and also may be thought to be unmanly."

The big questions, then, are these:

- Is the thesis *argued* rather than merely asserted, and
- is it argued *convincingly?*

Or, to put it another way,

- is the evidence adequate?

The writer certainly does argue (offer reasons) rather than merely assert, but does he offer enough evidence to make you think that his response is one that you can share? Has he helped you to enjoy the poem by seeing things that you may not have noticed—or has he said things that, however interesting, seem to you not to be in close contact with the poem as you see it?

✔ Checklist: Writing an Interpretation

❑ Do I know the work well enough—for instance, have I looked up the meanings of words that were unfamiliar to me—to offer a thoughtful interpretation?

❑ Have I discussed the work with classmates—or at least argued with myself—so that I can reasonably believe that my interpretation makes sense?

❑ What is my thesis, my main point? Can I state it in a sentence?

❑ Have I supported my thesis with evidence, using brief quotations from the text?

❑ Have I taken account of evidence that may seem to contradict my thesis?

❑ Have I kept my audience in mind?

❑ Have I given credit to all sources for borrowed words and also for borrowed ideas? (On avoiding plagiarism, see pages 327–29.)

FOR FURTHER INTERPRETATION, COMPARISON, AND WRITING

Perhaps you are familiar with Frost's much-admired poem "The Road Not Taken" (1920), you can find this poem, along with many others by Frost, at www.bartleby.com <http://www.bartleby.com/.>

1. Read and reread this poem carefully, jotting notes and asking questions about Frost's tone of voice, word choice, and organization. What is Frost saying in each line? What is he saying in each stanza? Then, write an interpretation of "The Road Not Taken," using as your model the essay that the student Darrel MacDonald wrote on "Stopping by Woods on a Snowy Evening."

2. Place these two Frost poems side by side and compare them. Is Frost's perspective on life the same in both poems? Different? The same in some ways yet different in others?

📖 SUGGESTIONS FOR FURTHER READING

The entries on *interpretation* in the reference works cited on pages 87–88 provide a good starting point, as does Steven Mailloux's entry on *interpretation* in *Critical Terms for Literary Study,* ed. Frank Lentricchia and Thomas McLaughlin, 2nd ed. (1995). Also of interest are E. D. Hirsch, *Validity in Interpretation* (1967); Paul B. Armstrong, *Conflicting Readings: Variety and Validity in Interpretation* (1990); and Umberto Eco, with Richard Rorty, Jonathan Culler, and Christine Brooke-Rose, *Interpretation and Overinterpretation* (1992). This last title includes three essays by Eco, with responses by Rorty, Culler, and Brooke-Rose, and a final "reply" by Eco. See also Joseph Margolis, *Interpretation Radical but Not Unruly: The New Puzzle of the Arts and History* (1995); and *Texts and Textuality: Textual Instability, Theory, and Interpretation,* ed. Philip Cohen (1997), which relates recent work in literary theory to the practices of scholarly editing of texts. For help with terms and concepts, see J. A. Cuddon, *A Dictionary of Literary Terms and Literary Theory* (revised by C. E. Preston), 4th ed. (2000), and Edward Quinn, *A Dictionary of Literary and Thematic Terms*, 2nd ed. (2006).

8

WHAT IS EVALUATION?

For all right judgment of any man or thing it is useful, nay, essential, to see his good qualities before pronouncing on his bad.

—Thomas Carlyle

To set up as a critic is to set up as a judge of values.

—I. A. Richards

You can never draw the line between aesthetic criticism and moral and social criticism. . . . You start with literary criticism, and however rigorous an aesthete you may be, you are over the frontier into something else sooner or later. The best you can do is to accept these conditions and know what you are doing when you are doing it.

—T. S. Eliot

CRITICISM AND EVALUATION

Although in ordinary usage *criticism* implies finding fault, and therefore implies evaluation—"this story is weak"—most literary criticism is *not* concerned with evaluation. It is chiefly concerned with *interpretation* (the setting forth of meaning) and with *analysis* (examination of relationships among the parts, or of causes and effects). For instance, an interpretation may argue that in *Death of a Salesman* (1949) by Arthur Miller, Willy Loman is the victim of a cruel capitalistic economy, and an analysis may show how the symbolic setting of the play (a stage direction tells us that "towering, angular shapes" surround the salesman's house) contributes to the meaning. In our discussion of "Form and Meaning" we saw that an analysis of Robert Frost's "The Span of Life" (page 85) called attention to the contrast between the meter of the first line (relatively uneven or irregular, with an exceptional number of heavy stresses) and the meter of

101

the second (relatively even and jingling). The analysis also called attention to the contrast between the content of the first line (the old dog) and the second (the speaker's memory of a young dog):

> The old dog barks backward without getting up.
> I can remember when he was a pup.

In our discussion we did not worry about whether this poem deserves an A, B, or C, nor about whether it was better or worse than some other poem by Frost, or by some other writer. For the most part, critics assume that the works they are writing about have value and are good enough to merit attention, and so critics largely concern themselves with other matters.

ARE THERE CRITICAL STANDARDS?

One approach to evaluating a work of literature, or, indeed, to evaluating anything, is to rely on personal taste. This approach is evident in a statement such as "I don't know anything about modern art, but I know what I like." The idea is old, at least as old as the Roman saying, *De gustibus non est disputandum* (There is no disputing tastes).

If we say, "This is a good work," or "This book is greater than that book," are we saying anything beyond "I like this" and "I like this better than that"? Are all expressions of evaluation really nothing more than expressions of taste? Most people believe that if there are such things as works of art, or works of literature, there must be standards by which they can be evaluated, just as most other things are evaluated by standards. The standards for evaluating a kitchen knife, for instance, are clear: It ought to cut cleanly, it ought not to need frequent sharpening, and it ought to feel comfortable in the hand. We may also want it to look nice and to be inexpensive, rustproof, and so on, but in any case we can state our standards. Similarly, there are agreed-on standards for evaluating figure skating, gymnastics, and fluency in language.

But what are the standards for evaluating literature? In earlier pages we have implied one standard: In a good work of literature, all of the parts contribute to the whole, making a unified work. Some people would add that mere unity is not enough; a work of high quality needs not only to be unified but needs also to be complex. The writer offers a "performance in words" (Frost's phrase), and when we read, we can see if the writer has performed well. If the stated content of the poem is mournful, yet the meter jingles, we can probably say that the performance is unsuccessful.

Here are some of the standards commonly set forth:

- Personal taste
- Truth, realism
- Moral content
- Aesthetic qualities, such as unity

We will look at some of these standards in detail.

Morality and Truth as Standards

"It is always a writer's duty to make the world better." Thus wrote Samuel Johnson (1709–84), in 1765, in his "Preface to Shakespeare." In this view, *morality* plays a large role; a story that sympathetically treats lesbian or gay love is, from a traditional Judeo-Christian perspective, probably regarded as a bad story, or at least not as worthy as a story that celebrates heterosexual married love. On the other hand, a gay or lesbian critic, or anyone not committed to traditional Judeo-Christian values, might regard the story highly because, in such a reader's view, it helps to educate readers and thereby does something "to make the world better."

But there are obvious problems. For one thing, a gay or lesbian story might strike even a reader with traditional values as a work that is effectively told, with believable and memorable characters, whereas a story of heterosexual married love might be unbelievable, awkwardly told, trite, or sentimental. How much value does one give to the ostensible content of the story, the obvious moral or morality, and how much value does one give to the artistry exhibited in telling the story?

People differ greatly about moral and religious issues. Edward FitzGerald's (1809–83) translation of *The Rubáiyát of Omar Khayyám* (1859) suggests that God doesn't exist, or—perhaps worse—if He does exist, He does not care about us. That God does not exist is a view held by many moral people; it is also a view rejected by many moral people. The issue then may become a matter of *truth*. Does the value of the poem depend on which view is right? In fact, does a reader have to subscribe to FitzGerald's view to enjoy (and to evaluate highly) the following stanza from the poem, in which FitzGerald suggests that the pleasures of this world are the only paradise that we can experience?

A book of verses underneath the bough,
A jug of wine, a loaf of bread—and thou
    Beside me singing in the wilderness—
Oh, wilderness were paradise enow!

Some critics can give high value to a literary work only if they share its beliefs, if they think that the work corresponds to reality. They measure the work against their vision of the truth.

Other readers can highly value a work of literature that expresses ideas they do not believe, arguing that literature does not require us to believe in its views. This theory claims literature gives a reader a strong sense of *what it feels like* to hold certain views—even though the reader does not share those views.

Take, for instance, a lyric poem in which Christina Rossetti (1830–94), a devout Anglican, expresses both spiritual numbness and spiritual hope. Here is one stanza from "A Better Resurrection":

My life is like a broken bowl,
  A broken bowl that cannot hold
One drop of water for my soul
  Or cordial in the searching cold;
Cast in the fire the perished thing;
  Melt and remould it, till it be
A royal cup for Him, my King:
  O Jesus, drink of me.

One need not be an Anglican suffering a crisis to find this poem of considerable interest. It offers insight into a state of mind, and the truth or falsity of religious belief is not at issue. Similarly, one can argue that although *The Divine Comedy* (c. 1310–14) by Dante Alighieri (1265–1321) is a deeply Roman Catholic work, the non-Catholic reader can read it with interest and pleasure because of (for example) its rich portrayal of a wide range of characters, the most famous of whom perhaps are the pathetic lovers Paolo and Francesca. In Dante's view, they are eternally damned because they were unrepentant adulterers, but a reader need not share this belief.

Other Ways to Think about Truth and Realism

Other solutions to the problem of whether a reader must share a writer's beliefs have been offered. One extreme view says that beliefs are irrelevant, because literature has nothing to do with truth. In this view, a work of art does not correspond to anything "outside" itself, that is, to anything in the real world. If a work of art has any "truth," it is only in the sense of being internally consistent. Thus Shakespeare's *Macbeth* is not making assertions about reality. *Macbeth* has nothing to do with the history of

Scotland, just as (in this view) Shakespeare's *Julius Caesar* has nothing to do with the history of Rome, although Shakespeare borrowed some of his material from history books. These tragedies are worlds in themselves— not to be judged against historical accounts of Scotland or Rome—and we are interested in the characters in the plays only as they exist *in the plays*. We may require that the characters be consistent, believable, and engaging, but we cannot require that they correspond to historical figures.

Literary works are neither true nor false; they are only (when success-ful) coherent and interesting. The poet William Butler Yeats (1865–1939) perhaps had in mind something along these lines when he said that you can refute a philosopher, but you cannot refute the Song of Sixpence. And indeed "Sing a song of sixpence, / Pocket full of rye," has endured for a couple of centuries, perhaps partly because it has nothing to do with truth or falsity; it has created its own engaging world.

And yet one can object, offering a commonsense response: Surely when we see a play, or read an engaging work of literature, whether it is old or new, we feel that somehow the work says something about the life around us, the real world. True, some of what we read—let us say, detec-tive fiction—is chiefly fanciful; we read it to test our wits, or to escape, or to kill time. But most literature seems to be connected to life. This com-monsense view, that literature is related to life, has an ancient history, and in fact almost everyone in the Western world believed it from the time of the ancient Greeks until the nineteenth century, and many people— including authors and highly skilled readers—still believe it today.

Certainly a good deal of literature, most notably the realistic short story and the novel, is devoted to giving a detailed picture that at least *looks like* the real world. One reason we read the fiction of Kate Chopin is to find out what "the real world" of Creole New Orleans in the late nineteenth century was like—as seen through Chopin's eyes. Writers of stories, novels, and plays are concerned about giving plausible, indeed precise and insightful, images of the relationships between people. Writ-ers of lyric poems presumably are specialists in presenting human feel-ings, such as the experience of love or of the loss of faith. We are invited to compare the writer's created world to the world that we live in, perhaps to be reminded that our own lives can be richer than they are.

The novelist D. H. Lawrence (1885–1930) offers a relevant com-ment in the ninth chapter of *Lady Chatterley's Lover* (1928). He is talk-ing about novels, but perhaps we can extend his view to all works of literature.

It is the way our sympathy flows and recoils that really determines our lives. And here lies the vast importance of the novel, properly handled. It can inform and lead into new places the flow of our sympathetic consciousness, and it can lead our sympathy away in recoil from things gone dead. Therefore, the novel, properly handled, can reveal the most secret places of life.

In Lawrence's view, we can evaluate literature in terms of its moral effect on the reader; the good novel, Lawrence claims, leads us into worlds—human relationships—that deserve our attention and leads us away from "things gone dead," presumably relationships and values—whether political, moral, or religious—that no longer deserve to survive.

Realism is not the writer's only tool. In *Gulliver's Travels* (1726) Jonathan Swift gives us a world of Lilliputians, people about six inches tall. Is his book pure fancy, unrelated to life? Not at all. We perceive that the Lilliputians are (except for their size) pretty much like ourselves, and we realize that their tiny stature is an image of human pettiness, an *un*realistic device that helps us to see the real world more clearly.

✍ A RULE FOR WRITERS

When you draft an essay, and when you revise it through successive drafts, imagine that you are explaining your position to someone who, quite reasonably, wants to hear the *reasons* that have led you to your conclusions and give the *evidence* that supports your reasons.

📖 SUGGESTIONS FOR FURTHER READING

Most of the reference works cited on page 100 include entries on *evaluation*. But for additional short discussions, see Chapter 18 ("Evaluation") in René Wellek and Austin Warren, *Theory of Literature*, 3rd ed. (1962); Chapter 5 ("On Value-Judgments") in Northrop Frye, *The Stubborn Structure* (1970); and Chapter 4 ("Evaluation") in John M. Ellis, *The Theory of Literary Criticism* (1974). For a longer discussion, see Chapters 10 and 11 ("Critical Evaluation" and "Aesthetic Value") in Monroe C. Beardsley, *Aesthetics* (1958). Also of interest is Joseph Strelka, ed., *Problems of Literary Evaluation* (1969). In Strelka's collection, you may find it best to begin with the essays by George Boas, Northrop Frye, and David Daiches, and then to browse in the other essays. Still useful is *The*

Intent of the Critic, ed. Donald A. Stauffer (1941), which includes essays by Edmund Wilson, Norman Foerster, John Crowe Ransom, and W. H. Auden that explore the relationship between criticism and evaluation. For examples of literary judgment making and the critical evaluation of poetry, we recommend Richard Howard, *Alone with America: Essays on the Art of Poetry in the United States Since 1950,* enl. ed. (1980); Helen Vendler, *Part of Nature, Part of Us: Modern American Poets* (1980); Vendler, *The Music of What Happens: Poems, Poets, Critics* (1988); William Logan, *Reputations of the Tongue: On Poets and Poetry* (1999); and two books by James Wood, *The Broken Estate: Essays on Literature and Belief* (2000) and *The Irresponsible Self: On Laughter and the Novel* (2004). The novelist and short-story writer John Updike (1932–2009) also wrote a great deal of stimulating literary criticism; his collections of essays and reviews, stylishly written and astute in their evaluations, include *Hugging the Shore* (1983), *Odd Jobs* (1991), and *More Matter: Essays and Criticism* (2000).

9

WRITING ABOUT LITERATURE: AN OVERVIEW

All art is at once surface and symbol. Those who go beneath the surface do so at their peril. Those who read the symbol do so at their peril.

—Oscar Wilde

In a symbol there is concealment and yet revelation.

—Thomas Carlyle

To be just, that is to say, to justify its existence, criticism should be partial, passionate, and political, that is to say, written from an exclusive point of view, but a point of view that opens the widest horizons.

—Charles Baudelaire

Nothing is as easy as it looks.

—Murphy's Law #23

THE NATURE OF CRITICAL WRITING

In everyday talk the most common meaning of **criticism** is something like "finding fault." And to be critical is to be censorious. But a critic can see excellences as well as faults. Because we turn to criticism with the hope that the critic has seen something we have missed, the most valuable criticism is not that which shakes its finger at faults but that which calls our attention to interesting things going on in the work of art. Here is a statement by the poet and critic W. H. Auden (1907–1973) suggesting that criticism is most useful when it calls our attention to things worth attending to:

> What is the function of a critic? So far as I am concerned, he can do me one or more of the following services:
> 1. Introduce me to authors or works of which I was hitherto unaware.
> 2. Convince me that I have undervalued an author or a work because I had not read them carefully enough.
> 3. Show me relations between works of different ages and cultures which I could never have seen for myself because I do not know enough and never shall.
> 4. Give a "reading" of a work which increases my understanding of it.
> 5. Throw light upon the process of artistic "Making."
> 6. Throw light upon the relation of art to life, science, economics, ethics, religion, etc.
>
> —*The Dyer's Hand* (1963), 8–9

Auden does not neglect the delight we get from literature, but he extends (especially in his sixth point) the range of criticism to include topics beyond the literary work itself. Notice, too, the emphasis on observing, showing, and illuminating, which suggests that the function of critical writing is not very different from the most common view of the function of imaginative writing.

SOME CRITICAL APPROACHES

Whenever we talk about a work of literature or of art, or, for that matter, even about a so-so movie or television show, what we say depends in large measure on certain conscious or unconscious assumptions that we make: "I liked it; the characters were very believable" (here the assumption is that characters ought to be believable); "I didn't like it; there was too much violence" (here the assumption is that violence ought not to be shown, or if it is shown it should be made abhorrent); "I didn't like it; it was awfully slow" (here the assumption probably is that there ought to be a fair amount of physical action, perhaps even changes of scene, rather than characters just talking); "I didn't like it; I don't think topics of this sort ought to be discussed publicly" (here the assumption is a moral one, that it is indecent to present certain topics); "I liked it partly because it was refreshing to hear such frankness" (here again the assumption is moral, and more or less the reverse of the previous one).

Professional critics, too, work from assumptions, but their assumptions are usually highly conscious, and such critics may define their assumptions at length. They regard themselves as, for instance, Freudian or Marxist or gay critics. They read all texts through the lens of a particular theory, and their focus enables them to see things that otherwise might go unnoticed. Most critics realize, however, that if a lens or critical perspective or interpretive strategy helps us to see certain things, it also limits our vision. They therefore regard their method not as an exclusive way of thinking but only as a useful tool.

What follows is a brief survey of the chief current approaches to literature. You may find, as you read these pages, that one or another approach sounds congenial, and you may want to make use of it in your reading and writing. On the other hand, it is important to remember that works of literature are highly varied, and, second, that we read them for various purposes—to kill time, to enjoy fanciful visions, to be amused, to explore unfamiliar ways of feeling, and to learn about ourselves. It is best, at least at the outset therefore, to respond to each text in the way that the text seems to require rather than to read all texts according to a single formula. You will find that some works will lead you to want to think about them from several angles. A play by Shakespeare may stimulate you to read a book about the Elizabethan playhouse, another book that offers a Marxist interpretation of the English Renaissance, and still another book that offers a feminist analysis of Shakespeare's plays. All of these approaches, and others, may help you to deepen your understanding of the literary works that you read.

Formalist Criticism (New Criticism)

Formalist criticism emphasizes the work as an independent creation, a self-contained unit, something to be studied in itself, not as part of some larger context, such as the author's life or a historical period. This kind of study is called *formalist criticism* because the emphasis is on the *form* of the work, the relationships between the parts—the construction of the plot, the contrasts between characters, the functions of rhymes, the point of view, and so on. Formalist critics explain how and why literary works—*these* words, in *this* order—constitute unique, complex structures that embody or set forth meanings.

Cleanth Brooks, a distinguished formalist critic, in an essay in the *Kenyon Review* (Winter 1951), set forth what he called his "articles of faith":

That literary criticism is a description and an evaluation of its object.

That the primary concern of criticism is with the problem of unity—the kind of whole which the literary work forms or fails to form, and the relation of the various parts to each other in building up this whole.

That the formal relations in a work of literature may include, but certainly exceed, those of logic.

That in a successful work, form and content cannot be separated.

That form is meaning.

Formalist criticism is, in essence, *intrinsic* criticism, rather than extrinsic, for it concentrates on the work itself, independent of its writer and the writer's background—that is, independent of biography, psychology, sociology, and history. The discussions of a proverb ("A rolling stone") and of a short poem by Frost ("The Span of Life") on page 85 are brief examples. In practice, of course, we usually bring outside knowledge to the work. A reader who is familiar with, say, *Hamlet* can hardly study some other tragedy by Shakespeare, let's say *Romeo and Juliet,* without bringing to the second play some conception of what Shakespearean tragedy is or can be. A reader of Alice Walker's *The Color Purple* (1982) inevitably brings outside material (perhaps the experience of being an African-American or some knowledge of the history of African-Americans) to the literary work. It is hard to talk only about *Hamlet* or *The Color Purple* and not at the same time talk about, or at least have in mind, aspects of human experience.

Formalist criticism begins with a personal response to the literary work, but it goes on to try to account for the response by closely examining the work. It assumes that the author shaped the poem, play, or story so fully that the work guides the reader's responses. The assumption that "meaning" is fully and completely presented within the text is not much in favor today, when many literary critics argue that the active or subjective reader (or even what Judith Fetterley, a feminist critic, has called "the resisting reader"), and not the author of the text, "makes" the meaning. Still, even if one grants that the reader is active, not passive or coolly objective, one can hold with the formalists that the author is active too, constructing a text that in some measure controls the reader's responses.

Formalist criticism usually takes one of two forms: **explication** (the unfolding of meaning, line by line or even word by word) or **analysis** (the examination of the relations of parts). The essay on Yeats's "The Balloon of the Mind" (pages 246–47) is an explication, a setting forth of the implicit meanings of the words. The essays on Kate Chopin's "The Story of an Hour" (pages 39–41) and on Tennessee Williams's *The Glass Menagerie* (pages 187–93) are analyses. The essay on Frost's "Stopping by Woods on a Snowy Evening" (pages 96–97) is chiefly an analysis but with some passages of explication.

Formalist criticism, also called the **New Criticism** (to distinguish it from the historical and biographical writing that in earlier decades had defined literary study), began to achieve prominence in the late 1920s and was dominant from the late 1930s until about 1970, and even today it is widely considered the best way for a student to begin to study a work of literature. Formalist criticism empowers the student; that is, the student confronts the work immediately and is not told first to spend days or weeks or months reading Freud and his followers in order to write a psychoanalytic essay, or reading Marx and Marxists in order to write a Marxist essay, or doing research in order to write a historical essay.

Deconstruction

Deconstruction, or deconstructive or poststructuralist criticism, can almost be characterized as the opposite of everything for which formalist criticism stands. Deconstruction begins with the assumption that language is unstable, elusive, unfaithful. (Language is all of these things because meaning is largely generated by opposition: *Hot* means something in opposition to *cold,* but a hot day may be 90 degrees whereas a hot oven is at least 400 degrees, and a "hot item" may be of any temperature.) Deconstructionists seek to show that a literary work (usually called "a text" or "a discourse") inevitably is self-contradictory. Unlike formalist critics—who hold that an author constructs a coherent work with a stable meaning, and that competent readers can perceive this meaning—deconstructionists hold that a work has no coherent meaning at the center.

Despite the emphasis on indeterminacy, one sometimes detects in deconstructionist interpretations a view associated with Marxism. This is the idea that authors are "socially constructed" from the "discourses of power" or "signifying practices" that surround them. Thus, although authors may think they are individuals with independent minds, their works usually reveal—unknown to the authors—powerful social, cultural, or philosophic assumptions. Deconstructionists "interrogate" a text, and they reveal what the authors were unaware of or had thought they had kept safely out of sight. Deconstructionists often find a rather specific meaning—though this meaning is one that might surprise the author.

Deconstruction is valuable insofar as—like the New Criticism—it encourages close, rigorous attention to the text. Furthermore, in its rejection of the claim that a work has a single stable meaning, deconstruction has had a positive influence on the study of literature. The problem with deconstruction, however, is that too often it is reductive, telling the same story about every text—that here, yet again, and again, we see how a text is incoherent and heterogeneous.

Reader-Response Criticism

Probably all reading includes some sort of response—"This is terrific," "This is a bore," "I don't know what's going on here"—and almost all writing about literature begins with some such response, but specialists in literature disagree greatly about the role that response plays, or should play, in experiencing literature and in writing about it.

At one extreme are those who say that our response to a work of literature should be a purely aesthetic response—a response to a work of art—and not the response we would have to something comparable in real life. To take an obvious point: If in real life we heard someone plotting a murder, we would intervene, perhaps by calling the police or by attempting to warn the victim. But when we hear Macbeth and Lady Macbeth plot to kill King Duncan, we watch with deep *interest;* we hear their words with *pleasure,* and maybe with horror and fascination we even look forward to seeing the murder and to what the characters then will say and what will happen to the murderers.

When you think about it, the vast majority of works of literature do not have a close, obvious resemblance to the reader's life. Most readers of *Macbeth* are not Scots, and no readers are Scottish kings or queens. (It is not just a matter of older literature; no readers of Toni Morrison's *Beloved* [1987] are nineteenth-century African-Americans.) The connections that readers make between themselves and the lives in most of the books they read are not, on the whole, connections based on ethnic or professional identities, but, rather, connections with states of consciousness—for instance, a young person's sense of isolation from the family, or a young person's sense of guilt for initial sexual experiences. Before we reject a work because it seems either too close to us ("I'm a man and I don't like the depiction of this man"), or on the other hand too far from our experience ("I'm not a woman, so how can I enjoy reading about these women?"), we should try to follow the advice of Virginia Woolf (1882–1941), who said, "Do not dictate to your author; try to become him." Nevertheless, some literary works of the past may today seem intolerable, at least in part. There are passages in Mark Twain's *Adventures of Huckleberry Finn* (1884), where African-Americans are stereotyped or called derogatory names, that deeply upset us today. We should, however, try to reconstruct the cultural assumptions of the age in which the work was written. If we do so, we may find that if in some ways it reflected its historical era, in other ways it challenged it.

Reader-response criticism, then, says that the "meaning" of a work is not merely something put into the work by the writer; the "meaning" is an interpretation created or constructed or produced by the reader as well as the writer. Stanley Fish, an exponent of reader-response theory, in *Is There a Text in This Class?* (1980), puts it this way: "Interpretation is not the art of construing but of constructing. Interpreters do not decode poems; they make them" (327).

But does every reader see his or her individual image in each literary work? Even *Hamlet,* a play that has generated an enormous range of interpretation, is universally seen as a tragedy, a play that deals with painful realities. If someone were to tell us that *Hamlet* is a comedy, and that the end, with a pile of corpses, is especially funny, we would not say, "Oh, well, we all see things in our own way." Rather, we would conclude that this person has misunderstood the play.

Many people who subscribe to one version or another of a reader-response theory would agree that they are concerned not with all readers but with what they call *informed readers* or *competent readers.* Informed or competent readers are familiar with the conventions of literature. They understand that in a play such as *Hamlet* the characters usually speak in verse. Such readers, then, do not express amazement that Hamlet often speaks metrically, and that he sometimes uses rhyme. These readers understand that verse is the normal language for most of the characters in the play, and therefore such readers do not characterize Hamlet as a poet. Informed, competent readers, in short, know the rules of the game.

There will still be plenty of room for differences of interpretation. Some people will find Hamlet not at all blameworthy; others will find him somewhat blameworthy; still others may find him highly blameworthy. In short, we can say that a writer works against a background that is *shared* by readers. As readers, we are familiar with various kinds of literature, and we read or see *Hamlet* as a particular kind of literary work, a tragedy, a play that evokes (in Shakespeare's words) "woe or wonder" (*Hamlet* 5.2.370), sadness and astonishment. Knowing (to a large degree) how we ought to respond, our responses are not merely private.

Archetypal (or Myth) Criticism

Carl G. Jung (1875–1961), the Swiss psychiatrist, in *Contributions to Analytical Psychology* (1928), postulates the existence of a "collective unconscious," an inheritance in our brains consisting of "countless typical experiences [such as birth, escape from danger, selection of a mate] of our ancestors." Few people today believe in an inherited "collective unconscious," but many people agree that certain repeated experiences, such as going to sleep and hours later awakening, or the perception of the setting and the rising sun, or of the annual death and rebirth of vegetation, manifest themselves in dreams, **myths,** and literature—in these instances, as stories of apparent death and rebirth. This **archetypal** plot of death and rebirth is said to be evident in Samuel Taylor Coleridge's *The Rime of the Ancient Mariner* (1798), for example. The ship suffers a deathlike calm and then is miraculously restored to motion, and, in a sort of parallel rebirth, the mariner moves from spiritual death to renewed perception of the holiness of life. Another archetypal plot is the Quest, which usually involves the testing and initiation of a hero, and thus essentially represents the movement from innocence to experience. In addition to archetypal plots there are archetypal characters; an archetype is any recurring unit. Among archetypal characters are the Scapegoat (as in Shirley Jackson's "The Lottery"), the Hero (savior, deliverer), the Terrible Mother (witch, stepmother—even the wolf "grandmother" in the tale of Little Red Riding Hood), and the Wise Old Man (father figure, magician).

Because, the theory holds, both writer and reader share unconscious memories, the tale an author tells (derived from the collective unconscious) may strangely move the reader, speaking to his or her collective unconscious. As the British scholar Maud Bodkin puts it, in *Archetypal Patterns in Poetry* (1934), something within us "leaps in response to the effective presentation in poetry of an ancient theme" (4). But this emphasis on ancient (or repeated) themes has made archetypal criticism vulnerable to the charge that it is reductive. The critic looks for certain characters or patterns of action and values the work if the motifs are there, meanwhile overlooking what is unique, subtle, distinctive, and truly interesting about the work. That is, a work is regarded as good if it closely resembles other works, with the usual motifs and characters. A second weakness in some archetypal criticism is that in the search for the deepest meaning of a work the critic may crudely impose a pattern, seeing (for instance) the Quest in every walk down the street.

If archetypal criticism sometimes seems far-fetched, it is nevertheless true that one of its strengths is that it invites us to use comparisons, and comparing is often an excellent way to see not only what a work shares with other works but what is distinctive in the work. The most successful practitioner of archetypal criticism was Northrop Frye (1912–91), whose numerous books help readers to see fascinating connections between works. For Frye's explicit comments about archetypal criticism, as well as for examples of such criticism in action, see especially his *Anatomy of Criticism* (1957) and *The Educated Imagination* (1964).

Historical Criticism

Historical criticism studies a work within its historical context. Thus, a student of *Julius Caesar, Hamlet,* or *Macbeth*—plays in which ghosts appear—may try to find out about Elizabethan attitudes toward ghosts. We may find that the Elizabethans took ghosts more seriously than we do, or, on the other hand, we may find that ghosts were explained in various ways, for instance, sometimes as figments of the imagination and some-times as shapes taken by the devil to mislead the virtuous. Similarly, a historical essay concerned with *Othello* may be devoted to Elizabethan attitudes toward Moors, or to Elizabethan ideas of love, or, for that mat-ter, to Elizabethan ideas of a daughter's obligations toward her father's wishes concerning her suitor. The historical critic assumes (and one can hardly dispute the assumption) that writers, however individualistic, are shaped by the particular social contexts in which they live. The goal of historical criticism is to understand how people in the past thought and felt. It assumes that such understanding can enrich our understanding of a particular work. The assumption is, however, disputable, because one may argue that the artist may *not* have shared the age's view on this or that. All of the half dozen or so Moors in Elizabethan plays other than *Othello* are villainous or foolish, but this evidence does not prove that *therefore* Othello is villainous or foolish.

Marxist Criticism

One form of historical criticism is **Marxist criticism,** named for Karl Marx (1818–83). Actually, to say "one form" is misleading because Marxist criticism today is varied, but essentially it sees history primarily as a struggle between socioeconomic classes, and it sees literature (and everything else) as the product of economic forces of the period.

For Marxists, economics is the "base" or "infrastructure"; on this base rests a "superstructure" of ideology (law, politics, philosophy, religion, and the arts, including literature), reflecting the interests of the dominant class. Thus, literature is a material product, produced—like bread or Barbie dolls—to be consumed in a given society. Marxist critics are concerned with Shakespeare's plays as part of a market economy—with show *business,* the economics of the theater, including payments to authors and actors, and revenue from audiences.

Few critics would disagree that works of art in some measure reflect the age that produced them, but most contemporary Marxist critics go further. First, they assert—in a repudiation of what has been called "'vulgar' Marxist theory"—that the deepest historical meaning of a literary work is to be found in what it does *not* say, what its ideology does not permit it to express. Second, Marxists take seriously Marx's famous comment that "the philosophers have only *interpreted* the world in various ways; the point is to *change* it." The critic's job is to change the world by revealing the economic basis of the arts.

Not surprisingly, most Marxists are skeptical of such concepts as "genius" and "masterpiece." These concepts, they say, are part of the bourgeois myth that idealizes the individual and detaches it from its economic context.

For an introduction to Marxist criticism, see Terry Eagleton, *Marxism and Literary Criticism* (1976).

New Historicism

A recent school of scholarship, called the **New Historicism,** insists that there is no "history" in the sense of a narrative of indisputable past events. Rather, the New Historicism holds that there is only our version—our narrative, our representation—of the past. In this view, each age projects its own preconceptions on the past; historians may think they are revealing the past but they are revealing only their own historical situation and their personal preferences. For example, in the nineteenth century and in

118   CHAPTER 9   WRITING ABOUT LITERATURE: AN OVERVIEW

the twentieth almost up to 1992, Columbus was represented as the heroic benefactor of humankind who discovered the New World. But even while plans were being made to celebrate the five-hundredth anniversary of his first voyage across the Atlantic, voices were raised in protest: Columbus did not "discover" a New World; after all, the indigenous people knew where they were, and it was Columbus who was lost, since he thought he was in India. In short, people who wrote history in, say, 1900 projected onto the past their current views (colonialism was a good thing), and people who in 1992 wrote history projected onto that same period a very different set of views (colonialism was a bad thing).

Similarly, ancient Greece, once celebrated by historians as the source of democracy and rational thinking, is now more often regarded as a society that was built on slavery and on the oppression of women. And the Renaissance, once glorified as an age of enlightened thought, is now often seen as an age that tyrannized women, enslaved colonial people, and enslaved itself with its belief in witchcraft and astrology. Thinking about these changing views, one feels the truth of the witticism that the only thing more uncertain than the future is the past.

On the New Historicism, see H. Aram Veeser, ed., *The New Historicism* (1989) and *The New Historicism Reader* (1994).

Biographical Criticism

One kind of historical research is *biography*, which for our purposes includes not only biographies but also autobiographies, diaries, journals, letters, and so on. What experiences did Mark Twain undergo? Are some of the apparently sensational aspects of *Adventures of Huckleberry Finn* in fact close to events that Twain experienced? If so, is he a "realist"? If not, is he writing in the tradition of the "tall tale"?

The really good biographies not only tell us about the life of the author but enable us to return to the literary texts with a deeper understanding of how they came to be what they are. If, for example, you read Alfred Habegger's biography of Emily Dickinson (2001), you will find a wealth of material concerning her family and the world she moved in—for instance, the religious ideas that were part of her upbringing.

Biographical study may illuminate even the work of a living author. If you are writing about the poetry of Adrienne Rich, you may want to consider what she has told us in many essays about her life, in *On Lies, Secrets, and Silence* (1979) and *Blood, Bread, and Poetry* (1986), especially about her relations with her father and her husband.

Psychological (or Psychoanalytic) Criticism

One form that biographical study may take is **psychological** or **psycho-analytic criticism,** which usually examines the author and the author's writings in the framework of Freudian psychology. A central doctrine of Sigmund Freud (1856–1939) is the Oedipus complex, the view that all males (Freud seems not to have made his mind up about females) unconsciously wish to displace their fathers and to sleep with their mothers. According to Freud, hatred for the father and love of the mother, normally repressed, may appear disguised in dreams. Works of art, like dreams, are disguised versions of repressed wishes.

In *Hamlet and Oedipus* (1949) Ernest Jones, amplifying some comments by Freud, argued that Hamlet delays killing Claudius because Claudius (who has killed Hamlet's father and married Hamlet's mother) has done exactly what Hamlet himself wants to do. For Hamlet to kill Claudius, then, would be to kill himself.

If this approach interests you, take a look at Norman N. Holland's *Psychoanalysis and Shakespeare* (1966) or Frederick Crews's study of Hawthorne, *The Sins of the Fathers* (1966). Crews finds in Hawthorne's work evidence of unresolved Oedipal conflicts, and he accounts for the appeal of the fictions thus: The stories "rest on fantasy, but on the shared fantasy of mankind, and this makes for a more penetrating fiction than would any illusionistic slice of life" (263). For applications to other authors, consider Simon O. Lesser's *Fiction and the Unconscious* (1957) or an anthology of criticism, *Literature and Psychoanalysis* (1983), ed. Edith Kurzweil and William Phillips.

Psychological criticism can also turn from the author and the work to the reader, seeking to explain why we, as readers, respond in certain ways. Why, for example, is *Hamlet* so widely popular? A Freudian answer is that it is universal because it deals with a universal (Oedipal) impulse. One can, however, ask whether it appeals as strongly to women as to men (again, Freud was unsure about the Oedipus complex in women) and, if so, why it appeals to them. Or, more generally, one can ask if males and females read in the same way.

Gender (Feminist, and Lesbian and Gay) Criticism

This last question brings us to **gender criticism.** As we have seen, writing about literature usually seeks to answer questions. Historical criticism, for instance, tries to answer such questions as "What did Shakespeare and his contemporaries believe about ghosts?" and "How did Victorian novelists and poets respond to Darwin's theory of evolution?" Gender criticism, too, asks questions. It is especially concerned with two issues, one about reading and one about writing: "Do men and women read in different ways" and "Do they write in different ways?"

Feminist criticism can be traced back to the work of Virginia Woolf (1882–1941), but chiefly it grew out of the women's movement of the 1960s. The women's movement at first tended to hold that women are pretty much the same as men and therefore should be treated equally, but much recent feminist criticism has emphasized and explored the differences between women and men. Because the experiences of the sexes are different, the argument goes, their values and sensibilities are different, and their responses to literature are different. Further, literature written by women is different from literature written by men. Works written by women are seen by some feminist critics as embodying the experiences of a minority culture—a group marginalized by the dominant male culture. (If you have read Charlotte Perkins Gilman's "The Yellow Wallpaper" [1892] or Susan Glaspell's "Trifles" [1916] you'll recall that these literary works themselves are concerned with the differing ways that males and females perceive the world.)

Of course, not all women critics are feminist critics, and not all feminist critics are women. Further, there are varieties of feminist criticism. For good introductions see Elaine Showalter, *The New Feminist Criticism: Essays on Women, Literature, and Theory* (1985), and *Feminisms: An Anthology of Literary Theory and Criticism,* ed. Robyn R. Warhol and Diane Price Herndl, 2nd ed. (1991). For the role of men in feminist criticism, see *Engendering Men*, ed. Joseph A. Boone and Michael Cadden (1990).

Feminist critics rightly point out that men have established the conventions of literature and that men have established the canon—the body of literature that is said to be worth reading. Speaking a bit broadly, in this patriarchal or male-dominated body of literature, men are valued for being strong and active, whereas women are expected to be weak and passive. Thus, in the world of fairy tales, the admirable male is the energetic hero (Jack the Giant-Killer) but the admirable female is the passive Sleeping Beauty. Active women such as the wicked stepmother or—a disguised form of the same thing—the witch are generally villainous. (There are of course exceptions, such as Gretel, in "Hansel and Gretel.") A woman hearing or reading the story of Sleeping Beauty or of Little Red Riding Hood (rescued by the powerful woodcutter) or any other work in which women seem to be trivialized will respond differently from a man. For instance, a woman may be socially conditioned into admiring Sleeping Beauty, but only at great cost to her mental well-being. A more resistant female reader may recognize in herself no kinship with the beautiful, passive Sleeping Beauty and may respond to the story indignantly. Another way to put it is this: The male reader perceives a romantic story, but the resistant female reader perceives a story of oppression.

For discussions of the ways in which, it is argued, women *ought* to read, you may want to look at *Gender and Reading*, ed. Elizabeth A. Flynn and Patrocinio P. Schweikart (1986), and especially at Judith Fetterley's *The Resisting Reader* (1978).

Feminist criticism has been concerned not only with the depiction of women and men in a male-determined literary canon and with female responses to these images, but also with yet another topic: women's writing. Women have had fewer opportunities than men to become writers of fiction, poetry, and drama—for one thing, they have been less well educated in the things that the male patriarchy valued—but even when they *have* managed to write, men sometimes have neglected their work simply because it is by a woman. Feminists have further argued that certain forms of writing have been especially the province of women—journals, diaries, and letters—and predictably, these forms have not been given adequate space in the traditional, male-oriented canon.

In 1972, in an essay titled "When We Dead Awaken: Writing as Re-Vision," the poet and essayist Adrienne Rich effectively summed up the matter:

> A radical critique of literature, feminist in its impulse, would take the work first of all as a clue to how we live, how we have been living, how we have been led to imagine ourselves, how our language has trapped as well as liberated us; and how we can begin to see—and therefore live—afresh. . . . We need to know the writing of the past and know it differently than we have ever known it: not to pass on a tradition but to break its hold over us.

Much feminist criticism concerned with women writers has emphasized connections between the writer's biography and her life. Suzanne Juhasz, in her introduction to *Feminist Critics Read Emily Dickinson* (1983), puts it this way:

> The central assumption of feminist criticism is that gender informs the nature of art, the nature of biography, and the relation between them. Dickinson is a woman poet, and this fact is integral to her identity.

Feminist criticism's sensitivity to the components of female experience in general and to Dickinson's identity as a woman generates essential insights about her. . . . Attention to the relationship between biography and art is a requisite of feminist criticism. To disregard it further strengthens those divisions continually created by traditional criticism, so that nothing about the woman writer can be seen whole. (1–5)

Lesbian and gay criticism have their roots in feminist criticism, which introduced many of the questions that these other, newer developments are now exploring.

Before turning to some of the questions that lesbian and gay critics address, it is necessary first to say that lesbian criticism and gay criticism are not symmetrical, chiefly because lesbian and gay relationships themselves are not symmetrical. Straight society has traditionally been more tolerant of—or blinder to—lesbianism than male homosexuality. Further, lesbian literary theory has tended to see its affinities more with feminist theory than with gay theory; that is, the emphasis has been on gender (male/female) rather than on sexuality (homosexuality/bisexuality/heterosexuality). On the other hand, some gays and lesbians have been writing what is now being called *Queer Theory*.

Now for some of the questions that this criticism addresses:

- Do lesbians and gays read in ways that differ from the ways straight people read?
- Do they write in ways that differ from those of straight people?
- How have straight writers portrayed lesbians and gays, and how have lesbian and gay writers portrayed straight women and men?
- What strategies did lesbian and gay writers use to make their work acceptable to a general public in an age when lesbian and gay behavior was unmentionable?

Examination of gender can help to illuminate literary works, but it should be added, too, that some—perhaps most—gay and lesbian critics write also as activists, reporting their findings not only to enable us to understand and to enjoy the works of, say, Whitman, but also to change society's view of sexuality. Thus, in *Disseminating Whitman* (1991), Michael Moon is impatient with earlier critical rhapsodies about Whitman's universalism. It used to be said that Whitman's celebration of the male body was a sexless celebration of brotherly love in a democracy, but the gist of Moon's view is that we must neither whitewash Whitman's poems with such high-minded talk nor reject them as indecent; rather, we must see exactly what Whitman is saying about a kind of experience that society had shut its eyes to and we must take Whitman's view seriously.

One assumption in much lesbian and gay critical writing is that although gender greatly influences the ways in which we read, reading is a skill that can be learned, and therefore straight people—aided by lesbian and gay critics—can learn to read, with pleasure and profit, lesbian and gay writers. This assumption also underlies much feminist criticism, which often assumes that men must stop ignoring books by women and must learn (with the help of feminist critics) how to read them, and, in fact, how to read—with newly opened eyes—the sexist writings of men of the past and present.

In addition to the titles mentioned earlier concerning gay and lesbian criticism, consult Eve Kosofsky Sedgwick, *Between Men: English Literature and Male Homosocial Desire* (1985), and an essay by Sedgwick, "Gender Criticism," in *Redrawing the Boundaries*, ed. Stephen Greenblatt and Giles Gunn (1992).

The following books also are illuminating: Annamarie Jagose, *Queer Theory: An Introduction* (1996); *Feminism Meets Queer Theory*, ed. Elizabath Weed and Naomi Schor (1997); *Hemingway and Women: Female Critics and the Female Voice*, ed. Lawrence R. Broer and Gloria Holland (2002); *Queer Theory*, ed. Iain Morland and Annabelle Willox (2005); Phyllis Rackin, *Shakespeare and Women* (2005); and *Gender in Modernism: New Geographies, Complex Intersections*, ed. Bonnie Kime Scott (2007). For the work of an influential theorist of gender, see *The Judith Butler Reader*, ed. Sara Salih (2004).

📖 SUGGESTIONS FOR FURTHER READING

Because a massive list of titles may prove discouraging rather than helpful, it seems advisable here to give a short list of basic titles. (Titles already mentioned in this chapter—which are good places to begin—are *not* repeated in the following list.)

Good selections of contemporary criticism can be found in *The Critical Tradition: Classic Texts and Contemporary Trends,* ed. David H. Richter, 3rd ed. (2006), and *The Norton Anthology of Literary Theory and Criticism,* ed. Vincent B. Leitch et al., 2nd ed. (2010).

For a readable introduction to various approaches, written for students who are beginning the study of literary theory, see Steven Lynn, *Texts and*

Contexts, 6th ed. (2010). For a more advanced survey that assumes some familiarity with the material, see a short book by K. M. Newton, *Interpreting the Text: A Critical Introduction to the Theory and Practice of Literary Interpretation* (1990). A third survey, though considerably longer than the books by Lynn and Newton, is narrower because it confines itself to a study of critical writings about Shakespeare: Brian Vickers, *Appropriating Shakespeare: Contemporary Critical Quarrels* (1993), offers a stringent appraisal of deconstruction, New Historicism, psychoanalytic criticism, feminist criticism, and Marxist criticism. For collections of essays on Shakespeare written from some of the points of view that Vickers deplores, see Patricia Parker and Geoffrey Hartman, eds., *Shakespeare and the Question of Theory* (1985), and John Drakakis, ed., *Shakespearean Tragedy* (1992).

Sympathetic discussions (usually two or three pages long) of each approach, with extensive bibliographic suggestions, are given in the appropriate articles in the four encyclopedic works by Harris; Makaryk; Groden and Kreiswirth; Payne; and Preminger and Brogan, listed on page 87 of Chapter 6, though only Groden and Kreiswirth (*The Johns Hopkins Guide*) discuss lesbian and gay criticism (under "Gay Theory and Criticism"). For essays discussing feminist, gender, Marxist, psychoanalytic, deconstructive, New Historicist, and cultural criticism—as well as other topics not covered in this chapter—see Stephen Greenblatt and Giles Gunn, eds., *Redrawing the Boundaries: The Transformation of English and American Literary Studies* (1992).

Formalist Criticism (The New Criticism)

Cleanth Brooks, *The Well Wrought Urn: Studies in the Structure of Poetry* (1947), especially Chapters 1 and 11 ("The Language of Paradox" and "The Heresy of Paraphrase"); W. K. Wimsatt, *The Verbal Icon* (1954), especially "The Intentional Fallacy" and "The Affective Fallacy"; Murray Krieger, *The New Apologists for Poetry* (1956); and, for an accurate overview of a kind of criticism often misrepresented today, Chapters 9–12 in Volume 6 of René Wellek, *A History of Modern Criticism: 1750–1950* (1986). For a good collection, see *Praising It New: The Best of the New Criticism*, ed. Garrick Davis (2008).

Deconstruction

Christopher Norris, *Deconstruction: Theory and Practice*, rev. ed. (1991); Vincent B. Leitch, *Deconstructive Criticism: An Advanced Introduction and Survey* (1983); Christopher Norris, ed., *What Is Deconstruction?* (1988); Christopher Norris and Andrew Benjamin, *Deconstruction and the Interests of Theory* (1989). For a negative assessment, consult John M. Ellis, *Against Deconstruction* (1989). More generally, see *Deconstruction: A Reader,* ed. Martin McQuillan (2001).

Reader-Response Criticism

Wolfgang Iser, *The Act of Reading: A Theory of Aesthetic Response* (1978); Wolfgang Iser, *Prospecting: From Reader Response to Literary Anthropology* (1993); Susan Suleiman and Inge Crossman, eds., *The Reader in the Text* (1980); Jane P. Tompkins, ed., *Reader-Response Criticism* (1980); Norman N. Holland, *The Dynamics of Literary Response* (1973, 1989); Steven Mailloux, *Interpretive Conventions: The Reader in the Study of American Fiction* (1982); Gerry Brenner, *Performative Criticism: Experiments in Reader Response* (2004).

Archetypal Criticism

G. Wilson Knight, *The Starlit Dome* (1941); Richard Chase, *Quest for Myth* (1949); Murray Krieger, ed., *Northrop Frye in Modern Criticism* (1966); Frank Lentricchia, *After the New Criticism* (1980). For a good survey of Frye's approach, see Robert D. Denham, *Northrop Frye and Critical Method* (1978). Also, *Rereading Frye: The Published and Unpublished Works,* ed. David Boyd and Imre Salusinszky (1999).

Historical Criticism

For a brief survey of some historical criticism of the first half of this century, see René Wellek, *A History of Modern Criticism: 1750–1950,* volume 6 (1986), Chapter 4 ("Academic Criticism"). E. M. W. Tillyard, *The Elizabethan World Picture* (1943), and Tillyard's *Shakespeare's History Plays* (1944), both of which relate Elizabethan literature to the beliefs of the age, are good examples of the historical approach. Also of interest is David Levin, *Forms of Uncertainty: Essays in Historical Criticism* (1992).

Marxist Criticism

Raymond Williams, *Marxism and Literature* (1977); Tony Bennett, *Formalism and Marxism* (1979); Lydia Sargent, ed., *Women and*

Revolution: A Discussion of the Unhappy Marriage of Marxism and Feminism (1981); and for a brief survey of American Marxist writers of the 1930s and 1940s, see Chapter 5 of volume 6 of René Wellek, *A History of Modern Criticism* (1986). Also helpful are Daniel Aaron, *Writers on the Left: Episodes in American Literary Communism* (1961, 1992); and Barbara Foley, *Radical Representations: Politics and Form in U.S. Proletarian Fiction, 1929–1941* (1993). Also stimulating are Terry Eagleton, *The Ideology of the Aesthetic* (1990), and *Marxist Shakespeares*, ed. Jean E. Howard and Scott Cutler Shershow (2001).

New Historicism

Historicizing Theory, ed. Peter C. Herman (2004); Stephen Greenblatt, *Renaissance Self-Fashioning from More to Shakespeare* (1980), especially the first chapter; Brook Thomas, *The New Historicism and Other Old-Fashioned Topics* (1991). Greenblatt's other influential books include *Shakespearean Negotiations: The Circulation of Social Energy in Renaissance England* (1988) and, with Catherine Gallagher, *Practicing New Historicism* (2000).

Biographical Criticism

Leon Edel, *Literary Biography* (1957); Estelle C. Jellinek, ed., *Women's Autobiography: Essays in Criticism* (1980); James Olney, *Metaphors of Self: The Meaning of Autobiography* (1981); and *Women, Autobiography, Theory: A Reader*, ed. Sidonie Smith and Julia Watson (1998). Important twentieth-century literary biographies are Richard Ellmann, *James Joyce* (1959, rev. ed., 1982); Juliet Barker, *The Brontës* (1994); Hermione Lee, *Virginia Woolf* (1997); Lyndall Gordon, *T. S. Eliot: An Imperfect Life* (1999); and Fred Kaplan, *The Singular Mark Twain: A Biography* (2003).

Psychological (or Psychoanalytical) Criticism

Edith Kurzweil and William Phillips, eds., *Literature and Psychoanalysis* (1983); Maurice Charney and Joseph Reppen, eds., *Psychoanalytic Approaches to Literature and Film* (1987); Madelon Sprengnether, *The Spectral Mother: Freud, Feminism, and Psychoanalysis* (1990); Frederick Crews, *Out of My System* (1975); and Graham Frankland, *Freud's Literary Culture* (2000). Helpful, too, is Anthony Storr, *Freud: A Very Short Introduction* (2001)

Gender (Feminist, and Lesbian and Gay) Criticism

Gayle Greene and Coppèlia Kahn, eds., *Making a Difference: Feminist Literary Criticism* (1985), including an essay by Bonnie Zimmerman on lesbian criticism; Catherine Belsey and Jane Moore, eds., *The Feminist Reader: Essays in Gender and the Politics of Literary Criticism* (1989); Toril Moi, ed., *French Feminist Thought* (1987); Elizabeth A. Flynn and Patrocinio P. Schweikart, eds., *Gender and Reading: Essays on Readers, Texts, and Contexts* (1986); Barbara Christian, *Black Feminist Criticism: Perspectives on Black Women Writers* (1985); Shoshana Felman, *What Does a Woman Want? Reading and Sexual Difference* (1993); Robert Martin, *The Homosexual Tradition in American Poetry* (1979); Kathryn R. Kent, *Making Girls into Women: American Women's Writing and the Rise of Lesbian Identity* (2003); and Rita Felski, *Literature After Feminism* (2003). Henry Abelove et al., eds., *The Lesbian and Gay Studies Reader* (1993), has only a few essays concerning literature, but it has an extensive bibliography on the topic.

Valuable reference works include *Encyclopedia of Feminist Literary Theory*, ed. Beth Kowaleski-Wallace (1997); *The Gay & Lesbian Literary Companion*, ed. Sharon Malinowski and Christa Brelin (1995); and *The Gay and Lesbian Literary Heritage: A Reader's Companion to the Writers and Their Works, from Antiquity to the Present*, ed. Claude J. Summers (1995). See also Summers, *Gay Fictions: Wilde to Stonewall: Studies in a Male Homosexual Literary Tradition* (1990); *Novel Gazing: Queer Readings in Fiction*, ed. Eve Kosofsky Sedgwick (1997); and Gregory Woods, *A History of Gay Literature: The Male Tradition* (1998). For further discussion of Queer Theory, see Annamarie Jagose, *Queer Theory: An Introduction* (1996); Alan Sinfield, *Cultural Politics—Queer Reading* (1994); and *Feminism Meets Queer Theory*, ed. Elizabeth Weed and Naomi Schor (1997). Also recommended is *The Columbia Anthology of Gay Literature*, ed. Byrne R. S. Fone (2001).

PART 3

Up Close: Thinking Critically about Literary Forms

10

WRITING ABOUT FICTION: THE WORLD OF THE STORY

There are only two or three human stories, and they go on repeating themselves as fiercely as if they had never happened before.

—Willa Cather

A novel that does not uncover a hitherto unknown segment of existence is immoral. Knowledge is the novel's only morality.

—Milan Kundera

Fiction is nothing less than the subtlest instrument for self-examination and self-display that mankind has yet invented.

—John Updike

PLOT AND CHARACTER

Plot has two meanings: (1) what happens, the basics of the narrative, and (2) the writer's arrangement or structuring of the material into a story. Thus, in the first sense, all tellings of the life of Abraham Lincoln have the same plot, but in the second sense, a writer who begins with the assassination in 1865 and then gives the earlier material is setting forth a plot that differs from one given by a writer who begins at the beginning of Lincoln's life.

It is usual to say that a plot (in the sense of an arrangement or structure) has an **introduction,** a **complication,** and a **resolution;** that is, it gets under way, then some difficulty or problem or complexity arises (usually a **conflict** of opposed wills or forces), and finally, there is some sort of settling down. A somewhat metaphoric way of putting it is to say that the plot is the tying and then the untying of a knot; the end is the **dénouement** (French for "untying").

A closely related way of looking at the organization of the happenings in many works of fiction is to see the plot as a pyramid or triangle. The German critic Gustav Freytag (1816–1895), in *Techniques of the Drama* (1863), introduced this conception in examining the five-act structure of plays, but it can be applied to some fiction, too. In this view, we begin either with an unstable situation or with an apparently stable situation that is soon disrupted; that is, some difficulty or problem or complexity arises (usually a **conflict** of opposed wills or forces). The early happenings, with their increasing tension, constitute a **rising action,** which culminates in a **climax** or **crisis** or **turning point.** (The word *climax* comes from a Greek word meaning "ladder." Originally, the climax was the entire rising action, but the word has come to mean the high point or end of the rising action.) What follows the decisive moment is the **falling action,** which ends in a stable situation— a situation that the reader takes to be final. The characters need not die; the reader feels, however, that nothing more is to be said about them.

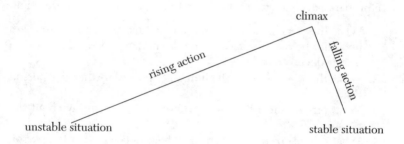

The diagram shows Freytag's pyramid. Remember that a story *need* not have this structure. Early fiction tends to have a good deal of physical action—wanderings, strange encounters, births, and deaths. But in some fiction, little seems to happen. These apparently plotless stories usually involve a *mental action*—a significant perception, a decision, a failure of the will—and the process of this mental action is the plot.

The sense of causality is in part rooted in **character.** Things happen, in most good fiction, at least partly because the people have certain personalities or characters (moral, intellectual, and emotional qualities) and, given their natures, because they respond plausibly to other personalities. What their names are and what they look like may help you to understand them, but the best guide to characters is what they do. As we get to know more about their drives and goals—especially the choices they make—we enjoy seeing the writer complete the portraits, finally presenting us with a coherent and credible picture of people in action.

In this view, plot and character are inseparable. Plot is a series not simply of happenings, but of happenings that come out of character, that reveal character, and that influence character. Henry James (1843–1916) puts it thus: "What is character but the determination of incident? What is incident but the illustration of character?" But, of course, characters are not defined only by what they do. The narrator often describes them, and the characters' words and dress reveal aspects of them.

You may want to set forth a character sketch, describing some person in a story or novel. You will probably plan to convey three things:

appearance,

personality, and

character—"character" here meaning not a figure in a literary work
   but the figure's moral or ethical values

In preparing a character sketch, take these points into consideration:

1. What the person says (but remember that what he or she says need not be taken at face value; the person may be hypocritical or self-deceived or biased).
2. What the person does—including, if possible, what the person thinks.
3. What others (including the narrator of the story) say about the person.
4. What others *do* (their actions may help indicate what the person could do but does not do), including what they *think* about others.
5. What the person looks like—face, body, clothes. These details may help convey the personality of the character, or they may in some measure help to disguise it.

Writing about a Character

A character sketch, such as "Holden Caulfield: Adolescent Snob or Suffering Saint?," may be complex and demanding, especially if the character (the figure) is complex. Notice that in this example the writer sees that Holden, the protagonist in J. D. Salinger's *The Catcher in the Rye* (1951), might be interpreted in two very different ways, as a snob or as a saint. In fact, the student who wrote the essay argued that Holden has touches of the adolescent snob but is chiefly a suffering saint.

An essay on a character is necessarily in some degree an interpretation, and such an essay has a thesis or argument holding it together. Usually, however, you will want to do more than set forth your view of a character. Probably, you will discuss the character's function or contrast him or her with other characters or trace the development of the character's personality. (One of the most difficult topics, the character of the narrator, will be discussed later in this chapter, under the heading "Point of View.") You will still want to keep in mind the five suggestions for getting at a character (as well as others on pages 173–174), but you will also want to go further, relating your findings to additional matters of the sort we will examine now.

Organizing an Analysis of a Character As you read and reread, you will highlight and annotate the text and jot down notes, recording (in whatever order they come to you) your thoughts about the character you are studying. Reading with a view toward writing, you'll want to

1. jot down traits as they come to mind ("kind," "forgetful," "enthusiastic") and
2. look back at the text, searching for supporting evidence (characteristic actions, brief supporting quotations), also looking for counterevidence so that you may modify your earlier impressions.

Brainstorming leads to an evaluation and a shaping of your ideas. Evaluating and shaping lead to a tentative outline. A tentative outline leads to the search for supporting evidence—the material that will constitute the body of your essay.

When you set out to write a first draft, review your annotations and notes, and see if you can summarize your view of the character in one or two sentences:

X is . . .

or

Although X is, . . . she is also . . .

That is, *try to formulate a thesis sentence or a thesis paragraph*—a proposition that you will go on to support.

You want to let your reader know early, probably in your first sentence—and almost certainly by the end of your first paragraph—which character you are writing about and what your overall thesis is.

Sometimes it is helpful to give yourself prompts to develop and define a thesis.[1] For example:

- During class discussion, some students said that . . . , but I disagree, and I disagree because. . . .
- When I first read X, I thought that . . . , but a second reading led me to change my mind. I now think that. . . .
- The most important thing to know about X is . . . , and it is important because. . . .
- In this essay, the question that I will ask and try to answer is. . . .
- In lecture and in class discussion, we focused on . . . , but I think that we also should consider. . . .
- There is evidence to support the view that . . . , but I think that there is even better evidence to support the view that. . . .

The body of your essay will be devoted to supporting your thesis. If you have asserted that although so-and-so is cruel and domineering he or she nevertheless is endowed with a conscience, you will go on in your essay to support those assertions with references to passages that demonstrate them. This support does *not* mean that you tell the plot of the whole work; an essay on a character is by no means the same as a summary of the plot. Because you must support your generalizations, you will have to make brief references to specific episodes that reveal his or her personality, and almost surely you will quote an occasional word or passage.

An essay on a character may be organized in many ways. Much will depend on your purpose and thesis. You may want to show how the character develops—gains knowledge or matures or disintegrates. Or you may want to show what the character contributes to the story or play as a whole. Or, to give another example, you may want to show that the character is unbelievable. Although no single organization is always right, two methods are common and effective.

One effective way of organizing an essay on a character is to let the organization of your essay follow closely the sequence of the literary work; you might devote a paragraph to the character as we first perceive him or her and then in subsequent paragraphs go on to show that this figure is later seen to be more complex than he or she at first appears. Such an essay may trace your changing responses.

---

[1] For these kinds of prompts, we are indebted to Gerald Graff and Cathy Birkenstein's stimulating book, *They Say/I Say: The Moves That Matter in Academic Writing* (2006).

A second effective way of organizing an essay on a character is to set forth, early in the essay, the character's chief strengths and weaknesses, and then to go on to study each trait you have listed. The organization would (in order to maintain the reader's interest) probably begin with the most obvious points and then move on to the less obvious, subtler points. The body of your essay is devoted to offering evidence that supports your generalizations about the character.

What about a concluding paragraph? The concluding paragraph ought *not* to begin with the obviousness of "Thus, we see," or "In conclusion," or "I recommend this story because. . . ." Especially if your essay has moved from the obvious traits to the more subtle and more important traits, and if your essay is fairly short (say, fewer than 500 words), a reader may not need a conclusion. Further, why blunt what you have just said by adding an unnecessary and merely repetitive summary? If you do feel that a conclusion is necessary, you may find it effective to write a summary of the character, somewhat as you did in your opening. For the conclusion, relate the character's character to the entire literary work; give the reader a sense of the role that the character plays.

A Sample Essay on a Character: "Holden's Kid Sister"

A student decided to write about Phoebe, Holden Caulfield's sister in *The Catcher in the Rye*. Before writing, he reread the book, highlighting certain passages about Phoebe. He then reviewed the text and jotted down some key ideas:

Phoebe Josephine Caulfield
   Holden's kid sister
      playful, funny, fun to be with
      likes movies
      invents new name (Weatherfield)
      good dancer
      academically good ("smart"; "good in all subjects")
        Actually, Holden says this, and as he somewhere says, he's
          a terrible liar—but here he's probably telling the truth.
          He wouldn't lie about her. (Does this point have to be
          proved?)
good listener (that's what H. needs; it seems that almost everyone else
  is trying to *tell* him some phoney stuff, but P. accepts him)

good listener *but* she doesn't always agree with him or approve of
 what he's doing.

>   Example: disapproves of his leaving school
>   BUT though she's upset by it, she sticks with him
>   Other examples needed?
> She's loyal—and she loves him. Does anyone else love him?

These note provided much of the first draft, which was submitted
to peer review. The student then revised the draft, partly in accordance
with the suggestions offered and partly in the light of his own further
thinking. Here is the final version.

Maxwell Bristol

Professor Lombardo

English Composition 2G

5 February 2011

Holden's Kid Sister

Phoebe Josephine Caulfield, Holden's ten-year-old sister in J. D.
Salinger's *The Catcher in the Rye*, is a child with a mind of her own.
She doesn't care for her middle name, and so on the first page of
one of her many notebooks she gives herself a new one: "Phoebe
Weatherfield Caulfield." She is, we gather, playful and imaginative,
but she is also in touch with reality, and able to get along well in the
world. She has friends, and at school she is "good in all subjects."
The quality that most impresses a reader, however, is not her
academic success but her loyalty to Holden, and even when she
criticizes Holden she does so out of deep love for him.

Since Holden is the narrator of the book, all that we know of
Phoebe is seen through his eyes, but there is no reason to doubt
his comments about her. Early in the book, in Chapter 10, he gives
us a long description, in the course of which he says that she is
"pretty and smart," a redhead, "skinny," and (more important, of
course) "affectionate." Later, Holden tells us that she shares his
taste in movies and that she is a perfect partner when she dances
with him. That is, Phoebe is on Holden's wavelength; the two can
move in harmony, and not only when they dance. She is a good
listener, and Holden desperately needs someone who can listen
to him because most of the people in his world are big talkers and
are trying to impose their own values on him.

This is not to say, however, that Phoebe approves of all of
Holden's actions. When she learns that he has left school, she is

upset with him, but the reader always feels that any criticism she makes proceeds from her love for Holden. She is so loyal to him that she wants to leave school and go with him when he tells her he plans to run away from New York and hitchhike to the West. Her loyalty, her refusal to leave him, causes him to abandon his desperate plan to flee.

Her sincerity and her love for Holden are not enough to restore him to mental health (at the end of the book we learn that he "got sick and all" and is now in some sort of asylum), but the reader knows that if any character in the book can provide the human warmth that Holden requires, that character is his bright, strong-willed, loving "kid sister."

The Student's Analysis Analyzed

- The title is informative and at least moderately interesting—more interesting, for example, than "Phoebe Caulfield."
- The writer does not cite pages because the instructor did not ask him to do so, but if your instructor asks you to give references, use the form prescribed. (On citations, see pages 327–40, 347–52.)
- The opening paragraph announces the topic, gives a brief description of Phoebe (her age, her imaginativeness), and ends by focusing on her most important trait, her love for Holden.
- The body of the essay (paragraphs 2 and 3) offers a few additional minor details, but chiefly it supports (by means of the comment on dancing) the earlier generalization that Phoebe is uniquely in harmony with Holden. It does not summarize the plot, but it does refer to certain episodes, and it interprets them in order to show how they reveal Phoebe's character.
- The final paragraph, the fourth, offers additional support (her plan to run away with Holden), and it concludes with a glance at the conclusion of the novel. The essay more or less echoes the chronology of the book, but these last sentences are not mere plot telling. Rather, they solidify the writer's view of Phoebe's character and her importance to Holden.

For a checklist concerned with writing about a character in fiction, see pages 173–74.

FORESHADOWING

The writer of fiction provides a coherent world in which the details work together. **Foreshadowing,** which eliminates surprise or at least greatly reduces it and thus prepares us for what will occur later, is a powerful tool in the hands of the writer of serious fiction.

James Joyce's "Araby" (1914)—it appears on pages 353–57—is an example of a story in which the beginning is a preparation for all that follows. Consider the first two paragraphs:

> North Richmond Street, being blind, was a quiet street except at the hour when the Christian Brothers' School set the boys free. An uninhabited house of two stories stood at the blind end, detached from its neighbours in a square ground. The other houses of the street, conscious of decent lives within them, gazed at one another with brown imperturbable faces.
>
> The former tenant of our house, a priest, had died in the back drawing-room. Air, musty from having been long enclosed, hung in all the rooms, and the waste room behind the kitchen was littered with old useless papers. Among these I found a few paper-covered books, the pages of which were curled and damp: *The Abbot,* by Walter Scott, *The Devout Communicant* and *The Memoirs of Vidocq.* I liked the last best because its leaves were yellow. The wild garden behind the house contained a central apple-tree and a few straggling bushes under one of which I found the late tenant's rusty bicycle pump. He had been a very charitable priest; in his will he had left all his money to institutions and the furniture of his house to his sister.

This story, like others, has at least three lives:

- when we read the story, sentence by sentence, trying to turn the sequence of sentences into a consistent whole;
- when we have finished reading the story and we think back on it as a whole; and
- when we reread a story, knowing already even as we read the first line how it will turn out at the end.

On the basis only of a reading of the first two paragraphs, what might you highlight or underline? Here are the words that one student marked:

blind	musty
quiet	kitchen was littered
set the boys free	leaves were yellow
brown imperturbable faces	wild garden . . . apple-tree
priest	charitable priest

No two readers will come up with exactly the same list (if you live on North Richmond Street, you will probably underline it and put an exclamation mark in the margin; if you attended a parochial school, you'll probably underline "Christian Brothers' School"), but most readers, despite their varied experience, would agree that Joyce is giving us a picture of what he elsewhere called the "paralysis" of Ireland. How the story will turn out is unknown to a first-time reader. Perhaps the paralysis will increase, or perhaps it will be broken. Joyce goes on adding sentence to sentence, trying to shape the reader's response, and the reader goes on reading, making meaning out of the sentences.

As we read further, we are not surprised to learn that the boy for a while manufactured quasi-religious experiences, religion being dead—remember the dead priest and his rusty bicycle pump. Shop boys sing "litanies," his girlfriend's name springs to his lips "in strange prayers," and his vision of her is a "chalice" that he carries "safely through a throng of foes." He plans to visit a bazaar, and he promises to bring her a gift; but after he has with some difficulty arrived at the bazaar, he is vastly disappointed by the trivial conversation of the attendants, by the counting of the day's receipts (money changers in the temple), and by the darkness ("the upper part of the hall was now completely dark"). The last line of the story runs thus: "Gazing up into the darkness I saw myself as a creature driven and derided by vanity; and my eyes burned with anguish and anger." Everything in the story coheres; the dead-end street, the dead priest, the rusty pump—all are perfect preludes to this story about a boy's recognition of the nothingness that surrounds him. The "vanity" that drives and derides him is not only the egotism that moved him to think he could bring the girl a fitting gift but also the nothingness that is spoken of in the biblical "Vanity of vanities, all is vanity."

In preparing to write about foreshadowing,

- Reread the story; now that you know how it ends, you will be able to see how certain early details are relevant to the ending.
- Underline or highlight these details, and perhaps jot down brief notes in the margins, such as "images of emptiness" or "later turns out ironically."
- At a later stage in the process of writing, you will find it useful to jot down on a sheet of paper key phrases from the text and to annotate them with such comments as "The first of many religious images" and "Same image appears later."

Organizing an Essay on Foreshadowing

What is the best way to organize an essay on foreshadowing? Probably you will work through the evidence chronologically, though your initial paragraph may discuss the end and indicate that the remainder of the essay will be concerned with tracing the way in which the author prepares the reader for this end and simultaneously maintains the right amount of suspense.

- If the suspense is too slight, we stop reading, not caring what comes next.
- If it is too great, possibly we are reading a story in which the interest depends entirely on some strange happening rather than a story with sufficiently universal application to make it worthy of a second reading.

Your essay may study the ways in which details gain in meaning as the reader gets farther into the story. Or it may study the author's failure to keep details relevant and coherent, the tendency to introduce material for its momentary value at the expense of the larger design. An essay on an uneven story may do both: It may show that although there are unfortunate irrelevancies, considerable skill is used in arousing and interestingly fulfilling the reader's expectations.

If you feel that the story is fundamentally successful, the organization of your thoughts may reflect your feelings. After an initial paragraph stating the overall position, you may discuss the failures and then go on at greater length to discuss the strengths, ending strongly on your main point. If you feel that the story is essentially a failure, perhaps first discuss its merits briefly and then go on to your main point—the unsatisfactory nature of the story.

SETTING AND ATMOSPHERE

Foreshadowing normally makes use of **setting.** The setting or environment in the first two paragraphs of Joyce's "Araby" is not mere geography, not mere locale: It provides an **atmosphere,** an air that the characters breathe, a world in which they move. Narrowly speaking, the setting is the physical surroundings—the furniture, the architecture, the landscape, the climate—and these often are highly appropriate to the characters who are associated with them. In Emily Brontë's *Wuthering Heights* (1847), the passionate Earnshaw family is associated with Wuthering Heights,

the storm-exposed moorland, whereas the mild Linton family is associated with Thrushcross Grange in the sheltered valley below. Hawthorne's
"Young Goodman Brown" (1835) also has two settings, Salem in the daytime and a nearby forest at night. A reader of the story probably comes to
believe that Salem is associated with order, decency, and the good, and
the dark forest with chaos and evil.

Setting includes not only the physical surroundings but a point or
several points in time. The background against which we see the characters and the happenings may be specified as morning or evening, spring
or fall, and this temporal setting in a good story will probably be highly
relevant; it will probably be part of the story's meaning, perhaps providing
an ironic contrast (think of the festive, carnival setting in Poe's "The Cask
of Amontillado," a story of a murder) or perhaps exerting an influence on
the characters.

Note: Although your instructor may ask you to write a paragraph describing the setting, more often he or she will want something more complicated, such as an essay on the *function* of the setting. For such an essay,
you may begin with a paragraph or two describing the setting or settings,
but be sure to go on to analyze the significance of this material.

SYMBOLISM

Writers of fiction do not write only about things that have happened to
them. They write about things they have seen or heard, and also about
thoughts and emotions.

Inevitably, writers use **symbols.** Symbols are neither puzzles nor colorful
details but are among the concrete embodiments that give the story its content. In "Ripe Figs" (pages 8–9), Maman-Nainaine tells Babette that when
the figs are ripe Babette can visit her cousins. Of course Maman may merely
be setting an arbitrary date, but as we read the story we likely feel—because
of the emphasis on the *ripening* of the figs, which occurs in the spring or early
summer—that the ripening of the figs in some way suggests the maturing of
Babette. If we do get such ideas, we will in effect be saying that the story is
not simply an anecdote about an old woman whose behavior is odd. True,
the narrator of the story, after telling us of Maman-Nainaine's promise, adds,
"Not that the ripening of figs had the least thing to do with it, but that is
the way Maman-Nainaine was." The narrator sees nothing special—merely
Maman-Nainaine's eccentricity—in the connection between the ripening of
the figs and Babette's visit to her cousins. Readers, however, may see more
than the narrator sees or says. They may see in Babette a young girl maturing;

they may see in Maman-Nainaine an older woman who, almost collaborating with nature, helps Babette to mature.

Writers use symbols because they want readers to perceive that certain characters or places or seasons or happenings have rich implications, stand for something more than what they are on the surface. How do writers help us to perceive these things? *By emphasizing them—* for instance, by describing them at some length—or *by introducing them at times when they might not seem strictly necessary,* or *by calling attention to them repeatedly.*

Consider, for example, Chopin's treatment of the season in which "The Story of an Hour" (page 20) takes place. The story has to take place at *some* time, but Chopin does not simply say, "On a spring day," or an autumn day, and let things go at that. Rather, she tells us about the sky, the trees, the rain, the twittering sparrows—and all of this in an extremely short story in which we might think there is no time for talk about the setting. After all, none of this material is strictly necessary to a story about a woman who has heard that her husband was killed in an accident, who grieves, then recovers, and then dies when he suddenly reappears.

Why, then, does Chopin give such emphasis to the season? Probably because she is using the season symbolically. In this story

- the spring is not just a bit of detail added for realism. Chopin puts considerable emphasis on it, loading it with suggestions of renewal, of the new life that Louise achieves for a moment.
- But here, a caution. To say that the spring in this story is symbolic is not to say that whenever spring appears in a story it always stands for renewal—or that whenever winter appears it always stands for death. Nor does it mean that since spring recurs, Louise will be reborn. In *this* story Chopin uses the season to convey certain specific implications.

Is the railroad also a symbol? Probably not—although readers may disagree. The railroad accident in "The Story of an Hour" may be just a railroad accident, essential to the plot but not to our sense of what the story is about. Chopin does not seem to be using the railroad to say something about modern travel, or about industrialism. The steam-propelled railroad train could be used symbolically, to say something about industrialism displacing an agrarian economy, but does Chopin give her train any such association? If she had wished to do so, she would probably have called attention to the enormous power of the train; she would have let us hear the shriek of its whistle and let us see the smoke pouring out of the smokestack and the intense fire burning in the engine, or she would have let us sense its indifference as it charged through the countryside, defacing the landscape and displacing farmworkers. Had she done so, it would be a different story. Or she might have made the train a symbol of fate overriding human desires, but, again, she does not endow her train with such suggestions. She gives virtually no emphasis to the train, so it is reasonable to believe that it has virtually no significance for the reader. (Incidentally, Chopin's father had died in a train accident, and so it is conceivable that the episode in the story had some special significance for Chopin, but that is a matter for a psychoanalytic interpretation.)

A Sample Essay on Setting as Symbol: "Spring Comes to Mrs. Mallard"

The following essay is about Kate Chopin's "The Story of an Hour" (page 230). If you have not yet read the story, take a moment now to do so.

Amy Jones, a first-year student, has provided her last notes, an outline that guided her while she wrote her first draft. Not all of the notes ended up in the final version, but they were helpful in shaping the essay.

thesis: setting here *not* place but time—springtime title?
    Chopin and Spring
    Chopin's Spring
    Mrs. M's Spring
    Mrs. M's Symbolic Spring
    Spring in "The Story of an Hour"
    Spring Comes to Mrs. M
    Setting as Symbol
    Setting as Symbol: Spring in . . .

setting in "Hour"
Define setting??? place *and* time
    Chopin doesn't give date (or city); but in a house
spring:
    "the tops of the trees . . . were all aquiver with the new spring"
        (parag. 5)
    "sparrows were twittering in the eaves" (parag. 5)

"There were patches of blue sky showing here and there
through the clouds" (parag. 6)
why clouds? brightness pushing through darkness, like
joyous new life pushing aside grief???
~~"spring days and summer days" special significance of~~
~~summer?? Or just means "lots of days"?~~
~~old way of life~~
~~"Louise, open the door! I beg; open the door"~~
elixir (near end) medicine???
doctors say died of heart disease
End with a quotation? Or with something about life turning to death?

Amy Jones
Professor Barnet
English 1G
11 April 2011

Spring Comes to Mrs. Mallard

Title implies thesis. Opening paragraph identifies author and story; topic (setting) is introduced.

In reading Kate Chopin's "The Story of an Hour" a reader is hardly aware of where the story is set. We are not told the country or the city, or the period, and so (if we think about it at all) we probably assume the story is set during Chopin's own lifetime, perhaps even during the year in which she wrote it, in Chopin's own territory, although there really is nothing very specific about Louisiana in this story. Nor do we learn, at the very beginning of the story, whether the action is taking place indoors or outdoors. However, since the story begins by telling us that Mrs. Mallard's sister, Josephine, gently breaks the news of the death of Mr. Mallard, we probably assume it is taking place at Mrs. Mallard's house. This assumption is confirmed a little later, when we hear that Mrs. Mallard, once she has heard the terrible news, "went away to her room alone" (67).

Transition ("But") leads to next point (that the season is emphasized).

But if Kate Chopin doesn't tell us anything about the society in which the figures in the story live, she tells us quite a bit about the time of the year during which the story takes place. The story is very short—only about two and a half pages—but Chopin finds space in which to tell us not only that the time is spring, but also that from a window in her room Mrs. Mallard

could see the tops of trees that were all aquiver with
the new spring life. The delicious breath of rain was
in the air. In the street below a peddler was crying his
wares. The notes of a distant song which some one
was singing finally reached her faintly, and countless
sparrows were twittering in the eaves. (67)

This is the fullest description of the time of year in the
story, but there are other shorter references, so we
can say that the springtime is given considerable
emphasis, considering how short the story is. For
instance, the quoted paragraph is followed by a shorter

paragraph that mentions "patches of blue sky" (67), and
in fact "blue sky" is mentioned again, two paragraphs
later. There is nothing especially remarkable about
the sky being blue, and so one might wonder why
Chopin bothers to tell us that the sky is blue when she
doesn't even tell us where her story is set. And then,
in the next paragraph, she tells us more about the sky:
"There was something coming to her. . . . What was
it? She did not know. . . . But she felt it creeping out of
the sky, reaching toward her through the sounds, the
scents, the color that filled the air" (67).

Given this emphasis on the spring air, we can now
see that Chopin is contrasting two aspects of setting,
the season versus the place, springtime versus the
closed room. The spring air is invading the room in
which Mrs. Mallard has locked herself. At first Mrs.
Mallard resists the mysterious invasion: "She was
beginning to recognize this thing that was approaching
to possess her, and she was striving to beat it back"
(68), but, the reader comes to understand, "this thing"
is the spirit of "the new spring life" which, we learned
earlier in the story, set the tops of the trees aquiver.
The trees, the swallows, and the blue sky are signs of
the spring, and the spring symbolizes life. The locked
room, where Mrs. Mallard goes to grieve, is a place
of mourning, of death, but Mrs. Mallard is a living

creature, and though she sincerely grieves she cannot shut out life.

Thesis is emphasized.

Now it is clear why Chopin did not bother to tell us in what city, or even in what kind of house, the action takes place. It doesn't matter. What does matter is the feeling of new life that Mrs. Mallard feels, and this can best be shown by relating it to springtime, a time of new life.

Concluding paragraph furthers the argument (passage about "elixir") and also, in its final sentences, wraps up essay.

Even though she has confined herself to her room, through the window Mrs. Mallard drinks the spring air. In Chopin's words, "She was drinking in the very elixir of life through that open window" (68). An elixir, according to *The American Heritage Dictionary*, fourth edition, is "a substance believed to maintain life indefinitely." This word is an effective word to describe the way Mrs. Mallard feels, as the sights and sounds of spring press upon her and give her a new sense of life. But of course although spring renews life indefinitely, each year bringing new vegetation, people do not live indefinitely. In fact Mrs. Mallard will live for less than an hour. Chopin does not make it clear to a reader whether Mrs. Mallard dies because she really has "heart trouble," as we are told in the first paragraph, or because she has lived an intense spring moment as an individual and so she cannot stand the thought of a lifetime with her husband. But what is perfectly clear is that one aspect of the setting—springtime, a season full of new life—is essential to convey to the reader a sense of Mrs. Mallard's new (and tragically brief) feelings.

[New page]

Work Cited

Documentation

Chopin, Kate. "The Story of an Hour." *An Introduction to Literature*. Ed. Sylvan Barnet, William Burto, and William E. Cain, 16th ed. New York: Longman, 2011. 67-68. Print.

POINT OF VIEW

The Dublin in "Araby" (pages 353–57) is the Dublin that James Joyce thought existed, but it must be remembered that although an author *writes* a story, someone else *tells* it. We hear the story from a particular **point of view,** and this point of view in large measure determines our response to the story. A wide variety of terms has been established to name differing points of view, but the following labels are among the most common. We may begin with two categories: third-person points of view (in which the **narrator** is not a participant in the story) and first-person points of view (in which the "I" who narrates the story plays a part in it).

Third-Person Narrators

The **third-person** or **nonparticipant point of view** itself has several subdivisions. At one extreme is the **omniscient narrator,** who knows everything that is going on and can tell us the inner thoughts of all the characters. The omniscient narrator may editorialize, pass judgments, re-assure the reader, and so forth, in which case he or she may sound like the author. Here is Thomas Hardy's editorially omniscient narrator in *Tess of the D'Urbervilles* (1891), telling the reader that Tess was mistaken in imagining that the countryside proclaimed her guilt:

> But this encompassment of her own characterization, based upon shreds of convention, peopled by phantoms and voices antipathetic to her, was a sorry and mistaken creation of Tess's fancy—a cloud of moral hobgob-lins by which she was terrified without reason.

Still, even this narrator is not quite Hardy; he does not allude to his other books, his private life, or his hope that the book will sell. If he is Hardy, he is only one aspect of Hardy, quite possibly a fictional Hardy, a disembod-ied voice with particular characteristics.

Another type of third-person narrator, **selective omniscient,** takes up what Henry James called a "center of consciousness," revealing the thoughts of one of the characters but (for the most part) seeing the rest of the characters from the outside only.

Wayne Booth, in a thoughtful study of Jane Austen's *Emma* (1816), explains the effectiveness of selective omniscience in this novel. He points out that Emma is intelligent, witty, beautiful, and rich. But she is flawed by pride, and, until she discovers and corrects her fault, she almost destroys herself and her friends. How may such a character be made sympathetic, so that we will hope for a happy conclusion to the comedy? "The solution to the problem of maintaining sympathy despite almost crippling faults," Booth says,

> was primarily to use the heroine herself as a kind of narrator, though in third person, reporting on her own experience. . . . By showing most of the story through Emma's eyes, the author insures that we shall travel with Emma rather than stand against her. It is not simply that Emma provides, in the unimpeachable evidence of her own conscience, proof that she has many redeeming qualities that do not appear on the surface; such evidence could be given with authorial commentary, though perhaps not with such force and conviction. Much more important, the sustained inside view leads the reader to hope for good fortune for the character with whom he travels, quite independently of the qualities revealed.
>
> —*The Rhetoric of Fiction,* 2nd ed. (1983), 245–46

Booth goes on to point out in a long and careful analysis that "sympathy for Emma can be heightened by withholding inside views of others as well as by granting them of her."

In writing about point of view, one tries to suggest what the author's choice of a particular point of view contributes to the story. Booth shows how Jane Austen's third-person point of view helps keep sympathetic a character who otherwise might be less than sympathetic. Notice that Booth states the problem—how to draw an intelligent but proud woman so that the reader will wish for a happy ending—and he presents his answer convincingly, moving from "It is not simply . . . " to "Much more important . . . " (to reverse the order would cause a drop in interest). He then moves from a discussion of the inside treatment of Emma to the outside treatment of the other characters, thus substantiating and enlarging his argument.

The third-person narrator, then, although not in the ordinary sense a character in the story, is an important voice in the story, who helps give shape to it. Another type of third-person narrator is the so-called **effaced narrator.** (Some critics use the term **dramatic point of view** or **objective point of view.**) This narrator does not seem to exist, for (unlike the editorially omniscient narrator) he or she does not comment in his or her own voice and (unlike the omniscient and selective omniscient narrators) does not enter any minds. It is almost improper to speak of an effaced narrator as "he" or "he or she," for no evident figure is speaking. The reader hears dialogue and sees only what a camera or a fly on the wall would see. The following example is from Hemingway's "The Killers" (1927):

> The door of Henry's lunchroom opened and two men came in. They sat down at the counter.
> "What's yours?" George asked them.
> "I don't know," one of the men said. "What do you want to eat, Al?"
> "I don't know," said Al. "I don't know what I want to eat."

But even an effaced narrator has a kind of personality. The story the narrator records may seem "cold" or "scientific" or "reportorial" or "objective," and such a **tone** or voice (attitude of the narrator, as it is detected) may be an important part of the story. The French critic Rémy de Gourmont's remark, quoted in Ezra Pound's *Literary Essays* (1954), is relevant: "To be impersonal is to be personal in a special kind of way. . . . The objective is one of the forms of the subjective."

In writing about a third-person narrator, speak of "the narrator" or "the speaker," not of "the author."

First-Person Narrators

To turn to **first-person, or participant, points of view:** The "I" who narrates the story (recall that at the end of "Araby" the narrator says, "I saw myself as a creature driven and derided by vanity") may be a major character in it (as he is in "Araby," in *The Catcher in the Rye*, and in Mark Twain's *Adventures of Huckleberry Finn*) or may be a minor character, a mere witness (Dr. Watson narrates tales about Sherlock Holmes, Nick Carraway narrates the story of Gatsby in *The Great Gatsby*). Of course, the narrator, even when a relatively minor character, is still a character, and, therefore, in some degree the story is about him or her. Although *The Great Gatsby* is primarily about Gatsby, it is also about Nick's changing perception of Gatsby.

First-person narrators may not fully understand their own report. Take Huck Finn in *Adventures of Huckleberry Finn*. In one passage Huck describes the "astonishing things" performed at a circus he witnesses, including a drunk who badgers the ringmaster until he is permitted to try to ride a horse. The drunk turns out to be an expert performer and is part of the circus act, but Huck thinks the ringmaster was genuinely deceived by a performer who "had got up that joke all out of his own head." In using Huck as the narrator, Mark Twain uses an **innocent eye,** a device in which a good part of the effect consists in the discrepancy between the narrator's imperfect awareness and the reader's superior awareness. Mark Twain makes much more important use of the device in another passage, when Huck is listening to Jim, an escaped slave:

> Jim talked out loud all the time while I was talking to myself. He was saying how the first thing he would do when he got to a free state he would go to saving up money and never spend a single cent, and when he got enough he would buy his wife, which was owned on a farm close to where Miss Watson lived; and then they would both work to buy the two children, and if their master wouldn't sell them, they'd get an Ab'litionist to go and steal them.
>
> It most froze me to hear such talk. He wouldn't ever dared to talk such talk in his life before. Just see what a difference it made in him the minute he judged he was about free. It was according to the old saying, "Give a nigger an inch and he'll take an ell." Thinks I, this is what comes of my not thinking. Here was this nigger, which I had as good as helped to run away, coming right out flat-footed and saying he would steal his children—children that belonged to a man I didn't even know; a man that hadn't ever done me no harm.
>
> I was sorry to hear Jim say that, it was such a lowering of him.

We hear *unconscious* irony in Huck's words, especially in his indignation that Jim "would steal his children—children that belonged to a man I didn't even know." We also hear in Huck's use of the n-word that he has absorbed the demeaning characterizations of African Americans common in the society—the slave South in the 1830s and 1840s—in which he has been raised. In short, Huck is an **unreliable narrator.** Unreliable narrators come in a variety of types: Narrators may be unreliable because (for example) they are naive children, or are senile, or are morally blind, or are caught up in a rage.

On the other hand, we sometimes feel that a first-person narrator (Conrad's Marlow in *Heart of Darkness* [1899] and several other novels is an example) is a very thinly veiled substitute for the author. Nevertheless, the words of a first-person narrator require the same kind of scrutiny that we give to the words of the other characters in a story or play. The reader must deduce the personality from what is said. For instance, the narrator of "Araby" never tells us that he was a good student, but we can deduce that he was a bookish boy until he fell in love: "I watched my master's face pass from amiability to sternness; he hoped I was not beginning to idle."

A first-person narrator is not likely to give us the help that an editorially omniscient narrator gives. We must deduce from this passage in "Araby" that the narrator's uncle drinks too much: "At nine o'clock I heard my uncle's latchkey in the hall-door. I heard him talking to himself and heard the hall-stand rocking when it had received the weight of his over-coat. I could interpret these signs." In a first-person narrative it is some-times difficult for the reader to interpret the signs. In a sense the author has given the reader two stories: the story the narrator tells and the story of a narrator telling a story.

Note: In writing about point of view in a first-person narrative such as *Adventures of Huckleberry Finn,* after an introductory remark to the effect that Huckleberry Finn narrates the story, use the character's name or a pronoun ("Huck fails to see . . . ") in speaking of the narrator.

Caution: Essays on narrative point of view have a way of slipping into essays on what the story is about. Point of view *is* relevant to the theme of the story, but if you are writing about point of view, keep this focus in sight, explaining, for instance, how it shapes the theme.

NOTES AND A SAMPLE ESSAY ON NARRATIVE POINT OF VIEW IN JAMES JOYCE'S "ARABY"

Here are some of the notes—a journal entry and a rough outline—and the final version of an essay on the narrator in Joyce's "Araby" (see pages 353–57). Doubtless some of the notes were based on passages that the student had underlined or highlighted in the text.

1st-person point of view, *but what sort of person?*

Several sorts

Opening ¶ seems <u>objective</u> point of view

Boy is sensitive to beauty: likes a book because pages are yellow

(334); plays in stable where he hears "music from the buckled

harness" (335);

Boy is shy: hardly talks to girl: "I had never spoken to her" (335);

"At last she spoke to me" (336) *Here narrator is <u>personal</u>, not objective omniscient*

But he plays with other boys; they don't seem to regard him as

different. Typical boy? Prob. not. "~~My eyes were often full~~

~~of tears" (335).~~ *But <u>not</u> from "the rough tribes from the cottages."*

But narrator is no longer a kid; grownup, looking back on

childhood; sometimes he *seems almost amused* by his

childhood ("Her name sprang to my lips at moments in

strange prayers and praise which I myself did not

understand," 335, *sometimes seems a bit hard on his*

earlier self: "all my foolish blood"; "What innumerable

follies laid waste my waking and sleeping   *So, a third aspect*

thoughts," 335); "~~My soul luxuriated~~ (336)   *to narrator*

Ending: very hard on self: "I saw myself as a creature   *The third*
                                                                aspect
driven and derided by vanity" (338)   *or maybe*
                                                                even
But opening is very different, unemotional. In fact, come to   *a fourth*

think of it, opening isn't even clearly a first-person narrator.
But there is a special personality in semicomic comment that
houses themselves were "conscious" of decent lives within them."

[Final draft]

Fumiko Jackson
Professor Stubbs
Core Writing 100
13 April 2011

The Three First-Person Narrators of Joyce's "Araby"

James Joyce's "Araby" is told by a first-person narrator, but
this point of view is not immediately evident to a reader. The story
at first seems to be told by an objective third-person narrator:

North Richmond Street, being blind, was a quiet street except at the hour when the Christian Brothers' School set the
boys free. An uninhabited house of two stories stood at the
blind end, detached from its neighbors in a square ground.
The other houses of the street, conscious of decent lives
within them, gazed at one another with brown imperturbable
faces. (137)

These words seem objective and omniscient, but the very next paragraph begins by saying, "The former tenant of our house. . . ." The word *our* indicates that the narrative point of view is first-person. On rereading the first paragraph of the story, a reader probably still feels that the paragraph is chiefly objective, but perhaps the reader now gets a little sense of an individualized speaker in the passage about the houses being "conscious of decent lives within them," and the houses have "imperturbable faces." That is, the narrator personifies the houses, making them "conscious" and rather smug. Apparently he is detached, and somewhat amused, as he thinks back to the middle-class neighborhood of his childhood.

In many passages, however, the narrator describes his romantic childhood without any irony. For instance, he says that when he was in love with the girl, his "body was like a harp and her words and gestures were like fingers running upon the wires" (138). We can say, then, that so far the narrator has two aspects: (1) an adult, who looks back objectively, or maybe with a little sense of irony, and (2) an adult who looks back almost nostalgically at himself when he was a child in love.

But there is a third aspect to the narrator, revealed in several passages. For instance, he says that the girl's name was "like a summons to all [his] foolish blood" (138) and that he engaged in "innumerable follies" (138). What may seem to be the strongest passage of this sort is at the very end of the story, and it is the strongest partly because it is in such an emphatic place: "Gazing up into the darkness I saw myself as a creature driven and derided by vanity" (141). But this passage is not exactly what it first seems to be. The narrator is *not* condemning himself, saying that as a child he was "driven and derided by vanity." He is saying, now, as an adult, that *at the time of the experience* he saw himself as driven and derided by vanity.

The fact that he says "I saw myself" is almost a way of saying "I saw myself, *falsely*, as. . . ." That is, the narrator makes it clear that he is giving the child's view, and the reader understands that the child was unusually sensitive. In several passages the narrator has distanced himself from the child (as in the "foolish blood" passage), but the reader does not see the child as foolish, just as highly romantic. The very fact that the narrator calls the child "foolish" is enough for a reader mentally to come to the child's defense and in effect say, "Oh, no, don't be so hard on yourself."

The earlier passages in which the narrator condemns his childhood experience thus serve to help the reader to take the child's part. And now, at the end of the story, when the narrator reports the child's severe judgment on himself, the reader leaps to the child's defense. If the narrator had *not* occasionally commented negatively on his childhood, readers might themselves have thought that the child was acting absurdly and also thought that the narrator was too pleased with himself, but since the narrator occasionally passes a negative judgment on the child and ends by telling us that the child judged himself severely, too, the reader almost certainly wants to reassure the child that his behavior was not nearly so bad as he thought it was—and in fact it was really quite touching.

In some ways, then, this narrator is an unreliable narrator. Such a narrator is usually a naive person, who doesn't understand what is really going on in the story. The narrator of "Araby" is not naive—he is obviously a sophisticated person—but sometimes is an unreliable guide so far as his own childhood goes. But because the narrator sometimes takes a critical view of his childhood, a reader mentally defends the child. The third (critical) aspect of the narrator, then, serves to make the reader value the child's behavior rather than judge it negatively.

[New page]

Work Cited

Joyce, James. "Araby." *An Introduction to Literature*. Ed. Sylvan Barnet, William Burto, and William E. Cain. 16th ed. New York: Longman, 2011. 137-41.Print.

The Student's Analysis Analyzed

- The **title** is engaging—the idea of *three* first-person narrators at first sounds paradoxical. And it probably is enough if a title is engaging and proves to be relevant. But keep in mind that the best title often is one that gives the reader a hint of your thesis. Here the title might have been "How Reliable Is the Narrator in 'Araby'?" or perhaps "Reliable and Unreliable Narrators in Joyce's 'Araby.'" The choice of a title is important.

- The **organization** is reasonable. It begins with the beginning and it ends with the end. Such an organization is not a requirement, but it is not to be shunned. Do not, however, allow such an organization to turn what should be an analytic essay into a long summary of the story. You are arguing a thesis, not writing a summary.

- The **proportions are good.** The thesis is that the third, or critical, voice in the essay is important in (paradoxically) getting sympathy for the boy, and so the third voice is given the most space.

- **Quotations** are used to let the reader know exactly what the writer is talking about. They are used as part of the argument, not as padding.

If you enjoyed Joyce's "Araby," you might want to read the other stories included with it in his *Dubliners*. Each one of them could serve as the basis for an essay on narrative point of view or an essay in which you compare its narrative point of view with that of "Araby." The first three stories, including "Araby," are written in the first-person, and the rest are in third-person. The complete text can be found at *Dubliners*: <http://www.doc.ic.ac.uk/~rac101/concord/texts/dubliners/> or at Project Gutenberg: <http://www.gutenberg.org/ebooks/2814>.

THEME: VISION OR ARGUMENT?

Because modern fiction makes subtle use of it, point of view can scarcely be neglected in a discussion of **theme**—what a story is about. Perhaps unfairly, modern criticism is usually unhappy when the author's voice, especially in older fiction, seems too controlling, explicit, or heavy-handed. We would rather see than be lectured. We are less impressed by "It was the stillness of an implacable force brooding over an inscrutable intention" (from Conrad's *Heart of Darkness*) than by this passage from the same book:

> Black shapes crouched, lay, sat between the trees, leaning against the trunks, clinging to the earth, half coming out, half effaced within the dim light, in all the attitudes of pain, abandonment, and despair. Another mine on the cliff went off, followed by a slight shudder of the soil

under my feet. The work was going on. The work! And this was the place where some of the helpers had withdrawn to die.

The second quotation, but not the first, gives us the sense of reality that we have come to expect from fiction. As the novelist Flannery O'Connor puts it in *Mystery and Manners* (1969), we expect a storyteller to speak "*with* character and action, not *about* character and action" (76).

Determining and Discussing the Theme

First, we can distinguish between *story* and *theme* in fiction. Story is concerned with "How does it turn out? What happens?" Theme is concerned with "What does it add up to? What motif holds the happenings together? What does it make out of life, and, perhaps, what wisdom does it offer?"

In a good work of fiction, the details add up, or, to use Flannery O'Connor's words, they are "controlled by some overall purpose." In F. Scott Fitzgerald's *The Great Gatsby* (1925), for example, there are many references to popular music, especially to jazz. These references contribute to our sense of the reality in Fitzgerald's depiction of America in the 1920s, but they do more: In context they help to comment on the shallowness of the white middle-class characters, and they sometimes (very gently) remind us of an alternative culture. One might study Fitzgerald's references to music with an eye toward getting a deeper understanding of what the novel is about.

PRELIMINARY NOTES AND A SAMPLE ESSAY ON THE THEME OF EUDORA WELTY'S "A WORN PATH"

Below are the notes and the final essay of a student, Jim Wayne, who chose to write about the theme of Eudora Welty's "A Worn Path." We recommend that you read the story first; it appears on pages 357–63 of this book.

After reading and rereading the story, the student jotted down a set of preliminary notes. Some were observations based on passages he had underlined, and others were questions that he wanted to think further about. The jottings include material specifically on the story, references to other writers, and general issues that the student found relevant to his reflections on the story's theme. When he reviewed these notes before preparing an outline and starting on a first draft, he deleted some of them, having decided that they were not useful for this essay. Still, they were worth jotting down, for often a writer can see what is useful and belongs in an outline only after he has collected a range of notes.

Preliminary Notes

My response: Enjoyable, carefully written, good details. Comic in places. Mysterious.

Not much happens. What is this story really about?

"Negro," "colored": What is Welty's attitude toward African-Americans? What is the relationship between the black woman and the white characters? Is Welty making a point through the story about blacks and whites in the South? The publication date is 1941—segregation was common then. "I know you old colored people," the white hunter says. Racial stereotypes. The gun—threat of violence? If the story is supposed to take place around the time of publication, Phoenix, "too old at the Surrender," would be about ninety.

White characters: hunter, lady in town, attendant & nurse at clinic. (Doctor's office? Hospital?)

colors: e.g., second paragraph—dark striped, bleached, "eyes were blue with age," golden, yellow, red, black, copper.

"chains"—chains worn in slavery.

Welty's point of view? (Note: Check for biog info about Welty.)

Details about Phoenix Jackson—peculiar name.

a phoenix:

1. A bird in Egyptian mythology that lived in the desert for 500 years and then consumed itself by fire, later to rise renewed from its ashes.

2. A person or thing of unsurpassed excellence or beauty; a paragon. (*American Heritage Dictionary*, 4th. ed.)

—"Phoenix rose carefully."

Random House Unabridged Dictionary says about the phoenix— "often an emblem of immortality or of idealism or hope."

Jackson:

Thomas Jonathan Jackson, known as "Stonewall." 1824-63.

American Confederate general who commanded troops at both
  battles of Bull Run (1861 and 1862) and directed the Shenandoah
  Valley campaign (1862). He was accidentally killed by his
  own troops at Chancellorsville (1863). (*Concise Columbia
  Encyclopedia*)

Names connected to the story's theme? Phoenix—rebirth, return,
  renewal.

No other character is named—not even grandson.

Significance of the title? Why not make "Phoenix" the title?

Descriptions of the woods ("deep and still") remind me of the
  forest in Hawthorne's story "Young Goodman Brown." Scary,
  weird. Check Frost's poem, the line "the woods are lovely,
  dark and deep."

Time of year: December, cold ("frozen"), Christmas—Christianity?
  Christian symbolism (birth of Jesus).

Places: From country to city.

Phoenix on a journey, a quest. "Through the maze now"—
  labyrinth. A traveler, a pilgrim. By herself—no one to help
  her on the way. But she is known at the clinic, has been there
  before.

Humor in the story? Phoenix talks to animals; crossing log across
  creek.

Is she crazy? But determination, dignity ("face very solemn"). Does
  she trick the hunter? The attendant? Clever, shrewd.

Phoenix is poor—has to walk, even her cane made from an umbrella,
  she sees the nickel, called a "charity case," "Charity" marked
  in the clinic book when she gets the medicine.

Emphasis on her old age. But makes the trip anyway—love for her
  grandson. Where are the parents?

Puzzling details: "like a festival figure in some old parade," "pearly
  cloud of mistletoe."

Supernatural elements—Ghost, scarecrow, spell.

"God watching me the whole time."

Grandson is important, but not a character in the story. Why not?
  Or *can* we say he is a character? But we don't see him, except
  in the talk of others.

Phoenix's reaction when asked about grandson—hard to figure
    out.

"We is the only two left in the world"—what does that mean?

Is the grandson left by himself while Phoenix goes to the city? Just
    how sick is the child? Hallucinations, imaginings, etc. Forgetful.
    Is there really a grandson? Alive or dead?

Ending—gift of the windmill. Sign of love between Phoenix and
    grandson.

Assignment says "A Worn Path" last story in Welty's collection *A
    Curtain of Green and Other Stories*. Reasons why this story a
    good one for ending a book of stories?

Interesting for a white author to end with story about a black
    character. Would story work if Phoenix were white?

Focus paper on main character? Phoenix J. herself as theme?—
    meaning of her life as meaning of story?

Most striking thing about Phoenix: her trip—because she loves her
    grandson.

Sounds sentimental, but story doesn't feel that way. How does
    Welty do that?

Titles for paper?—connect to discussion of theme. Phoenix = Love.
    Phoenix's Love
    The Bond of Love
    Flight of the Phoenix
    Rising from the Ashes
    Rising into Love

These jottings show the amount of preliminary work that this student did. Sometimes we imagine (or hope) that if we stare at a story or
poem long enough, we will eventually "find something to write about."
But remember:

- Good writers realize that a topic and an outline do not appear by
  magic from the pages of the assigned text.
- Writers must become *engaged* with the text, asking questions and
  thinking about it and taking notes to make the topic and outline
  begin to take shape.

In short, to write well, you have to be both an active reader and an active,
alert, question-asking writer.

Jim Wayne
Critical Interpretation, Section A
Professor Katz
27 February 2011

Rising into Love

In Eudora Welty's short story "A Worn Path," not much happens. The main character, Phoenix Jackson, an elderly African-American woman, takes a long and difficult walk to the city of Natchez. She overcomes obstacles, has encounters with animals and talks to them, meets a white hunter, and finally reaches her destination, the clinic, where she speaks briefly with an attendant and a nurse. But the point of Welty's story is not in the plot; it is in the character of Phoenix Jackson herself. Phoenix loves her grandson and takes this difficult journey for him. In her own way, she is a moral heroine, and through her Welty shows that love is the source of personal strength and human connection.

From the very beginning, Welty suggests that Phoenix's trip is a challenging one for her. It is a cold December day, and Phoenix herself is "very old and small." She probably is about ninety, since she was too old to go to school at the end of the Civil War (1865), and the story seems to be set at about the time it was published, in 1941. We see Phoenix "coming along a path," her journey under way, as if Phoenix has already been walking for a long time. She seems not to have much or any money; she has to walk to town though it is far away, and even her cane, we learn, is "thin" and "small," made from an umbrella. But Phoenix is special, intriguing, even paradoxical, someone whom Welty wants us to notice and care about. She moves from side to side somehow balancing "heaviness and lightness"; she is "neat and tidy" but she almost trips over her shoelaces (perhaps she is too old to bend over to tie them); and she is old and worn-out yet filled with a purpose. Welty's description of her is vivid with details of color; Phoenix's eyes "were blue with age," she has a "golden color" in her forehead, and a "yellow burning" on her cheeks.

Phoenix is more than a little eccentric. She chats with animals, has a few words for the thorns that catch at her dress, and holds her cane "fiercely" as she prepares to cross the log. These details are comic, but Welty uses them to make Phoenix more endearing;

she is not poking fun at her character, for these touches show the struggles that Phoenix faces and her efforts to prevail against them.

This is not a story that emphasizes race relations or racism, but Welty tells us from the start that Phoenix is black, and other details reinforce this point. "Seems like there is chains about my feet," says Phoenix, a detail that brings to mind the chains worn by black people during slavery. Later, Phoenix refers to "the Surrender," the end of the Civil War, which took place when the Confederate general Robert E. Lee surrendered his forces to the Union general Ulysses S. Grant. Perhaps for some readers, the name Jackson evokes one of the South's greatest war heroes, the legendary General Thomas "Stonewall" Jackson. Phoenix is a solitary figure, known only to a very few people, but, I think Welty is saying, Phoenix is in her own private way as brave, resourceful, and determined as a public military hero.

Phoenix is on a journey, a quest; she is a traveler, a solitary pilgrim—no one accompanies her—who is intent upon reaching her goal. She fears she will not get there in time, at one point crying "thick tears." And she suffers from dreams and hallucinations, believing for a moment that a boy is handing her a piece of cake and, shortly thereafter, she reaches toward a ghost that turns out to be a scarecrow. But Welty describes the landscape in terms that make it frightening to the reader, too: "Big dead trees, like black men with one arm, were standing in the purple stalks of the withered cotton field. There sat a buzzard." Phoenix's trip tires and frightens her, and Welty makes certain that we understand why; we might not be elderly or have failing eyesight or hearing ("my senses is gone"), but such a landscape—Phoenix calls it a "maze," a labyrinth—would unnerve us too.

Still, Phoenix is strong and clever. Along the way, she meets a man, a *white* man, a hunter with a gun and a hunting dog (the dog is on a chain and growls at another dog). He helps her and is not mean or unkind, but he treats Phoenix as an inferior, calling her "Granny" and saying, "I know you old colored people." She, however, is sharper than he is, tricking him to get the nickel that falls from his pocket, just as she later prompts the clinic attendant to give her a nickel and not just a "few" pennies.

At the clinic, Phoenix's strength and resolve continue to be tested. The attendant is gruff and demeaning ("a charity case, I suppose"), and the nurse is only slightly more polite, asking "Aunt Phoenix" to take a seat but saying to her, "Tell us quickly about your grandson, and get it over."

The grandson, we now learn, is the reason for Phoenix's journey to Natchez. She has made the trip to buy (or to be given) the medicine that the child needs, and old, weary Phoenix is the only person who can perform this deed. The child's parents are not referred to; perhaps they have left or have died. For Phoenix, her grandson is as precious as the Christ child, whose birth is celebrated this "Christmas time" of year. He is sickly, but Phoenix is certain "He going to last": Her love for him will keep him alive. Phoenix leaves the clinic with the medicine and a bit of money to buy the boy a toy windmill as a Christmas present.

Welty uses Phoenix to teach a powerful lesson about selflessness and love. *Phoenix* is the name of "a bird in Egyptian mythology that lived in the desert for 500 years and then consumed itself by fire, later to rise renewed from its ashes." It is a symbol for "a person or thing of unsurpassed excellence or beauty; a paragon." Phoenix Jackson is an elderly black woman in the segregated South; she is poor and uneducated. Yet she is, Welty implies, a figure of grandeur nonetheless, like the great phoenix of mythology. The trip to Natchez renews Phoenix each time that she makes it, intensifying yet again her bond of love to her grandson.

Southern society places Phoenix Jackson low on its social scale, but she strikes the reader as a better person than anyone she meets: She embodies love. If a less gifted author had written the story, it might have seemed sentimental or preachy. But Welty's portrait—comic and poignant at the same time—makes the moral lesson come alive. The others in the story pay little attention to Phoenix Jackson, but Welty makes her unforgettable to us.

[New Page]

Works Cited

American Heritage Dictionary. 4th ed. Boston: Houghton Mifflin, 2002. 1046. Print.

Welty, Eudora. "A Worm Path." *An Introduction to Literature*. Ed. Sylvan Barnet, William Burto, and William E. Cain. 16th ed. New York: Longman, 2011. 30–35. Print.

A Brief Overview of the Essay

- Jim Wayne's title is a good one because it anticipates an important point that the paper makes; his opening paragraph states the thesis clearly—that Phoenix is a heroic figure. He uses quotations as evidence to support his generalizations, and his final paragraph brings the essay to a nice conclusion.
- We think that Jim's paper is a good one, and we hope that you agree. Still, could this paper be made even better? Imagine that you were asked to read it during the class's work on peer review. What suggestions, if any, would you offer?
- Are there additional details in the text that Jim could have drawn upon? Do you think he has defined the theme of the story as well as he could have? Has he made his argument convincing to the reader? When you look back over his preliminary notes, do you see questions and ideas that he could have included in the paper to make it better?
- Reread the paper line by line. Can you improve the style, word choices, sentences, and paragraphs? Mark up and make insertions on the copy of the paper here.

✔ Checklist: Writing about Theme

❑ What is the theme—the main idea—suggested by this literary work?

❑ Does the title of the work provide a clue to the main idea, the theme of the work?

❑ Does one character seem to be the author's spokesperson? If so, why do we trust this character more than another?

❑ Do certain symbols convey the theme?

❑ What evidence—what details in the work—support the view that such-and-such is the theme?

❑ Does the theme pervade the work, or does it appear only here and there, at key moments?

❑ Is the theme a vision of life, an argument, a piece of propaganda?

Basing the Paper on Your Own Responses

In his preliminary work, this student made use of a dictionary, and at one point he consulted an encyclopedia. (Notice that in the paper he footnoted the dictionary because he quoted at length directly from it. He did not cite the encyclopedia because he took from it only some "common knowledge" facts about Stonewall Jackson that are widely known and not in dispute; on this point, see pages 327–28.) The student thus developed his ideas and plan for the paper from his own reading of "A Worn Path," his reflections on and his feelings about it, his previous literary experiences—in a word, from lots of thoughtful work on the assigned topic, which was to write an essay of 1,000 words on the theme of "A Worn Path."

All of us have experienced moments of self-doubt when faced with an assignment, especially one that represents a new challenge or that calls on us to examine a particularly complex poem or story. It is tempting to head right away to the library to track down secondary sources. But unless your instructor indicates otherwise, you should follow this student's example, basing the paper that you write on your own response to the literary work.

- Have faith in your instincts and intuitions.
- Make use of and develop your analytical skills.

Do not underestimate how much you can achieve on your own, with just the text and two or three basic reference works for help with the meanings of words and references to places, historical figures, characters in myth or legend, and the like.

A Note on Secondary Sources

Sometimes an instructor will tell the class as a whole, or will state in answer to a question, that you "may use secondary sources if you want to." You may indeed want to, because the story has aroused your curiosity and made you eager to learn all that you can about the author and the work. Or else—this can happen on occasion—after some real effort of your own, you have found that you cannot quite figure out the story and believe you would benefit from placing your responses alongside those of other readers—scholars and critics—who know the subject well.

Be aware of the nature of the assignment, however. *This* assignment on the theme of "A Worn Path" is not a research paper as such, and it does not call for the approach that is covered extensively later in this book (see Chapter 17).

If you choose to do outside reading in secondary sources for such an assignment, follow these guidelines:

- For any kind of paper, if you make use of someone else's insights, you need to say so and cite the source.
- Do not pull two or three books at random from the library shelves. You might get lucky: Maybe they will be good books for your work. But they might not be, and the result would then be that you have wasted your time or been misled by a book that has not won general respect from the community of scholars.
- Remember that there are *levels* of reference material, and that you might do best to move step-by-step through them even if you are seeking sources in a somewhat informal way.

If, for example, you decide that you wish to consult two or three good sources for your study of Welty's "A Worn Path," proceed in this fashion:

1. General works—reference, overview, bibliography.

For your point of departure, you could select *The Oxford Companion to Women's Writing in the United States,* ed. Cathy N. Davidson and Linda Wagner-Martin (1995). Included in this book of more than 1,000 pages is a helpful entry on Welty's life and writings, with a paragraph of bibliography.

Two similar books are *Contemporary Novelists* (1991), in the series Contemporary Writers of the English Language, and *Modern American Women Writers* (1991), whose consulting editor is Elaine Showalter and whose general editors are Lea Baechler and A. Walton Litz. Another, more recent, is *American Women Writers, 1900-1945: A Bio-bibliographical Critical Sourcebook*, ed. Laurie Champion (2000).

How are such books located? We give detailed advice in Chapter 17. Here it is sufficient to recommend that you "search" in the online library catalog for women writers, American women writers, contemporary authors, and similar categories. Even better: Seek out the reference librarians and ask them for guidance. Or your instructor may recommend a title or two.

These general works will assist you in identifying reference material on the author or topic you have picked or been assigned.

2. Reference works and bibliographies for the author or topic.

For Welty, they include:

The Eudora Welty Newsletter (published twice a year, beginning in Winter 1977). Stays up-to-date with coverage of primary and secondary sources.

W. U. McDonald, Jr., "An Unworn Path: Bibliographical and Textual Scholarship on Eudora Welty," *Southern Quarterly* 20 (Summer 1982): 101-108.

Pearl Amelia McHaney, "A Eudora Welty Checklist, 1973-1986," in *Welty: A Life in Literature,* ed. Albert J. Devlin (1987), 266-302.

Victor H. Thompson, *Eudora Welty: A Reference Guide* (1976). Covers secondary studies from 1936 to 1975.

3. Important books on the author or topic.

The reference works and bibliographies will lead you to the most important books on Welty. Since you are focusing on one of her stories, you probably would want to consult Carol Ann Johnston, *Eudora Welty: A Study of the Short Fiction* (1997), and Peter Schmidt, *The Heart of the Story: Eudora Welty's Short Fiction.* (1991).

4. Biographies.

Studies of the author's life can sometimes be helpful for an interpretive essay, giving information about the biographical context for the story or insight into the author's intentions. Two such works are Suzanne Marrs, *Eudora Welty: A Biography* (2005), and Ann Waldron, *Eudora: A Writer's Life* (1998).

5. Primary Sources.

Many writers of fiction have also written poems, autobiographies, literary essays, travel essays, or other kinds of work. Their journals or letters perhaps have been published. Sometimes too they have done work in other media, other artistic forms. Eudora Welty, for example, was an important photographer. Various sorts of primary sources can help to illuminate features of a story—a comment in a letter about the story's theme, or, in Welty's case, a photograph that we might find to be connected in character and theme to the story we are examining in an essay. See Pearl Amelia McHaney, ed., *Eudora Welty as Photographer: Photographs by Eudora Welty* (2009); Eudora Welty, *The Eye Of The Story: Selected Essays and Reviews* (1978); and Eudora Welty, *One Writer's Beginnings* (1984).

There are many journal articles on Welty's short fiction and on "A Worn Path" in particular, as well as collections of book reviews and critical essays, general books on southern writing, and additional primary sources. Use the right strategy for the task at hand. It is one thing to seek a few sources to stimulate your thinking for a short analytical paper, and another thing to embark on a full-fledged research assignment.

Be aware, too, that for this *kind* of paper, too much research may prove a hindrance rather than a help. Locating good sources takes time. You might be better off if you returned to the text itself to develop your own responses. Do some pre-writing, try a rough outline, and explicate a key passage. Your best resource is yourself.

So much, on just about everything, is now available on the Internet. Often it is tempting to do a search, using the name of the author or the title of the story, to see what results turn up. And some good, relevant material indeed might turn up. But it is important for us to be aware, as we will say again later, that the Internet must be used critically and with care. You need to know the nature of the sources you locate—are they reliable or not? And you will want to recall too that usually the best, or most of the best, print sources can be found only in the library, not online. Neither of the two biographies of Welty, listed above, is available online. Nor are Welty's *The Eye of the Story* and *One Writer's Beginnings*.

A SECOND ESSAY ABOUT THEME: NOTES AND THE FINAL VERSION OF AN ESSAY ON SHIRLEY JACKSON'S "THE LOTTERY"

Here are the preliminary notes and the final essay of a student who chose to write about the theme of Jackson's "The Lottery." The story is widely available in anthologies and is currently available online as well, in the American Literature Short Story Library: <http://www.american literature.com/Jackson/SS/TheLottery.html>

Nat Komor, after reading and rereading the story online, jotted down the following notes as a sort of preliminary outline. Some of the notes were based on passages he had underlined. Notice that the jottings include some material specifically on the story and other material—references to the outside world—that is relevant to what the writer takes to be the theme of the story. When he reviewed his notes before starting on a first draft, the writer deleted about a third of them, having decided that they were not especially useful for his essay. Still, they were worth jotting down; only in retrospect can a writer clearly see which notes are useful.

Is Jackson saying that human nature is evil? Prob. no; here, people just follow a tradition, and don't examine it. Mr. Warner defends lottery, saying "There's *always* been a lottery." No real argument in defense of it.

We are least conscious of the things we take for granted; ~~I recall someone's saying "a fish is not aware of water until it is out of it."~~

examples of blindly following society's customs

compulsory schooling (how many people that the gov't has no right to require kids to go to school)

school is 5 days a week, why not 4 or 6? Why is a college degree 4 years and not 3 or 5?

segregation (until 1960s)

~~women not permitted to drive in Saudi Arabia~~

~~women must wear voil in Saudi Arabia~~

eating of meat; might a vegetarian society not look with horror at our habit of eating meat?

slavery (thought to be "natural" by almost all societies until nineteenth century)

thoughtless following of custom in "The Lottery"

~~exact words of ritual lost, but still necessary to address "each person approaching"~~

~~original box gone, but present box said to be made of parts of previous box~~

lottery an established ritual: "The lottery was conducted—as were the square dances, the teenage club, the Halloween program—by Mr. Summers, who had time and energy to devote to civic activities." *Important*: the lottery is a civic activity, a social action, a *summer* (pun?) ritual.

Evil? Certainly yes, since killing an innocent, but no one in the story says it's evil.

BUT Adams does say that in the north village "they're talking of giving up the lottery," and his wife says "Some places have already quit lotteries."

Also: a girl whispers, "I hope it's not Nancy," so at least one
        person feels uneasy about the whole thing
Are these people evil? No, they seem pretty decent. They just don't
    much question what they are doing, and they do something
    terrible
the box
    black = death?
    made out of pieces of old box
    "faded," "splintered badly": does this symbolize a need for
        a new tradition?
the papers
        earlier, wood chips. At end, wind blows away slips of paper?
            Symbolic of life fluttering away? (Prob. not)
the three-legged stool
        symbolic? If so, of what?

possible title

    The Violent Lottery
    The Irrational Lottery
    We All Participate in "The Lottery"
    The Meaning of the Lottery
    Human Nature

A lot of the material here is good, though some of it would be more
suited for an essay on symbolism, and it is chiefly this material that the writer
wisely deleted in preparing to draft an essay on the theme of Jackson's story.
After writing a draft and then revising it, Nat Komor submitted the revision
to a group for peer review. Ultimately, he turned in the following essay.

Nat Komor
Professor Lee
English 101B
7 March 2011
                We All Participate in "The Lottery"
        The townsfolk in Shirley Jackson's "The Lottery" engage in a
horrible ritual. They stone an innocent person to death. It would
be horrible enough if the person they stoned were guilty of some
crime, and stoning was a form of capital punishment that the society
practiced, but in the case of "The Lottery" the person is not guilty

of any crime. Tessie Hutchinson simply has the bad luck to pick the wrong slip of paper from a box, a paper marked with a black spot.

The people in this unnamed town every year hold a lottery, to find a victim. On the whole, they seem to believe that the lottery is necessary, or is natural; at least they hardly question it. True, Mr. Adams says that in the north village "they're talking of giving up the lottery," and his wife says that "Some places have already quit lotteries," but that's about as much as one hears of anybody's questioning this institution of society. Probably most of the people in the village would agree with Old Man Warner, who says that people who talk about giving up the lottery are a "pack of crazy fools." He adds, "There's *always* been a lottery," and that seems to be about the best answer that anyone can give. Of course the people don't take any special pleasure in the lottery, and there is at least one expression of sympathy, when a girl says, "I hope it's not Nancy." On the whole, however, the people seem to believe that the lottery must be held, and someone has to die.

It's important to notice that the lottery is one of the "civic activities," that is, it is part of the regular life of these people, part (so to speak) of the air they breathe. For the most part they don't question the lottery any more than we question compulsory education, the length of the school year, or the eating of meat. When one thinks about it, one might ask why the government should have the power to compel parents to send children to school, or, for that matter, why a child shouldn't have the right to leave school whenever he or she feels like it. Why should children have almost no rights? People simply don't bother to think about this issue, or about many others. For instance, I can imagine that a member of a vegetarian society must be horrified by the way almost all Americans think nothing of raising animals (bringing life into the world) for the sole purpose of eating them. We just accept these things, without thinking, but from the view of another culture they may be horrible customs.

What Jackson seems to be saying to her readers is this: "Unthinkingly you follow certain conventions. These conventions seem to you to be natural, and for the most part they are harmless, but some of them are barbaric and destructive." That is, Jackson is telling us to examine our lives, and to stop assuming that all our customs are right. Some of the beliefs we share today may, in time, come to be seen as being as evil as slavery or murder.

The Student's Analysis Analyzed

The **title** is effective: It announces the thesis; readers familiar with the story presumably now want to know what sort of evidence will be produced that will justify the accusation that "we all" are participants in this horrible activity.

The **introductory paragraph** briefly summarizes the story but it is not just a summary, a brief retelling of the plot. It includes a moral response.

The second and third paragraphs—largely the **body** of the essay—introduce *evidence to support the writer's thesis*, the thesis announced in the title. In the first of these two paragraphs the evidence consists of the brief quotations spoken by Old Man Warner; in the second of the two middle paragraphs the supporting evidence consists of references to our school system and to our meat-eating habit, that is, to two things that most people take for granted. By the end of the third paragraph, then, the writer has made his case (insofar as a case can be made in such brief space) that, like the people in Jackson's story, most of us do not examine some fundamental aspects of our society.

In the **concluding paragraph** the essayist clarifies his interpretation of the story and more directly relates it to our lives. Notice that he avoids such weak phrasing as "In conclusion, I believe that" or "Thus we may say." On the contrary, he boldly invents words for Shirley Jackson and forces the reader to think about them.

The writer's, thesis is, in effect, "The story is an indictment of *our* society." Suppose someone were to reply to him, "The story is just a fantasy, meant as a shocker. Relax, it has nothing to do with you or me; it's a story, an entertaining piece, sort of like sci-fi." Would you agree or not? Why?

📖 SUGGESTIONS FOR FURTHER READING

E. M. Forster's *Aspects of the Novel* (1927) remains an engaging introduction to the art of prose fiction by an accomplished practitioner. Other highly readable books by story writers and novelists include: Flannery O'Connor, *Mystery and Manners* (1969); William Gass, *Fiction and the Figures of Life* (1971); Eudora Welty, *The Eye of the Story* (1977); John Updike, *Hugging the Shore* (1983), *Odd Jobs* (1991), and *More Matter: Essays and Criticism* (1999); and John Gardner, *The Art of Fiction* (1983).

For academic studies, see Robert Scholes and Robert Kellogg, *The Nature of Narrative* (1966), on oral as well as written fiction; Robert Liddell, *Robert Liddell on the Novel* (1969), a volume combining two earlier books by Liddell—*A Treatise on the Novel* and *Some Principles of Fiction*; Norman Friedman, *Form and Meaning in Fiction* (1975); Seymour Chatman, *Story and Discourse* (1978); and Wayne C. Booth, *The Rhetoric of Fiction*, 2nd ed. (1983).

Some of the best modern studies are included in *Forms of Modern Fiction*, ed. William Van O'Connor (1948); *Critiques and Essays on Modern Fiction, 1920–1951*, ed. John W. Aldridge (1952); *Approaches to the Novel: Materials for a Poetics*, ed. Robert Scholes, rev. ed. (1966); and *The Theory of the Novel: New Essays*, ed. John Halperin (1974). For essays defining the short story and sketching its history, see Susan Lohafer and Jo Ellyn Clarey, eds., *Short Story Theory at a Crossroads* (1989). Also helpful are Valerie Shaw, *The Short Story: A Critical Introduction* (1983), and Thomas Riggs, *Reference Guide to Short Fiction*, 2nd ed. (1998).

Examples of contemporary approaches include Susan Lanser, *The Narrative Act: Point of View in Fiction* (1981); Peter Brooks, *Reading for the Plot: Design and Intention in Narrative* (1984); David Lodge, *The Art of Fiction, Illustrated from Classic and Modern Texts* (1993); and *Understanding Narrative*, ed. James Phelan and Peter J. Rabinowitz (1994).

Among recent studies, we recommend Margaret Anne Doody, *The True Story of the Novel* (1995), an important study of the genre from its classical sources through the eighteenth century; *Cultural Institutions of the Novel*, ed. Deidre Lynch and William B. Warner (1996), a collection of essays on the novel from the perspectives of "comparative literature and transnational cultural studies"; and *Theory of the Novel: A Historical Approach*, ed. Michael McKeon (2000), an anthology of classic essays.

See also McKeon's influential, *The Origins of the English Novel, 1600–1740* (1987; new ed., 2002). Also recommended is a massive, multiauthored reference work: *The Novel*, ed. Franco Moretti (2006), in two volumes.

Among journals devoted to narrative are *Journal of Narrative Technique, Modern Fiction Studies, Novel: A Forum*, and *Studies in Short Fiction*.

✔ Checklist: Getting Ideas for Writing about Fiction

Here are questions that may stimulate ideas about stories. Not every question is relevant to every story, but if after reading a story and thinking about it, you then review these pages, you will find some questions that will help you to think further about the story and to get ideas.

It is best to do your thinking with a pen or pencil in hand. If some of the following questions seem to you to be especially relevant to the story you will be writing about, jot down your initial responses, interrupting your writing only to glance again at the story when you feel the need to check the evidence.

Title

❑ Is the title informative? What does it mean or suggest? Did the meaning seem to change after you read the story? Does the title help you to formulate a theme?

❑ If you had written the story, what title would you use?

Plot

❑ Does the plot grow out of the characters, or does it depend on chance or coincidence? Did something at first strike you as irrelevant that later you perceived as relevant? Do some parts continue to strike you as irrelevant?

❑ Does *surprise* play an important role, or does foreshadowing? If surprise is very important, can the story be read a second time with any interest? If so, what gives it this further interest?

❑ What *conflicts* does the story include? Conflicts of one character against another? Of one character against the setting, or against society? Conflicts within a single character?

❑ Are the conflicts resolved? If so, how?

❑ Are certain episodes narrated out of chronological order? If so, were you puzzled? Annoyed? On reflection, does the arrangement of episodes seem effective? Why or why not? Are certain situations repeated? If so, what do you make of the repetitions?

❑ List the major structural units of the story. In a sentence or two summarize each unit that you have listed.

❑ In a sentence summarize the conclusion or resolution. Do you find it satisfactory? Why, or why not?

Character

❑ List the traits of the main characters.

❑ Which character chiefly engages your interest? Why?

❑ What purposes do minor characters serve? Do you find some who by their similarities and differences define each other or define the major character? How else is a particular character defined—by his or her words, actions (including thoughts and emotions), dress, setting, narrative point of view? Do certain characters act differently in the same, or in a similar, situation?

❑ How does the author reveal character? By explicit authorial (editorial) comment, for instance, or, on the other hand, by revelation through dialogue? Through depicted action? Through the actions of other characters? How are the author's methods especially suited to the whole of the story?

❑ Is the behavior plausible—that is, are the characters well motivated?

❑ If a character changes, why and how does he or she change? (You may want to jot down each event that influences a change.) Or did you change your attitude toward a character not because the character changes but because you came to know the character better?

❑ Are the characters round or flat (Forster's terms)? That is, are they complex or, on the other hand, highly typical (for instance, one-dimensional representatives of a social class or age)? Are you chiefly interested in a character's psychology, or does the character strike you as standing for something, such as honesty or the arrogance of power?

❑ How has the author caused you to sympathize with certain characters? How does your response—your sympathy or lack of sympathy—contribute to your judgment of the conflict?

Point of View

❑ Who tells the story? How much does the narrator know? Does the narrator strike you as reliable? What effect is gained by using this narrator?

❑ How does the point of view help shape the theme? After all, the basic story of Little Red Riding Hood—what happens—remains unchanged whether told from the wolf's point of view or the girl's, but if we hear the story from the wolf's point of view, we may feel that the story is about terrifying yet pathetic compulsive behavior; if from the girl's point of view, about terrified innocence and male violence.

❑ Does the narrator's language help you to construct a picture of the narrator's character, class, attitude, strengths, and limitations? (Jot down some evidence, such as colloquial or—on the other hand—formal expressions, ironic comments, figures of speech.) How far can you trust the narrator? Why?

Setting

❑   Do you have a strong sense of the time and place? Is the story very much about, say, New England Puritanism, or race relations in the South in the late nineteenth century, or midwestern urban versus small-town life? If time and place are important, how and at what points in the story has the author conveyed this sense? If you do not strongly feel the setting, do you think the author should have made it more evident?

❑   What is the relation of the setting to the plot and the characters? (For instance, do houses or rooms or their furnishings say something about their residents? Is the landscape important?) Would anything be lost if the descriptions of the setting were deleted from the story or if the setting were changed?

Symbolism

❑   Do certain characters seem to you to stand for something in addition to themselves? Does the setting—whether a house, a farm, a landscape, a town, a period—have an extra dimension?

❑   Do certain actions in the story—for instance, entering a forest at night, or shutting a door, or turning off a light—seem symbolic? If so, symbolic of what?

❑   If you do believe that the story has symbolic elements, do you think they are adequately integrated within the story, or do they strike you as being too obviously stuck in?

Style

❑   Style may be defined as *how* the writer says what he or she says. It is the writer's manner of expression. The writer's choice of words, of sentence structure, and of sentence length are all aspects of style. Example: "Shut the door," and "Would you mind closing the door, please," differ substantially in style. Another example: Lincoln begins the Gettysburg Address by speaking of "Four score and seven years ago," that is, by using language that has a biblical overtone. If he had said, "Eighty-seven years ago," his style would have been different.

❑   How would you characterize the style? Simple? Understated? Figurative? Or what, and why?

❑   How has the point of view shaped or determined the style?

❑   Do you think that the style is consistent? If it is not—for instance, if there are shifts from simple sentences to highly complex ones—what do you make of the shifts?

Theme

❑   Do certain passages—the title, some of the dialogue, some of the de-
    scription, the names of certain characters—seem to you to point es-
    pecially toward the theme? Do you find certain repetitions of words
    or pairs of incidents highly suggestive and helpful in directing your
    thoughts toward stating a theme?
❑   Is the meaning of the story embodied in the whole story, or does it
    seem stuck, for example, in certain passages of editorializing?
❑   Suppose someone asked you to state the point—the theme—of the
    story. Could you? And if you could, would you say that the theme of a
    particular story reinforces values you hold, or does it to some degree
    challenge them?

Documentation

❑   Have I given credit to all sources for borrowed words and also for
    borrowed ideas? (On avoiding plagiarism, see page 327–29.)

✔   Checklist: Getting Ideas for Writing about a Film Based on a Work of Literature

Many novels and short stories have been turned into films, and the relationship between film and fiction is a popular topic for courses. If your
instructor asks you to write about a film version of a work of fiction, these
questions may help to bring your impressions out into the open and provide topics for essays.

Preliminaries

❑   Is the title significant? If the title of the film differs from the title of
    the published story, account for and evaluate the change. (Consider,
    for example, the slight but significant difference between the title of
    Thomas Hardy's novel "Jude the Obscure" [1895] and the title cho-
    sen for the film "Jude" [1996].)

Plot, Character, Setting, and Theme

❑   Does the film closely follow its original or not? Is the use of the
    camera straightforward, or highly creative? Are there, for in-
    stance, shots from high or low angles, slow or fast motion that
    present effectively or else distort features of the original work?
    (Robert Enrico's *An Occurrence at Owl Creek Bridge* [1962] is a

close adaptation of Ambrose Bierce's story, and yet it is visually interesting.)

❏ How faithful is the film to the story in plot and in character? Evaluate the changes, if any. Are the additions or omissions due to the medium or to a crude or faulty interpretation of the original?

❏ Does the film do violence to the theme of the original?

❏ Can film deal as effectively with inner action or mental processes as with external, physical action? In a given film, how is the inner action conveyed? By voice-over? Or by visual equivalents?

❏ How effectively does the film convey the setting or settings that the author chose for the story?

❏ Does the editing—for instance, frequent sharp juxtapositions, or slow panoramic shots—convey qualities that the story writer conveyed by means of sentence length and structure?

❏ Are shots and sequences adequately developed, or do they seem (in film terminology) jerky? (A shot may be jerky by being extremely brief or at an odd angle; a sequence may be jerky by using discontinuous images or fast cuts. Sometimes, of course, jerkiness may be desirable.) If such cinematic techniques as wipes, dissolves, and slow motion are used, are they meaningful and effective?

❏ Are the actors appropriately cast? Was it a mistake to cast Robert Redford as Gatsby in Jack Clayton's film version of *The Great Gatsby* (1974)? Is Gwyneth Paltrow the right choice for the leading role in the film version (1996) of Jane Austen's novel *Emma*? John Huston, in his film (1951) of Stephen Crane's *The Red Badge of Courage* (1895), a novel about cowardice and courage in the Civil War, used Audie Murphy, one of the most highly decorated and best-known heroes of World War II, as Henry Fleming, the young soldier who flees from battle but later gets a second chance to fight bravely. What is the effect of this casting?

Symbolism

❏ If in the story certain objects acquire symbolic meanings, are these same objects similarly used in the film? Or does the film introduce new symbols? Is the lighting in the film realistic or symbolic? Both?

Soundtrack

❏ Does the soundtrack offer more than realistic dialogue? In the film adaptation of "An Occurrence at Owl Creek Bridge," for instance, we hear—much louder than normal—the sound of soldiers' boots on railroad ties and we even hear the sound of the hangman's rope rubbing on a crossbeam. Is the music appropriate and functional? (Music may, among other things, imitate natural sounds, give a sense of locale or of ethnic group, suggest states of mind, provide ironic commentary, or—by repeated melodies—help to establish connections.) Are volume, tempo, and pitch—whether of music or of such sounds as the wind blowing or cars moving—used to stimulate emotions?

Overall Effect

❑   What is your overall response to the film? Do you find the literary work more compelling, more stimulating, than the film, or do you think that the film is better? What above all defines your experience of the literary work? And the experience of the film? Can one medium do something, or some things, that the other cannot?

James Joyce's story "Araby" is included in his collection *Dubliners* (1914), which is available online. The last and longest story in *Dubliners* is "The Dead," which describes Gabriel Conroy and his wife's time together at an annual holiday party hosted by Gabriel's aunts. A beautiful film version, directed by John Huston and starring his daughter Angelica Huston, released in 1987, is faithful to Joyce's story in its action and dialogue, with only minor changes. It is widely available on DVD (be sure that you watch the complete 83-minute version) and makes for a rewarding comparison with the text of the story as Joyce wrote it.

11

GRAPHIC FICTION

"What is the use of a book," thought Alice, "without pictures?"
—Lewis Carroll

LETTERS AND PICTURES

Literature is, literally speaking, made out of letters ("literature," "literally," "literate," and "letters" all come from a Latin word, *littera,* "letter"). A person who can read letters is literate. Yet today we also hear about *visual literacy,* which means "the ability to understand visual things." In this usage, "literacy" is metaphoric. One does not literally (again that word!) read a picture; one looks at it and either understands it or does not understand it. In the following pages, in order to help prepare you to read a story that is partly told by means of pictures, we will be talking about achieving visual literacy, that is, achieving the ability to understand pictures, to "read" pictures—specifically, pictures that are used to tell stories.

The good news is that if you have spent any time at all looking at comic strips you already know a great deal about how to "read" pictures that tell stories.

- You know, for instance, that you should read the pictures and the words from left to right. (If you were brought up in China or Japan, you would begin at the right and read the first column downward, then the next column, again reading downward, unless the book were a Western-style book.)
- You also know that in the usual comic strip a box represents a particular scene; the next box may show the same characters, but at a later moment in time.
- You know that human actions can be conveyed by showing figures in certain postures (walking, eating, etc.) and making certain gestures (pointing, making a fist).

- You know that emotions can be conveyed by facial expressions (think of the Smiley Face, where a few dots and a curve say it all).
- You know that the setting can easily be established (a tree indicates the outdoors, the Capitol Building indicates Washington, D.C.).
- You also know that when a heavy object is depicted on the ground, with the word "bang" in large thick letters next to it, a character has just dropped the object.
- And you know that the words enclosed in a "balloon" above the character's head are the words that the character is speaking.
- If the words are represented not by letters but by such symbols as @, #, and !, you know that the character is cursing or using dirty language.
- You also know that if the line that encloses these words is scalloped, or looks something like a cloud, the words represent *thoughts* rather than utterances.

In short, you know the conventions that enable you to understand what the cartoonist/story-teller is saying; you can follow the story, the narrative conveyed by words and pictures. You are already visually literate.

Nevertheless, because you may not have developed the habit of reading images closely, taking in all the subtleties that they may offer, we will consider what it means to read pictures.

The first thing we want to say is that although there is some truth in some contexts to the statement that a picture is worth a thousand words, pictures are not very good at telling *stories*. Think of any familiar story— let's say (to take an example in our text) the story of King Solomon and the two women who claimed to be the mother of an infant. Solomon ordered a servant to bring the sword, and to divide the living child so that each woman could have half. A sword was brought (here we give the text of the Revised Standard Version)

> then the woman whose son was alive said to the king, because her heart yearned for her son, "Oh, no my lord, give her [i.e., the other woman] the living child, and by no means slay it." But the other said, "It shall be neither mine nor yours: divide it." Then the king answered and said, "Give the living child to the first woman, and by no means slay it; she is its mother." (I Kings 3.26-27)

We could draw striking images of the story—if we had the talent!—for instance, an image of two women quarreling over an infant, an image of a servant entering with a massive sword, and an image of the infant being handed over to one woman. But we think it would be impossible by images alone to tell the story, which essentially leads the reader to draw two conclusions:

- A loving mother will give up a child rather than let it die, and
- Solomon was a wise judge.

Tradition says that in the Middle Ages, when most people were illiterate, pictures such as those in stained glass windows were "the Bible of the people." These windows did tell stories—but the stories could be understood only if the viewers were already familiar with verbal tellings. Similarly, such narratives as those on Trajan's Column (built 113 CE), adorned with images of the Roman emperor's victories and in the Bayeux Tapestry (late eleventh century), depicting the French invasion of England, show us lots of energetic figures, but to *understand* what is going on, we must already know the story.

Having made the point that pictures are not very good at telling stories, we now admit that they *can* tell a simple story. Look, for instance, at the painting by Grant Wood, *Death on Ridge Road*. The title—words!—tells you what

Grant Wood (American, 1892-1942), *Death on the Ridge Road*, 1935.
Oil on masonite; frame: 39 × 46 1/16 in. (99 × 117 cm), Williams College Museum of Art, Williamstown, MA, gift of Cole Porter, (47.1.3). Art © Figge Art Museum, successor to the Estate of Nan Wood Graham/Licensed by VAGA, New York.

the picture is about, but even if you found the picture in the attic, with no title affixed, you could infer what is about to happen, what story the picture tells.

A big black car, apparently a limousine, is going to collide with a truck.

We think all viewers will agree with this statement, and perhaps we can go a little further. (First, let us mention that the cars are black, the truck is red, the grass is green, and the sky is darkening.)

- Given that the cars are black—in this context, an ominous color—that the sky shows a storm brewing, that the intersecting diagonals of the limousine and the truck imply conflict, and that the two telephone poles tip in opposite ways, the picture makes one uneasy.
- Apparently the limousine was behind the car that is now at the bottom of the picture; in order to pass the car, the limo must have crossed into the left lane, and it is now cutting to the right in order to return to its proper lane.
- The telephone pole is of course a telephone pole, but, in this context of vehicles about to collide, we perceive the pole also as a cross that turns the pretty landscape with its winding road into a cemetery.
- The picture may cause us to moralize along these lines: "Death comes unexpectedly," "Even in lovely rural surroundings death can be present."

But, again, even if a viewer has such thoughts—and we think these thoughts are supported by the picture—the picture itself tells a very simple story:

A car, having passed on the left another car, is cutting back to the right, and will in a moment collide with a truck coming over a hill.

It does *not* tell us anything about the minds of the people involved in the accident to come. Conceivably a viewer may conjecture that the driver of the limousine was impatient, driving behind a guy in a dinky car going at twenty miles an hour, and—such is the temperament of the rich men who drive big cars, or of their chauffeurs—this driver has confidently and recklessly crossed the dividing line, entered the left lane, zoomed in front of the slowpoke, and now (here we return to the facts in the picture) is cutting back into the right-hand lane, too near the truck to avoid a crash. But this interpretation of the character of the driver cannot be supported by the picture. For all we know, the smaller car may have stalled in the middle of the road, and the driver of the limousine—maybe a very cautious woman—was forced to go around the stalled car.

TOPIC FOR WRITING

Grant Wood's most famous painting is *American Gothic*, a picture that shows a man and a woman standing in front of their home, a house with a window shaped like a gothic (pointed) arch. (If you are unfamiliar with the picture, you can easily find it with a Google search.) Do you see a story, a narrative a sequence of events, in this picture? If so, what is the story? If you do not see a story, invent a very short one, a story that might plausibly use this picture as an illustration of some episode.

READING AN IMAGE: A SHORT STORY TOLD IN ONE PANEL

As we indicated in our discussion of the story of King Solomon, pictures are not good at conveying states of mind, motivations, reflections, or judgments. Still, pictures can communicate meanings, and we look now at a picture that is accompanied by words. Tony Carrillo, born and raised in Tempe, Arizona, conceived *F Minus* when he was a sophomore at Arizona State University. The strip is currently syndicated in more than a hundred newspapers.

F Minus: © 2010 CARRILLO, Dist. by UFS, Inc.

For the moment, let us pretend that the picture did not exist, and we were given only this text:

> One day, in a quiet office building somewhere, a small calculator suddenly became self-aware.
>
> In eight seconds, it plotted the extinction of all mankind.
> Then the battery died.
> Two weeks later, it was thrown away.

We do not want to make extravagant claims but we think this is pretty good as a mini sci-fi story. We hear much about the possibility that some day there may be machines that "think," and we hear even more about technology getting out of control and possibly destroying its creators. In the words of the novelist and essayist Elias Canetti(1905–1994), "The planet's survival has become so uncertain that any effort, any thought that presupposes an assured future amounts to a mad gamble." So the graphic story begins with something fantastic yet something that we hear about and that we can imagine may become real:

> One day, in a quiet office building somewhere, a small calculator suddenly became self-aware.
> In eight seconds, it plotted the extinction of all mankind.

Here is an engaging combination of vagueness ("One day," "somewhere") and of the highly specific ("In eight seconds"); that is, things in a leisurely once-upon-a-time land suddenly come down to a matter of seconds. The vague fairy-tale world of "one day" has been transformed into a real time, and the "small calculator" is now a big threat. Like all good fiction, each sentence of this tiny story stimulates the reader to wonder, "What happens next?"

What does happen after the calculator "plotted the extinction of all mankind"? "Then the battery died." Well, that makes sense. We had not anticipated this happening, but, again, the happening that is narrated is plausible, and we are relieved, satisfied. In a sense the story is over—the battery is dead, so what more can be said?—but we see additional words:

> Two weeks later, it was thrown away.

We think this ending is masterful. E. M. Forster's comment in *Aspects of the Novel* (1927) about a good plot comes to mind:

> Shock, followed by the feeling, "Oh, that's all right," is a sign that all is well with plot: characters, to be real, ought to run smoothly, but a plot ought to cause surprise.

It is as if we heard a joke, laughed, and thought we had heard the end of the matter—and then the narrator went on to top the joke, giving us a second, unexpected joke that builds on the first joke, a line that, after we have heard it, seems inevitable and utterly conclusive. The calculator, once an enormous menace, fails to be of even the slightest significance because—as is entirely natural, if we can speak of naturalness in connection with a mechanical device—the battery dies. The story seems to be over, there is nothing more to say. But there *is* more to say. The battery-dead calculator is not even noticed for two weeks, and then, when presumably it somehow comes to some unspecified person's attention, it is unceremoniously discarded, "thrown away."

What is convincing is not simply that A is followed by B and B is followed by C, but that there is a *logic* to the sequence, even (may we say?) a *truth* to the sequence. Notice, too, that the artist-writer does not moralize; rather, it is the reader-viewer who draws conclusions.

The theme is a great one, the humbling of the ambitious. Shakespeare often treated it, for instance in *Richard II*, where the king meditates on his "state" (i.e., high status, exalted rank) and sees death as an "antic" (buffoon, jester) mocking even a king:

Within the hollow crown
That rounds the mortal temples of a King
Keeps Death his court and there the antic sits,
Scoffing his state and grinning at his pomp,
Allowing him a breath, a little scene,
To monarchize, be feared and kill with looks,
Infusing him with self and vain conceit,
As if this flesh which walls about our life,
Were brass impregnable, and humored thus
Comes at the last and with a little pin
Bores through his castle wall, and farewell king! (3.2.160-70)

We are not claiming that the story about the calculator is in the same league with *Richard II*, but we do find it memorable. We think the *text* of this graphic story makes a good short-short story, even without the picture.

The cartoonist might simply have drawn a calculator, but he cleverly—is it too much to say brilliantly?—put two eyes into the liquid crystal display and thus animated the whole thing. The calculator *does* seem to be a person, does it not? So the story becomes enriched by the image. We can call this sort of thing "graphic fiction," but, to go back to our earlier point, the truth is that the picture doesn't tell the story. It merely enriches a story that is told in words.

Yet our last sentence is unfair. The image does not "merely" enrich the words; the picture is central to the story. If the story consisted only of text, or if all of the text were written above or below the picture, the story would not be as effective. We admit it: The image—the visual material—is integral.

And that is our point: The best graphic fiction does not merely illustrate the verbal story; rather, the images are inseparable from the words. The story is text-and-image, not just text-adorned-with-image.

12

WRITING ABOUT DRAMA

*Drama is based on the mistake. . . . all good drama has two move-
ments, first the making of the mistake, then the discovery that it
was a mistake.*

—W. H. Auden

*The theater is supremely fitted to say, "Behold! These things are."
Yet most dramatists employ it to say: "This moral truth can be
learned from beholding this action."*

—Thornton Wilder

The essays you write about plays will be similar to analytic essays about fiction. Unless you are writing a review of a performance, you probably will
not try to write about all aspects of a play. Rather, you will choose some significant topic. For instance, if you are writing about Tennessee Williams's
The Glass Menagerie (1945), you might compare the aspirations of Jim
O'Connor and Tom Wingfield, or you might compare Tom's illusions with
those of his sister, Laura, and his mother, Amanda. Or you might examine
the symbolism, perhaps limiting your essay to the glass animals or extend-
ing it to include other symbols, such as the fire escape, the lighting, and the
victrola. Similarly, if you are writing an analysis, you might decide to study
the construction of one scene of a play, or, if the play does not have a great
many scenes, even the construction of the entire play.

A list of questions on pages 214–15 may help you to find a topic for
the particular play you choose.

A SAMPLE ESSAY

The following essay discusses the structure of *The Glass Menagerie*. It
mentions various characters, but, because its concern is with the arrangement of scenes, it does not examine any of the characters in detail. An
essay might be devoted to Williams's assertion that "There is much to
admire in Amanda, and as much to love and pity as there is to laugh at,"
but an essay on the structure of the play is probably not the place to talk
about Williams's characterization of Amanda.

Preliminary Notes

After deciding to write on the structure of the play, with the goal of seeing the overall pattern, the student reread *The Glass Menagerie,* jotted down some notes, briefly summarizing each of the seven scenes, with an occasional comment, and then he typed them. On rereading the typed notes, he made deletions and he added observations in handwriting.

These notes enabled the student to prepare a rough draft, which he then submitted to some classmates for peer review. (On peer review, see pages 37–38.)

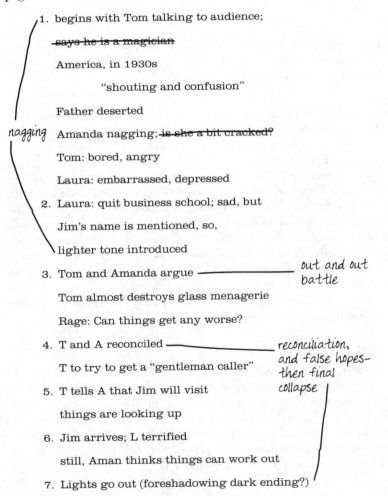

1. begins with Tom talking to audience;

   ~~says he is a magician~~

   America, in 1930s

      "shouting and confusion"

   Father deserted

nagging   Amanda nagging; ~~is she a bit cracked?~~

   Tom: bored, angry

   Laura: embarrassed, depressed

2. Laura: quit business school; sad, but

   Jim's name is mentioned, so,

   lighter tone introduced

3. Tom and Amanda argue ——————— *out and out battle*

   Tom almost destroys glass menagerie

   Rage: Can things get any worse?

4. T and A reconciled ——————— *reconciliation, and false hopes— then final collapse*

   T to try to get a "gentleman caller"

5. T tells A that Jim will visit

   things are looking up

6. Jim arrives; L terrified

   still, Aman thinks things can work out

7. Lights go out (foreshadowing dark ending?)

Jim a jerk, clumsy; breaks unicorn, but L doesn't seem to mind.

Maybe he <u>is</u> the right guy to draw her into normal world. Jim

reveals he is engaged:

"Desolation."

Tom escapes into merchant marine, but can't escape memories.

Speaks to audience.

L. blows out candles (does this mean he forgets her? No,

because he is remembering her right now. I don't get it, if

the candles are supposed to be symbolic.)

Notice that the final version of the essay, printed below, is *not* merely a summary (a brief retelling of the plot). Although it does indeed include summary, it is devoted to showing *how* the scenes are related.

Elaine Hugard
Professor Swann
English Composition 2B
9 May 2011

Title is focused; it announces topic and thesis.

Opening paragraph closes in on thesis.

The Solid Structure of *The Glass Menagerie*

In the "Production Notes" Tennessee Williams calls *The Glass Menagerie* a "memory play," a term that the narrator in the play also uses. Memories often consist of fragments of episodes which are so loosely connected that they seem chaotic, and therefore we might think that *The Glass Menagerie* will consist of very loosely related episodes. However, the play covers only one episode, and though it gives the illusion of random talk, it has a firm structure and moves steadily toward a foregone conclusion.

Reasonable organization; the paragraph touches on the beginning and the end.

Tennessee Williams divides the play into seven scenes. The first scene begins with a sort of prologue and the last scene concludes with a sort of epilogue that is related to the prologue. In the prologue Tom addresses the audience and comments on the 1930s as

Brief but effective quotations.

a time when America was "blind" and was a place of "shouting and confusion." Tom also mentions that our lives consist of expectations, and though he does not say that our expectations are unfulfilled, near the end of the prologue he quotes a postcard that his father wrote to the family he deserted: "Hello—Goodbye." In the epilogue Tom tells us that he followed his "father's footsteps," deserting the family. And just before the epilogue, near the end of Scene VII, we see what can be considered another desertion: Jim explains to Tom's sister Laura that he is engaged and therefore cannot visit Laura again. Thus the end is closely related to the beginning, and the play is the steady development of the initial implications.

Useful generalization based on earlier details.

Chronological organization is reasonable. Opening topic sentence lets readers know where they are going.

The first three scenes show things going from bad to worse. Amanda is a nagging mother who finds her only relief in talking about the past to her crippled daughter, Laura, and her frustrated son, Tom. When she was young she was beautiful and was eagerly courted by rich young men, but now the family is poor and this harping on the past can only bore or infuriate Tom and embarrass or depress Laura, who have no happy past to look back to, who see no happy future, and who can only be upset by Amanda's insistence that they should behave as she behaved long ago.

Brief plot summary supports thesis.

The second scene deepens the despair: Amanda learns that the timorous Laura has not been attending a business school but has retreated in terror from this confrontation with the contemporary world. Laura's helplessness is made clear to the audience, and so is Amanda's lack of understanding. Near the end of the second scene, however, Jim's name is introduced; he is a boy Laura had a crush on in high school, and so the audience gets a glimpse of a happier Laura and a sense that possibly Laura's world is wider than the stifling tenement in which she and her mother and brother live. But in the third scene things get worse, when Tom and Amanda have so violent an argument that they are no longer on speaking terms. Tom is so angry with his mother that he almost by accident destroys his sister's treasured collection of glass animals, the fragile lifeless world which is her refuge. The apartment is literally full of the "shouting and confusion" that Tom spoke of in his prologue.

Useful summary and transition.

The first three scenes have revealed a progressive worsening of relations; the next three scenes reveal a progressive improvement in relations. In Scene IV Tom and his mother are reconciled, and Tom reluctantly—apparently in an effort to make up with his mother—agrees to try to get a friend to come to dinner so that Laura will have "a gentleman caller." In Scene V Tom tells his mother that Jim will come to dinner on the next night, and Amanda brightens because she sees a possibility of security for Laura at last. In Scene VI Jim arrives, and despite Laura's initial terror, there seems, at least in Amanda's mind, to be the possibility that things will go well.

The seventh scene, by far the longest, at first seems to be fulfilling Amanda's hopes. Despite the ominous fact that the lights go out because Tom has not paid the electric bill, Jim is at ease. He is an insensitive oaf, but that doesn't seem to bother Amanda, and almost miraculously he manages to draw Laura somewhat out of her sheltered world. Even when Jim in his clumsiness breaks the horn of Laura's treasured glass unicorn, she is not upset. In fact, she is almost relieved because the loss of the horn makes the animal less "freakish" and he "will feel more at home with the other horses." In a way, of course, the unicorn symbolizes the crippled Laura, who at least for the moment feels less freakish and isolated now that she is somewhat reunited with society through Jim. But this is a play about life in a blind and confused world, and though in a previous age the father escaped, there can be no escape now. Jim reveals that he is engaged, Laura relapses into "desolation," Amanda relapses into rage and bitterness, and Tom relapses into dreams of escape.

The essayist is thinking and commenting, not merely summarizing the plot.

In a limited sense Tom does escape. He leaves the family and joins the merchant marine, but his last speech or epilogue tells us that he cannot escape the memory of his sister: "Oh, Laura, Laura, I tried to leave you behind me, but I am more faithful than I intended to be!" And so the end of the last scene brings us back again to the beginning of the first scene: We are still in a world of "the blind" and of "confusion." But now at the end of the play the darkness is deeper; the characters are lost forever in their unhappiness as Laura "blows the candles out," the darkness being literal but also symbolic of their extinguished hopes.

Useful, thoughtful summary of thesis.

Numerous devices, such as repeated references to the absent father, to Amanda's youth, to Laura's victrola, and of course to Laura's glass menagerie help to tie the scenes together into a unified play. But beneath these threads of imagery, and recurring motifs, is a fundamental pattern that involves the movement from nagging (Scenes I and II) to open hostilities (Scene III) to temporary reconciliation (Scene IV) to false hopes (Scenes V and VI) to an impossible heightening of false hopes and then, in a swift descent, to an inevitable collapse (Scene VII). Tennessee Williams has constructed his play carefully. G. B. Tennyson says that a "playwright must 'build' his speeches, as the theatrical expression has it" (13). But a playwright must do more, he must also build his play out of scenes. Like Ibsen, if Williams had been introduced to an architect he might have said, "Architecture is my business too."

[New page]

Works Cited

Tennyson, G. B. *An Introduction to Drama.* New York: Holt, 1967. Print.

Williams, Tennessee. *The Glass Menagerie. An Introduction to Literature.* Ed. Sylvan Barnet, William Burto, and William E. Cain. 16th ed. New York: Longman, 2011. 855-900. Print.

The danger in writing about structure, especially if one proceeds by beginning at the beginning and moving steadily to the end, is that one will simply repeat the plot. This essay on *The Glass Menagerie* manages to say things about the organization of the plot even as it tells the plot. It has a point, hinted at in the pleasantly paradoxical title, developed in the body of the essay, and wrapped up in the last line.

TYPES OF PLAYS

Most of the world's great plays written before the twentieth century may be regarded as one of two kinds: **tragedy** or **comedy.** Roughly speaking, tragedy dramatizes the conflict between the vitality of the individual life and the laws or limits of life. The tragic hero reaches a height, going beyond the experience of others but at the cost of his or her life. Comedy dramatizes the vitality of the laws of social life. In comedy, the good life is seen to reside in the shedding of an individualism that isolates, in favor of a union with a genial and enlightened society. These points must be amplified a bit before we go on to the point that any important play does much more than can be put into such simple formulas.

Tragedy

Tragic heroes usually go beyond the standards to which reasonable people adhere; they do some fearful deed that ultimately destroys them. This deed is often said to be an act of **hubris,** a Greek word meaning something like "overweening pride." It may involve, for instance, violating a taboo, such as that against taking life. But if the hubristic act ultimately destroys the man or woman who performs it, it also shows that person to be in some way more fully a living being—a person who has experienced life more fully, whether by heroic action or by capacity for enduring suffering—than the other characters in the play. Othello kills Desdemona, Lear gives away his crown and banishes his one loving daughter, Antony loses his share of the Roman Empire, but all of these men seem to live more fully than the other characters in the plays—for one thing, they experience a kind of anguish unknown to those who surround them and who outlive them. (If the hero does not die, he or she usually is left in some deathlike state, as is the blind Oedipus in *King Oedipus*.)

In tragedy, we see humanity pushed to an extreme; in agony and grief the hero enters a world unknown to most and reveals magnificence. After his or her departure from the stage, we are left in a world of littler people. The closing lines of almost any of Shakespeare's tragedies may be used to illustrate the point. *King Lear*, for example, ends thus:

> The oldest hath borne most: we that are young
> Shall never see so much, nor live so long.

If you are writing about a tragedy, you might consider whether the points just made are illustrated in your play. Is the hero guilty of hubris? Does the hero seem a greater person than the others in the play? An essay examining such questions probably requires not only a character sketch but also some comparison with other characters.

Tragedy commonly involves **irony** of two sorts: unconsciously ironic deeds and unconsciously ironic speeches. **Ironic deeds** have consequences more or less the reverse of what the doer intends. Macbeth thinks that by killing Duncan he will gain happiness, but he finds that his deed brings him sleepless nights. Brutus thinks that by killing Caesar he will bring liberty to Rome, but he brings tyranny. In an **unconsciously ironic speech,** the speaker's words mean one thing to him or her but something more significant to the audience, as when King Duncan, baffled by Cawdor's treason, says:

> There's no art
> To find the mind's construction in the face:
> He was a gentleman on whom I built
> An absolute trust.

At this moment Macbeth, whom we have already heard meditating the murder of Duncan, enters. Duncan's words are true, but he does not apply them to Macbeth, as the audience does. A few moments later Duncan praises Macbeth as "a peerless kinsman." Soon Macbeth will indeed become peerless, when he kills Duncan and ascends to the throne.[1] Sophocles' use of ironic deeds and speeches is so pervasive, especially in *King Oedipus,* that **Sophoclean irony** has become a critical term. Here is a critic summarizing the ironies of *King Oedipus:*

> As the images unfold, the enquirer turns into the object of enquiry, the hunter into the prey, the doctor into the patient, the investigator into the criminal, the revealer into the thing revealed, the finder into the thing found, the savior into the thing saved ("I was saved, for some dreadful destiny"), the liberator into the thing released ("I released your feet from the bonds which pierced your ankles" says the Corinthian messenger), the accuser becomes the defendant, the ruler the subject, the teacher not only the pupil but also the object lesson, the example.
>
> —Bernard Knox, "Sophocles' Oedipus,"
> in *Tragic Themes in Western
> Literature,* ed. Cleanth Brooks (1955), 10–11

Notice the neatness of that sentence; it is long, but it does not ramble, it does not baffle, and it does not suggest a stuffy writer. The verb *turns* governs the first two-thirds, and after the second long parenthetical statement, when the messenger's speech may cause the reader to forget the verb, the writer provides another verb, *becomes.*

When the deed backfires or has a reverse effect, as happens with Macbeth's effort to gain happiness, we have what Aristotle called a **peripeteia,** or a **reversal.** When a character comes to perceive what has happened (Macbeth's "I have lived long enough: my way of life / Is fall'n into the sere, the yellow leaf"), he experiences (in Aristotle's language) an **anagnorisis,** or **recognition.** Strictly speaking, for Aristotle the recognition was a matter of literal identification, for example, that Oedipus is the son of a man he killed. In *Macbeth,* the recognition in this sense is that Macduff, "from his mother's womb / Untimely ripped," is the man who fits the prophecy that Macbeth can be conquered only by someone not "of woman born."

In his analysis of drama Aristotle says that the tragic hero comes to grief through his **hamartia,** a term sometimes translated as **tragic flaw** but perhaps better translated as **tragic error.** Thus, it is a great error for

---

[1] *Dramatic irony* (ironic deeds or happenings, and unconsciously ironic speeches) must be distinguished from *verbal irony,* which is produced when the speaker is *conscious* that his or her words mean something different from what they say.

Othello to trust Iago and to strangle Desdemona, for Lear to give away his kingdom, and for Macbeth to decide to help fulfill the prophecies. If we hold to the translation *flaw*, we begin to hunt for a fault in their characters, and we say, for instance, that Othello is gullible, Lear self-indulgent, Macbeth ambitious, or some such thing. In doing this, we may overlook their grandeur. Take a single example: Iago boasts he can dupe Othello because

> The Moor is of a free and open nature
> That thinks men honest that but seem to be so.

We ought to hesitate before we say that a man who trusts men because they seem to be honest has a flaw.

The text of Aristotle's *Poetics*, translated by Ingram Bywater and published in 1920, can be found at Project Gutenberg: <http://www .gutenberg.org/ebooks/6763>. An earlier translation, by S. H. Butcher, published in 1902, is available at The Internet Classics Archive: <http:// classics.mit.edu/Aristotle/poetics.html>.

Writing about Tragedy When writing about tragedy, the most common essay topic is on the tragic hero. Too often, however, the hero is judged according to a formula: He or she must be noble, must have a flaw, must do a fearful deed, must recognize the flaw, must die. The previous paragraph suggests that Shakespeare's practice makes doubtful one of these matters, the flaw. Be similarly cautious about accepting the rest of the package unexamined. (This book has several times urged you to trust your feelings; do not assume that what you have been taught about tragedy—in these pages or elsewhere—must always be true and that you should, therefore, trust such assertions even if they go against your own responses to a given play.) On the other hand, if *tragedy* is to have any meaning—any use as a term—it must have some agreed-upon attributes.

An essay that seeks to determine whether a particular character is a tragic character ought at its outset to make clear its conception of tragedy and the degree of rigidity, or flexibility, with which it will interpret some or all of its categories. For example, it may indicate that although nobility is essential, nobility is not equivalent to high rank. A middle-class figure with certain mental or spiritual characteristics may, in such a view, be an acceptable tragic hero.

An essay closely related to the sort we have been talking about measures a character by some well-known theory of tragedy. For example, one can measure Willy Loman, in *Death of a Salesman* (1949), against Arthur Miller's essays on tragedy, in *The Theater Essays of Arthur Miller* (1978), or against Aristotle's remarks on tragedy. The organization of such an essay is usually not a problem: Isolate the relevant aspects of the theoretical statement, and then examine the character to see if, point by point, he illustrates them. But remember that even if Willy Loman fulfills Arthur Miller's idea of a tragic figure, you need not accept him as tragic; conversely, if he does not fulfill Aristotle's idea, you need not deny him tragic status. Aristotle may be wrong.

✔ Checklist: Writing about Tragedy

❑ What causes the tragedy? Is it a flaw in the central character? a mistake (*not* the same thing as a flaw) made by this character? an outside force, such as another character or fate?
❑ Is the tragic character defined partly by other characters, for instance, by characters who help us to sense what the character *might* have done, or who in some other way reveal the strengths or weaknesses of the protagonist?
❑ Does a viewer know more than the tragic figure knows? more than most or all of the characters know?
❑ Does the tragic character achieve any sort of wisdom at the end of the play?
❑ To what degree do you sympathize with the tragic character?
❑ Is the play depressing? If not, why not?

Comedy

Although a **comedy** ought to be amusing, plays that are called comedies are not just collections of jokes. Rather, they are works that are entertaining throughout and that end happily.

In comedy, the fullest life is seen to reside within enlightened social norms: At the beginning of a comedy we find banished dukes, unhappy lovers, crabby parents, jealous husbands, and harsh laws, but at the end we usually have a unified and genial society, often symbolized by a marriage feast to which everyone, or almost everyone, is invited. Early in Shakespeare's *A Midsummer Night's Dream,* for instance, we meet quarreling young lovers and a father who demands that his daughter either marry a man she does not love or enter a convent. Such is the Athenian law. At the end of the play the lovers are properly matched, to everyone's satisfaction.

Speaking broadly, most comedies fall into one of two classes: **satiric comedy** and **romantic comedy.** In satiric comedy the emphasis is on the obstructionists—the irate fathers, hardheaded businessmen, and other members of the Establishment who at the beginning of the play seem to hold all the cards, preventing joy from reigning. They are held up to ridicule because they are repressive monomaniacs enslaved to themselves, acting mechanistically (always irate, always hardheaded) instead of responding genially to the ups and downs of life. The outwitting of these obstructionists, usually by the younger generation, often provides the resolution of the plot. Ben Jonson (1572–1637), Molière (1627–73), and George Bernard Shaw (1856–1950) are in this tradition; their comedy, according to an ancient Roman formula, "chastens morals with ridicule"; that is, it reforms folly or vice by laughing at it. In romantic comedy (one thinks of A *Midsummer Night's Dream, As You Like It,* and *Twelfth Night*) the emphasis is on a pair or pairs of delightful people who engage our sympathies as they run their obstacle race to the altar. Obstructionists are found here, too, but the emphasis is on festivity.

Writing about Comedy Essays on comedy often examine the nature of the humor. Why is an irate father, in this context, funny? Or why is a young lover, again in this context, funny? Commonly, one will find that at least some of the humor is in the disproportionate nature of their activities (they get terribly excited) and in their inflexibility. In both of these qualities they are rather like the cat in animated cartoons who repeatedly chases the mouse to his hole and who repeatedly bangs his head against the wall. The following is a skeleton of a possible essay on why Jaques in Shakespeare's *As You Like It* is amusing:

> Jaques is insistently melancholy. In the Eden-like Forest of Arden, he sees only the dark side of things.

> His monomania, however, is harmless to himself and to others; because it causes us no pain, it may entertain us.

> Indeed, we begin to look forward to his melancholy speeches. We delight in hearing him fulfill our expectations by wittily finding gloom where others find mirth.

We are delighted, too, to learn that this chastiser of others has in fact been guilty of the sort of behavior he chastises.

At the end of the play, when four couples are wed, the inflexible Jaques insists on standing apart from the general rejoicing.

Such might be the gist of an essay. It needs to be supported with details, and it can be enriched, for example, by a comparison between Jaques's sort of jesting and Touchstone's, but it is at least a promising draft of an outline.

In writing about comedy you may be concerned with the function of one scene or character, but whatever your topic, you may find it helpful to begin by trying to decide whether the play is primarily romantic or primarily satiric (or something else). One way of getting at this is to ask yourself to what degree you sympathize with the characters. Do you laugh with them, sympathetically, or do you laugh at them, regarding them as at least somewhat contemptible?

✔ Checklist: Writing about Comedy

❑ Do the comic complications arise chiefly out of the personalities of the characters (for instance, pretentiousness or amorousness) or out of the situations (for instance, mistaken identity)?

❑ What are the chief goals of the figures? Do we sympathize with these goals, or do we laugh at persons who pursue them? If we laugh, *why* do we laugh?

❑ What are the personalities of those who oppose the central characters? Do we laugh at them, or do we sympathize with them?

❑ What is funny about the play? Is the comedy high (including verbal comedy) or chiefly situational and physical?

❑ Is the play predominantly genial, or is there a strong satiric tone?

❑ Does the comedy have any potentially tragic elements in it? Might the plot be slightly rewritten so that it would become a tragedy?

❑ What, if anything, do the characters learn by the end of the play?

ASPECTS OF DRAMA

Theme

If we have perceived the work properly, we ought to be able to formulate its **theme,** its underlying idea, and perhaps we can even go so far as to say its moral attitudes, its view of life, its wisdom. Some critics, it is true, have argued that the concept of theme is meaningless. They hold that *Macbeth,* for example, gives us only an extremely detailed history of one imaginary man. In this view, *Macbeth* says nothing to you or me; it says only what happened to some imaginary man. Even *Julius Caesar* says nothing about the historical Julius Caesar or about the nature of Roman politics. On this we can agree; no one would offer Shakespeare's play as evidence of what the historical Caesar said or did. But surely the view that the concept of theme is meaningless and that a work tells us only about imaginary creatures is a desperate one. We *can* say that we see in *Julius Caesar* the fall of power or (if we are thinking of Brutus) the vulnerability of idealism.

To the reply that these are mere truisms, we can counter: Yes, but the truisms are presented in such a way that they take on life and become a part of us rather than remain things of which we say, "I've heard it said, and I guess it's so."

A brief illustration may be helpful here. A critic examining Ibsen's achievements begins by trying to see what some of the plays are in fact about.

> We must not waste more than a paragraph on such fiddle-faddle as the notion that *Ghosts* is a play about venereal disease or that *A Doll's House* is a play about women's rights. On these terms, *King Lear* is a play about housing for the elderly and *Hamlet* is a stage-debate over the reality of spooks. Venereal disease and its consequences are represented onstage in *Ghosts;* so, to all intents and purposes, is incest; but the theme of the play is inherited guilt, and the sexual pathology of the Alving family is an engine in the hands of that theme. *A Doll's House* represents a woman imbued with the idea of becoming a person, but it proposes nothing categorical about women becoming people; in fact, its real theme has nothing to do with the sexes. It is the irrepressible conflict of two different personalities which have founded themselves on two radically different estimates of reality.
> —Robert M. Adams, "Ibsen on the Contrary," in *Modern Drama,* ed. Anthony Caputi (1966), 345

Such a formulation can be most useful; a grasp of the theme enables us to see what the plot is really all about, what the plot suggests in its universal meaning or applicability.

Some critics (influenced by Aristotle's statement that a drama is an imitation of an action) use **action** in a sense equivalent to *theme.* In this sense, the action is the underlying happening—the inner happening—for example, "the enlightenment of someone" or "the coming of unhappiness" or "the finding of the self by self-surrender." One might say that the theme of *Macbeth* is embodied in some words that Macbeth himself utters: "Blood will have blood." This is not to say that these words and no other words embody the theme or the action. The literary critic Francis Fergusson (1904-1986) suggests that another expression in *Macbeth*, to the effect that Macbeth "outran the pauser, reason," describes the action of the play:

> To "outrun" reason suggests an impossible stunt, like lifting oneself by one's own bootstraps. It also suggests a competition or race, like those of nightmare, which cannot be won. As for the word "reason," Shakespeare associates it with nature and nature's order, in the individual soul, in society, and in the cosmos. To outrun reason is thus to violate nature itself, to lose the bearings of common sense and of custom, and to move into a spiritual realm bounded by the irrational darkness of Hell one way, and the superrational grace of faith the other way. As the play develops before us, all the modes of this absurd, or evil, or supernatural, action are attempted, the last being Malcolm's and Macduff's acts of faith.
> —*The Human Image in Dramatic Literature* (1957), 118

Critics such as Fergusson, who are influenced by Aristotle's *Poetics*, assume that the dramatist conceives of an action and then imitates it or sets it forth by means of first a plot and characters and then by means of language, gesture, and perhaps spectacle and music. When the Greek comic dramatist Menander (342–292 BCE) told a friend he had finished his play and now had only to write it, he must have meant that he had the action or the theme firmly in mind and had worked out the plot and the requisite characters. All that remained was to set down the words.

Plot

Plot is variously defined, sometimes as equivalent to *story* (in this sense a synopsis of *Julius Caesar* has the same plot as *Julius Caesar*) but more often, and more usefully, as the dramatist's particular *arrangement* of the story. Because Shakespeare's *Julius Caesar* begins with a scene dramatizing an encounter between plebeians and tribunes, its plot is different from that of a play on Julius Caesar in which such a scene (not necessary to the story) is omitted. The scholar Richard G. Moulton (1849–1924), discussing the early part of Shakespeare's plot in *Julius Caesar*, examines the relationship between the first two scenes.

> The opening scene strikes appropriately the key-note of the whole action. In it we see the tribunes of the people—officers whose whole

raison d'être is to be the mouthpiece of the commonalty—restraining their own clients from the noisy honors they are disposed to pay Caesar. To the justification in our eyes of a conspiracy against Caesar, there could not be a better starting-point than this hint that the popular worship of Caesar, which has made him what he is, is itself reaching its reaction-point. Such a suggestion moreover makes the whole play one complete *wave* of popular fickleness from crest to crest.

The second is the scene upon which the dramatist mainly relies for the *crescendo* in the justification of the conspirators. It is a long scene, elaborately contrived so as to keep the conspirators and their cause before us at their very best, and the victim at his very worst.

—*Shakespeare as a Dramatic Artist* (1893), 188–189

Moulton's discussion of the plot continues at length. One may argue that he presents too favorable a view of the conspirators (when he says we see the conspirators at their best, he seems to overlook their fawning), but that is not our concern here; here we have been talking about the process of examining juxtaposed scenes, a process that Moulton's words illustrate well.

Handbooks on the drama often suggest that a plot (arrangement of happenings) should have a **rising action,** a **climax,** and a **falling action.** Such a plot may be diagrammed as a pyramid: The tension rises through complications or **crises** to a climax, at which point the climax is the apex, and the tension allegedly slackens as we witness the **dénouement** (unknotting). Shakespeare sometimes used a pyramidal structure, placing his climax neatly in the middle of what seems to us to be the third of five acts. Roughly the first half of *Romeo and Juliet,* for example, shows Romeo winning Juliet, but when in 3.1 he kills her cousin Tybalt, Romeo sets in motion (it is often said) the second half of the play, the losing of Juliet and of his own life. Similarly, in *Julius Caesar* Brutus rises in the first half of the play, reaching his height in 3.1 with the death of Caesar, but later in this scene he gives Mark Antony permission to speak at Caesar's funeral, and thus he sets in motion his own fall, which occupies the second half of the play. In *Macbeth,* the protagonist attains his height in 3.1 ("Thou hast it now: King"), but he soon perceives that he is going downhill:

> I am in blood
> Stepped in so far, that, should I wade no more,
> Returning were as tedious as go o'er.

In *Hamlet,* the protagonist proves to his own satisfaction Claudius's guilt in 3.2, by the play within the play, but almost immediately he begins to worsen his position by failing to kill Claudius when he is an easy target (3.3) and by contaminating himself with the murder of Polonius (3.4).

No law demands such a structure, and looking for the pyramid might lead us to overlook all the crises but the middle one. The Irish poet and playwright William Butler Yeats (1865–1939) once suggestively diagrammed a good plot not as a pyramid but as a line moving diagonally upward, punctuated by several crises. And it has been said that in Samuel Beckett's *Waiting for Godot* (1952), "nothing happens, twice." Perhaps it is sufficient to say that a good plot has its moments of tension, but that the location of these moments will vary with the play. They are the product of **conflict,** but it should be noted that not all conflict produces tension; there is conflict but little tension in a ball game when the home team is ahead 10–0 in the ninth inning.

Regardless of how a plot is diagrammed, the **exposition** is the part that tells the audience what it has to know about the past, the **antecedent action.** Two gossiping servants who tell each other that after a year away in Paris the young master is coming home tomorrow with a new wife are giving the audience the exposition. The exposition in Shakespeare's *The Tempest* is almost ruthlessly direct: Prospero tells his naive daughter, "I should inform thee farther," and for about 150 lines he proceeds to tell her why she is on an almost uninhabited island. Prospero's harangue is punctuated by his daughter's professions of attention, but the Elizabethans (and the Greeks) sometimes tossed out all pretense at dialogue and began with a **prologue,** like the one spoken by the Chorus at the opening of *Romeo and Juliet:*

> Two households, both alike in dignity
> > In fair Verona, where we lay our scene,
> From ancient grudge break to new mutiny,
> > Where civil blood makes civil hands unclean.
> From forth the fatal loins of these two foes
> > A pair of star-crossed lovers take their life. . . .

But the exposition may also extend far into the play, being given in small, explosive revelations.

Exposition has been discussed as though it consists simply of informing the audience about events, but exposition can do much more. It can give us an understanding of the characters who themselves are talking about other characters, it can evoke a mood, and it can generate tension. When we summarize the opening act and treat it as "mere exposition," we are probably losing what is in fact dramatic in it. Moulton, in his analysis of the first two scenes in *Julius Caesar,* does not make the mistake of thinking that the first scenes exist merely to tell the audience certain facts.

Exposition usually includes **foreshadowing.** Details given in the exposition, which we may at first take as mere background, often turn out to be highly relevant to later developments. For instance, in the short first scene of *Macbeth,* the Witches introduce the name of Macbeth, but in such words as "fair is foul" and "when the battle's lost and won" they also give glimpses of what will happen: Macbeth will become foul, and although he will seem to win (he becomes king), he will lose the most important battle. Similarly, during the exposition in the second scene we learn that Macbeth has loyally defeated Cawdor, who betrayed King Duncan, and Macbeth has been given Cawdor's title. Later we will find that, like Cawdor, Macbeth betrays Duncan: In giving us the background about Cawdor, the exposition is also telling us (though we don't know it when we first see or read the play) something about what will happen to Macbeth.

✔ Checklist: Writing about Plot

In writing about an aspect of plot, you may consider one of the following topics:

- ❏ Is the plot improbable? If so, is the play, therefore, weak?
- ❏ Does a scene that might at first glance seem unimportant or even irrelevant serve an important function?
- ❏ If certain actions that could be shown onstage take place offstage, what is the reason? In *Macbeth,* why do you suppose the murder of Duncan takes place offstage, whereas Banquo and Macduff's family are murdered onstage? Why, then, might Shakespeare have preferred not to show us the murder of Duncan? What has he gained? (A good way to approach this sort of question is to think of what your own reaction would be if the action were shown onstage.)
- ❏ If the play has several conflicts—for example, between pairs of lovers or between parents and their children and also between the parents themselves—how are these conflicts related? Are they parallel? Or contrasting?
- ❏ Does the arrangement of scenes have a structure? For instance, do the scenes depict a rise and then a fall?
- ❏ Does the plot seem satisfactorily concluded? Are there any loose threads? If so, is the apparent lack of a complete resolution a weakness in the play?

An analysis of plot, then, will consider the arrangement of the episodes and the effect of juxtapositions, as well as the overall story. A useful essay could be written on the function of one scene. Such an essay may point out, for example, that the long, comparatively slow scene (4.3) in *Macbeth,* in which Malcolm, Macduff, an English doctor, and Ross converse near the palace of the king of England, is not so much a leisurely digression as may at first be thought. After reading it closely, you may decide that it has several functions. For example, it serves to indicate the following:

1. The forces that will eventually overthrow Macbeth are gathering.
2. Even good men must tell lies during Macbeth's reign.
3. Macbeth has the vile qualities that the virtuous Malcolm pretends to have.
4. Macbeth has failed—as the king of England has not—to be a source of health to the realm.

It will take an effort to come to these or other conclusions, but once you have come to such ideas (probably by means of brainstorming and listing; see pages 22–25), the construction of an essay on the function of a scene is fairly simple: An introductory paragraph announces the general topic and thesis—an apparently unnecessary scene will be shown to be functional—and the rest of the essay demonstrates the functions, usually in climactic order if some of the functions are more important than others.

How might you organize such an essay? If you think all of the functions are equally important, perhaps you will organize the material from the most to the least obvious, thereby keeping the reader's attention to the end. If, on the other hand, you believe that although justifications for the scene can be imagined, the scene is nevertheless unsuccessful, say so; announce your view early, consider the alleged functions one by one, and explain your reasons for finding them unconvincing as you take up each point.

Sometimes an analysis of the plot will examine the relationships between the several stories in a play: *A Midsummer Night's Dream* has supernatural lovers, mature royal lovers, young Athenian lovers, a bumpkin who briefly becomes the lover of the fairy queen, and a play (put on by the bumpkins) about legendary lovers. How these are held together and how they define each other and the total play are matters that concern anyone looking at the plot of *A Midsummer Night's Dream.*

Characterization and Motivation

Characterization, or personality, is defined most obviously, as in fiction (see pages 132–35, 173–74), by what the characters do (a stage direction tells us that "Hedda paces up and down, clenching her fists"), by what they say (she asks her husband to draw the curtains), by what others say about them, and by the setting in which they move.

The characters are also defined in part by other characters whom they in some degree resemble. Hamlet, Laertes, and Fortinbras have each lost their fathers, but Hamlet spares the praying King Claudius, whereas Laertes, seeking vengeance on Hamlet for murdering Laertes' father, says he would cut Hamlet's throat in church; Hamlet meditates about the nature of action, but Fortinbras leads the Norwegians in a military campaign and ultimately acquires Denmark. Here is the Shakespeare scholar and literary critic Kenneth Muir (1907–1996) commenting briefly on the way Laertes helps us see Hamlet more precisely. Notice how Muir first offers a generalization, then supports it with details, and finally, drawing a conclusion from the details he has just presented, offers an even more important generalization that effectively closes his paragraph.

> In spite of Hamlet's description of him as "a very noble youth," there is a coarseness of fibre in Laertes which is revealed throughout the play. He has the stock responses of a man of his time and position. He gives his sister copybook advice; he goes to Paris (we are bound to suspect) to tread the primrose path; and after his father's death and again at his sister's grave he shows by the ostentation and "bravery of his grief" that he pretends more than he really feels. He has no difficulty in raising a successful rebellion against Claudius, which suggests that the more popular prince could have done the same. Laertes, indeed, acts more or less in the way that many critics profess to think Hamlet ought to act; and his function in the play is to show precisely the opposite. Although Hamlet himself may envy Laertes' capacity for ruthless action we ought surely to prefer Hamlet's craven scruples.
>
> —*Shakespeare: The Great Tragedies* (1961), 12–13

Muir has not exhausted the topic in this paragraph. If you are familiar with *Hamlet* you may want to think about writing an entire essay comparing Hamlet with Laertes.

Other plays provide examples of such **foils,** or characters who set one another off. Macbeth and Banquo both hear prophecies, but they act and react differently; Brutus is one kind of assassin, Cassius another, and

Casca still another. In *Waiting for Godot,* the two tramps Didi and Gogo are contrasted with Pozzo and his slave, Lucky, the former two suggesting the contemplative life, the latter two the practical or active (and, it turns out, mistaken) life.

Any analysis of a character, then, will have to take into account, in some degree, the other characters who help show what he or she is, who help set forth his or her motivation (grounds for action, inner drives, goals).

Conventions

Artists and their audience have some tacit—even unconscious—agreements. When we watch a motion picture and see an image dissolve and then reappear, we understand that some time has passed. Such a device, unrealistic but widely accepted, is a **convention.** In the theater, we sometimes see on the stage a room, realistic in all details except that it lacks a fourth wall; were that wall in place, we would see it and not the interior of the room. We do not regret the missing wall, and, indeed, we are scarcely aware that we have entered into an agreement to pretend that this strange room is an ordinary room with the usual number of walls. Sometimes the characters in a play speak verse, although outside the theater no human beings speak verse for more than a few moments. Again we accept the device because it allows the author to make a play, and we want a play. In *Hamlet* the characters are understood to be speaking Danish, in *Julius Caesar* Latin, in *A Midsummer Night's Dream* Greek, yet they all speak English for our benefit.

Two other conventions are especially common in older drama: the **soliloquy** and the **aside.** In the former, although a solitary character speaks his or her thoughts aloud, we do not judge him or her to be a lunatic; in the latter, a character speaks in the presence of others but is understood not to be heard by them, or to be heard only by those to whom he or she directs those words.

The soliloquy and the aside strike us as artificial—and they are. But they so strike us only because they are no longer customary. Because we are accustomed to it, we are not bothered by the artificiality of music accompanying dialogue in a motion picture. The conventions of the modern theater are equally artificial but are so customary that we do not notice them. The Elizabethans, who saw a play acted without a break, would probably find strange our assumption that, when we return to the auditorium after a ten-minute intermission, the ensuing action may be supposed to follow immediately the action before the intermission.

Costumes, Gestures, and Settings

The language of a play, broadly conceived, includes the costumes that the characters wear, the gestures that the characters make, and the settings in which the characters move. As Ezra Pound says, "The medium of drama is not words, but persons moving about on a stage using words."

We will begin with **costume,** specifically with Nora Helmer's changes of costume in Ibsen's *A Doll's House.* In the first act, Nora wears ordinary clothing, but in the middle of the second act she puts on "a long, many-colored shawl" when she frantically rehearses her tarantella. The shawl is supposed to be appropriate to the Italian dance, but surely its multitude of colors also expresses Nora's conflicting emotions, her near hysteria, expressed, too, in the fact that "her hair comes loose and falls down over her shoulders," but "she doesn't notice." The shawl and her disheveled hair, then, *speak* to us as clearly as the dialogue does.

In the middle of the third act, after the party and just before the showdown, Nora appears in her "Italian costume," and her husband, Torvald, wears "evening dress" under an open black cloak. She is dressed for a masquerade (her whole life has been a masquerade, it turns out), and Torvald's formal suit and black cloak express the stiffness and the blight that have forced her to present a false front throughout their years of marriage. A little later, after Nora sees that she never really has known her husband for the selfish creature he is, she leaves the stage, and when she returns she is "in an everyday dress." The pretense is over. She is no longer Torvald's "doll." When she finally leaves the stage—leaving the house—she "Wraps her shawl around her." This is not the "many-colored shawl" she used in rehearsing the dance, but the "big, black shawl" she wears when she returns from the dance. The blackness of this shawl signifies the death of her old way of life; Nora is now aware that life is not child's play.

Ibsen did not invent the use of costumes as dramatic language; it goes back to the beginnings of drama, and one has only to think of Hamlet's "inky cloak" or of Lear tearing off his clothing or of the fresh clothing in which Lear is garbed after his madness to see how eloquently costumes can speak. To this may be added the matter of disguises—for example, Edgar's disguise in *King Lear*—which are removed near the end of plays, when the truth is finally revealed and the characters can be fully themselves. In short, the removal of disguises *says* something.

Gestures, too, are a part of the language of drama. Helmer "playfully pulls [Nora's] ear," showing his affection—and his domineering condescension; Nora claps her hands; Mrs. Linde (an old friend of Nora's) "tries to read but seems unable to concentrate"; and so forth. All such gestures clearly and naturally convey states of mind. One of the most delightful and revealing gestures in the play occurs when, in the third act, Helmer demonstrates to Mrs. Linde the ugliness of knitting ("Look here: arms pressed close to the sides") and the elegance of embroidering ("... with your right [hand] you move the needle—like this—in an easy, elongated arc"). None of his remarks throughout the play is quite so revealing of his absurdity as is this silly demonstration.

Drama of the nineteenth and early twentieth centuries (for example, the plays of Ibsen, Anton Chekhov, and Clifford Odets) is often thought to be "realistic," but even a realistic playwright or stage designer selects his or her materials. A realistic **setting** (indication of the locale), then, can say a great deal, can serve as a symbol. Here is Ibsen on nonverbal devices:

> I can do quite a lot by manipulating the prosaic details of my plays so that they become theatrical metaphors and come to mean more than what they are; I have used costume in this way, lighting, scenery, landscape, weather; I have used trivial every-day things like inky fingers and candles; and I have used living figures as symbols of spiritual forces that act upon the hero. Perhaps these things could be brought into the context of a modern realistic play to help me to portray the modern hero and the tragic conflict which I now understand so well.
>
> —Quoted by JOHN NORTHAM, "Ibsen's Search for the Hero."
> In *Ibsen: A Collection of Critical Essays*, ed. R. Fjelde
> (Englewood Cliffs, N.J.: Prentice-Hall, 1965), 99.

In the setting of *Hedda Gabler* (1890), for example, Ibsen uses two suggestive details as more than mere background: Early in the play Hedda is distressed by the sunlight that shines through the opened French doors, a detail that we later see reveals her fear of the processes of nature. More evident and more pervasive is her tendency, when she cannot cope with her present situation, to move to the inner room, at the rear of the stage, in which hangs a picture of her late father. Over and over again in Ibsen we find the realistic setting of a nineteenth-century drawing room, with its heavy draperies and its bulky furniture, conveying his vision of a bourgeois world that oppresses the individual who struggles to affirm other values.

Twentieth-century dramatists are often explicit about the symbolic qualities of the setting. Here is an example from Arthur Miller's description of the set in *Death of a Salesman:*

Before us is the Salesman's house. We are aware of towering, angular shapes behind it, surrounding it on all sides. Only the blue light of the sky falls upon the house and forestage; the surrounding area shows an angry glow of orange. As more light appears, we see a solid vault of apartment houses around the small, fragile-seeming home.

This cannot be skipped or skimmed. These directions and the settings they describe are symbols that give the plays their meaning. Not surprisingly, Miller's play has Marxist overtones. Miller (notice the "solid vault of apartment houses" that menaces the salesman's house) is concerned with social forces that warp the individual. An essay might examine in detail the degree to which the setting contributes to the theme of the play.

Because Shakespeare's plays were performed in broad daylight on a stage that (compared with Ibsen's and Miller's) made little use of scenery, he had to use language to manufacture his settings. But the attentive ear or the mind's eye responds to these settings, too. Early in *King Lear,* when Lear reigns, we hear that we are in a country "With plenteous rivers, and wide-skirted meads"; later, when Lear is stripped of his power, we are in a place where "For many miles about / There's scarce a bush."

In any case, a director must provide some sort of setting—even if only a bare stage—and this setting will be part of the play. A recent production of *Julius Caesar* used great cubes piled on top of each other as the background for the first half of the play, suggesting the pretensions and the littleness of the figures who strutted on the stage. In the second half of the play, when Rome is in the throes of a civil war, the cubes were gone; a shaggy black carpet, darkness at the rear of the stage, and a great net hanging above the actors suggested that they were wretched little creatures groping in blindness. In writing a review of a production, you will want to pay some attention to the function of the setting.

A SAMPLE ESSAY ON SETTING IN DRAMA: "WHAT THE KITCHEN IN *TRIFLES* TELLS US"

One of our students, Margaret Hammer, wrote a short essay on setting in Susan Glaspell's *Trifles.* The play is readily available in most introductory anthologies of literature and the text is also available online, as part of the Electronic Text Center at the University of Virginia; for the link, do a search for Glaspell Trifles University of Virginia. The student has kindly allowed us to use her preliminary notes as well as the final version of her essay.

setting

  physical location: kitchen of farmhouse

  historical time; probably early 20th century—but not especially
        relevant also time of day: Not esp. relevant

only one setting here—but, come to think of it, there is the setting that
        we see, and the setting that we are told about in the dialogue.
        Are they the same??

Certainly wife must have thought that gloomy husband was indeed
        part of her "setting," part of the environment she was stuck
        with.

Can we say that the characters themselves who live here (John Wright,
        and wife Minnie) contribute to the setting? Are part of the
        setting?

Text says: "gloomy" (opening stage direction)

  kitchen messy—but we learn that this must be UNusual

  kitchen cold (much talk about cold, about need for stove)—(GET
  EXAMPLES)

  The coldness is a sort of sign (symbol?) of Mr. Wright.

  Helps to explain motivation for murder.

THESIS : gloomy and physically cold setting reveals character of
        husband, life Mrs. Wright was forced to live.

Now for the final version of the essay that emerged from these notes.

  Margaret Hammer
  Professor Gagosian
  English Composition 100F
  15 April 2011

                    What the Kitchen in *Trifles* Tells Us
        Susan Glaspell's *Trifles* is a one-act play with only one setting.
  It cannot show us, therefore, a strong contrast such as we might
  see in the first two scenes of *Hamlet*, where at the start we encounter soldiers on guard during a cold night, and then, in the second

scene, we are taken into the king's splendid court. Nevertheless, as we read *Trifles* we *do* become aware of a contrast: We see an untidy kitchen, with "dirty" towels (847), bread left unbaked, a cupboard closet with a "mess" of preserves (847), and a table "one half of which is clean, the other half messy" (849), but we hear about a pleasant woman who in happier days sang in the church choir, and who was an excellent quilter. The reader, or the spectator at the play, inevitably concludes that the gloomy and messy kitchen is *not* typical of the woman who worked in it. But what *is* it typical of?

In the first stage direction of the play Glaspell tells us what the spectator sees: "The kitchen in the now abandoned farmhouse of John Wright, a gloomy kitchen, and left without having been put in order . . . " (845). Later we hear that we are near Omaha (845), but nothing much is made of the particular part of the United States where the play is set. What much *is* made of is the fact that the kitchen is cold, that "it never seemed a very cheerful place" (848), and—here we get something crucial—that no "place'd be any cheerfuller for John Wright's being in it" (848). In short, the cold, cheerless, gloomy place is almost a symbol of the farmer, John Wright, and (perhaps surprisingly) the kitchen does not represent the woman who doubtless spent much of her time in it.

As the play progresses, we hear that the Wright house, "down in a hollow," is "a lonesome place" (851), but the central fact—the point repeatedly made in the play—is how cold the kitchen is, and the reader or viewer comes to identify the setting with John Wright himself, a man who was "like a raw wind that gets to the bone" (851).

The mess in the kitchen provides Mrs. Hale and Mrs. Peters with information as to what drove Mrs. Wright to murder her husband, but the "gloomy" kitchen itself provides information about Mr. Wright, and about the miserable life that he forced his wife to live.

[New Page]

Work Cited

Glaspell, Susan. "Trifles." *An Introduction to Literature,* Ed. Sylvan Barnet, William Burto, and William E. Cain. 16th ed. New York: Longman, 2011. 845-54. Print.

The Student's Analysis Analyzed

We think Margaret Hammer has done a very good job explaining the role of the setting in *Trifles*. What are some of the things that make the essay effective?

- The title is engaging, and hints at the thesis (that the setting is important).
- The first paragraph makes a relevant comparison with another work that the student has studied. The comparison is not window-dressing: it makes the important point that a single setting can convey a good deal.
- The second paragraph focuses on the point that the kitchen is cold and cheerless—and that in these respects it is like the farmer, John Wright, and *not* like the woman who worked there.
- The third paragraph pretty much makes the same point as the second, and in fact we would have combined the second and third paragraphs. If each of these paragraphs had been long— say, eight or ten sentences apiece—we might have kept them as two paragraphs, but, given their relative brevity, we think a reader can take both at once.
- The final paragraph briefly and emphatically reiterates the thesis.

📖 SUGGESTIONS FOR FURTHER READING

Among useful reference works are Stanley Hochman, ed., *McGraw-Hill Encyclopedia of World Drama*, 5 vols., 2nd ed. (1984); Phyllis Hartnoll, ed., *The Oxford Companion to the Theatre*, 4th ed. (1983); and Martin Banham, ed., *The Cambridge Guide to Theatre* (1995). See also J. L. Styan, *Modern Drama in Theory and Practice*, 3 vols. (1981). Another helpful resource is *Theatre, Theory, Theatre: The Major Critical Texts from Aristotle and Zeami to Soyinka and Havel*, ed. Daniel Gerould (2000).

Useful introductions to the nature of drama are Eric Bentley, *The Life of the Drama* (1964); J. L. Styan, *The Elements of Drama* (1969); and J. L. Styan, *The English Stage: A History of Drama and Performance* (1996). More specialized studies are Eric Bentley, *The Playwright as Thinker* (1946); C. W. E. Bigsby, *A Critical Introduction to Twentieth-Century American Drama*, 3 vols. (1982–85); Sue Ellen Case, *Feminism and the Theatre* (1984); and Susan Bennett, *Theatre Audiences: A Theory of Pro-*

duction and Reception (1990). We also recommend the essays in *Shakespeare in the Theatre: An Anthology of Criticism*, ed. Stanley Wells (1997).

Recent work includes: Sanford Sternlicht, *A Reader's Guide to Modern American Drama* (2002); *The Cambridge History of British Theatre*, ed. Peter Thomson et al., 3 vols. (2004); Kenneth Pickering, *Key Concepts in Drama and Performance* (2005); Julia A. Walker, *Expressionism and Modernism in the American Theatre: Bodies, Voices, Words* (2005); and *Feminist Futures?: Theatre, Performance, Theory*, ed. Elaine Aston and Geraldine Harris (2006), Martin Meisel, *How Plays Work: Reading and Performance* (2007).

A quarterly journal, *Modern Drama,* publishes articles on American and English drama from 1850 to the present.

✔ Checklist: Getting Ideas for Writing about Drama

The following questions will help you to formulate ideas for an essay on a play.

Plot and Conflict

❏ Does the exposition introduce elements that will be ironically fulfilled? During the exposition do you perceive things differently from the way the characters perceive them?

❏ Are certain happenings or situations recurrent? If so, what significance do you attach to them?

❏ If there is more than one plot, do the plots seem to you to be related? Is one plot clearly the main plot and another plot a subplot, a minor variation on the theme?

❏ Take one scene of special interest and indicate the structure, for example, from stability at the beginning to the introduction of an instability, and then to a new sort of stability or resolution.

❏ Do any scenes strike you as irrelevant?

❏ Are certain scenes so strongly foreshadowed that you anticipated them? If so, did the happenings in these scenes merely fulfill your expectations, or did they also in some way surprise you?

❏ What kinds of conflict are there? One character against another, one group against another, one part of a personality against another part in the same person?

❏ How is the conflict resolved? By an unambiguous triumph of one side or by a triumph that is also in some degree a loss for the triumphant side? Do you find the resolution satisfying, or unsettling, or what? Why?

Character

❑ What are the traits of the chosen character?
❑ A dramatic character is not likely to be thoroughly realistic, a copy of someone we might know. Still, we can ask if the character is consistent and coherent. We can also ask if the character is complex or is, on the other hand, a rather simple representative of some human type.
❑ How is the character defined? Consider what the character says and does and what others say about him or her and do to him or her. Also consider other characters who more or less resemble the character in question, because the similarities—and the differences—may be significant.
❑ How trustworthy are the characters when they characterize themselves? When they characterize others?
❑ Do characters change as the play goes on, or do we simply know them better at the end? If characters change, *why* do they change?
❑ What do you make of the minor characters? Are these characters merely necessary to the plot, or are they foils to other characters? Or do they serve other functions?
❑ If a character is tragic, does the tragedy seem to proceed from a moral flaw, from an intellectual error, from the malice of others, from sheer chance, or from some combination of these?
❑ What are the character's goals? To what degree do you sympathize with them? If a character is comic, do you laugh *with* or *at* the character?
❑ Do you think the characters are adequately motivated?
❑ Is a given character so meditative that you feel he or she is engaged less in a dialogue with others than in a dialogue with the self? If so, do you feel that this character is in large degree a spokesperson for the author, commenting not only on the world of the play but also on the outside world?

Nonverbal Language

❑ If the playwright does not provide full stage directions, try to imagine for a least one scene what gestures and tones might accompany each speech. (The first scene is often a good one to try your hand at.)
❑ What do you make of the setting? Does it help reveal character? Do changes of scene strike you as symbolic? If so, symbolic of what?

✔ Checklist: Getting Ideas for Writing about a Film Based on a Play

Preliminaries

❑   Is the title of the film the same as the title of the play? If not, what is implied?

Dramatic Adaptations

❑   Does the film closely follow its original and neglect the potentialities of the camera? Or does it so revel in cinematic devices that it distorts the original?

❑   Does the film do violence to the theme of the original? Is the film better than its source? Are the additions or omissions due to the medium or to a crude or faulty interpretation of the original?

Plot and Character

❑   Can film deal as effectively with inner action—mental processes— as with external, physical action? In a given film, how is the inner action conveyed? Laurence Olivier used voice-over for sections of Hamlet's soliloquies—that is, we hear Hamlet's voice but his lips do not move.

❑   Are shots and sequences adequately developed, or do they seem jerky? (A shot may be jerky by being extremely brief or at an odd angle; a sequence may be jerky by using discontinuous images or fast cuts. Sometimes, of course, jerkiness may be desirable.) If such cinematic techniques as wipes, dissolves, and slow motion are used, are they meaningful and effective?

❑   Are the characters believable?

❑   Are the actors appropriately cast?

Soundtrack

❑   Does the soundtrack offer more than realistic dialogue? Is the music appropriate and functional? (Music may, among other things, imitate natural sounds, give a sense of locale or of ethnic group, suggest states of mind, provide ironic commentary, or—by repeated melodies—establish connections.) Are volume, tempo, and pitch— whether of music or of such sounds as the wind blowing or cars moving—used to stimulate emotions?

A STUDENT'S ESSAY ON A FILMED VERSION OF A PLAY: "BRANAGH'S FILM OF HAMLET"

What follows is Will Saretta's review, published in a college newspaper, of Kenneth Branagh's film version of *Hamlet* (1996).

Branagh's Film of *Hamlet*

Kenneth Branagh's *Hamlet* opened last night at the Harman Auditorium and will be shown again on Wednesday and Thursday at 7:30 p.m. According to the clock the evening will be long—the film runs for four hours, and in addition there is one ten-minute intermission—but you will enjoy every minute of it.

Well, almost every minute. Curiously, the film begins and ends relatively weakly, but most of what occurs in between is good and much of it is wonderful. The beginning is weak because it is too strong; Bernardo, the sentinel, offstage says "Who's there?" but before he gets a reply he crashes onto the screen and knocks Francisco down. The two soldiers grapple, swords flash in the darkness, and Francisco finally says, "Nay, answer me. Stand and unfold yourself." Presumably Branagh wanted to begin with a bang, but here, as often, more is less. A quieter, less physical opening in which Bernardo, coming on duty, hears a noise and demands that the maker of the noise identify himself, and Francisco, the sentinel on duty, rightly demands that the newcomer identify *himself*, would catch the uneasiness and the mystery that pervades the play much better than does Branagh's showy beginning.

Similarly, at the end of the film, we get too much. For one thing, shots of Fortinbras's army invading Elsinore alternate with shots of the duel between Hamlet and King Claudius's pawn, Laertes, and they merely distract us from what really counts in this scene, the duel itself, which will result in Hamlet's death but also in Halmet's successful completion of his mission to avenge his father. Second, at the very end we get shots of Fortinbras's men pulling down a massive statue of Hamlet Senior, probably influenced by television and newspaper shots of statues of Lenin being pulled down when the Soviet Union was dissolved a few years earlier.

This is ridiculous; *Hamlet* is not a play about the fall of Communism, or about the one form of tyranny replacing another. Shakespeare's *Hamlet* is not about the triumph of Fortinbras. It is about Hamlet's brave and ultimately successful efforts to do what is right, against overwhelming odds, and to offer us the consolation that in a world where death always triumphs there nevertheless is something that can be called nobility.

What, then, is good about the film? First, the film gives us the whole play, whereas almost all productions, whether on the stage or in the movie house, give us drastically abbreviated versions. Although less is often more, when it comes to the text of *Hamlet*, more is better, and we should be grateful to Branagh for letting us hear all of the lines. Second, it is very well performed, with only a few exceptions. Jack Lemmon as Marcellus is pretty bad, but fortunately the part is small. Other big-name actors in small parts—Charlton Heston as the Player King, Robin Williams as Osric, and Billy Crystal as the First Gravedigger—are admirable. But of course the success or failure of any production of *Hamlet* will depend chiefly on the actor who plays Hamlet, and to a considerable degree on the actors who play Claudius, Gertrude, Polonius, Ophelia, Laertes, and Horatio. There isn't space here to comment on all of these roles, but let it be said that Branagh's Prince Hamlet is indeed princely, a man who strikes us as having the ability to become a king, not a wimpy whining figure. When at the end Fortinbras says that if Hamlet had lived to become king, he would "have proved most royal," we believe him. And his adversary, King Claudius, though morally despicable, is a man of great charm and great ability. The two men are indeed "mighty opposites," to use Hamlet's own words.

Branagh's decision to set the play in the late nineteenth century rather than in the Elizabethan period of Shakespeare's day and rather than in our own day contributes to this sense of powerful forces at work. If the play were set in Shakespeare's day, the men would wear tights, and if it were set in our day they would wear suits or trousers and sports jackets and sweaters, but in the film all of the men wear military costumes (black for Hamlet, scarlet for Claudius, white for Laertes) and the women wear ball gowns of the Victorian period. Branagh gives us a world that is closer to our own than would Elizabethan costumes, but yet it is, visually at least, also distant enough to convey a sense of grandeur, which modern dress cannot suggest. Of course *Hamlet* can be done in modern dress, just as *Romeo and Juliet* was done, successfully, in the recent film starring Claire Danes and Leonardo DiCaprio, set in a world that seemed to be Miami Beach, but *Romeo and Juliet* is less concerned with heroism and grandeur than *Hamlet* is, so Branagh probably did well to avoid contemporary costumes.

Although Branagh is faithful to the text, in that he gives us the entire text, he knows that a good film cannot be made merely by recording on film a stage production, and so he gives us handsome shots of landscape, and of rich interiors—for instance, a great mirrored hall—that would be beyond the resources of any theatrical production. I have already said that at the end, when Fortinbras's army swarms over the countryside and then invades the castle we get material that is distracting, indeed irrelevant, but there are also a few other distractions. It is all very well to let us *see* the content of long narrative speeches (for instance, when the Player King talks of the fall of Troy and the death of King Priam and the lament of Queen Hecuba, Branagh shows us these things, with John Gielgud as Priam and Judi Dench as Hecuba, performing in pantomime), but there surely is no need for us to see a naked Hamlet and a naked Ophelia in bed, when Polonius is warning Ophelia that Hamlet's talk of love cannot be trusted. Polonius's warning is not so long or so undramatic that we need to be entertained visually with an invention that finds not a word of support in the text. On the contrary, all of Ophelia's lines suggest that she would not be other than a dutiful young woman, obedient to the morals of the times and to her father's authority. Yet another of Branagh's unfortunate inventions is the prostitute who appears in Polonius's bedroom during Polonius's interview with Reynaldo. A final example of unnecessary spectacle is Hamlet's killing of Claudius: He hurls his rapier the length of the hall, impaling Claudius, and then like some 1930s movie star he swings on the chandelier and drops down on Claudius to finish him off.

But it is wrong to end this review by pointing out faults in Branagh's film of *Hamlet*. There is so much in this film that is exciting, so much that is moving, so much that is ..., well, so much that is *Hamlet* (which is to say that is a great experience), that the film must be recommended without reservation. Go to see it. The four hours will fly.

A postscript: It is good to see that Branagh uses color-blind casting. Voltemand, Fortinbras's Captain, and the messenger who announces Laertes's return are black—the messenger is a black woman—although of course medieval Denmark and Elizabethan England and, for that matter, Victorian England, would not have routinely included blacks. These performers are effective, and it is appropriate that actors of color take their place in the world's greatest play.

✔ Checklist: Topics for Critical Thinking and Writing

❏ Does the writer give adequate evidence to support his favorable comments on the play?
❏ Does he give evidence to support his unfavorable comments?
❏ Given the writer's overall evaluation of the film, do you agree with his strategy of devoting first and last paragraphs to praising the play?
❏ Do you think the writer apportioned his space well, or should he have spent more time on the weaknesses, or more time on the strengths? Why?
❏ Do you find the comments about the late-nineteenth-century settings relevant and thoughtful, or irrelevant and not very perceptive? Explain.
❏ Do you find the *postscript* intrusive? Explain.
❏ If you have seen the film, do you more or less agree with the reviewer? Do you think that the reviewer neglected to make certain points that you would have made in your review?

13

WRITING ABOUT
POETRY

The figure a poem makes. It begins in delight and ends in wisdom. . . . It inclines to the impulse, it assumes direction with the first line laid down, it runs a course of lucky events, and ends in a clarification of life—not necessarily a great clarification, such as sects and cults are founded on, but in a momentary stay against confusion.

—Robert Frost

THE SPEAKER AND THE POET

The **speaker** or **voice** or **mask** or **persona** (Latin for "mask") that speaks a poem is not usually identical with the poet who writes it. The author assumes a role, or counterfeits the speech of a person in a particular situation. Robert Browning (1812–89), for instance, in "My Last Duchess" (1842) invented a Renaissance duke who, in his palace, talks about his first wife and his art collection with an emissary from a count who is negotiating to offer his daughter in marriage to the duke.

In reading a poem, then, the first and most important question to ask yourself is this: Who is speaking? If an audience and a setting are suggested, keep them in mind, too, although they are not always indicated in a poem. Emily Dickinson's "Wild Nights—Wild Nights!" (1861) is the utterance of an impassioned lover, but we need not assume that the beloved is actually in the presence of the lover. In fact, since the second line says, "Were I with Thee," the reader must assume that the person addressed is *not* present. The poem apparently represents a state of mind—a sort of talking to oneself—rather than an address to another person.

Emily Dickinson (1830–86)

WILD NIGHTS—WILD NIGHTS![1]

Wild Nights—Wild Nights,
Were I with Thee
Wild Nights should be
Our luxury!   4

Futile—the Winds
To a Heart in port—
Done with the Compass—
Done with the Chart!   8

Rowing in Eden
—Ah, the Sea!
Might I but moor—Tonight—
In Thee.   12

Questions to Stimulate Ideas about "Wild Nights—Wild Nights!" This chapter will end with a checklist of many questions that you may ask yourself to get ideas for writing about any poem. Here, however, are a few questions about this particular poem, to help you to think about it:

1. How does this poem communicate the speaker's state of mind? For example, in the first stanza (lines 1–4), what—beyond the meaning of the words—is communicated by the repetition of "Wild Nights"? In the last stanza (lines 9–12), what is the tone of "Ah, the Sea!"? (*Tone* means something like "emotional coloring," as when one speaks of a "businesslike tone," a "bitter tone," or an "eager tone.")

2. Paraphrase (put into your own words) the second stanza. What does this stanza communicate about the speaker's love for the beloved? Compare your paraphrase and the original. What does the form of the original sentences (the *omission*, for instance, of the verbs of lines 5 and 6 and of the subject in lines 7 and 8) communicate?

3. Paraphrase the last stanza. How does "Ah, the Sea!" fit into your paraphrase? If you had trouble fitting it in, do you think the poem would be better off without it? If not, why not?

---

[1]Emily Dickinson, "Wild nights—wild nights!" Reprinted by permission of the publishers and the Trustees of Amherst College from *The Poems of Emily Dickinson*, Thomas H. Johnson, ed., Cambridge, Mass: The Belknap Press of Harvard University Press, Copyright © 1951, 1979, 1983 by the President and Fellows of Harvard College.

Although the voice speaking a poem often clearly is *not* the author's, in many other poems the voice does have the ring of the author's own voice, and to make a distinction between speaker and author may at times seem perverse. In fact, some poetry (especially contemporary American poetry) is highly autobiographical. Still, even in autobiographical poems it may be convenient to distinguish between author and speaker. The speaker of a given poem is, for instance, Sylvia Plath (1932–63) in her role as parent, or Sylvia Plath in her role as daughter.

Often we can develop our interpretive skill, and deepen our appreciation of an author, by moving from one of his or her poems to another, and then to still others. Reading the author's range of work and, in either analytical essays or journal or notebook entries, writing about the poems we encounter: these are rewarding activities that enrich our literary experience. For this reason we suggest that you visit an excellent Internet site maintained by the Academy of American Poets. There you will discover hundreds of poems by a great many poets, past and present:<http://www.poets.org/>.

Do a search for Emily Dickinson, and you will find thirty or more of her poems, which you will enjoy reading and which could serve as good points of comparison and contrast with "Wild Nights—Wild Nights!." In particular we recommend: "I'm Nobody! Who are you?" and "The Soul selects her own Society." But read and reread all of the Dickinson poems on this site and choose your own favorites.

The Language of Poetry: Diction and Tone

How is a voice or mask or persona created? From the whole of language, the author selects certain words and grammatical constructions; this selection constitutes the persona's **diction.** It is, then, partly by the diction that we come to know the speaker of a poem. Just as in life there is a difference between people who speak of a *belly button*, a *navel*, and an *umbilicus*, so in poetry there is a difference between speakers who use one word rather than another. Of course, it is also possible that all three of these words are part of a given speaker's vocabulary, but the speaker's choice among the three would depend on the situation; that is, in addressing a child, the speaker would probably use the word *belly button;* in addressing an adult other than a family member or close friend, the speaker might be more likely to use *navel;* and if the speaker is a physician addressing an audience of physicians, he or she might be most likely to use *umbilicus.* This is only to say that the dramatic situation in which one finds oneself helps to define oneself and establish the particular role that one is playing.

Some words are used in virtually all poems: *I, see, and,* and the like. Often the grammatical constructions in which they appear defines the speaker. In Dickinson's "Wild Nights—Wild Nights!," such expressions as "Were I with Thee" and "Might I" indicate an educated speaker.

Speakers have attitudes toward

- themselves,
- their subjects,
- and their audiences,

and, consciously or unconsciously, they choose their words, pitch, and modulation accordingly; all these add up to their tone. In written literature, tone must be detected without the aid of the ear, although it's a good idea to read poetry aloud, trying to find the appropriate tone of voice; that is, the reader must understand by the selection and sequence of words the way the words are meant to be heard—playfully, angrily, confidentially, ironically. The reader must catch what Frost calls "the speaking tone of voice somehow entangled in the words and fastened to the page for the ear of the imagination."

A good way to begin your exploration of a speaker's tone of voice is to read the poem aloud. This oral performance of the poem helps to give us a feeling for the rhythm of the lines, the placement and effect of pauses, the impact of words and images and their relationship to one another. As you read a poem aloud, ask yourself: How does this speaker sound? Another form for the question might be: How would I respond if someone spoke to me in this tone of voice?

We now will examine the tone of voice in a sonnet (see pages 256) by the American poet Edna St. Vincent Millay (1892–1950), a contemporary of Robert Frost and T. S. Eliot. Do your best not only to *see* the words on the page, but to *hear* them.

I, being born a woman and distressed
By all the needs and notions of my kind,
Am urged by your propinquity to find
Your person fair, and feel a certain zest   4
To bear your body's weight upon my breast:
So subtly is the fume of life designed,
To clarify the pulse and cloud the mind,
And leave me once again undone, possessed.   8
Think not for this, however, the poor treason
Of my stout blood against my staggering brain,

I shall remember you with love, or season
My scorn with pity,—let me make it plain: 12
I find this frenzy insufficient reason
For conversation when we meet again.

[1923]

Remember an obvious point: You have the words of the poem in front of you. It is the words of the poem that you respond to, and that you *work with* when you prepare an analytical paper. In a sense you are never at a loss about what to say: There is always something to say because you always have the poet's words to study and reflect upon—their sounds, their meanings and implications.

At the end of the first line, for instance, consider the word "distressed," which is perhaps a surprise in relation to the "I" that opens Millay's poem. The first-person speaker initially seems decisive; "I" at the start of a line or sentence nearly always has an assertive effect, of someone taking a stand or speaking his or her mind. By the end of the first line the "I" of this speaker is "distressed." Though we may wonder: Is she *really*, or is she, instead, ironically aware of the expectation that since she is a "woman," she is biologically destined to be "distressed" in a typical female way?

As we move more deeply into the poem, we'll find that it engages this conflict or tension: The tone shifts, as the speaker is sometimes inside, sometimes outside, the role that society (in the 1920s) expects a woman to occupy. Is the speaker strong and assertive, or not? Does the speaker *sound* assertive, or not?

"Distress" is an intriguing word, which reveals even more about the speaker's tone. It derives from a Latin word for "hinder," and when used as a transitive verb, it means: "to cause strain, anxiety, or suffering to; law: to hold the property of (a person) against the payment of debts; to mar or otherwise treat (an object of fabric, for example) to give the appearance of an antique or of heavy prior use." It also has an older sense: "To constrain or overcome by harassment." Used as a noun, "distress" suggests "anxiety or mental suffering; severe strain resulting from exhaustion or an accident; acute physical discomfort; physical deterioration, as of a highway, caused by hard use over time: pavement distress; the condition of being in need of immediate assistance: a motorist in distress." The resonances, the meanings, of this word lead us into the emotions of the speaker—how she feels, and how she sounds as she describes how she feels.

"Propinquity" (line 3) is another word that plays a key role in evoking the speaker's tone. Here, we might expect a simpler word (e.g., "nearness"), but Millay is seeking the distance, detachment, and irony that the more unusual, Latinate "propinquity" (which derives from the Latin word for "near") offers. Propinquity implies "proximity; nearness; kinship; similarity in nature." It is the kind of word that many of us may need to look up in a dictionary, and the strangeness of the word-choice tells us something about the distinctive tone of voice that Millay is seeking to create, a tone that is ironic and formal about highly charged issues of female identity, erotic feeling, and sexual desire.

One more example—"fume," as in line 6. Fume as a noun means "vapor, gas, or smoke, especially if irritating, harmful, or strong; a strong or acrid odor; a state of resentment or vexation." As a verb, it means "to emit fumes; to rise in fumes; to feel or show resentment or vexation." One might have expected to find here the phrase "scheme of life" or "span of life." And it is this expectation that Millay is working with—or, rather, against. "Fume" may imply "perfume"; both words derive from the Latin word for "smoke." "Fume" is also in an odd relationship to the passive voice "designed": We do not know who or what did the designing, and it sounds a little awkward or (deliberately) obscure to say that a "fume" (vaporous, gassy) is "designed."

Many readers admire Millay's first book, *Renascence and Other Poems*, published in 1917. It includes twenty-three poems, six of which are sonnets. Take a few moments to read and jot down your responses to two of the sonnets: "Thou art not lovelier than lilacs,—no," and "If I should learn, in some quite casual way." How would you describe the speaker's tone of voice in these sonnets, and, furthermore, how would you contrast the tone in them with that in "I being born a woman and distressed"?

Millay's book can be accessed online at Bartleby.com: Great Books Online, in the section on Verse:<http://www.bartleby.com/>.

✍ A RULE FOR WRITERS

Explore both the meanings and the sounds of the words that poets use. Seek to become—as Robert Frost recommended—not only an "eye reader" but also an "ear reader."

We now turn to a poem by Robert Frost and make use of our approach to tone and diction in the planning and development of an analytical paper.

Writing about the Speaker:
Robert Frost's "The Telephone"

Robert Frost once said that:

everything written is as good as it is dramatic. . . . [A poem is] heard as sung or spoken by a person in a scene—in character, in a setting. By whom, where and when is the question. By the dreamer of a better world out in a storm in autumn; by a lover under a window at night.

Suppose, in reading a poem Frost published in 1916, we try to establish "by whom, where, and when" it is spoken. We may not be able to answer all three questions in great detail, but let us see what the poem suggests. As you read it, you'll notice—alerted by the quotation marks—that the poem has *two* speakers; the poem is a tiny drama. The closing quotation marks at the end of line 9 signal to us that the first speech is finished.

Robert Frost (1874–1963)

THE TELEPHONE

"When I was just as far as I could walk
From here today
There was an hour
All still
When leaning with my head against a flower   5
I heard you talk.
Don't say I didn't, for I heard you say—
You spoke from that flower on the window sill—
Do you remember what it was you said?"

"First tell me what it was you thought you heard."   10

"Having found the flower and driven a bee away,
I leaned my head,
And holding by the stalk,
I listened and I thought I caught the word—
What was it? Did you call me by my name   15
Or did you say—
Someone said 'Come'—I heard it as I bowed."

"I may have thought as much, but not aloud."

"Well, so I came."

Suppose we ask:

- Who are these two speakers?
- What is their relationship?
- What's going on between them?
- Where are they?

These questions cannot be answered with absolute certainty, but some answers are more probable than others. For instance, line 8 ("You spoke from that flower on the window sill") suggests that the speakers are in a room, probably of their home—rather than, say, in a railroad station—but we can't say whether they live in a farmhouse or in a village, town, or city, or in an apartment.

We will put the questions (even if they may turn out to be unanswerable) into a more specific form.

Questions

1. One speaker speaks lines 1–9, 11–17, and 19. The other speaks lines 10 and 18. Can you tell the gender of each speaker? Certainly, probably, or not at all? On what do you base your answer?
2. Try to visualize this miniature drama. In line 7 the first speaker says, "Don't say I didn't. . . . " What happens—what do you see in your mind's eye—after line 6 that causes the speaker to say this?
3. Why do you suppose the speaker of lines 10 and 18 says so little? How would you characterize the tone of these two lines? What sort of relationship do you think exists between the two speakers?
4. How would you characterize the tone of lines 11–17? Of the last line of the poem?

If you have not jotted down your responses, consider doing so before reading what follows.

Journal Entries

Given questions somewhat like these, students were asked whether they could identify the speakers by sex, to speculate on their relationship, and then to add whatever they wished to say. One student recorded the following thoughts:

These two people care about each other—maybe husband and wife, or lovers—and a man is doing most of the talking, though I can't prove it. He has walked as far as possible—that is, as far as possible and still get back on the same day—and he seemed to hear the other person call him. He claims that she spoke to him "from that flower on the window sill," and that's why I think the second person is a woman. She's at home, near the window. Somehow I even imagine she was at the window near the kitchen sink, maybe working while he was out on this long walk.

Then she speaks one line; she won't say if she did or didn't speak. She is very cautious or suspicious: "First tell me what it was you thought you heard." Maybe she doesn't want to say something and then have her husband embarrass her by saying, "No, that's not what I thought." Or maybe she just doesn't feel like talking. Then he claims that he heard her speaking through a flower, as though the flower was a telephone, just as though it was hooked up to the flower on the window sill. But at first he won't say what he supposedly heard, or "thought" he heard. Instead, he says that maybe it was someone else: "Someone said 'Come.' " Is he teasing her? Pretending that she may have a rival?

Then she speaks—again just one line, saying, "I may have thought as much, but not aloud." She won't admit that she did think this thought. And then the man says, "Well, so I came." Just like that; short and sweet. No more fancy talk about flowers as telephones. He somehow (through telepathy?) got the message, and so here he is. He seems like a sensitive guy, playful (the stuff about the flowers as telephones) but also he knows when to stop kidding around.

Another student also identified the couple as a man and a woman and thought that this dialogue occurs after a quarrel:

As the poem goes on, we learn that the man wants to be with the woman, but it starts by telling us that he walked as far away from her as he could. He doesn't say why, but I think from the way the woman speaks later in the poem, they had a fight and he walked out. Then, when he stopped to rest, he thought he heard her voice. He really means that he was thinking of her and he was hoping she was thinking of him. So he returns, and he tells her he heard her calling him, but he pretends he heard her call him through a flower on their window sill. He can't admit that he was thinking about her. This seems very realistic to me; when someone feels a bit ashamed, it's sometimes hard to admit that you were wrong, and you want the other person to tell you that things are OK anyhow. And judging from line 7, when he says "Don't say I didn't," it seems that she is going to interrupt him by denying it. She is still angry, or maybe she doesn't want to make up too quickly. But he wants to pretend that *she* called him back. So when he says, "Do you remember what it was you said?" she won't admit that she *was* thinking of him, and she says, "First tell me what it was you thought you heard." She's testing him a little. So he goes on, with the business about flowers as telephones, and he says "someone" called him. He understands that she doesn't want to be pushed into forgiving him, so he backs off. Then she is willing to admit that she did think about him, but still she doesn't quite admit it. She is too proud to say openly that she wants him back but she does say, "I *may* have thought as much. . . . " And then, since they both have preserved their dignity and also have admitted that they care about the other, he can say, "Well, so I came."

Further Thoughts about "The Telephone"

1. In a paragraph or two, *evaluate* one of these two entries recorded by students. Do you think the comments are weak, plausible, or convincing, and *why* do you think so? Can you offer additional supporting evidence, or counterevidence?

2. Two small questions: In a sentence or two, offer a suggestion why in line 11 Frost wrote, "and driven a bee away." After all, the bee plays no role in the poem. Second, in line 17 Frost has the speaker say, "I heard it as I bowed." Of course, "bowed" rhymes with "aloud," but let's assume that the need for a rhyme did not dictate the choice of this word. Do you think "I heard it as I bowed" is better than "I heard it as I waited" or "I heard it as I listened"? Why?

"The Telephone" is included in Frost's book *Mountain Interval*, published in 1920. In one of his earlier books, *North of Boston*, published in 1915, you will find a longer, more emotionally charged and intense poem about a relationship, "Home Burial." Notice the ways in which Frost uses dialogue in this poem, counterpointing it with the speaker's (that is, the narrator's) descriptions of the setting and scene. You can find this poem in the Verse section, under Frost, on Bartleby.com: <http://www.bartleby.com/>.

FIGURATIVE LANGUAGE

Robert Frost said, "Poetry provides the one permissible way of saying one thing and meaning another." This is an exaggeration, but it shrewdly suggests the importance of figurative language—saying one thing in terms of something else. Words have their literal meanings, but they can also be used so that something other than the literal meaning is implied. "My love is a rose" is, literally, nonsense, for a person is not a five-petaled, many-stamened plant with a spiny stem. But the suggestions of rose (at least for Robert Burns [1759–96], the Scottish poet who compared his beloved to a rose in the line, "My love is like a red, red rose") include "delicate beauty," "soft," and "perfumed," and, thus, the word *rose* can be meaningfully applied—figuratively rather than literally—to "my love." The girl is fragrant; her skin is perhaps like a rose in texture and (in some measure) color; she will not keep her beauty long. The poet has communicated his perception very precisely.

People who write about poetry have found it convenient to name the various kinds of figurative language. Just as the student of geology employs such special terms as *kames* and *eskers,* the student of literature employs special terms to name things as accurately as possible. The following paragraphs discuss the most common terms.

In a **simile,** items from different classes are explicitly compared by a connective such as *like, as,* or *than,* or by a verb such as *appears* or *seems.* (If the objects compared are from the same class, for example, "Tokyo is like Los Angeles," no simile is present.)

Float like a butterfly, sting like a bee.

—MUHAMMAD ALI

It is a beauteous evening, calm and free.
The holy time is quiet as a Nun,
Breathless with adoration.

—WILLIAM WORDSWORTH

All of our thoughts will be fairer than doves.

—ELIZABETH BISHOP

Seems he a dove? His feathers are but borrowed.

—SHAKESPEARE

A **metaphor** asserts the identity, without a connective such as *like* or a verb such as *appears,* of terms that are literally incompatible.

Umbrellas clothe the beach in every hue.

—ELIZABETH BISHOP

> The
> whirlwind fife-and-drum of the storm bends the salt
> marsh grass.
>
> —MARIANNE MOORE

In the following poem, Keats's excitement on reading George Chapman's sixteenth-century translation of the Greek poet Homer is communicated first through a metaphor and then through a simile:

John Keats (1795–1821)

ON FIRST LOOKING INTO CHAPMAN'S HOMER

Much have I traveled in the realms of gold,	
And many goodly states and kingdoms seen;	
Round many western islands have I been	
Which bards in fealty° to Apollo hold.	*loyalty* 4
Oft of one wide expanse had I been told,	
That deep-browed Homer ruled as his demesne:°	*property*
Yet did I never breathe its pure serene°	*vast expanse*
Till I heard Chapman speak out loud and bold:	8
Then felt I like some watcher of the skies	
When a new planet swims into his ken;	
Or like stout Cortez when with eagle eyes	
He stared at the Pacific—and all his men	12
Looked at each other with a wild surmise—	
Silent, upon a peak in Darien.°	*in Central America*

We might pause for a moment to take a closer look at Keats's poem. If you write an essay on the figurative language in this sonnet, you will probably discuss the figure involved in asserting that reading is a sort of traveling (it brings us to unfamiliar worlds) and especially that reading brings us to realms of gold: the experience of reading is valuable. "Realms of gold" not only continues and modifies the idea of reading as travel, but in its evocation of El Dorado (an imaginary country in South America, thought to be rich in gold and, therefore, the object of search by Spanish explorers of the Renaissance) it introduces a suggestion of the Renaissance appropriate to a poem about a Renaissance translation of Homer. The figure of traveling is amplified in the next few lines, which assert that the "goodly states and kingdoms" and "western islands" are ruled by poets who owe allegiance to a higher authority, Apollo.

The beginning of the second sentence (line 5) enlarges this already spacious area with its reference to "one wide expanse," and the ruler of this area (unlike the other rulers) is given the dignity of being named. He is Homer, "deep-browed," "deep" suggesting not only his high or perhaps furrowed forehead but the profundity of the thoughts behind the forehead. The speaker continues the idea of books as remote places, but now he also seems to think of this place as more than a rich area; instead of merely saying that until he read Chapman's translation he had not "seen" it (as in line 2) or "been" there (line 3), he says he never breathed its air; that is, the preciousness is not material but ethereal, not gold but something far more exhilarating and essential.

This reference to air leads to the next dominant image, that of the explorer of the illimitable skies (so vast is Homer's world) rather than of the land and sea. But the explorer of the skies is imagined as watching an *oceanic* sky. In hindsight we can see that the link was perhaps forged earlier in line 7, with "serene" (a vast expanse of air *or* water); in any case, there is an unforgettable rightness in the description of the suddenly discovered planet as something that seems to "swim" into one's ken.

After this climactic discovery we return to the Renaissance Spanish explorers (though Balboa, not Cortez, was the first white man to see the Pacific) by means of a simile that compares the speaker's rapture with Cortez's as he gazed at the expanse before him. The writer of an essay on the figurative language in a poem should, in short, call attention to the aptness (or ineptness) of the figures and to the connecting threads that make a meaningful pattern.

Two types of metaphor deserve special mention. In **synecdoche** the whole is replaced by the part, or the part by the whole. For example, "bread," in "Give us this day our daily bread," replaces all sorts of food. In **metonymy** something is named that replaces something closely related to it. For example, James Shirley (1596–1666) names certain objects ("scepter and crown," and "scythe and spade"), using them to replace social classes (powerful people and poor people) to which the objects are related:

> Scepter and crown must tumble down
> And in the dust be equal made
> With the poor crooked scythe and spade.

The attribution of human feelings or characteristics to abstractions or to inanimate objects is called **personification.**

> Memory,
> that exquisite blunderer.
>
> —AMY CLAMPITT

> There's Wrath who has learnt every trick of guerilla warfare,
> The shamming dead, the night-raid, the feinted retreat.
>
> —W. H. AUDEN

> Hope, thou bold taster of delight.
>
> —RICHARD CRASHAW

Crashaw's personification, "Hope, thou bold taster of delight," is also an example of the figure called **apostrophe,** an address to a person or thing not literally listening. Wordsworth begins a sonnet by apostrophizing John Milton:

> Milton, thou shouldst be living at this hour,

and Allen Ginsberg (1926–97) apostrophizes "gusts of wet air":

> Fall on the ground, O great Wetness.

What conclusions can we draw about figurative language?

First, figurative language, with its literally incompatible terms, forces the reader to attend to the connotations (suggestions, associations) rather than to the denotations (dictionary definitions) of one of the terms.

Second, although figurative language is said to differ from ordinary discourse, it is found in ordinary discourse as well as in literature. "It rained cats and dogs," "War is hell," "Don't be a pig," "Mr. Know-all," and other tired figures are part of our daily utterances. But through repeated use, these, and most of the figures we use, have lost whatever impact they once had and are only a shade removed from expressions that, though once figurative, have become literal: the *eye* of a needle, a *branch* office, the *face* of a clock.

Third, good figurative language is usually concrete, condensed, and interesting. The concreteness lends precision and vividness; when Keats writes that he felt "like some watcher of the skies / When a new planet swims into his ken," he more sharply characterizes his feelings than if he had said, "I felt excited." His simile isolates for us a precise kind of excitement, and the metaphoric "swims" vividly brings up the oceanic aspect of the sky. The effect of the second of these three qualities, condensation, can be seen by attempting to paraphrase some of the figures. A paraphrase will commonly use more words than the original, and it will have less impact—as the gradual coming of night usually has less impact on us than a sudden darkening of the sky, or as a prolonged push has less impact than a sudden blow. The third quality, interest, is largely dependent on the previous two; the successful figure often makes us open our eyes wider and take notice. Keats's "deep-browed Homer" arouses our interest in Homer as "thoughtful Homer" or "meditative Homer" does not. Similarly, when William Butler Yeats says

> An aged man is but a paltry thing,
> A tattered coat upon a stick, unless
> Soul clap its hands and sing, and louder sing
> For every tatter in its mortal dress,

the metaphoric identification of an old man with a scarecrow jolts us out of all our usual unthinking attitudes about old men as kind, happy folk who are content to have passed from youth into age.

Preparing to Write about Figurative Language

As you prepare to write about figurative language, consider

1. the areas from which the images are drawn (for instance, religion, exploration, science, commerce, nature);
2. the kinds of images (for instance, similes, metaphors, overstatements, understatements);
3. any shifts from one type of imagery to another (for instance, from similes to metaphors, or from abundant figures of speech to literal speech) and the effects that the shifts arouse in you; and
4. the location of the images (perhaps they are concentrated at the beginning of the poem or in the middle or at the end) and if parts of the poem are richer in images than other parts, consider their effect on you.

If you underline or highlight images in your text or in a copy of the poem that you have written or typed, you will be able to see patterns, and you can indicate the connections by drawing arrows or by making lists of related images. Thinking about these patterns, you will find ideas arising about the ways in which the poem makes its effect.

Imagery and Symbolism

When we read *rose*, we may call to mind a picture of a rose, or perhaps we are reminded of the odor or texture of a rose. Whatever in a poem appeals to any of our senses (including sensations of heat as well as of sight, smell, taste, touch, sound) is an image. In short, images are the sensory content of a work, whether literal or figurative. When a poet says "My rose" and is speaking about a rose, we have no figure of speech—though we still have an image. If, however, "My rose" is a shortened form of "My love is a rose," some would say that the poet is using a metaphor; but others would say that because the first term is omitted ("My love is"), the rose is a **symbol.** A poem about the transience of a rose might compel the reader to feel that the transience of female beauty is the larger theme even though it is never explicitly stated.

Some symbols are **conventional symbols**—people have agreed to accept them as standing for something other than their literal meanings: A poem about the cross is probably about Christianity; similarly, the rose has long been a symbol for love. In Virginia Woolf's novel *Mrs. Dalloway* (1925), the husband communicates his love by proffering this conventional symbol: "He was holding out flowers—roses, red and white roses. (But he could not bring himself to say he loved her; not in so many words.)" Objects that are not conventional symbols, however, may also give rise to rich, multiple, indefinable associations. The following poem uses the traditional symbol of the rose, but in a nontraditional way.

William Blake (1757–1827)

THE SICK ROSE

O rose, thou art sick.
The invisible worm
That flies in the night,
In the howling storm,
Has found out thy bed
Of crimson joy,
And his dark secret love
Does thy life destroy.

A reader might argue that the worm is invisible (line 2) merely because it is hidden within the rose, but an "invisible worm / That flies in the night" is more than a long, slender, soft-bodied, creeping animal, and a rose that has, or is, a "bed / Of crimson joy" is more than a gardener's rose.

Blake's worm and rose suggest things beyond themselves—a stranger, more vibrant world than the world we are usually aware of. They are symbolic, although readers will doubtless differ in their interpretations. Perhaps we find ourselves half thinking, for example, that the worm is male, the rose female, and that the poem is about the violation of virginity. Or that the poem is about the destruction of beauty: Woman's beauty, rooted in joy, is destroyed by a power that feeds on her. But these interpretations are not fully satisfying: The poem presents a worm and a rose, yet it is not merely about a worm and a rose. These references resonate, stimulating our thoughts toward something else, but the something else is elusive. This is not to say, however, that symbols mean whatever any reader says they mean. A reader could scarcely support an interpretation arguing that the poem is about the need to love all aspects of nature. Not all interpretations are equally valid; it's the writer's job to offer a reasonably persuasive interpretation.

A **symbol,** then, is an image so loaded with significance that it is not simply literal, and it does not simply stand for something else; it is both itself *and* something else that it richly suggests, a manifestation of something too complex or too elusive to be otherwise revealed. Blake's poem is about a blighted rose and at the same time about much more.

STRUCTURE

The arrangement of the parts, the organization of the entire poem, is its **structure.** Sometimes a poem is divided into blocks of, say, four lines each, but even if the poem is printed as a solid block, it probably has some principle of organization—for example, from sorrow in the first two lines to joy in the next two, or from a question in the first three lines to an answer in the last line.

Consider this short poem by an English poet of the seventeenth century.

Robert Herrick (1591–1674)

UPON JULIA'S CLOTHES

Whenas in silk my Julia goes,
Then, then (methinks) how sweetly flows
That liquefaction of her clothes.
Next, when I cast mine eyes, and see
That brave° vibration, each way free,   *splendid*
O, how that glittering taketh me.

Annotating and Thinking about a Poem

David Thurston, a student, began thinking about this poem by copying it, double-spaced, and by making the following notes on his copy.

Upon Julia's Clothes

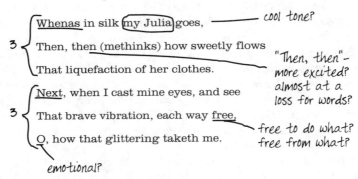

Whenas in silk (my Julia) goes,   ——— *cool tone?*

3   Then, then (methinks) how sweetly flows

That liquefaction of her clothes.   *"Then, then"– more excited? almost at a loss for words?*

Next, when I cast mine eyes, and see

3   That brave vibration, each way free,   *free to do what? free from what?*

O, how that glittering taketh me.

emotional?

The student got further ideas by thinking about several of the questions that, at the end of this chapter (pages 264–68), we suggest you ask yourself while rereading a poem. Among the questions are these:

Does the poem proceed in a straightforward way, or at some point or points does the speaker reverse course, altering his or her tone or perception?

What is the effect on you of the form?

With such questions in mind, the student was stimulated to see if Herrick's poem has a reversal or change and, if so, how it is related to the structure. After rereading the poem several times, thinking about it in the light of these questions and perhaps others, he produced the following notes:

Two stanzas, each of three lines, with the same structure
Basic structure of 1st stanza: When X (one line), then Y (two lines)
Basic structure of second stanza: Next (one line), then Z (two lines)

When he marked the text after reading the poem a few times, he noticed that the last line—an exclamation of delight ("O, how that glittering taketh me")—is much more personal than the rest of the poem. A little further thought enabled him to refine this last perception:

Although the pattern of stanzas is repeated, the somewhat analytic, detached tone of the beginning ("Whenas," "Then," "Next") changes to an open, enthusiastic confession of delight in what the poet sees.

Further thinking led to this:

> Although the title is "Upon Julia's Clothes," and the first five lines describe Julia's silken dress, the poem finally is not only about Julia's clothing but about the effect of Julia (moving in silk that liquefies or seems to become a liquid) on the poet.

This is a nice observation, but when the student looked again at the poem the next day and started to write about it, he found that he was able to refine his observation.

> Even at the beginning, the speaker is not entirely detached, for he speaks of "*my* Julia."

In writing about Herrick's "Upon Julia's Clothes," David Thurston reported, the thoughts did not come quickly or neatly. After two or three thoughts, he started to write. Only after drafting a paragraph and rereading the poem did he notice that the personal element appears not only in the last line ("taketh *me*") but even in the first line ("*my* Julia"). For almost all of us, the way to get to a good final essay is to read, to think, to jot down ideas, to write a draft, and to revise and revise again. Having gone through such processes, the student came up with this excellent essay.

The Student's Essay: "Herrick's Julia, Julia's Herrick"

By the way, the student did not hit on the final version of his title ("Herrick's Julia, Julia's Herrick") until shortly before he typed his final version. His preliminary title was

> Structure and Personality in
> Herrick's "Upon Julia's Clothes"

That is a bit heavy-handed, but at least it is focused, as opposed to such an uninformative title as "On a Poem." He soon revised his tentative title to

> Julia, Julia's Clothing, and Julia's Poet

That is a good title: It is neat, and it is appropriate; it moves (as the poem and the essay do) from Julia and her clothing to the poet. It does not tell the reader exactly what the essay will be about, and three uses of Julia may be one too many, but it does stimulate the reader's interest. The essayist's final title, however, is even better:

Herrick's Julia, Julia's Herrick

Again, it is neat (the balanced structure, and structure is part of the student's topic), less repetitive, and it moves (as the poem itself moves) from Julia to the poet.

David Thurston
Professor Wong
English 1H
15 February 2011

Herrick's Julia, Julia's Herrick

Robert Herrick's "Upon Julia's Clothes" begins as a description of Julia's clothing and ends as an expression of the poet's response not just to Julia's clothing but to Julia herself. Despite the apparently objective or detached tone of the first stanza and the first two lines of the second stanza, the poem finally conveys a strong sense of the speaker's excitement.

The first stanza seems to say, "Whenas" X (one line), "Then" Y (two lines). The second stanza repeats this basic structure of one line of assertion and two lines describing the consequence: "Next" (one line), "then" (two lines). But the logic or coolness of "Whenas," "Then," and "Next," and of such rather scientific language as *liquefaction* (a more technical-sounding word than "melting") and *vibration* is undercut by the breathlessness or excitement of "Then, then" (that is very different from a simple "Then"). It is also worth mentioning that although there is a personal rather than a fully detached note even in the first line, in "*my* Julia," this expression scarcely reveals much feeling. In fact, it reveals a touch of male chauvinism, a suggestion that the woman is a possession of the speaker's. Not until the last line does the speaker reveal that, far from Julia being his possession, he is possessed by Julia: "O, how that glittering taketh me." If he begins coolly, objectively, and somewhat complacently and uses a structure that suggests a somewhat detached mind, in the exclamatory "O" he nevertheless at last confesses (to our delight) that he is enraptured by Julia.

Other things might be said about this poem. For instance, the writer says nothing about the changes in the meter and their possible value in the poem. Nor does he say anything about the sounds of any of the words (he might have commented on the long vowels in "sweetly flows" and shown how the effect would have been different if instead of "sweetly flows" Herrick had written "swiftly flits"). But such topics might be material for another essay. Furthermore, another reader might have found the poem less charming—even offensive in its exclusive concern with Julia's appearance and its utter neglect of her mind. Still, this essay is, in itself, an interesting and perceptive discussion of the way the poet used a repeated structure to set forth a miniature drama in which observation is, at the end, replaced by emotion.

Some Kinds of Structure

Repetitive Structure

Although every poem has its own structure, if we stand back from a given poem we may see that the structure is one of three common sorts: repetitive, narrative, or logical. **Repetitive structure** is especially common in lyrics that are sung, where a single state of mind is repeated from stanza to stanza so that the stanzas are pretty much interchangeable. Here is a passage from Walt Whitman's "By Blue Ontario's Shore" (1881) that has a repetitive structure:

> I will confront these shows of the day and night,
> I will know if I am to be less than they,
> I will see if I am not as majestic as they,
> I will see if I am not as subtle and real as they,
> I will see if I am to be less generous than they.

Narrative Structure

In a poem with a **narrative structure** (we are not talking about "narrative poems," poems that tell a story, such as Homer's *Odyssey* or Coleridge's *Rime of the Ancient Mariner*, but about a kind of lyric poem) there is a sense of advance. Blake's "The Sick Rose" (page 236) is an example. What comes later in the poem could not come earlier. The poem seems to get somewhere, to settle down to an end. A lyric in which the speaker at first grieves and then derives comfort from the thought that at least he was once in love similarly has a narrative structure. Here is a short poem with a narrative structure.

William Wordsworth (1770–1850)

A SLUMBER DID MY SPIRIT SEAL

> A slumber did my spirit seal;
> I had no human fears:
> She seemed a thing that could not feel
> The touch of earthly years.

> No motion has she now, no force;
> She neither hears nor sees;
> Rolled round in earth's diurnal° course,   *daily*
> With rocks, and stones, and trees.

In the first stanza the (first four lines) *did* and *seemed* establish the time as the past; in the second stanza *now* establishes the time as the present. In the blank space between the stanzas the woman has died. If we were required to summarize the stanzas very briefly, we might for the first stanza come up with "I thought she could not die," and for the second, "She is dead." But the poem is not so much about the woman's life and death as about the speaker's response to her life and death.

Logical Structure

The third kind of structure commonly found is **logical structure.** The speaker argues a case and comes to some sort of conclusion. Probably the most famous example of a poem that moves to a resolution through an argument is Andrew Marvell's "To His Coy Mistress" (1681). The speaker begins, "Had we but world enough, and time" (that is, "if"), and for twenty lines he sets forth what he might do. At the twenty-first line he says, "But," and he indicates that the preceding twenty lines, in the subjunctive, are not a description of a real condition. The real condition (as he sees it) is that Time oppresses us, and he sets this idea forth in lines 21–32. In line 33 he begins his conclusion, "Now therefore," clinching it in line 45 with "Thus." Here is another example of a poem with a logical structure.

> *John Donne (1573–1631)*
> THE FLEA
>
> Mark but this flea, and mark in this
> How little that which thou deniest me is:
> It sucked me first, and now sucks thee,
> And in this flea our two bloods mingled be.
> Thou knowest that this cannot be said   5
> A sin, nor shame, nor loss of maidenhead;
>   Yet this enjoys before it woo,
>   And pampered swells with one blood made of two,
>   And this, alas, is more than we would do.
>
> O stay, Three lives in one flea spare,   10
> Where we almost, yea, more than married are;

This flea is you and I, and this
Our marriage bed and marriage temple is.
Though parents grudge, and you, we're met
And cloistered in these living walls of jet.   15
    Though use° make you apt to kill me,   *custom*
    Let not to that, self-murder added be,
    And sacrilege, three sins in killing three.

Cruel and sudden! Hast thou since
Purpled thy nail in blood of innocence?   20
Wherein could this flea guilty be,
Except in that drop which it sucked from thee?
Yet thou triumph'st and saist that thou
Find'st not thyself, nor me, the weaker now.
    'Tis true. Then learn how false fears be;   25
    Just so much honor, when thou yield'st to me,
    Will waste, as this flea's death took life from thee.

The speaker is a lover who begins by assuring his mistress that sexual intercourse is of no more serious consequence than a flea bite. Between the first and second stanzas the woman has apparently threatened to kill the flea, moving the lover to say in line 10, "O stay, Three lives in one flea spare." In this second stanza he reverses his argument, now insisting on the importance of the flea, arguing that since it has bitten both man and woman it holds some of their lives, as well as its own. Unpersuaded of its importance, the woman kills the flea between the second and third stanzas; and the speaker uses her action to reinforce his initial position when he says, beginning in line 25, that the death of the flea has no serious consequences and her yielding to him will have no worse consequences.

One of the best known and most beloved of older anthologies of poetry is *The Golden Treasury of the Best Songs and Lyrical Poems in the English Language*, edited by the British critic and poet Francis Turner Palgrave (1824–97), published in 1861 and revised and expanded in later editions. Robert Frost said that *The Golden Treasury* was his favorite book, and he added that, after many readings of it over many years, he had come to know all of its poems by heart. You might enjoy perusing this volume for its own sake but also as an opportunity to look for and study poems that use a repetitive, narrative, or logical structure. *The Golden Treasury* can be found online at several sites, including Bartleby.com, under Verse (Anthologies):<http://www.bartleby.com/verse/>.

Verbal Irony

Among the most common devices in poems with logical structure (although this device is employed elsewhere, too) is **verbal irony.** The speaker's words mean more or less the opposite of what they seem to say. Sometimes it takes the form of **understatement,** as when Andrew Marvell's speaker in "To His Coy Mistress" remarks with cautious wryness, "The grave's a fine and private place / But none, I think, do there embrace," or when Sylvia Plath sees an intended suicide as "the big strip tease." One special form of understatement, *litotes*, uses a negative to imply the opposite. Thus, "He's not very smart" does not mean exactly what it says—that he is not very smart, is merely of average intelligence. It means that he is the opposite of "very smart" (it means "He is stupid"). Sometimes verbal irony takes the form of **overstatement,** or **hyperbole,** as when John Donne's speaker says that in the flea he and the lady are "more than married." Intensely emotional contemporary poems, such as those of Plath, often use irony to undercut—and thus make acceptable—the emotion.

Paradox

Another common device in poems with a logical structure is **paradox,** the assertion of an apparent contradiction, as in "This flea is you and I." But again it must be emphasized that irony and paradox are not limited to poems with a logical structure. In "Auld Lang Syne," there is the paradox that the remembrance of joy evokes sadness, and there is understatement in "we've wandered mony a weary fitt," which stands (roughly) for something much bigger, such as "we have had many painful experiences."

EXPLICATION

In Chapter 4, which included a discussion of Langston Hughes's "Harlem" and also an Explication Checklist (page 50), we saw that an explication is a line-by-line commentary on what is going on in a text. (*Explication* literally means "unfolding," or "spreading out.") Although your explication will for the most part move steadily from the beginning to the end of the selection, try to avoid writing along these lines (or, one might say, along this one line): "In line one . . . , In the second line . . . , In the third line . . . ,"; that is, don't hesitate to write such things as

> The poem begins . . . In the next line . . . The speaker immediately adds
> . . . She then introduces . . . The next stanza begins by saying . . .

An explication is not concerned with the writer's life or times, and it is not a paraphrase (a rewording)—although it may include paraphrase if a passage in the original seems unclear because of an unusual word or an unfamiliar expression. On the whole, however, an explication goes beyond paraphrase, seeking to make explicit what the reader perceives as implicit in the work. To this end it calls attention, as it proceeds, to the implications of

- words, especially of their tone (repetitions, shifts in levels of diction, for instance, from colloquial to formal language, or from ordinary language to technical language);
- figures of speech;
- length of sentences (since an exceptionally short or exceptionally long sentence conveys a particular effect);
- sound effects, such as alliteration and rhyme; and
- structure (for instance, a question in one stanza, and the answer in the next, or a generalization and then a particularization, or a contrast of some sort).

An explication makes *explicit* what is implicit, especially in the words. It sets forth the reader's sense of the precise meaning of the work, word by word, or phrase by phrase, or line by line.

A Sample Explication of Yeats's "The Balloon of the Mind"

Consider this short poem (published in 1917) by William Butler Yeats (1865–1939). The "balloon" in the poem is a dirigible, a blimp.

William Butler Yeats

THE BALLOON OF THE MIND

Hands, do what you're bid:
Bring the balloon of the mind
That bellies and drags in the wind
Into its narrow shed.

Annotations and Journal Entries

A student began thinking about the poem by copying it, double-spaced. Then she jotted down her first thoughts.

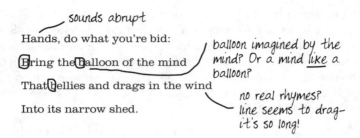

sounds abrupt

Hands, do what you're bid:

Bring the Balloon of the mind   *balloon imagined by the mind? Or a mind like a balloon?*

That Bellies and drags in the wind

Into its narrow shed.   *no real rhymes? line seems to drag— it's so long!*

Later the student wrote some notes in a journal.

I'm still puzzled about the meaning of the words, "The balloon of the mind." Does "balloon of the mind" mean a balloon that belongs to the mind, sort of like "a disease of the heart"? If so, it means a balloon that the mind *has*, a balloon that the mind possesses, I guess by imagining it. Or does it mean that the mind is *like* a balloon, as when you say, "He's a pig of a man," meaning he is like a pig, he is a pig? Can it mean both? What's a balloon that the mind imagines? Something like dreams of fame, wealth? Castles in Spain?

Is Yeats saying that the "hands" have to work hard to make dreams a reality? Maybe. But maybe the idea really is that the mind is *like* a balloon—hard to keep under control, floating around. Very hard to keep the mind on the job. If the mind is like a balloon, it's hard to get it into the hangar (shed).

"Bellies." Is there such a verb? In this poem it seems to mean something like "puffs out" or "flops around in the wind." Just checked *The American Heritage Dictionary*, and it says "belly" can be a verb, "to swell out," "to bulge." Well, you learn something every day.

A later entry:

OK; I think the poem is about a writer trying to keep his balloon-like mind under control, trying to keep it working at the job of writing something, maybe writing something with the "clarity, unity, and coherence" I keep hearing about in this course.

Here is the student's final version of the explication.

Yeats's "Balloon of the Mind" is about writing poetry, specifically about the difficulty of getting one's floating thoughts down in lines on the page. The first line, a short, stern, heavily stressed command to the speaker's hands, perhaps implies by its severe or impatient tone that these hands will be disobedient or inept or careless if not watched closely: The poor bumbling body so often fails to achieve the goals of the mind. The bluntness of the command in the first line is emphasized by the fact that all the subsequent lines have more syllables. Furthermore, the first line is a grammatically complete sentence, whereas the thought of line 2 spills over into the next lines, implying the difficulty of fitting ideas into confining spaces, that is, of getting one's thoughts into order, especially into a coherent poem.

Lines 2 and 3 amplify the metaphor already stated in the title (the product of the mind is an airy but unwieldy balloon), and they also contain a second command, "Bring." Alliteration ties this command "*B*ring" to the earlier "*b*id"; it also ties both of these verbs to their object, "*b*alloon," and to the verb that most effectively describes the balloon, "*b*ellies." In comparison with the abrupt first line of the poem, lines 2 and 3 themselves seem almost swollen, bellying and dragging, an effect aided by using adjacent unstressed syllables ("of the," "[bell]ies and," "in the") and by using an eye rhyme ("mind" and "wind") rather than an exact rhyme. And then comes the short last line: Almost before we could expect it, the cumbersome balloon—here the idea that is to be packed into the stanza—is successfully lodged in its "narrow shed." Aside from the relatively colorless "into," the only words of more than one syllable in the poem are "balloon," "bellies," and "narrow," and all three emphasize the difficulty of the task. But after "narrow"—the word itself almost looks long and narrow, in this context like a hangar—we get the simplicity of the monosyllable "shed." The difficult job is done, the thought is safely packed away, the poem is completed—but again with an off rhyme ("bid" and "shed"), for neatness can go only so far when hands and mind and a balloon are involved.

The reader of an explication needs to see the text, and if the explicated text is short, it is advisable to quote it all. Remember, your imagined audience probably consists of your classmates; even if they have already read the work you are explicating, they have not memorized it, and so you helpfully remind them of the work by quoting it.

- You may quote the entire text at the outset, or
- you may quote the first unit (for example, a stanza), then explicate that unit, and then quote the next unit, and so on.
- And if the poem or passage of prose is longer than, say, six lines, it is advisable to number each line at the right for easy reference.

Reminder: For an Explication Checklist, see page 50.

The Internet site Bartleby.com, in its Verse listings, includes three volumes of poems by William Butler Yeats: *The Wind Among the Reeds* (1899), *Responsibilities and Other Poems* (1916), and *The Wild Swans at Coole* (1919). For further work in explication, and in comparison and contrast, you might turn to these volumes, for reading and browsing. In particular we recommend "To a Child Dancing in the Wind," in *Responsibilities*, and "The Wild Swans at Coole." <http://www.bartleby.com/verse/>.

RHYTHM AND VERSIFICATION: A GLOSSARY FOR REFERENCE

Rhythm

Rhythm (most simply, in English poetry, **stresses** at regular intervals) has a power of its own. A highly pronounced rhythm is common in such forms of poetry as charms, college yells, and lullabies; all are aimed at inducing a special effect magically. It is not surprising that *carmen,* the Latin word for poem or song, is also the Latin word for charm and the word from which our word *charm* is derived.

In much poetry, rhythm is only half heard, but its presence is suggested by the way poetry is printed. Prose (from Latin *prorsus,* "forward," "straight on") keeps running across the paper until the right-hand margin is reached; then, merely because the paper has given out, the writer or printer starts again at the left, with a small letter. But verse (Latin *versus,* "a turning") often ends well short of the right-hand margin. The next line begins at the left—usually with a capital—not because paper has run out but because the rhythmic pattern begins again. Lines of poetry are continually reminding us that they have a pattern.

Note that a mechanical, unvarying rhythm may be good to put the baby to sleep, but it can be deadly to readers who want to stay awake. Poets vary their rhythm according to their purposes; they ought not to be so regular that they are (in W. H. Auden's words) "accentual pests." In competent hands, rhythm contributes to meaning; it says something.

Ezra Pound has a relevant comment: "Rhythm *must* have meaning. It can't be merely a careless dash off, with no grip and no real hold to the words and sense, a tumty tum tumty tum tum ta."

Consider this description of Hell from John Milton's *Paradise Lost* (1667) (stressed syllables are marked by ´; unstressed syllables by ˘):

Rócks, cáves, lákes, féns, bógs, déns, aňd shádes ŏf déath.

The normal line in *Paradise Lost* is written in iambic feet—alternate unstressed and stressed syllables—but in this line Milton immediately follows one heavy stress with another, helping to communicate the "meaning"—the oppressive monotony of Hell. As a second example, consider the function of the rhythm in two lines by Alexander Pope (1688–1744):

Wheň Ájaž strivés somĕ rock's vást weigʹht to ˘thrów.
Tʹhe liňe tóo lábors, aňd tʹhe wórds móve slów.

The stressed syllables do not merely alternate with the unstressed ones; rather, the great weight of the rock is suggested by three consecutive stressed words, "rock's vast weight," and the great effort involved in moving it is suggested by another three consecutive stresses, "line too labors," and by yet another three, "words move slow." Note, also, the abundant pauses within the lines. In the first line, unless one's speech is slovenly, one must pause at least slightly after *Ajax, strives, rock's, vast, weight,* and *throw.* The grating sounds in *Ajax* and *rock's* do their work, too, and so do the explosive *t*'s. When Pope wishes to suggest lightness, he reverses his procedure, and he groups *un*stressed syllables:

Not so, when swift Camilla scours the plain,
Flíes o'eʹr th' ˘unbéndiňg córn, aňd skíms aʹlong thĕ máin.

This last line has twelve syllables and is, thus, longer than the line about Ajax, but the addition of *along* helps communicate lightness and swiftness because in this line neither syllable of *along* is strongly stressed. If *along* is omitted, the line still makes grammatical sense and becomes more regular, but it also becomes less imitative of lightness.

The regularity of a line may be meaningful, too. Shakespeare begins a sonnet thus:

Wheň Í dŏ cóunt tʹhe clóck tʹhat télls thĕ timé.

This line about a mechanism runs with appropriate regularity. (It is worth noting that "*count* the *c*lock" and "*t*ells the *t*ime" emphasize the regularity by the repetition of sounds and syntax.) But notice what Shakespeare does in the middle of the next line:

And see the brave day sunk in hideous night.

The three heavy stresses, on "brave day sunk," are oppressive; one might almost say they hang weights on the day, sinking it in the night.

The technical vocabulary of **prosody** (the study of the principles of verse structure, including meter, rhyme and other sound effects, and stanzaic patterns) is large. An understanding of these terms will not turn anyone into a poet, but it will enable you to write about some aspects of poetry more efficiently. The following are the chief terms of prosody.

Meter

Most poetry written in English has a pattern of stressed (**accented**) sounds, and this pattern is the **meter** (from the Greek word for "measure"). Strictly speaking, we really should not talk of "unstressed" or "unaccented" syllables, since to utter a syllable—however lightly—is to give it some stress. It is really a matter of *relative* stress, but the fact is that *unstressed* and *unaccented* are parts of the established terminology of versification.

In a line of poetry, the **foot** is the basic unit of measurement. It is on rare occasions a single stressed syllable; generally a foot consists of two or three syllables, one of which is stressed. The repetition of feet, then, produces a pattern of stresses throughout the poem.

Two cautions:

1. A poem will seldom contain only one kind of foot throughout; significant variations usually occur, but one kind of foot is dominant.

2. In reading a poem, we chiefly pay attention to the sense, not to a presupposed metrical pattern. By paying attention to the sense, we often find (reading aloud is a great help) that the stress falls on a word that according to the metrical pattern would be unstressed. Or a word that according to the pattern would be stressed may be seen to be unstressed. Furthermore by reading for sense that not all stresses are equally heavy; some are almost as light as unstressed syllables we discover. To repeat: We read for sense, allowing the syntax to help indicate the stresses.

Metrical Feet   The most common feet in English poetry are the six listed here.

Iamb (adjective: **iambic**): one unstressed syllable followed by one stressed syllable. The iamb, said to be the most common pattern in English speech, is surely the most common in English poetry. The following example has four iambic feet:

Mӳ heárt iš líke ă síng -ĭng bírd.

—CHRISTINA ROSSETTI

Trochee (trochaic): one stressed syllable followed by one unstressed.

Wé wĕre vérӳ tíreď, wé wĕre vérӳ mérrӳ

—EDNA ST. VINCENT MILLAY

Anapest (anapestic): two unstressed syllables followed by one stressed.

Thĕre ăre mán -y whŏ sáy thăt ă dóg hăs hĭs dáy.

—DYLAN THOMAS

Dactyl (dactylic): one stressed syllable followed by two unstressed. This trisyllabic foot, like the anapest, is common in light verse or verse suggesting joy, but its use is not limited to such material, as Longfellow's long narrative poem *Evangeline* (1847) shows. Thomas Hood's sentimental "The Bridge of Sighs" begins:

Táke hĕr up ténderlӳ.

Spondee (spondaic): two stress syllables; most often used as substitute for an iamb or trochee.

Smárt láď, tŏ slíp betímes awáy.

—A. E. HOUSMAN

Pyrrhic: two unstressed syllables; it is often not considered a legitimate foot in English.

Metrical Lines A metrical line consists of one or more feet and is named for the number of feet in it. The following names are used:

> **monometer:** one foot   **pentameter:** five feet
>
> **dimeter:** two feet   **hexameter:** six feet
>
> **trimeter:** three feet   **heptameter:** seven feet
>
> **tetrameter:** four feet

A line is scanned for the kind and number of feet in it, and the **scansion** tells you if it is, say, anapestic trimeter (three anapests):

> As Ĭ cáme tŏ thĕ edǵe ŏf thĕ woóds.
>
> —ROBERT FROST

Or, in another example, iambic pentameter:

> Thĕ súmmĕr thúndĕr, lĭke ă woódĕn béll
>
> —LOUISE BOGAN

A line ending with a stress has a **masculine ending;** a line ending with an extra unstressed syllable has a **feminine ending.** The **caesura** (usually indicated by the symbol //) is a slight pause within the line. It need not be indicated by punctuation (notice the fourth and fifth lines in the following quotation), and it does not affect the metrical count:

> Awake, my St. John!//leave all meaner things
> To low ambition,//and the pride of kings.
> Let us//(since Life can little more supply
> Than just to look about us//and to die)   4
> Expatiate free//o'er all this scene of Man;
> A mighty maze!//but not without a plan;
> A wild,//where weeds and flowers promiscuous shoot;
> Or garden,//tempting with forbidden fruit.   8
>
> —ALEXANDER POPE

The varying position of the caesura helps to give Pope's lines an informality that plays against the formality of the pairs of rhyming lines.

An **end-stopped line** concludes with a distinct syntactical pause, but a **run-on line** has its sense carried over into the next line without syntactical pause. The running-on of a line is called **enjambment.** In the following passage, only the first is a run-on line:

Yet if we look more closely we shall find
Most have the seeds of judgment in their mind:
Nature affords at least a glimmering light;
The lines, though touched but faintly, are drawn right.
—ALEXANDER POPE

Meter produces **rhythm,** recurrences at equal intervals, but rhythm (from a Greek word meaning "flow") is usually applied to larger units than feet. Often it depends most obviously on pauses. A poem with run-on lines will have a different rhythm from a poem with end-stopped lines even though both are in the same meter. And prose, though it is unmetrical, may also have rhythm.

In addition to being affected by syntactical pause, rhythm is affected by pauses attributable to consonant clusters and to the length of words. Polysyllabic words establish a different rhythm from monosyllabic words, even in metrically identical lines. One may say, then, that rhythm is altered by shifts in meter, syntax, and the length and ease of pronunciation. Even with no such shift, even if a line is repeated word for word, a reader may sense a change in rhythm. The rhythm of the final line of a poem, for example, may well differ from that of the line before even though in other respects the lines are identical, as in Frost's "Stopping by Woods on a Snowy Evening," which concludes by repeating "And miles to go before I sleep." One may simply sense that this final line ought to be spoken, more slowly and with more stress on "miles."

Patterns of Sound

Though rhythm is basic to poetry, **rhyme**—the repetition of the identical or similar stressed sound or sounds—is not. Rhyme is pleasant in itself; it suggests order; and it also may be related to meaning, for it brings two words sharply together, often implying a relationship, as in the now trite *dove* and *love* or in the more imaginative *throne* and *alone.*

Perfect or **exact rhyme:** Differing consonant sounds are followed by identical stressed vowel sounds, and the following sounds, if any, are identical (*foe–toe; meet–fleet; buffer–rougher*). Notice that perfect rhyme involves identity of sound, not of spelling. *Fix* and *sticks,* like *buffer* and *rougher,* are perfect rhymes.

Half rhyme (or off-rhyme): Only the final consonant sounds of the words are identical; the stressed vowel sounds, as well as the initial consonant sounds, if any, differ (*soul–oil; mirth–forth; trolley–bully*).

Eye rhyme: The sounds do not in fact rhyme, but the words look as though they would rhyme *(cough–bough)*.

Masculine rhyme: The final syllables are stressed and, after their differing initial consonant sounds, are identical in sound *(stark–mark; support–retort)*.

Feminine rhyme (or double rhyme): Stressed rhyming syllables are followed by identical unstressed syllables *(revival–arrival; flatter–batter)*. **Triple rhyme** is a kind of feminine rhyme in which identical stressed vowel sounds are followed by two identical unstressed syllables *(machinery–scenery; tenderly–slenderly)*.

End rhyme (or terminal rhyme): The rhyming words occur at the ends of the lines.

Internal rhyme: At least one of the rhyming words occurs within the line (Oscar Wilde's "Each narrow *cell* in which we *dwell*").

Alliteration: Sometimes defined as the repetition of initial sounds ("All the *aw*ful *au*guries" or "*B*ring me my *b*ow of *b*urning gold"), and sometimes as the prominent repetition of a consonant ("a*f*ter li*f*e's *f*itful *f*ever").

Assonance: The repetition, in words of proximity, of identical vowel sounds preceded and followed by differing consonant sounds. Whereas *tide* and *hide* are rhymes, *tide* and *mine* are assonantal.

Consonance: The repetition of identical consonant sounds and differing vowel sounds in words in proximity *(fail–feel; rough–roof; pitter–patter)*. Sometimes, consonance is more loosely defined merely as the repetition of a consonant *(fail–peel)*.

Onomatopoeia: The use of words that imitate sounds, such as *hiss* and *buzz*. A common mistaken tendency is to see onomatopoeia every-where—for example, in *thunder* and *horror*. Many words sometimes thought to be onomatopoeic are not clearly imitative of the thing they refer to; they merely contain some sounds that, when we know what the word means, seem to have some resemblance to the thing they denote. The Victorian poet Alfred, Lord Tennyson's lines from "Come Down, O Maid" are an example of onomatopoeia:

> The moan of doves in immemorial elms
> And murmuring of innumerable bees.

✍ A RULE FOR WRITERS

In referring to a word or a letter, it is common to use quotation marks, but italics perhaps are better and many instructors now prefer them.

In an early poem, "The Lake Isle of Innisfree," Yeats ends the first stanza by saying that he will have

> a hive for the honey-bee,
> And live alone in the bee-loud glade.

Yeats is trying to convey the sound of bees buzzing, not only by the word *bee,* which itself has a buzzing sound, but also by the *v* of *hive* and *live,* and by the long *o* of *alone,* and the long *a* of *glade.* Probably, too, the *n's*—a nasal sound—in *honey, alone,* and *in* contribute to the humming effect.

Stanzaic Patterns

Lines of poetry are commonly arranged into a rhythmical unit called a **stanza** (from an Italian word meaning "room" or "stopping place"). Usually, all the stanzas in a poem have the same rhyme pattern. A stanza is sometimes called a **verse,** though *verse* may also mean a single line of poetry. (In discussing stanzas, rhymes are indicated by identical letters. Thus, *a b a b* indicates that the first and third lines rhyme with each other, while the second and fourth lines are linked by a different rhyme. An unrhymed line is denoted by *x.*) Common stanzaic forms in English poetry are the following:

Couplet: a stanza of two lines, usually, but not necessarily, with end rhymes. *Couplet* is also used for a pair of rhyming lines. The **octosyllabic couplet** is iambic or trochaic tetrameter:

> Had we but world enough, and time,
> This coyness, lady, were no crime.

> —ANDREW MARVELL

Heroic couplet: a rhyming couplet of iambic pentameter, often "closed," that is, containing a complete thought, with a fairly heavy pause at the end of the first line and a still heavier one at the end of the second. Commonly, a parallel or an *antithesis* (contrast) is found within a line or between the two lines. It is called *heroic* because in England, especially in the eighteenth century, it was much used for heroic (epic) poems.

> Some foreign writers, some our own despise;
> The ancients only, or the moderns, prize.

> —ALEXANDER POPE

Triplet (or **tercet**): a three-line stanza, usually with one rhyme.

Whenas in silks my Julia goes
Then, then (methinks) how sweetly flows
That liquefaction of her clothes.

—ROBERT HERRICK

Quatrain: a four-line stanza, rhymed or unrhymed. The **heroic** (or **elegiac**) **quatrain** is iambic pentameter, rhyming *a b a b*.

Sonnet: a fourteen-line poem, predominantly in iambic pentameter. The rhyme is usually according to one of the two following schemes. The **Italian** (or **Petrarchan**) **sonnet** has two divisions: the first eight lines (rhyming *a b b a a b b a*) are the **octave;** the last six (rhyming *c d c d c d,* or a variant) are the **sestet**. Keats's "On First Looking into Chapman's Homer" (page 232) is an Italian sonnet. The second kind of sonnet, the **English** (or **Shakespearean**) **sonnet,** is arranged usually into three quatrains and a couplet, rhyming *a b a b c d c d e f e f g g*. Many sonnets have a marked correspondence between the rhyme scheme and the development of the thought. Thus, an Italian sonnet may state a generalization in the octave and a specific example in the sestet. Or an English sonnet may give three examples—one in each quatrain—and draw a conclusion in the couplet.

Blank Verse and Free Verse

A good deal of English poetry is unrhymed, much of it in **blank verse,** that is, unrhymed iambic pentameter. Introduced into English poetry by Henry Howard, the earl of Surrey, in the middle of the sixteenth century, it became the standard medium (especially in the hands of Christopher Marlowe and Shakespeare) of English drama late in the century. A passage of blank verse that has a rhetorical unity is sometimes called a **verse paragraph.**

The second kind of unrhymed poetry fairly common in English, especially in the twentieth century, is **free verse** (or **vers libre**), which has rhythmical lines varying in length, adhering to no fixed metrical pattern, and usually unrhymed. The pattern is often largely based on repetition and parallel grammatical structure. Here is a sample of free verse.

Walt Whitman (1819–92)

WHEN I HEARD THE LEARN'D ASTRONOMER

When I heard the learn'd astronomer,
When the proofs, the figures, were ranged in columns before me,

When I was shown the charts and diagrams, to add, divide, and
    measure them,
When I sitting heard the astronomer where he lectured with much
    applause in the lecture-room,
How soon unaccountable I became tired and sick,   5
Till rising and gliding out I wander'd off by myself,
In the mystical moist night-air, and from time to time,
Look'd up in perfect silence at the stars.

What can be said about the rhythmic structure of this poem?
Rhymes are absent, and the lines vary greatly in the number of syllables, ranging from 9 (the first line) to 23 (the fourth line), but when
we read the poem we sense a rhythmic structure. The first four lines
obviously hang together, each beginning with "When"; indeed, three of
these four lines begin "When I." We may notice, too, that each of these
four lines has more syllables than its predecessor (the numbers are 9,
14, 18, and 23); this increase in length, like the initial repetition, is a
kind of pattern.

In the fifth line, however, which speaks of fatigue and surfeit, there is
a shrinkage to 14 syllables, offering an enormous relief from the previous
swollen line with its 23 syllables. The second half of the poem—the pattern established by "When" in the first four lines is dropped, and in effect
we get a new stanza, also of four lines—does not relentlessly diminish the
number of syllables in each succeeding line, but it *almost* does so: 14, 14,
13, 10.

The second half of Whitman's poem, thus, has a pattern, and this
pattern is more or less the reverse of the first half of the poem. We may
notice, too, that the last line (in which the poet, now released from the
oppressive lecture hall, is in communion with nature) is very close to an
iambic pentameter line; the poem concludes with a metrical form said to
be the most natural in English.

The effect of naturalness or ease in this final line, moreover, is increased by the absence of repetitions (e.g., not only of "When I," but even
of such syntactic repetitions as "charts and diagrams," "tired and sick,"
"rising and gliding") that characterize most of the previous lines. This final
effect of naturalness is part of a carefully constructed pattern in which
rhythmic structure is part of meaning. Though at first glance free verse
may appear unrestrained, as T. S. Eliot (a practitioner) said, "No *vers* is
libre for the man who wants to do a good job"—or for the woman who
wants to do a good job.

In recent years poets who write what earlier would have been called free verse have characterized their writing as **open form.** Such poets as Charles Olson, Robert Duncan, and Denise Levertov reject the "closed form" of the traditional, highly patterned poem, preferring instead a form that seems spontaneous or exploratory. To some readers the unit seems to be the phrase or the line rather than the group of lines, but Denise Levertov insists that the true writer of open form poetry must have a "form sense"; she compares such a writer to "a sort of helicopter scout flying over the field of the poem, taking aerial photos and reporting on the state of the forest and its creatures—or over the sea to watch for the schools of herring and direct the fishing fleet toward them."[2] And, Levertov again, "Form is never more than a *revelation* of content."

PREPARING TO WRITE ABOUT PROSODY

- Once you have decided to write about some aspect of verse structure—whether meter, rhyme, or other sound effects—write your own copy of the poem (or passage from a long poem), triple-spaced so that you will have plenty of room for your annotations. Number the lines, and print or photocopy several copies because you may find it useful to put metrical annotations on one copy, annotations concerning effects such as alliteration and consonance within lines on another, and annotations concerning the rhyme scheme on yet another.
- Read the poem aloud several times. Make sure you are reading for sense and are not imposing too regular a metrical pattern.
- Mark the stresses, and in the margins call attention to all departures (or probable departures) from the overall metrical pattern.
- Circle letters of words that are connected, for instance by alliteration or by assonance, and see if the connections are meaningful. The identity of sound may, for instance, reinforce identity or similarity of meaning (as in "born and bred"), or the identity of sound may provide an ironic contrast ("born and blasted"). Again, jot down marginal notes expanding your observations.
- Mark the rhyme scheme, and in your marginal notes call attention to imperfect rhymes. *Caution:* The pronunciation of some words has changed over the centuries. In the eighteenth

---

[2]"Some Notes on Organic Form," reprinted in *The Poetics of the New American Poetry*, ed. Donald M. Allen and Warren Tallman (1973), 316–317.

century, for instance, *line* and *join* (pronounced *jine*) were
perfect rhymes.

- Prepare a tentative organization. If you are planning to write
  on all aspects, you probably will want to write first about one
  aspect—let's say the overall structure of sounds imposed by the
  rhyme—then about meter, and then about other sound effects
  such as assonance and consonance. When you have finished a
  draft you may well discover that for this particular poem, a
  different organization is preferable, but you ought to begin with
  a tentative plan, and—equally or more important—you ought to
  be prepared to modify your plan after you finish a first draft.

A SAMPLE ESSAY ON METRICS: "SOUND AND SENSE IN A. E. HOUSMAN'S 'EIGHT O'CLOCK'"

Here is an excellent analysis by a student, Julia Jeffords. Notice that she
quotes the poem and indicates the metrical pattern and that she proceeds
chiefly by explaining the effect of the variations or departures from the
norm in the order in which they occur.

Notice, too, that although it is a good idea to announce your thesis
early—that is, in the first paragraph—this writer does *not* say, "This paper
will show that Housman effectively uses rhythm to support his ideas" or
some such thing. It is sufficient that the writer announces her topic in the
title and again, in slightly different words, in the first sentence (the paper will "analyze the effects of sounds and rhythms in Housman's 'Eight
O'Clock'"). We know where we will be going, and we read with even a bit
of suspense, looking to see what the analysis will produce.

Julia Jeffords
Professor Nicholas
College Writing 200
12 February 2011

Sound and Sense in A. E. Housman's "Eight O'Clock"

Before trying to analyze the effects of sounds and rhythms in
A. E. Housman's "Eight O'Clock" (1922) it will be useful to quote
the poem and to indicate which syllables are stressed and which
are unstressed. It must be understood, however, that the following scansion is relatively crude because it falsely suggests that all
stressed syllables (marked ˊ) are equally stressed, but of course

they are not: In reading the poem aloud, one would stress some
of them relatively heavily, and one would stress others only a trifle
more than the unstressed syllables. It should be understood, too,
that in the discussion that follows the poem some other possible
scansions will be proposed.

> He stood, | and heard | the steeple
>   Sprinkle | the quar | ters on | the mor | ning town.
> One, two, | three, four, | to mar | ket-place | and people
>   It tossed | them down.
> Strapped, noosed, | nighing | his hour.
>   He stood | and coun | ted them | and cursed | his luck;
> And then | the clock | collec | ted in | the tower
>   Its strength, | and struck.

As the first line of the second stanza makes especially clear,
the poem is about a hanging at eight o'clock, according to the title.
Housman could have written about the man's thoughts on the justice
or injustice of his fate, or about the reasons for the execution,
but he did not. Except for the second line of the second stanza—
"He stood and counted them and cursed his luck"—he seems to
tell us little about the man's thoughts. But the poem is not merely a
narrative of an event; the sound effects in the poem help to convey
an idea as well as a story.

The first line establishes an iambic pattern. The second line
begins with a trochee ("Sprinkle"), not an iamb, and later in the
line possibly "on" should not be stressed even though I marked
it with a stress and made it part of an iambic foot, but still the line
is mainly iambic. The poem so far is a fairly jingling description of
someone hearing the church clock chiming at each quarter of the
hour. Certainly, even though the second line begins with a stress,
there is nothing threatening in "Sprinkle," a word in which we
almost hear a tinkle.

But the second half of the first stanza surprises us, and
maybe even jolts us. In "One, two, three, four" we get four
consecutive heavy stresses. These stresses are especially
emphatic because there is a pause, indicated by a comma, after
each of them. Time is not just passing to the chimes of a clock:

This is a countdown, and we sense that it may lead to something significant. Moreover, the third line, which is longer than the two previous lines, does not end with a pause. This long line (eleven syllables) runs on into the next line, almost as though once the countdown has begun there is no stopping it. But then we do stop suddenly because the last line of the stanza has only four syllables—far fewer than we would have expected. In other words, this line stops unexpectedly because it has only two feet. The first line had three feet, and the second and third lines had five feet. Furthermore, this short, final line of the stanza ends with a heavy stress in contrast to the previous line, which ends with an unstressed syllable, "péoplĕ." As we will see, the sudden stopping at the end is a sort of preview of a life cut short. Perhaps it is also a preview of a man dropping through a trapdoor and then suddenly stopping when the slack in the hangman's rope has been taken up.

In the first line of the second stanza the situation is made clear, and it is also made emphatic by three consecutive stresses: "Strápped, nóosed, nighǐng his hoúr." The pauses before the first three stresses make the words especially emphatic. And though I have marked the first two words of the next line "Hĕ stoód," possibly "He" should be stressed too. In any case even if "He" is not heavily stressed, it is certainly stressed more than the other unstressed syllables, "and," "-ed" (in "counted"), and "his." Similarly in the third line of the stanza an effective reading might even stress the first word as well as the second, thus: "Ánd thén." And although normal speech would stress only the second syllable in "colléctĕd," in this poem the word appears after "clock," and so one must pause after the *k* sound in "clock" (one simply can't say "clock collected" without pausing briefly between the two words), and the effect is to put more than usual stress on the first syllable, almost turning it into "cólléctĕd." And so this line really can reasonably be scanned like this:

And thén the clóck colléctĕd in the tówer

And again the third line of the stanza runs over into the fourth, propelling us onward. The final line surely begins with a stress, even though "Its" is not a word usually stressed, and so in the final line we begin with two strong stresses, "Íts stréngth." This line, like the last line of the first stanza, is unusually short, and it, too, ends with a heavy stress. The total effect, then, of the last two lines of this stanza is of a clock striking, not just sprinkling music but forcefully and emphatically and decisively striking. The pause after "strength" is almost like the suspenseful pause of a man collecting his strength before he strikes a blow, and that is what the clock does:

> Ánd thén the clóck colléctéd ín the tówer

> Íts stréngth and strúck.

If "clock collected" has in its *k* sounds a sort of ticktock effect, the clock at the end shows its force, for when it strikes the hour, the man dies.

I said near the beginning of this essay that Housman did not write about the man's thoughts about the justice or injustice of the sentence, and I think this is more or less true, but if we take into account the sound effects in the poem we can see that in part the poem is about the man's thoughts: He sees himself as the victim not only of his "luck" but of this machine, this ticking, unstoppable contraption that strikes not only the hours but a man's life.

The Student's Analysis Analyzed

- The **title** suggests Julia Jeffords's topic, and the first sentence of the **opening paragraph** states it without doubt: "the effects of sounds and rhythms" in a particular poem. This paragraph also includes sentences whereby the author indicates her awareness that not everyone will scan the poem exactly as she does. Willingness to concede differences of opinion is a good argumentative strategy; it establishes the writer as a person who is open-minded.
- The writer provides the reader with **the text of the poem,** marked with her sense of the stresses. Do not expect your reader to read your paper and also to be thumbing through a book to find the poem.
- The **organization** is simple but adequate. The writer begins at the beginning and moves through the poem to its end.

- In her **final paragraph** she interestingly modifies an assertion she made earlier, that Housman "did not write about the man's thoughts about the justice or injustice of the sentence." She now shows that, in a way, the metrical effects—her chief topic—do tell us something about the victim's thoughts. This modification is not a contradiction. If indeed she now sees that Housman did write about these topics, she should have revised the earlier passage. But the earlier passage remains true, at least in a broad sense. Housman did not write about the victim's thoughts about justice. What the writer is saying, at the end of her essay, is that the metrical effects *do* in some degree get us into the mind of the victim, helping us to see him as someone struck down by an implacable machine.

An Internet site we have mentioned before, Bartleby.com, includes the full text of one of A. E. Housman's best-known volumes of verse, *A Shropshire Lad* (1986). In it you will find a number of poems that show a careful connection between sound and sense. You might select one for comparison and contrast with "Eight O'Clock," such as "Loveliest of trees, the cherry now" or "The time you won your town the race." <http://www.bartleby.com/verse/>.

📖 SUGGESTIONS FOR FURTHER READING

Alex Preminger and T. V. F. Brogan, eds., *The New Princeton Encyclopedia of Poetry and Poetics* (1993), is an indispensable reference work, with entries ranging from a few sentences to half a dozen or so pages on prosody, genres, critical approaches, and so on. See also Ross Murfin and Supryia M. Ray, *The Bedford Glossary of Critical and Literary Terms*, 3rd ed. (2008).

On prosody, see Paul Fussell, *Poetic Meter and Poetic Form,* rev. ed. (1979), and John Hollander, *Rhyme's Reason,* 3rd ed. (2001). A cogent book on the same topic is Robert Pinsky, *The Sounds of Poetry: A Brief Guide* (1998). Barbara Herrnstein Smith, *Poetic Closure: A Study of the Way Poems End* (1968), is an interesting study. For poets talking about their art, see *The Poet's Work: 29 Masters of 20th Century Poetry on the Origins and Practice of Their Art,* ed. Reginald Gibbons (1979). For good discussions (with interesting visual materials) of thirteen American poets from Whitman to Sylvia Plath, see *Voices and Visions: The Poet in America,* ed. Helen Vendler (1987).

Other insightful books are Christopher Ricks, *The Force of Poetry* (1984); Frank Kermode, *An Appetite for Poetry* (1989); and John Hollander, *The Work of Poetry* (1997). For a collection of essays illustrating contemporary theory, see *Lyric Poetry: Beyond New Criticism* (1985), ed. Chaviva Hosek and Patricia Parker. A huge book that doubles as a reference work and a history of poetry is Michael Schmidt, *Lives of the Poets* (1999). We also suggest you take a look at *Touchstones: American Poets on a Favorite Poem*, ed. Robert Pack and Jay Parini (1996).

Recent studies include: Virginia Jackson, *Dickinson's Misery: A Theory of Lyric Reading* (2005); Helen Vendler, *Invisible Listeners: Lyric Intimacy in Herbert, Whitman, and Ashbery* (2005); and Mutlu Konuk Blasing, *Lyric Poetry: The Pain and the Pleasure of Words* (2007).

✔ Checklist: Getting Ideas for Writing about Poetry

If you are going to write about a fairly short poem (say, under thirty lines), it is a good idea to copy out the poem, writing or typing it triple-spaced. By writing it out you will be forced to notice details, down to the punctuation. After you have copied the poem, proofread it carefully against the original. Catching an error—even the addition or omission of a comma—may prompt you to notice a detail in the original that you might otherwise have overlooked. And now that you have the poem with ample space between the lines, you have a worksheet with room for jottings.

A good essay is based on a genuine response to a poem; a response may be stimulated in part by first reading the poem aloud and then considering the following questions.

First Response

❏   What was your response to the poem on first reading? Did some parts especially please or displease you or puzzle you? After some study—perhaps checking the meanings of some of the words in a dictionary and reading the poem several times—did you modify your initial response to the parts and to the whole?

Speaker and Tone

❏   Who is the speaker? (Consider age, sex, personality, frame of mind, and tone of voice.) Is the speaker defined fairly precisely (for instance, an older woman speaking to a child), or is the speaker simply a voice meditating? (Jot down your first impressions, then reread the poem and make further jottings, if necessary.)

❑ Do you think the speaker is fully aware of what he or she is saying, or does the speaker unconsciously reveal his or her personality and values? What is your attitude toward this speaker?

❑ Is the speaker narrating or reflecting on an earlier experience or attitude? If so, does he or she convey a sense of new awareness, such as of regret for innocence lost?

Audience

❑ To whom is the speaker speaking? What is the situation, including time and place? (In some poems, a listener is strongly implied, but in others, especially those in which the speaker is meditating, there may be no audience other than the reader, who "overhears" the speaker.)

Structure and Form

❑ Does the poem proceed in a straightforward way, or at some point or points does the speaker reverse course, altering his or her tone or perception? If there is a shift, what do you make of it?

❑ Is the poem organized into sections? If so, what are these sections— stanzas, for instance—and how does each section (characterized, perhaps, by a certain tone of voice, or a group of rhymes) grow out of what precedes it?

❑ What is the effect on you of the form—say, quatrains (stanzas of four lines) or blank verse (unrhymed lines of ten syllables)? If the sense overflows the form, running without pause from, for example, one quatrain into the next, what effect is created?

Center of Interest and Theme

❑ What is the poem about? Is the interest chiefly in a distinctive character, or in meditation? That is, is the poem chiefly psychological or chiefly philosophical?

❑ Is the theme stated explicitly (directly) or implicitly? How might you state the theme in a sentence? What is lost by reducing the poem to a statement of a theme?

Diction

❑ How would you characterize the language? Colloquial, or elevated, or what?

❏ Do certain words have rich and relevant associations that relate to other words and define the speaker or the theme or both?

❏ What is the role of figurative language, if any? Does it help to define the speaker or the theme?

❏ What do you think is to be taken figuratively or symbolically, and what literally?

Sound Effects

❏ What is the role of sound effects, including repetitions of sound (for instance, alliteration) and of entire words, and shifts in versification?

❏ If there are off-rhymes (such as, *dizzy* and *easy,* or *home* and *come*), what effect do they have on you? Do they, for instance, add a note of tentativeness or uncertainty?

❏ If there are unexpected stresses or pauses, what do they communicate about the speaker's experience? How do they affect you?

14

POEMS AND PICTURES

Painting is poetry which is seen and not heard,
and poetry is painting which is heard but not seen.

—Leonardo da Vinci

Are there, one may ask, significant correspondences among the arts? If we talk about rhythm in a painting, are we talking about a quality similar to rhythm in a poem? Are the painter's colors comparable to the poet's images? Does it make sense to say, as Goethe (1749–1832) said, that architecture is frozen music? Or to call architecture "music in space"? Many artists of one sort have felt that their abilities ought to enable them to move into a "sister art," and they have tried their hand at something outside their specialty, usually with no great success. For instance, the painter Edgar Degas (1834–1917) tried to write sonnets but could not satisfy even himself. When he complained to his friend, the poet Stéphane Mallarmé, that he couldn't write poems even though he had plenty of ideas, Mallarmé replied, "You don't write poems with ideas; you write them with words."

Painters have been moved, for many centuries, to illustrate texts. More than two thousand years ago the painters of Greek vases illustrated the Greek myths, and from the Middle Ages onward artists have illustrated the Bible. Conversely, poets have been moved to write about paintings or sculptures. Among the well-known poems about artworks—texts and images of most are available on the Internet—are these:

W. H. Auden, "Musée des Beaux Arts" (about Pieter Brueghel's *Landscape with the Fall of Icarus*)
Gwendolyn Brooks, "The Chicago Picasso" (about a Cubist sculpture)

Rita Dove, "The Great Piece of Turf" (about Dürer's painting with
   this title)
Robert Fagles, *I, Vincent* (a book of poems about paintings by van
   Gogh)
Jane Flanders, "Van Gogh's Bed" (about van Gogh's *Vincent's Bed*)
Donald Hall, "Munch's Scream" (about Munch's *The Scream*)
Robert Hayden, "Monet's Waterlilies"
Edward Hirsch, "Edward Hopper and the House by the Railroad"
   (about Hopper's *House by the Railroad*)
Ted Kooser, "Prisoners from the Front" (about Winslow Homer's
   painting with this title)
Henry Wadsworth Longfellow, "The Cross of Snow" (about an
   engraving in a magazine, based on a photograph 1875 by William
   Henry Jackson of "The Mountain of the Holy Cross")
Edwin Markham, "The Man with the Hoe" (about Millet's painting
   with this title)
Anne Sexton, "The Starry Night" (about van Gogh's *The Starry
   Night*)
John Updike, "Before the Mirror" (about Picasso's *Girl Before a
   Mirror*)
William Carlos Williams, "The Great Figure" (about Charles
   Demuth's *I Saw the Figure Five in Gold*)
William Carlos Williams, "The Dance" (about Brueghel's *Peasant
   Dance*)
Samuel Yellen, "Nighthawks" (about Edward Hopper's painting
   with this title)

Despite Mallarmé's witty remark that poems are made not with ideas
but with words (and despite Archibald MacLeish's assertion that "A poem
should not mean / But be"), of course poems use ideas, and of course they
have meanings. When you see a painting that is the subject of a poem, you
might think about the following questions:

- What is your first response to the painting? In interpreting
  the painting, consider the subject matter, the composition (for
  instance, balanced masses, as opposed to an apparent lack of
  equilibrium), the technique (for instance, vigorous brushstrokes
  of thick paint, as opposed to thinly applied strokes that leave no
  trace of the artist's hand), the color, and the title.
- Now that you have read the poem, do you see the painting in a
  somewhat different way?

- To what extent does the poem illustrate the painting, and to what extent does it depart from the painting and make a very different statement?
- Beyond the subject matter, what (if anything) do the two works have in common?

A POEM AND A SAMPLE STUDENT ESSAY

Vincent van Gogh, *The Starry Night*, 1889.
Oil on canvas, 29 × 36 ¼ in. [73.7 × 92.1 cm.]. Museum of Modern Art, New York. Acquired through Lillie P. Bliss Bequest/Art Resource.

Read (preferably aloud) Anne Sexton's "The Starry Night," which was inspired by van Gogh's painting of the same name. Then read the student's essay that we reprint after the poem.

Anne Sexton

Anne Sexton (1928–1974) was born in Newton, Massachusetts. She attended Garland Junior College, married at twenty, and began a life as a housewife. After a mental breakdown at the age of twenty-eight she took up writing poetry at the suggestion of a therapist. She published many books of poetry, the third of which, *Live or Die* (1966), won a Pulitzer Prize, as well as a number of children's books (co-authored with the poet Maxine Kumin). Despite her literary success, her life was deeply troubled. She committed suicide in 1974.

THE STARRY NIGHT

That does not keep me from having a terrible need of—shall I say the word—religion. Then I go out at night to paint the stars.
                                        —Vincent van Gogh in a letter to his brother

The town does not exist
except where one black-haired tree slips
up like a drowned woman into the hot sky.
The town is silent. The night boils with eleven stars.
Oh starry starry night! This is how   5
I want to die.

It moves. They are all alive.
Even the moon bulges in its orange irons
to push children, like a god, from its eye.
The old unseen serpent swallows up the stars.   10
Oh starry starry night! This is how
I want to die:

into that rushing beast of the night,
sucked up by the great dragon, to split
from my life with no flag,   15
no belly,
no cry.

                                                                [1961]

Tina Washington
Professor Serno
English 10G
12 November 2008

                    Two Ways of Looking at a Starry Night
        About a hundred years ago Vincent van Gogh looked up into
the sky at night and painted what he saw, or what he felt. We know
that he was a very religious man, but even if we had not heard
this in an art course or read it in a book we would know it from

his painting *The Starry Night*, which shows a glorious heaven, so bright that the stars all have halos. Furthermore, almost in the lower center of the picture is a church, with its steeple rising above the hills and pointing to the heavens.

Anne Sexton's poem is about this painting, and also (we know from the line she quotes above the poem) about van Gogh's religious vision of the stars. But her poem is not about the heavenly comfort that the starry night offered van Gogh. It is a poem about her wish to die. As I understand the poem, she wants to die in a blaze of light, and to become extinct. She says, in the last line of the poem, that she wants to disappear with "no cry," but this seems to me to be very different from anything van Gogh is saying. His picture is about the glorious heavens, not about himself. Or if it is about himself, it is about how wonderful he feels when he sees God's marvelous creation. Van Gogh is concerned with praising God as God expresses himself in nature; Anne Sexton is concerned with expressing her anguish and with her hope that she can find extinction. Sexton's world is not ruled by a benevolent God but by an "old unseen serpent." The night is a "rushing beast," presided over by a "great dragon."

Sexton has responded to the painting in a highly personal way. She is not trying to put van Gogh's picture into words that he might approve of. Rather, she has boldly used the picture as a point of departure for her own word-picture.

[New page]

Work Cited

Sexton, Anne. "The Starry Night." *An Introduction to Literature*. Ed. Sylvan Barnet, William Burto, and William E. Cain. 16th ed. New York: Longman, 2011. 727. Print.

TOPICS FOR CRITICAL THINKING AND WRITING

1. Do you agree with this student's analysis, especially her point that Sexton's poem is a point of departure for her own word-picture?

2. Has the student cited and examined passages from the poem in a convincing way?

3. In general, do you think poets are obliged to be faithful to the paintings that they write about, or do poets enjoy the freedom—a kind of poetic license—to interpret a painting just as they choose, doing with it whatever the purpose of their poem requires?

THE LANGUAGE OF PICTURES

It may sound odd to talk about the "language" of pictures and about "reading" pictures, but pictures, like words, convey messages. Advertisers know this, and that is why their advertisements for soft drinks include images of attractive young couples frolicking at the beach. The not-so-hidden message of this visual language is that consumers of these products are healthy, prosperous, relaxed, and sexually attractive.

Like verbal compositions (such as stories, poems, and even vigorous sentences), many pictures are carefully constructed, built up in a certain way in order to make a statement. To cite an obvious example, in medieval religious pictures Jesus or Mary may be shown larger than the surrounding figures to indicate their greater spiritual status. But even in realistic paintings the more important figures are likely to be given a greater share of the light or a more central position than the lesser figures. Such devices of composition are fairly evident in paintings, but we occasionally forget that photographs too are almost always constructed things. The photographer—even the amateur just taking a candid snapshot—adjusts a pillow under the baby's head, or suggests that the subject may want to step out of the shadow; then the photographer backs up a little and bends his or her knees before clicking the shutter. Even when photographing something inanimate, the photographer searches for the best view, waits for a cloud to pass, and perhaps pushes out of the range of the camera some trash that would spoil the effect of a lovely fern growing beside a rock. The photographer Minor White was speaking for almost all photographers when he said, "I don't take pictures, I make them."

And we often make our photographs for a special purpose—for instance, to have a souvenir of a trip, or to show grandparents what the new baby looks like. Even professional photographers have a variety of purposes—for instance, to sell automobiles or to provide wedding portraits or to show how rich or how poor some people are. Sometimes these purposes can be mingled. During the depression of the early 1930s, for instance, the Resettlement Administration employed photographers such as Dorothea Lange to help convince the nation that migrant workers and dispossessed farmers needed help. With such a picture as Lange's *Migrant Mother*, these photographers were, so to speak, selling something, but they were also reporting the news and serving a noble social purpose.

Here are questions that may help you to think about pictures.

WRITING ABOUT PICTURES

What are the basic things to look for in understanding the language of pictures? One can begin almost anywhere, but we will begin with the relationship among the parts:

- Do the figures share the space evenly, or does one figure overpower another, taking most of the space or the light?
- Are the figures harmoniously related, perhaps by a similar stance or shared action? Or are they opposed, perhaps by diagonals thrusting at each other? Generally speaking, diagonals may suggest instability, except when they form a triangle resting on its base. Horizontal lines suggest stability, as do vertical lines when connected by a horizontal line. Circular lines are often associated with motion, and sometimes (especially by men) with the female body and fertility. These simple formulas, however, must be applied cautiously, for they are not always appropriate.
- In a landscape, what is the relation between humans and nature? Are the figures at ease in nature, or are they dwarfed by it? Are they earthbound, placed beneath the horizon, or (because the viewpoint is low) do they stand out against the horizon and perhaps seem in touch with the heavens, or at least with open air? Do the natural objects in the landscape somehow reflect the emotions of the figures in it?
- If the picture is a portrait, how do the furnishings and the background and the angle of the head or the posture of the head and body (and of course, the facial expression) contribute to our sense of the *character* of the person portrayed?
- What is the effect of light in the picture? Does it produce sharp contrasts, brightly illuminating some parts and throwing others into darkness? Or does it, by means of gentle gradations, unify

most or all of the parts? Does the light seem theatrical or natural, disturbing or comforting? If the picture is in color, is the color realistic or is it expressive, or both?

You can stimulate your responses to pictures by asking yourself two kinds of questions:

- *What is this doing?* Why is this figure here and not there, why is this tree so brightly illuminated, why are shadows omitted, why is this seated figure leaning forward like that?
- *Why do I have this response?* Why do I find this figure pathetic, this landscape oppressive, this child revoltingly sentimental but that child fascinating?

The first of these questions, "What is this doing?," requires you to identify yourself with the artist, wondering perhaps whether the fence or the side of the house is the better background for this figure, or whether both figures should sit or stand. *The second question, "Why do I have this response?,"* requires you to trust your feelings. If you are amused, repelled, unnerved, or soothed, assume that these responses are appropriate and follow them up—at least until further study of the work provokes other responses.

COMPARING AND CONTRASTING

Elsewhere in this book we talk in some detail about writing a comparison (pages 56–59), but here we want to make a few large points. The writer Howard Nemerov once said, "If you really want to see something, look at something else." He was talking about the power of comparison to illuminate. We compare X and Y, not for the sake of making lists of similarities and differences, but for the sake of seeing X (or Y) more clearly. Our understanding of one work may be heightened by thinking about it in comparison with another work.

We begin this discussion of seeing differences by taking the word "seeing" literally; we will look not at a work of literature but at a photograph of Sitting Bull and Buffalo Bill, taken by a Canadian photographer, William Notman (1826–1891). Buffalo Bill—William F. Cody—got his name from his activities as a supplier of buffalo meat for workers on the Kansas Pacific Railway, but his fame came chiefly from his exploits as an army scout and a fighter against the Sioux Indians, and later from Buffalo

Bill's Wild West. Buffalo Bill's Wild West was a show consisting of mock battles with Indians, an attack on a stagecoach, and feats of horsemanship and sharpshooting. Sitting Bull, a Sioux chief, had defeated Custer at the Battle of Little Bighorn ten years before this picture was taken, but he had fled to Canada soon after the battle. In 1879 he was granted amnesty and returned to the United States, and in 1885 he appeared in Buffalo Bill's Wild West. The photograph, titled *Foes in '76, Friends in '85*, was used to publicize the show.

William Notman, *Foes in '76, Friends in '85*.
© Wendy White/Alamy.

Suppose we want to think about the picture of Sitting Bull and Buffalo Bill in order to deepen our understanding of it and to share our understanding with others. To say that the photograph's dimensions are such-and-such or even to say that it shows two people is merely to describe it, not to offer anything that can be called analytic thinking. But if we look more closely, and compare the two figures, our mind is energized. (Strictly speaking, to *compare* is to take note of similarities, and to *contrast* is to take note of differences, but in ordinary usage *compare* covers both activities.) Comparing greatly stimulates the mind; by comparing X with Y, we notice things that we might otherwise pass over. Suppose we ask these questions:

- What resemblances and differences do we see in the clothes of the two figures?
- What do their facial expressions tell us?
- How do their poses compare?
- Is the setting significant?

If we try to answer these and other questions that come to mind, we may find ourselves jotting down phrases and sentences along these lines:

Buffalo Bill is in fancy clothing: shiny boots, a mammoth buckle, a decorated jacket

BB is striking a pose—very theatrical, his right hand on his heart, his head tilted slightly back, his eyes looking off as though gazing into the future. He seems to be working hard to present a grand image of himself.

Sitting Bull simply stands there, apparently looking downward. One feels that he is going along with what is expected of him.

Sitting Bull lets BB have upper hand—literally—on his gun.

BB in effect surrounds SB (Bill's shoulder is behind Sitting Bull and Bill's left leg is in front of him).

ANALYZING AND EVALUATING EVIDENCE

If we continue to look closely, we probably notice that the landscape is fake—not the great outdoors but a set, a painted backdrop and probably a fake grass mat. If we see these things, we may formulate the thesis that Buffalo Bill here is all show biz, and that Sitting Bull retains his dignity.

And if in our essay we support these assertions by pointing to evidence, we are demonstrating critical thinking.

Here is the final paragraph from an essay that a student wrote on this picture:

> Buffalo Bill is obviously the dominant figure in this photograph, but he is not the outstanding one. His efforts to appear great only serve to make him appear small. His attempt to outshine Sitting Bull strikes us as faintly ridiculous. We do not need nor want to know any more about Buffalo Bill's personality; it is spread before us in the picture. Sitting Bull's inwardness and dignity make him more interesting than Buffalo Bill, and make us wish to prove our intuition and to ascertain that this proud Sioux was a great chief.

We think this analysis is excellent, but when we did some of our own research on Buffalo Bill we found that he was more complicated and more interesting than we at first thought. But that is another story.

THINKING CRITICALLY: ARGUING WITH ONESELF, ASKING QUESTIONS, AND COMPARING— E. E. CUMMINGS'S "BUFFALO BILL 'S"

Here is a short poem by E. E. Cummings, probably written in 1917, the year Buffalo Bill died, but not published until 1920. Cummings did not give it a title, but included it in a group of poems called "Portraits." (In line 6, "pigeons" are clay targets used in skeet shooting or in exhibitions of marksmanship.)

> Buffalo Bill 's
> defunct
>   who used to
> ride a watersmooth-silver
>   stallion
> and break onetwothreefourfive pigeonsjustlikethat
>   Jesus
> he was a handsome man
>   and what i want to know is
> how do you like your blueeyed boy
> Mister Death

Read the poem, preferably aloud, at least two or three times, and with as open a mind as possible. Do not assume that, because the photograph shows us a man for whom we probably would not want to work, this poem necessarily conveys the same attitude.

Ultimately you will want to ask your own questions about the poem and about your responses, but for a start you may find it useful to put down tentative answers to some or all of these questions. We say "tentative" answers because when you think about them, you will almost surely begin to question them and thus improve your responses.

1. What is the speaker's attitude toward Buffalo Bill? (How do you know? What evidence can you point to?)
2. In line 6, why do you suppose the poet runs the words together?
3. Why do you think Cummings spaces the poem as he does? One student suggested that the lines form an arrowhead pointing to the right. Do you find merit in this suggestion? If not, what better explanation(s) can you offer?
4. What do you make of the address to "Mister Death"? Why "Mister Death" rather than "Mr. Death" or "Death"? If Mister Death could speak, what answer do you think he might give to the speaker's question?
5. What do you make of the use of "defunct" (as opposed to "dead") in line 2?
6. What do you make of "Jesus" in line 7? What is the effect of placing the word on a line by itself? Is Cummings being blasphemous? Is he inviting us to compare Buffalo Bill with Jesus? Again, support your response with evidence.
7. Some readers have said that Cummings is satirizing Buffalo Bill, others that he is satirizing death. Do you agree with either of these views? Why? (In a sentence or two define *satire*—feel free to consult a dictionary—and perhaps give a clear example. By the way, it is possible to satirize the common human fear of death, but can death be satirized? How might that be done? And what would be the point?)

A WRITING ASSIGNMENT: CONNECTING A PICTURE WITH A WORK OF LITERATURE

Your instructor may ask you to comment on an image—a drawing, a painting, a photograph, or even a sculpture—in connection with a work of literature. An obvious pairing would be Keats's poem "Ode on a Grecian Urn" and a photograph of a Greek vase, or perhaps even a Greek vase in a museum in your vicinity. Another example: The American painter Thomas Hart Benton (1889–1975) illustrated three works by Mark Twain: *The Adventures of Tom Sawyer, Adventures of Huckleberry Finn,* and *Life on the Mississippi.* You might compare one or more of Benton's pictures with the material Benton illustrated: Does Benton interestingly depict the episode? Why, or why not?

Here is a very short essay by a student who wrote about Notman's photograph (page 275) of Buffalo Bill. The assignment was to find a picture of Buffalo Bill and to relate it, in a paragraph or two, to Cummings's poem.

Sebastian Welch

Professor Tajik

Composition 100 S

5 February 2011

Two Views of Buffalo Bill

William Notman's photograph "Foes in '76, Friends in '85" reveals a show-off guy, wearing fancy clothing and gesticulating melodramatically. But why shouldn't he show off? First of all, he is in show business. We don't expect modesty from a man who is billed as an Indian fighter, an expert marksman, a fearless guide, and so forth. Second, and most important, Buffalo Bill was *very* good at what he did. He must have been, or his act couldn't have been the success, year after year, that it was.

E. E. Cummings catches the double nature of Bill, the show-biz hype, but also the genuine accomplishment. Cummings begins with a line that, by means of the somewhat inflated—almost absurdly pretentious—word "defunct," brings us into the world of show business, the world of hype. But the rest of the poem stresses his real achievements. Buffalo Bill was a man who could

break onetwothreefourfive pigeonsjustlikethat

By running the words together, Cummings indicates that the clay pigeons (clay disks tossed into the air for a marksman to shoot at) were tossed in rapid succession, that is, Bill did not have time to take careful aim but was so skilled that he could easily hit a moving target.

Well, a man who can do this, a man who can hit five moving targets in quick succession, has a right to wear fancy clothing and to adopt a melodramatic pose. He is a showman, and there is nothing wrong with a showman's acting like a showman. If there is an answer to the speaker's question ("how do you like your blueeyed boy / Mister Death") the answer must be that Mister Death likes him very much: Buffalo Bill was a man of great ability, someone who did his thing to perfection, and Mister Death can't hope for anyone more adept. We might almost say that the poet admires Buffalo Bill almost as much as Buffalo Bill must have admired himself. And, at least as far as one reader goes, the poet has succeeded in making Buffalo Bill an admirable figure.

TOPIC FOR WRITING

Do you find this mini-essay engaging? Why, or why not?

15

WRITING ABOUT AN
AUTHOR IN DEPTH

A poem is best read in the light of all the other poems ever written. We read A the better to read B (we have to start somewhere; we may get very little out of A). We read B the better to read C, C the better to read D, D the better to go back and get something more out of A. Progress is not the aim, but circulation. The thing is to get among the poems where they hold each other apart in their places as the stars do.

—Robert Frost

If you have read several works by an author, whether tragedies by Shakespeare or detective stories about Sherlock Holmes by Sir Arthur Conan Doyle, you know that authors often return to certain genres and themes (tragedy for Shakespeare, crime for Conan Doyle), yet each treatment is different. *Hamlet* and *Romeo and Juliet* are both tragedies and share certain qualities that we think of as Shakespearean, yet each is highly distinctive.

When we read several works by an author, we find ourselves thinking about resemblances and differences. We enjoy seeing the author take up again a theme (nature, or love, or immortality, for example) or explore once more the possibilities of a literary form (the sonnet, blank verse, the short story). We may find that the author has handled things differently and that we are getting a sense of the writer's variety and development.

Sometimes we speak of the shape or the design of the author's career, meaning that the careful study of the writings has led us to an understanding of the narrative—with its beginning, middle, and end—that the writings tell across a period of time. Often, once we read one poem by an author and find it intriguing or compelling, we are enthusiastic about reading more: Are there other poems like this one? What kinds of poems were written before or after this one? Our enjoyment and understanding of one poem impel us to enjoy and understand other poems and make us curious about the place that each one occupies in a larger structure, the shape or design of the author's career.

Frost's words, quoted at the beginning of this chapter, imply a good strategy to follow when you are assigned to write about an author in depth. Begin with a single work and then move outward from it, making connections to works that show interesting similarities or differences. With Frost, for example, you might begin with "Stopping by Woods on a Snowy Evening" and explore his use of woods in other poems. You will find that he sometimes sets them (as in this poem) against the village or city, and that he sometimes sets their darkness against the light of the stars. Each poem is a work in itself, but it is also part of a larger whole.

Usually, for an assignment of this kind, the focus will be on poems or short stories. Unless the course is a seminar devoted to a single author, or two authors, your instructor probably will not have room on the syllabus for two novels by the same writer. The most you are likely to get is a week or two on Robert Frost or Emily Dickinson, or on the short stories of James Joyce or Eudora Welty. When you reach these points on the syllabus, you want to know both how to explicate a single text and how to present an in-depth analysis of several of them at once.

A CASE STUDY: WRITING ABOUT LANGSTON HUGHES

For a course on twentieth-century literature, a student, Mark Bradley, was assigned to write about a theme (which he had to define himself) in a selection of poems by Langston Hughes (1902–67).

Hughes is best known for his poetry, but he was also a short story writer, a dramatist, an essayist, and an editor. He was born in Joplin, Missouri; grew up in Lawrence, Kansas, and Cleveland, Ohio; and spent a year living in Mexico before entering Columbia University in 1921. He left Columbia the following year and traveled extensively in Europe, returning to the United States in the mid-1920s. During these years, Hughes pursued his academic studies at Lincoln University in Pennsylvania (graduating in 1929) and published his first two books of verse, *The Weary Blues* (1926) and *Fine Clothes to the Jew* (1927). He also took part in the Harlem Renaissance, an important literary and cultural movement of the 1920s and 1930s that celebrated and supported the efforts of African-American writers and artists; in Hughes's words, it fostered "the expression of our individual dark-skinned selves." Hughes's many literary achievements, drawing upon spirituals, blues, jazz, and folk expression, and his rich, productive career have led his biographer, Arnold

Rampersad, to describe him as "perhaps the most representative black American writer."

The student started by closely studying a poem by Hughes that had caught his attention when he made his way through a group of poems for the first time. Here is the poem, and then the journal entry that he wrote:

THE SOUTH[1]

The lazy, laughing South
With blood on its mouth.
The sunny-faced South,
    Beast-strong,
    Idiot-brained.
The child-minded South
Scratching in the dead fire's ashes
For a Negro's bones.
    Cotton and the moon,
    Warmth, earth, warmth,
    The sky, the sun, the stars,
    The magnolia-scented South.
Beautiful, like a woman,
Seductive as a dark-eyed whore,
    Passionate, cruel,
    Honey-lipped, syphilitic—
    That is the South.
And I, who am black, would love her
But she spits in my face.
And I, who am black,
Would give her many rare gifts
But she turns her back upon me.
    So now I seek the North—
    The cold-faced North,
    For she, they say,
    Is a kinder mistress,
And in her house my children
May escape the spell of the South.

[1922]

The poem "The South" surprised me. It wasn't what I expected. I thought Hughes would attack the South for being racist—he wrote the poem in the 1920s, when segregation was everywhere in the South. He says some harsh things about the South: "Beast-strong, / Idiot-brained." But he also says that the South is attractive in some ways, and I'm not convinced that when he brings in the North at the end, he really believes that the North is superior.

His curiosity kindled by this poem, the student made it his point of departure for the thematic paper he was assigned. He judged that if he worked intensively on this poem and came to know it well, he could review other Hughes poems and see how they were both like and unlike the one with which he had begun.

In reading an author's poems or stories in depth, and in preparing to write about an important issue, feature of style, or theme in them, you will find the following questions useful:

- What subject matter recurs in the author's work?
- Do certain views—attitudes toward life—emerge?
- Does a particular personality take shape?
- Does the author show a fondness for certain literary devices, such as irony, symbolism, metaphor?
- Do any of the poems or stories strike you as highly *un*representative of the author?
- Take note of the dates of publication: Do you detect changing views or changing techniques?
- Does one work seem the key to the others? Does one work strike you as very closely related in some way to another?
- How do your perceptions change when you place two authors— say, Hughes and Frost, or Joyce and Welty—alongside one another for intensive study? What do they illuminate about one another's central themes and literary style? Does one show greater range in style and subject than the other?

When you write about an author's work in depth, remember to keep in mind the length of the assignment and the choice of examples. You want to treat the right number of examples for the space you are given and, furthermore, to provide sufficient detail in your analysis of each of them.

Preparing an outline can be valuable. It will lead you to think carefully about the examples that you have selected for your argument and the main idea about each one that you will present. Like Mark Bradley, whose paper we will turn to in a moment, you might begin by examining one poem in depth and then proceed to relate it to key passages in other poems. Or maybe you will find one passage in a poem so significant that it—rather than the entire poem—can serve as a good beginning. Whichever strategy you choose, when you review your rough draft mark off the amount of space that you have devoted to each example. Ask yourself:

- Is this example clearly connected to my argument as a whole?
- Have I not only referred to the example but also provided adequate quotation from it?
- Have I made certain to *comment* on the passage? Passages do not interpret themselves. You have to explicate and explain them.
- Has each example received its due? There is no easy rule of thumb for knowing how much space each example should be given. Some passages are more complicated than others; some demand more intensive scrutiny. But you will be well on the way toward handling this aspect of the paper effectively if you are self-aware about your choices.

From the poem "The South" and his journal entry, the student went on to explore other poems by Hughes. Here they are, followed by his essay.

RUBY BROWN[2]

She was young and beautiful
And golden like the sunshine
That warmed her body.
And because she was colored
Mayville had no place to offer her,
Nor fuel for the clean flame of joy
That tried to burn within her soul.

One day,
Sitting on old Mrs. Latham's back porch
Polishing the silver,
She asked herself two questions
And they ran something like this:
What can a colored girl do
On the money from a white woman's kitchen?
And ain't there any joy in this town?

Now the streets down by the river
Know more about this pretty Ruby Brown,
And the sinister shuttered houses of the bottoms
Hold a yellow girl
Seeking an answer to her questions.
The good church folk do not mention
Her name any more.

But the white men,
Habitués of the high shuttered houses,
Pay more money to her now
Than they ever did before,
When she worked in their kitchens.

[1926]

BALLAD OF THE LANDLORD[3]

Landlord, landlord,
My roof has sprung a leak.
Don't you 'member I told you about it
Way last week?

Landlord, landlord,
These steps is broken down.
When you come up yourself
It's a wonder you don't fall down.

Ten Bucks you say I owe you?
Ten Bucks you say is due?
Well, that's Ten Bucks more'n I'll pay you
Till you fix this house up new.

What? You gonna get eviction orders?
You gonna cut off my heat?
You gonna take my furniture and
Throw it in the street?

Um-huh! You talking high and mighty.
Talk on—till you get through.
You ain't gonna be able to say a word
If I land my fist on you.

---

[3]Langston Hughes, "Ballad of the Landlord" from *The Collected Poems of Langston Hughes* by Langston Hughes, edited by Arnold Rampersad with David Roessel, Associate Editor, copyright © 1994 by the Estate of Langston Hughes. Used by permission of Alfred A. Knopf, a division of Random House, Inc, (print), and by permission of Harold Ober Associates Incorporated (electronic).

Police! Police!
Come and get this man!
He's trying to ruin the government
And overturn the land!

Copper's whistle!
Patrol bell!
Arrest.

Precinct Station.
Iron cell.
Headlines in press:

MAN THREATENS LANDLORD

. .

TENANT HELD NO BAIL

. .

JUDGE GIVES NEGRO 90 DAYS IN COUNTY JAIL.

[1940]

Mark Bradley
Professor Bell
English 1C: Critical Interpretation
25 March 2011

A National Problem: Race and Racism
in the Poetry of Langston Hughes

One of Langston Hughes's concerns in his poetry is to show
that racism is a national problem, and that it is a mistake to pretend
that it affects only the South. In his poem "The South," Hughes
criticizes the racist attitudes that pervade the southern states, yet
he ends with only a hesitant embrace of the North. In other poems,
such as "Ruby Brown" and "Ballad of the Landlord," it is not racism
in the South that is the crucial fact; it is instead the presence of
racism everywhere in the United States.

"The South" begins with a line that sounds appealing: "The
lazy, laughing South." But then Hughes turns sharply to a different
kind of image in the second line: "With blood on its mouth." Line 3
echoes line 1: "The sunny-faced South"; and then the next two lines
challenge it: "Beast-strong, / Idiot-brained." Hughes continues:

The child-minded South
Scratching in the dead fire's ashes
For a Negro's bones.

Here Hughes is attacking the evil of lynching, by which black men were hanged, shot, or burned to death on the mere suspicion of having committed a crime or somehow threatened white supremacy. According to one source that I consulted, from 1882 to 1901 the annual number of lynchings "usually exceeded 100," and though the numbers declined somewhat in the twentieth century, there were still eighty-three lynchings in 1919, just several years before Hughes published his poem (Foner and Garraty 685).

Hughes is moved by the beauties of the southern landscape, but he knows that the South is cruel and contemptuous, and that it will not return to him the love he feels for it:

> And I, who am black, would love her
> But she spits in my face.

Hughes then says that he will "seek the North," but his words are very qualified and cautious:

> So now I seek the North—
> The cold-faced North,
> For she, they say,
> Is a kinder mistress,
> And in her house my children
> May escape the spell of the South.

"Cold-faced" not only refers to the cold northern weather but also implies something "cold" about northern interactions with other people. The South, Hughes says at one point, is dangerously "seductive" (line 14), but the North may be at the other extreme—distant, chilly in its response to newcomers. Hughes does not know for certain how he will be treated in the North. He has heard reports—"they say"; but possibly the reports will prove inaccurate. "May escape the spell of the South," he writes, which is more tentative than saying will escape. Most important, he doesn't expect his own life will be better, though maybe his children's lives will.

It is possible that "Ruby Brown" is a southern poem, a story about life in the South, but it is interesting that Hughes doesn't say explicitly that it is. This is the story of a "young and beautiful" woman who wants the good things of life but who will never be able to afford them on the wages she receives as a servant. Hughes shows her turning to a grim life as a prostitute.

Hughes intends for readers to understand Ruby Brown's story as one that has occurred countless times. It is a story about racism—how racism drives people to despair and corruption. "Mayville" sounded to me at first like the name of a southern town, but according to an atlas that I consulted, all of the towns named Mayville in the United States are in the North (Michigan, New York, North Dakota, Wisconsin). For Hughes, racism is a problem for the United States as a whole because its effects are evident throughout the nation.

"Ballad of the Landlord" is also about despair, but it is about anger and resistance, too, and, like "Ruby Brown," it recounts an incident that could happen anywhere. The speaker of the first twenty lines is indignant at the shabby condition of the building he lives in; he talks back to the landlord and threatens him with violence: "If I land my fist on you." But Hughes's real point in this poem is that an African-American who stands up for his rights is immediately perceived as a danger to the community. Everybody calls for the police and declares that this black man is a revolutionary who aims to overthrow the government and hurl the country into chaos. The final lines, in capital letters, indicate how the media broadcast a version of events that confirms racist stereotypes. It is true that the man does threaten the landlord, but that is only because he himself has been mistreated.

Someone could claim that Hughes locates "Ballad of the Landlord" in the North, just as it could be argued that "Ruby Brown" is a poem about a woman in a southern locale. But, again, if Hughes had wanted to make this clear to his readers, he could have done so. He chooses not to, because he is aiming to make readers aware of the national evil of racism.

[New page]

Works Cited

Foner, Eric, and John A. Garraty, eds. *The Reader's Companion to American History*. Boston: Houghton Mifflin, 1991. Print.

Hughes, Langston. *Collected Poems*. Ed. Arnold Rampersad. New York: Knopf, 1994. Print.

The New Cosmopolitan World Atlas. Chicago: Rand McNally, 1992. Print.

A Brief Overview of the Essay

- Focus on the title and the opening and closing paragraphs. Are they effective?
- Elsewhere in this book (page 48) there is an explication of Hughes's poem "Harlem." How might this poem be integrated into the analysis that the student gives?
- The student did not comment on the dates of publication of the poems. Was this a mistake?
- The student used two reference works. Do you think that they make his analysis more convincing? Explain.

To develop your ability to study and write about an author in depth, you might enjoy reading more short stories by James Joyce and Eudora Welty, two of the authors featured in this book. Joyce's "Araby" (pages 353–57) is included in *Dubliners* (1914), and Welty's "A Worn Path" (pages 357–63) is the last story in *A Curtain of Green* (1941). *Dubliners*, as we noted earlier (page 155), is available on the Internet.

What is the relationship of each Joyce or Welty story to the others in the collection? What comparisons, contrasts, and connections among the stories, and between the authors, come to mind as you read the two books? How does each author present character, handle dialogue, describe setting, structure plot, explore and develop themes?

For studying an author or authors in depth, make good use of the strategy of preliminary note taking illustrated in the section of this book on "A Worn Path" (pages 357–63). For studying an author in depth in a research paper, consult the discussion of research strategies and print and Internet resources in Chapter 17.

PART 4

Inside: Style, Format, and Special Assignments

16

STYLE AND FORMAT

Style is character.

—Joan Didion

Some writers confuse authenticity, which they ought always to aim at, with originality, which they should never bother about.

—W. H. Auden

PRINCIPLES OF STYLE

Writing is hard work (Lewis Carroll's school in *Alice's Adventures in Wonderland* taught reeling and writhing), and there is no point fooling ourselves into believing that it is all a matter of inspiration. Evidence abounds that many of the poems, stories, plays, and essays that seem to flow so effortlessly as we read them were in fact the product of innumerable revisions. "Hard labor for life" was Joseph Conrad's view of his career as a writer. This labor for the most part is directed not to prettifying language but to improving one's thoughts and then getting the words that communicate these thoughts exactly.

Hard work is not guaranteed to pay off, but failure to work hard is sure to result in writing that will strike the reader as confused. It won't do to comfort yourself with the thought that you have been misunderstood. You may know what you *meant to say*, but your reader is the judge of what you *have said*.

Big books have been written on the elements of good writing, but the best way to learn to write is to generate ideas by such methods as annotating the text, listing, brainstorming, free writing, and making entries in a journal. Then, with some ideas at hand, you can write a first draft, which you will revise—perhaps in light of comments by your peers—and later will revise again, and yet again. After you hand your essay in, your instructor will annotate it. Study the annotations an experienced reader puts on your essay. In revising the annotated passages, you will learn what your weaknesses are. After drafting your next essay, put it aside for a day or so; when you reread it, preferably aloud, you may find much that bothers you. If the argument does not flow, check to see whether your organization is reasonable and whether you have made adequate transitions. Do not hesitate to delete interesting but irrelevant material that obscures the argument. Make the necessary revisions again and again if time permits. Revision is indispensable if you wish to avoid (in W. Somerset Maugham's words) "the impression of writing with the stub of a blunt pencil."

Still, a few principles can be briefly set forth here. On the eighteenth-century author Samuel Johnson's belief that we do not so much need to be taught as to be reminded, these principles are brief imperatives rather than detailed instructions. They will not suppress your particular voice. Rather, they will get rid of static, enabling your voice to come through effectively. You have something to say, but you can say it only after your throat is cleared of "Well, what I meant was," and "It's sort of, well, you know." Your readers do *not* know; they are reading in order *to* know. The paragraphs that follow are attempts to help you let your individuality speak clearly.

Get the Right Word

Denotation
Be sure the word you choose has the right explicit meaning, or **denotation.** Do not say "tragic" when you mean "pathetic," "sarcastic" when you mean "ironic," "free verse" when you mean "blank verse," "disinterested" when you mean "uninterested."

Connotation
Be sure the word you choose has the right association or implication—that is, the right **connotation.** Here are three examples of words with the wrong connotations for their contexts: "The heroic spirit is not dead. It still *lurks* in the hearts of men." (Lurks suggests a furtiveness inappropriate to the heroic spirit. Something like *lives* or *dwells* is needed.) "Close study will *expose* the strength of Woolf's style." (*Reveal* would be better than *expose* here; *expose* suggests that some weakness will be brought to light, as in "Close study will expose the flimsiness of the motivation.") "Although Creon suffers, his suffering is not great enough to *relegate* him to the role of tragic hero." (In place of *relegate,* we need something like *elevate* or *exalt.*)

Concreteness

Catch the richness, complexity, and uniqueness of things. Do not write "Here one sees his lack of emotion" if you really mean, "Here one sees his indifference" or "his iciness" or "his impartiality" or whatever the exact condition is. Instead of "The clown's part in *Othello* is very small," write, "The clown appears in only two scenes in *Othello*" or "The clown in *Othello* speaks only thirty lines." (*Very*, as in *very small* or *very big*, is almost never the right word. A role is rarely "very big"; it "dominates" or "overshadows" or "is second only to. . . .")

In addition to using the concrete word and the appropriate detail, use illustrative **examples.** Northrop Frye, writing about the perception of rhythm, illustrates his point:

> Ideally, our literary education should begin, not with prose, but with such things as "this little pig went to market"—with verse rhythm reinforced by physical assault. The infant who gets bounced on somebody's knee to the rhythm of "Ride a cock horse" does not need a footnote telling him that Banbury Cross is twenty miles northeast of Oxford. He does not need the information that "cross" and "horse" make (at least in the pronunciation he is most likely to hear) not a rhyme but an assonance. . . . All he needs is to get bounced.
>
> —*The Well-Tempered Critic* (1963), 25

Frye does not say our literary education should begin with "simple rhymes" or with "verse popular with children." He says "with such things as 'this little pig went to market,'" and then he goes on to add "Ride a cock horse." We know exactly what he means. Notice, too, that we do not need a third example. Be detailed, but know when to stop.

 A RULE FOR WRITERS

Keep in mind Mark Twain's comment, "The difference between the *almost* right word and the *right* word is really a large matter—'tis the difference between the lightning bug and the lightning."

Technical Language and Jargon

The members of almost every profession or trade—indeed, almost all people who share any specialized interest, for example cooking or baseball—use the vocabulary of their field. Learning a new discipline involves learning a new vocabulary, a new set of **technical terms**. Film critics talk about *long shots* and *anamorphic lenses.* Freudians talk of *cathect, libido,* and the *oral phase;* literary critics talk of *metonymy, pentameter,* and *selective omniscience.* Properly used, technical language communicates information concisely and clearly, and it can create a comfortable bond between speakers, or between the writer and the readers. Outsiders may object to such language, but their objections show only that they are unfamiliar with the language that specialists use when they speak concisely to each other.

Jargon, on the other hand, is inflated, pretentious language. It is sometimes used in an effort to impress readers rather than to communicate clearly. But (for instance) there is no need to speak of "a preliminary overall strategizing concept" when "plan" will do. The sad thing about inflated language is that it muffles the writer's voice: If the writer has any individuality, it is suppressed by puffed up talk.

✍🏻 A RULE FOR WRITERS

Use technical terms when necessary, and make sure that you define them if you think your readers may be unfamiliar with them. Do not confuse inflated language with technical language.

Repetition and Variation

Although some repetitions—say, of words like *surely* or *it is noteworthy*—reveal a tic that ought to be cured by revision, don't be afraid to repeat a word if it is the best word. The following paragraph repeats *interesting, paradox, Salinger, what makes,* and *book;* notice also *feel* and *feeling:*

> The reception given to *Franny and Zooey* in America has illustrated again the interesting paradox of Salinger's reputation there; great public enthusiasm, of the *Time* magazine and Best Seller List kind, accompanied by a repressive coolness in the critical journals. What makes this a paradox is that the book's themes are among the most ambitiously highbrow, and its craftsmanship most uncompromisingly virtuoso. What makes it an interesting one is that those who are most patronising about the book are those who most resemble its characters; people whose ideas and language in their best moments resemble Zooey's. But they feel they ought not to enjoy the book. There is a very strong feeling in American literary circles that Salinger and love of Salinger must be discouraged.
>
> —MARTIN GREEN, *Re-Appraisals* (1965), 197

Repetition, a device necessary for continuity and clarity, holds the paragraph together. Variations occur: *"Franny and Zooey"* becomes "the book," and then instead of "the book's" we get "its." Similarly, "those who" becomes "people," which in turn becomes "they." Such substitutions, which neither confuse nor distract, keep the paragraph from sounding like a broken phonograph record.

Pronouns are handy substitutes, and they ought to be used, but other substitutes need not always be sought. An ungrounded fear of repetition often produces a vice known as *elegant variation:* Having mentioned *Franny and Zooey*, an essayist next speaks of "the previously mentioned work," then of "the tale," and finally of "this work of our author." This vice is far worse than repetition; it strikes the reader as silly.

Pointless variation of this sort, however, is not to be confused with a variation that communicates additional useful information, such as "these two stories about the Glass family"; this variation is entirely legitimate, indeed necessary, for it furthers the discussion. But elegant variation can be worse than silly; it can be confusing, as in "My first *theme* dealt with plot, but this *essay* deals with character." The reader wonders if the writer means to suggest that an essay is different from a theme.

Observe in these lucid sentences by the critic Helen Gardner the effective repetition of *end* and *beginning:*

> *Othello* has this in common with the tragedy of fortune, that the end in no way blots out from the imagination the glory of the beginning. But the end here does not merely by its darkness throw up into relief the brightness that was. On the contrary, beginning and end chime against each other. In both the value of life and love is affirmed.
>
> —*The Noble Moor* (1956), 203

The substitution of *conclusion* or *last scene* for the second *end* would be worse than pointless; it would destroy Gardner's claim that there is *identity,* or correspondence, between beginning and end.

Do not repeat a word if it is being used in a different sense. Get a different word. Here are two examples of the fault: "This theme deals with the theme of the novel." (The first *theme* means "essay"; the second means "underlying idea," "motif.") "Caesar's *character* is complex. The comic *characters,* too, have some complexity." (The first *character* means "personality"; the second means "persons," "figures in the play.")

✍ A RULE FOR WRITERS

Do not repeat the same words in the same position in more than two consecutive sentences unless you are doing so for emphasis. Similarly, do not begin consecutive paragraphs with the same words ("This poem is . . . This poem is") unless you have a good reason.

The Sound of Sense

Avoid awkward repetitions of sound, as in "The story is marked by a remarkable mystery," "The reason the season is Spring . . . ," "Circe certainly . . . ," "This is seen in the scene in which. . . ." These irrelevant echoes call undue attention to the words and thus get in the way of the points you are making. But wordplay can be effective when it contributes to meaning. Gardner's statement that in the beginning and the end of *Othello* "the value of life and love is affirmed" makes effective use of the similarity in sound between *life* and *love*. Her implication is that these two things that sound alike are closely related, an idea that reinforces her contention that the beginning and the end of the play are in a way identical.

Write Effective Sentences

Economy

Say everything relevant, but say it in the fewest words possible. The wordy sentence

> There are a few vague parts in the story that give it a mysterious quality.

may be written more economically as

> A few vague parts in the story give it a mysterious quality.

Nothing has been lost by deleting "There are" and "that." Even more economical is

> A few vague parts add mystery to the story.

The original version says nothing that the second version does not say, and says nothing that the third version—nine words versus fifteen—does not say. If you find the right nouns and verbs, you can often delete adjectives and adverbs. (Compare "a mysterious quality" with "mystery.") Another example of wordiness is "Sophocles' tragic play *Antigone* is mistitled because Creon is the tragic hero, and the play should be named for him." These twenty words can be reduced, with no loss of meaning, to nine words: "Sophocles' *Antigone* is mistitled; Creon is the tragic hero."

Something is wrong with a sentence if you can delete words and not sense the loss. A chapter in a recent book on contemporary theater begins:

> One of the principal and most persistent sources of error that tends to bedevil a considerable proportion of contemporary literary analysis is the assumption that the writer's creative process is a wholly conscious and purposive type of activity.

There is something of interest here, but it comes along with a lot of hot air. Why that weaseling (*"tends* to bedevil," "a *considerable* proportion"), and why "type of activity" instead of "activity"? Those spluttering *p*'s ("principal and most persistent," "proportion," "process," "purposive") are a giveaway; the writer is letting off steam, not thinking. Pruned of the verbiage, what he says adds up to this:

> One of the chief errors bedeviling much contemporary criticism is the assumption that the writer's creative process is wholly conscious and purposive.

Or

> Contemporary critics often mistakenly assume the writers are in complete control of their efforts.

Or

> Too many critics wrongly assume that writers are fully conscious of their creative process and its aims.

Or

> Contemporary criticism tends to regard the writing process as wholly defined by the writer's conscious intentions.

If he were to complain that this revision deprives him of his style, might we not fairly reply that what he calls his style is a tangle of deadwood?

Cut out all the deadwood, but in cutting it out, do not cut out supporting detail. Supporting detail is wordiness only when the details are so numerous and obvious that they offend the reader's intelligence.

The **passive voice** (wherein the subject of a sentence is the object of the action) is a common source of wordiness. Do not say, "This story was written by Melville"; instead, say, "Melville wrote this story." The revision is one-third shorter, and it says everything that the longer version says. Yet sometimes the passive voice, although less vigorous, may be preferable to the active voice. Changing "The novel was received in silence" to "Readers neglected the novel" makes the readers' response more active than it was. The passive catches the passivity of the response. Furthermore, the revision makes "readers" the subject, but the true subject is (as in the original) the novel.

✔ Checklist: Revising for Conciseness

❑ Does every word count? Can any words or phrases be cut without loss of meaning?

❑ Are there any empty or pretentious words such as *situation, factor, virtually, significant,* and *utilize?*

❑ Do intensifiers such as *very, truly,* and *rather* weaken your sentences?

❑ Are there any roundabout or long-winded locutions? Do you say, for example, *at that point in time* when you mean *then,* or *for the simple reason that* when you mean *because?*

❑ Do sentences get off to a fast start? Can you cut any sentences that open with "it is . . . that"?

❑ Can you replace forms of the verbs *to be, to have,* and *to make* with precise and active verbs?

❑ Are there any redundancies or negative constructions?

❑ Can any sentences be improved by using subordination?

Parallels

Use parallels to clarify relationships. Few of us are likely to compose such deathless parallels as "I came, I saw, I conquered" or "of the people, by the people, for the people," but we can see to it that coordinate expressions correspond in their grammatical form. A parallel such as "He liked to read and to write" (instead of "He liked reading and to write") makes its point neatly. No such neatness appears in "Virginia Woolf wrote novels, delightful letters, and penetrating stories." The reader is left wondering what value the novels have. If one of the items has a modifier, usually all should have modifiers. Notice how the omission of "the noble" in the following sentence would leave a distracting gap: "If the wicked Shylock cannot enter the fairy story world of Belmont, neither can the noble Antonio."

Other examples of parallels are "Mendoza longs to be an Englishman and to marry the girl he loves" (*not* "Mendoza longs to be an Englishman and for the girl he loves"); "He talked about metaphors, similes, and symbols" (*not* "He talked about metaphors, similes, and about symbols"). If one wishes to emphasize the leisureliness of the talk, one might put it thus: "He talked about metaphors, about similes, and about symbols." The repetition of *about* in this version is not wordiness; because it emphasizes the leisureliness, it does some work in the sentence. Notice in the next example how Helen Gardner's parallels ("in the," "in his," "in his," "in the") lend conviction:

> The significance of *Othello* is not to be found in the hero's nobility alone, in his capacity to know ecstasy, in his vision of the world, and in the terrible act to which he is driven by his anguish at the loss of that vision. It lies also in the fact that the vision was true.
> —*The Noble Moor*, 205

Subordination

Make sure that the less important element is subordinate to the more important. In the following example the first clause, summarizing the writer's previous sentences, is a subordinate or dependent clause; the new material is made emphatic by being put into two independent clauses:

> As soon as the Irish Literary Theatre was assured of a nationalist backing, it started to dissociate itself from any political aim, and the long struggle with the public began.

The second and third clauses in this sentence, linked by *and,* are coordinate—that is, of equal importance.

We have already discussed parallels ("I came, I saw, I conquered") and pointed out that parallel or coordinate elements should appear so in the sentence. The following line gives time and eternity equal treatment: "Time was against him; eternity was for him." The quotation about the Irish Literary Theatre is a **complex sentence**. It begins with a subordinate clause ("As soon as the Irish Literary Theatre was assured of a nationalist backing), and then adds two independent clauses. A **complex sentence** (an independent clause and one or more subordinate clauses) does not give equal treatment to each clause; whatever is outside the independent clause is subordinate, less important. Consider this sentence:

> Aided by Miss Horniman's money, Yeats dreamed of a poetic drama.

The writer puts Yeats's dream in the independent clause, subordinating the relatively unimportant Miss Horniman. (Notice that emphasis by subordination often works along with emphasis by position. Here the independent clause comes *after* the subordinate clause; the writer appropriately put the more important material in the more emphatic position.)

Had the writer wished to give Miss Horniman more prominence, the passage might have run:

> Yeats dreamed of a poetic drama, and Miss Horniman subsidized that dream.

Here Miss Horniman at least stands in an independent clause, linked to the previous independent clause by *and.* The two clauses, and the two people, are now of approximately equal importance.

If the writer had wanted to emphasize Miss Horniman and to deemphasize Yeats, he might have written:

> While Yeats dreamed of a poetic drama, Miss Horniman provided the money.

Here, Yeats is reduced to the subordinate clause, and Miss Horniman is given the dignity of the only independent clause. Again notice that the important point is also in the emphatic position, near the end of the sentence. A sentence is likely to sprawl if an independent clause comes first, followed by a long subordinate clause of less importance, such as the sentence you are now reading.

In short, although simple sentences have their place, they make everything of equal importance. Because everything is not of equal importance, you must often write complex and compound-complex sentences, subordinating some things to other things.

✍ A RULE FOR WRITERS

Gain emphasis not by using italics and exclamation marks but by putting the right words into the right clauses.

Write Unified and Coherent Paragraphs

Unity

A unified paragraph is a group of sentences (rarely a single sentence) on a single idea. The idea may have several twists or subdivisions, but all the parts—the sentences—should form a whole that can be summarized in one sentence. A paragraph is, to put the matter a little differently, one of the major points supporting your thesis. If your essay is some 500 words long—about two double-spaced typewritten pages—you probably will not break it down into more than four or five parts or paragraphs. (But you *should* break your essay down into paragraphs, that is, coherent blocks that give the reader a rest between them. One page of typing is about as long as you can go before the reader needs a slight break.) A paper of 500 words with a dozen paragraphs is probably faulty not because it has too many ideas but because it has too few *developed* ideas. A short paragraph—especially one consisting of a single sentence—is usually anemic; such a paragraph may be acceptable when it summarizes a highly detailed previous paragraph or group of paragraphs, or when it serves as a transition between two complicated paragraphs, but usually summaries and transitions can begin the next paragraph.

Each paragraph has a unifying idea, which may appear as a **topic sentence.** Most commonly, the topic sentence is the first sentence, forecasting what is to come in the rest of the paragraph; or it may be the second sentence, following a transitional sentence. Less commonly, it is the last sentence, summarizing the points that the paragraph's earlier sentences have made. Least commonly—but thoroughly acceptable—the topic sentence may appear nowhere in the paragraph, in which case the paragraph has a **topic idea**—an idea that holds the sentences together although it has not been explicitly stated. Whether explicit or implicit, an idea must unite the sentences of the paragraph. If your paragraph has only one or two sentences, the chances are that you have not adequately developed its idea. You probably have not provided sufficient details—perhaps including brief quotations—to support your topic sentence or your topic idea.

A paragraph can make several points, but the points must be related, and the nature of the relationship must be indicated so that the paragraph has a single unifying point. Here is a brief paragraph that may seem to make two points but that, in fact, holds them together with a topic idea. The author is the critic Edmund Wilson:

> James Joyce's *Ulysses* was an attempt to present directly the thoughts and feelings of a group of Dubliners through the whole course of a summer day. *Finnegans Wake* is a complementary attempt to render the dream fantasies and the half-unconscious sensations experienced by a single person in the course of a night's sleep.
>
> —*The Wound and the Bow* (1947), 243

Wilson's topic idea is that *Finnegans Wake* complements *Ulysses*. Notice that the sentence about *Finnegans Wake* concludes the paragraph. Not surprisingly, Wilson's essay is about that book, and the structure of the paragraph allows him to get into his subject.

The next example may seem to have more than one subject (Samuel Richardson and Henry Fielding were contemporaries; they were alike in some ways; they were different in others), but again the paragraph is unified by a topic idea (although Richardson and Fielding were contemporaries and were alike in some ways, they differed in important ways):

> The names of Richardson and Fielding are always coupled in any discussion of the novel, and with good reason. They were contemporaries, writing in the same cultural climate (*Tom Jones* was published in 1719, a year after *Clarissa*). Both had genius and both were widely recognized immediately. Yet they are utterly different in their tastes and temperaments, and therefore in their visions of city and country, of men and women, and even of good and evil.
>
> —ELIZABETH DREW, *The Novel* (1963), 59

This paragraph, like Edmund Wilson's, closes in on its subject.

The beginning and especially the end of a paragraph are usually the most emphatic parts. A beginning may offer a generalization that the rest of the paragraph supports. Or the early part may offer details, preparing for the generalization in the later part. Or the paragraph may move from cause to effect. Although no rule can cover all paragraphs (except that all must make a point in an orderly way), one can hardly go wrong in making the first sentence either a transition from the previous paragraph or a statement of the paragraph's topic. Here is a sentence that makes a transition and states the topic: "Not only narrative poems but also meditative poems may have a kind of plot." This sentence gets the reader from plot in narrative poetry (which the writer has been talking about) to plot in meditative poetry (which the writer goes on to talk about).

Coherence

If a paragraph has not only unity but also a structure, then it has coherence; its parts fit together. Make sure that each sentence is properly related to the preceding and the following sentences. One way of gaining coherence is by means of transitions—words such as *furthermore, on the other hand,* and *but.* These words let the reader know how a sentence is related to the previous sentence.

Nothing is wrong with such obvious transitions as *moreover, however, but, for example, this tendency, in the next chapter,* and so on, but

(1) these transitions should not *start* every sentence (they can be buried thus: "Zora Neale Hurston, moreover, . . . "), and (2) they need not appear anywhere in the sentence. The point is not that transitions must be explicit, but that the argument must proceed clearly. The gist of a paragraph might run thus: "Speaking broadly, there were in the Renaissance two comic traditions. . . . The first. . . . The second. . . . The chief difference. . . . But both traditions. . . ."

> ## ✍ A RULE FOR WRITERS
> Use signal words or phrases that will help your readers know where you are taking them.

Introductory Paragraphs

Beginning one of his long poems, the Romantic poet George Gordon, Lord Byron (1788–1824) aptly wrote, "Nothing so difficult as a beginning." Almost all writers—professionals as well as amateurs—find that the beginning paragraphs in their drafts are false starts. Do not worry too much about the opening paragraphs of your draft; you'll almost surely want to revise your opening later anyway, and when writing a first draft you merely need something—almost anything may do—to get you going. Though on rereading you will probably find that the first paragraph or two should be replaced, those opening words at least helped you break the ice.

In your finished paper the opening cannot be mere throat clearing. It should be interesting and informative. Do not paraphrase your title ("Sex in *1984*") in your first sentence: "This theme will study the topic of sex in *1984*." The sentence contains no information about the topic here, at least none beyond what the title already gave, and no information about you, either—that is, no sense of your response to the topic, such as might be present in, say, "In George Orwell's *1984* the rulers put a lot of energy into producing antisexual propaganda, but Orwell never convinces us of the plausibility of all of this activity."

Often you can make use of a quotation, either from the work or from a critic. After all, if a short passage from the work caught your attention and set you thinking and stimulated you to develop a thesis, it may well provide a good beginning for your essay.

Here is a nice opening from a chapter on Norman Mailer, in a book by Richard Poirier: "Mailer is an unusually repetitious writer. Nearly all writers of any lasting interest are repetitious." The first sentence, simple though it is, catches our attention; the second gives the first a richer meaning than we had attributed to it. Poirier then goes on to give examples of major writers who are obsessed with certain topics, and he concludes the paragraph with a list of Mailer's obsessions.

Such an opening paragraph is a slight variant on a surefire method: *You cannot go wrong in stating your thesis* in your opening paragraph, moving from a rather broad view to a narrower one. If you look at the sample essays in this book, you will see that most good opening paragraphs clearly indicate the writer's thesis. Here is an introductory paragraph, written by a student, on the ways in which Shakespeare manages in some degree to present Macbeth sympathetically:

> Near the end of *Macbeth*, Malcolm speaks of Macbeth as a "dead butcher" (5.8.69), and there is some—perhaps much—truth in this characterization. Macbeth is the hero of the play, but he is also the villain. And yet to call him a villain is too simple. Despite the fact that he murders his king, his friend Banquo, and even the utterly innocent Lady Macduff and her children, he engages our sympathy, largely because Shakespeare continually reminds us that Macbeth never (despite appearances) becomes a cold-blooded murderer. Macbeth's violence is felt not only by his victims but by Macbeth himself; his deeds torture him, plaguing his mind. Despite all his villainy, he is a man with a conscience.

✍ A RULE FOR WRITERS

The introductory paragraph usually identifies the work(s) and it indicates the writer's thesis, but whatever it says, it must be interesting.

Concluding Paragraphs

With conclusions, as with introductions, say something interesting. It is not of the slightest interest to say "Thus we see . . . [here the writer echoes the title and the first paragraph]." Some justification may be made for a summary at the end of a long paper because the reader may have half forgotten some of the ideas presented thirty pages earlier, but a paper that can be held easily in the mind needs something different. In fact, if your paper is short—say two or three pages—you may not need to summarize or to draw a conclusion. Just make sure that your last sentence is a good one and that the reader does not expect anything further.

If you do feel that a concluding paragraph (as opposed to a final paragraph) is appropriate or necessary, make sure that you do not merely echo what you have already said. A good concluding paragraph may round out the previous discussion, normally with a few sentences that summarize (without the obviousness of "We may now summarize"), but it may also draw an inference that has not previously been expressed. To draw such an inference is not to introduce a new idea—a concluding paragraph is hardly the place for a new idea—but to see the previous material from a fresh perspective.

A good concluding paragraph closes the issue while enriching it. Notice how the two examples that follow wrap things up and, at the same time, open out by suggesting a larger frame of reference.

The first example is the conclusion to Norman Friedman's "Point of View in Fiction." In this discussion of the development of a critical concept, Friedman catalogs various points of view and then spends several pages arguing that the choice of a point of view is crucial if certain effects are to be attained. The omniscient narrator of a novel who comments on all that happens, Friedman suggests, is only one choice for fiction, and an author may willingly sacrifice this freedom for a narrower point of view if he or she wishes to make certain effects. Friedman concludes:

> All this is merely to say, in effect, that when an author surrenders in fiction, he does so in order to conquer; he gives up certain privileges and imposes certain limits in order the more effectively to render his story-illusion, which constitutes artistic truth in fiction. And it is in the service of this truth that he spends his creative life.
>
> —*PMLA* 70 (1955): 1184

Friedman devotes the early part of his paragraph to a summary of what has preceded, and then in the latter part he puts his argument in a new perspective.

A second example of a concluding paragraph that restates the old and looks toward the new comes from Richard B. Sewall's discussion of *The Scarlet Letter*.

> Henry James said that Hawthorne had "a cat-like faculty of seeing in the dark"; but he never saw through the dark to radiant light. What light his vision reveals is like the fitful sunshine of Hester's and Dimmesdale's

meeting in the forest—the tragic opposite of Emerson's triumphant gleaming sun that "shines also today."

—*The Vision of Tragedy* (1959), 91

Again, do not feel that you must always offer a conclusion in your last paragraph. Especially if your paper is short—let's say fewer than five pages—when you have finished your analysis or explication it may be enough to stop. If, for example, you have been demonstrating throughout your paper that in *Julius Caesar* Shakespeare condensed the time (compared to his historical source) and thus gave the happenings in the play an added sense of urgency, you scarcely need to reaffirm this point in your last paragraph. Probably it will be conclusion enough if you offer your final evidence in a well-written sentence and then stop.

✍ A RULE FOR WRITERS

In your final paragraph(s), don't merely summarize, do not say "in conclusion," do not introduce a totally new point, and do not apologize. do not merely repeat your main idea, but emphasize it, perhaps with an effective quotation, perhaps by picking up something from the beginning of the essay and thus bringing your readers full circle.

✔ Checklist: Revising Paragraphs

❑ Does the paragraph say anything? Does it have substance?

❑ Does the paragraph have a topic sentence? If so, is it in the best place? If the paragraph does not have a topic sentence, might one improve the paragraph? Or does it have a clear topic idea?

❑ If the paragraph is an opening paragraph, is it interesting enough to attract and to hold a reader's attention? If it is a later paragraph, does it easily evolve out of the previous paragraph, and lead into the next paragraph?

❑ Does the paragraph contain some principle of development, for instance, from cause to effect, or from general to particular?

❑ Does each sentence clearly follow from the preceding sentence? Have you provided transitional words or cues to guide your reader? Would it be useful to repeat certain key words, for clarity?

❏   What is the purpose of the paragraph? Do you want to summarize, or give an illustration, or concede a point, or what? Is your purpose clear to you, and does the paragraph fulfill your purpose?

❏   Is the closing paragraph effective, and not an unnecessary restatement of the obvious?

Write Emphatically

All that has been said about getting the right word, about effective sentences, and about paragraphs is related to the matter of **emphasis.** But we can add a few points here. The first rule (it will be modified in a moment) is: Be emphatic. But do not attempt to achieve emphasis by a *style* consisting *chiefly of italics* and *exclamation* marks!!! Do not rely on such expressions as "very important," "definitely significant," and "really beautiful." The proper way to be emphatic is to find the right word, to use appropriate detail, to subordinate the lesser points, and to develop your ideas reasonably.

The beginning and the end of a sentence (and of a paragraph) are emphatic positions; of these two positions, the end is usually the more emphatic. Here is a sentence that properly moves to an emphatic end:

> Having been ill treated by Hamlet and having lost her father, Ophelia goes mad.

If the halves are reversed, the sentence peters out:

> Ophelia goes mad because she has been ill treated by Hamlet and she has lost her father.

Still, even this version is better than the shapeless:

> Having been ill treated by Hamlet, Ophelia goes mad, partly, too, because she has lost her father.

The important point, that she goes mad, is dissipated by the lame addition of words about her father. In short, avoid anticlimaxes such as "Macbeth's deed is reprehensible and serious."

The usual advice, build to emphatic ends, needs modification. Don't write something that sounds like an advertisement for *The Blood of Dracula:* "In her eyes DESIRE! In her veins—the blood of a MONSTER!!!" Be emphatic but courteous and sensible; do not shout.

Notes on the Dash and the Hyphen

1. A **pair of dashes**—here is an example—is used to insert and set off additional information. A pair of dashes is, in effect, like a pair of commas or like a pair of parentheses (see the preceding commas, and the parentheses here), but the dashes are more emphatic—some people would say more breathless—and therefore they should be used sparingly.

2. **To indicate a dash,** type two hyphens without hitting the spacebar before, between, or after them.

3. **Hyphenate "century" when it is used as an adjective.** "Nineteenth-century authors often held that. . . ." But: "Eliot, born in the nineteenth century, often held that. . . ." The principle is: Use a hyphen to join words that are used as a single adjective, for example, a "six-volume work," "an out-of-date theory," and so "a nineteenth-century author." Notice that the hyphen is neither preceded nor followed by a space.

REMARKS ABOUT MANUSCRIPT FORM

Basic Manuscript Form

Much of what follows is nothing more than common sense.

- Use good-quality 8½-by-11-inch paper. Make a photocopy, or print out a second copy, in case the instructor's copy goes astray.
- Unless your instructor says otherwise, **double-space** and print on one side of the page only.
- Use **one-inch margins** on all sides.
- **Number the pages** of your essay. Type the numbers; do not write them in by hand.
- On the first page, below the top margin and flush with the left-hand margin, put **your full name,** your **instructor's name,** the **course number** (including the section), and the **date,** one item per line, double-spaced.
- **Center the title** of your essay. Remember that the title is important—it gives the readers their first glimpse of your essay.
- **Create your own title**—one that reflects your topic or thesis. For example, a paper on Shirley Jackson's "The Lottery" should not be called "The Lottery" but might be called

Suspense in Shirley Jackson's "The Lottery"

or

Is "The Lottery" Rigged?

or

Jackson's "The Lottery" and Scapegoat Rituals

These titles do at least a little in the way of arousing a reader's interest.

- **Capitalize the title thus:** Begin the first word of the title with a capital letter, and capitalize each subsequent word except articles (*a, an, the*), conjunctions (*and, but, if, when,* etc.), and prepositions (*in, on, with,* etc.):

A Word on Behalf of Mrs. Mitty

Notice that you do *not* enclose your title in quotation marks, and you do not italicize it—though if it includes the title of a story, *that* is enclosed in quotation marks, or if it includes the title of a novel or play, *that* is italicized, thus:

Jackson's "The Lottery" and the Scapegoat Tradition

and

Gender Stereotypes in *Macbeth*

- **After writing your title, double-space,** indent five spaces, and begin your first sentence.
- Unless your instructor tells you otherwise, **staple** the pages together. (Do not use a stiff binder; it will only add to the bulk of the instructor's stack of papers.)
- Extensive revisions should have been made in your drafts, but one or two minor **last-minute revisions** may be made—neatly—on the finished copy. Proofreading may catch typographical errors, and you may notice some small weaknesses.

Quotations and Quotation Marks

First, a word about the *point* of using quotations. Do not use quotations to pad the length of a paper. Rather, give quotations from the work you are discussing so that

- your readers will see evidence from the text or other material you are discussing and (especially in a research paper)
- your readers will know what some of the chief interpretations are and what your responses to them are.

Note: The next few paragraphs do not discuss how to include citations of pages, a topic discussed in the next chapter under "How to Document: Footnotes, Internal Parenthetical Citations, and a List of Works Cited (MLA Format)."

✍ A RULE FOR WRITERS

If you quote, *comment* on the quotation. Let the reader know what you make of it and why you quote it. A quotation does not interpret itself. That is your job.

Additional principles:

1. **Identify the speaker or writer of the quotation** so that the reader is not left with a sense of uncertainty. Usually, in accordance with the principle of letting readers know where they are going, this identification precedes the quoted material, but occasionally it may follow the quotation, especially if it will provide something of a pleasant surprise. For instance, in a discussion of Flannery O'Connor's stories, you might quote a disparaging comment on one of the stories and then reveal that O'Connor herself was the speaker.

2. If the quotation is part of your own sentence, **be sure to fit the quotation grammatically and logically into your sentence.**

Incorrect: Holden Caulfield tells us very little about "what my lousy childhood was like."

Correct: Holden Caulfield tells us very little about what his "lousy childhood was like."

3. **Indicate any omissions or additions.** The quotation must be exact. Any material that you add—even one or two words—must be enclosed within square brackets, thus:

Hawthorne tells us that "owing doubtless to the depth of the gloom at that particular spot [in the forest], neither the travellers nor their steeds were visible."

If you wish to omit material from within a quotation, indicate the omission by three spaced periods. If your sentence ends in an omission, add a closed-up period and then three spaced periods to indicate the omission. The following example is based on a quotation from the sentences immediately preceding this one:

> The instructions say, "If you . . . omit material from within a quotation, [you must] indicate the omission. . . . If your sentence ends in an omission, add a closed-up period and then three spaced periods. . . .

Notice that although material preceded "If you," periods are not needed to indicate the omission because "If you" began a sentence in the original. Customarily, initial and terminal omissions are indicated only when they are part of the sentence you are quoting. Even such omissions need not be indicated when the quoted material is obviously incomplete—when, for instance, it is a word or phrase.

✍ A RULE FOR WRITERS

Use brackets and ellipses only when you must. Such devices can prove confusing to the reader, who wonders what you have changed or omitted. Further, too many brackets and ellipses look awkward on the page.

---

4. **Distinguish between short and long quotations,** and treat each appropriately. *Short quotations* (usually defined as fewer than five lines of typed prose or three lines of poetry) are enclosed within quotation marks and embedded—that is, they are run into the text (rather than being set off, without quotation marks), as in the following example:

> Hawthorne begins the story by telling us that "Young Goodman Brown came forth at sunset into the street at Salem village," thus at the outset connecting the village with daylight. A few paragraphs later, when Hawthorne tells us that the road Brown takes was "darkened by all of the gloomiest trees of the forest," he begins to associate the forest with darkness—and a very little later with evil.

If your short quotation is from a poem, be sure to follow the capitalization of the original, and use a slash mark (with a space before and after it) to indicate separate lines. Give the line numbers, if your source gives them, in parentheses, immediately after the closing quotation marks and before the closing punctuation, thus:

> In Adrienne Rich's "Aunt Jennifer's Tigers," Rich says that "Uncle's wedding band / Sits heavily upon Aunt Jennifer's hand" (7–8). The band evidently is a sign of her oppression.

To set off a *long quotation* (five or more typed lines of prose or three or more lines of poetry), indent the entire quotation ten spaces from the left margin. Usually, a long quotation is introduced by a clause ending with a colon—for instance, "The following passage will make this point clear:" or "The closest we come to hearing an editorial voice is a long passage in the middle of the story:" or some such lead-in. After typing your lead-in, double-space, and then type the quotation, indented and double-spaced.

5. **Commas and periods go inside the quotation marks.**

> Chopin tells us in the first sentence that "Mrs. Mallard was afflicted with heart trouble," and in the last sentence the doctors say that Mrs. Mallard "died of heart disease."

Exception: If the quotation is immediately followed by material in parentheses or in square brackets, close the quotation, then give the parenthetical or bracketed material, and then—after the closing parenthesis or bracket—put the comma or period.

> Chopin tells us in the first sentence that "Mrs. Mallard was afflicted with heart trouble" (22), and in the last sentence the doctors say that Mrs. Mallard "died of heart disease" (24).

Semicolons, colons, and dashes go outside the closing quotation marks.

Question marks and exclamation points go inside if they are part of the quotation, outside if they are your own.

In the following passage from a student's essay, notice the difference in the position of the question marks. The first is part of the quotation, so it is enclosed within the quotation marks. The second question mark, however, is the student's, so it comes after the closing quotation mark.

The older man says to Goodman Brown, "Sayest thou so?" Doesn't a reader become uneasy when the man immediately adds, "We are but a little way in the forest yet"?

Quotation Marks or Italics?

Use quotation marks around titles of short stories and other short works—that is, titles of chapters in books, essays, and poems that might not be published by themselves. Italicize titles of books, periodicals, collections of essays, plays, and long poems such as Coleridge's *The Rime of the Ancient Mariner*. Word-processing software will let you use italic type.

A Note on the Possessive

It is awkward to use the possessive case for titles of literary works and secondary sources. Rather than "*The Great Gatsby*'s final chapter," write instead "the final chapter of *The Great Gatsby*," not "*The Oxford Companion to American Literature*'s entry on Emerson," but "the entry on Emerson in *The Oxford Companion to American Literature*."

17

WRITING A
RESEARCH PAPER

Research is formalized curiosity. It is poking and prying with a purpose.

—Zora Neale Hurston

When we have arrived at the question, the answer is already near.
—Ralph Waldo Emerson

WHAT RESEARCH IS NOT, AND WHAT RESEARCH IS

Because a research paper requires its writer to collect and interpret evidence—usually including the opinions of earlier investigators—one sometimes hears that a research paper, unlike a critical essay, is not the expression of personal opinion. But such a view is unjust both to criticism and to research. A critical essay is not a mere expression of personal opinions; if it is any good, it offers evidence that supports the opinions and thus persuades the reader of their objective rightness. And a research paper is in the final analysis largely personal, because the author continuously uses his or her own judgment to evaluate the evidence, deciding what is relevant and convincing. A research paper is not the mere presentation of what a dozen scholars have already said about a topic; it is a thoughtful evaluation of the available evidence, and so it is, finally, an expression of what the author thinks the evidence adds up to.

PRIMARY AND SECONDARY MATERIALS

The materials of literary research can be conveniently divided into two sorts, primary and secondary. The *primary materials,* or original sources, are the real subject of study; the *secondary materials* are critical and historical accounts already written about these primary materials. For example, Langston Hughes wrote poems, stories, plays, and essays: They are the primary materials. We include several of his poems in this book (see Chapter 15). If you want to study his ways of representing African-American speech or his representations of whites, or his collaboration with Zora Neale Hurston, you will read the primary material—his own writings (and Hurston's, in the case of the collaborative work). But in an effort to reach a thoughtful understanding of some aspect of his work, you will also want to look at later biographical and critical studies of his books and perhaps also at scholarly writing on such topics as jazz and Black English. You may even find yourself looking at essays that do not specifically mention Hughes, but that nevertheless may prove helpful.

A second example: If you are concerned with Charlotte Perkins Gilman's representation of medical treatment for women in her story "The Yellow Wallpaper," Gilman's story and her autobiographical writings are primary material, and you might also consider primary material to be the medical discussions of the period, especially the writings of S. Weir Mitchell, a physician who treated Gilman. Articles and books about Gilman and about medicine in the late nineteenth century, however, are secondary sources.

Locating Material: First Steps

The easiest way to locate articles and books on literature written in a modern language—that is, on a topic other than literature of the ancient world—is to consult the

> *MLA International Bibliography of Books and Articles in the*
> *Modern Languages and Literatures (1922–),*

which, until 1969, was published as part of *PMLA* (*Publications of the Modern Language Association*) and since 1969 has been published separately. Many college and university libraries now offer the *MLA International Bibliography* as part of their package of online resources for research, and it is up to date.

The *MLA International Bibliography* lists scholarly studies—books as well as articles in academic journals—published in a given year. The print version of the bibliography runs to more than one volume, but material on writing in English (including, for instance, South African authors who write in English) is in one volume. To see what has been published on Langston Hughes in a given year, then, you turn to the section on American literature (as opposed to English, Canadian, or Irish), and then to the subsection labeled 1900–2002, to see if anything that seems relevant is listed.

Because your time is limited, you probably cannot read everything published on your topic. At least for the moment, therefore, you will use only the last five or ten years of this bibliography. Presumably, any important earlier material will have been incorporated into some of the recent studies listed, and if, when you read these recent studies, you find references to an article from, say, 1975 that sounds essential, you can read that article too.

Although the *MLA International Bibliography* includes works on American literature, if you are doing research on an aspect of American literature you may want to begin with

American Literary Scholarship (1963–),

an annual publication noted for its broad coverage of articles and books on major and minor American writers, and especially valuable for its frank comments on the material that it lists.

On some recent topics—for instance, the arguments for and against dropping *Adventures of Huckleberry Finn* from high school curricula—there may be few or no books, and there may not even be material in the scholarly journals indexed in the *MLA International Bibliography*. Popular magazines, however, such as *Atlantic, Ebony,* and *Newsweek*—unlisted in the *MLA*—may include some useful material. These magazines, and about 200 others, are indexed in the

Readers' Guide to Periodical Literature (1900–).

If you want to write a research paper on the controversy over *Adventures of Huckleberry Finn,* or on the popular reception given to Kenneth Branagh's films of Shakespeare's *Henry V, Much Ado about Nothing,* and *Hamlet,* you can locate material (for instance, reviews of Branagh's films) through the *Readers' Guide.* For that matter, you can also locate reviews of older films, such as Olivier's films of Shakespeare's plays, by consulting the volumes for the years in which the films were released.

Once again, we should note that many libraries are making online versions of these and similar resources available for research. Some students (and faculty) prefer to use the books on the shelf, but the electronic editions have significant advantages: Often, it is easier to perform "searches" using them; and in many cases they are updated well before the next print editions are published.

Other Bibliographic Aids

There are hundreds of guides to publications and to reference works. *The Oxford Companion to African American Literature*, edited by William L. Andrews, Frances Smith Foster, and Trudier Harris (1997), provides detailed entries on authors; literary works; and many literary, historical, and cultural topics and terms, as well as suggestions for further reading. The *Reader's Guide to Literature in English,* edited by Mark Hawkins-Dady (1996), is a massive work (nearly 1,000 pages) that gives thorough summaries of recent critical and scholarly writing on English and American authors.

How do you find such books? Two invaluable guides to reference works (that is, to bibliographies and to such helpful compilations as handbooks of mythology, place names, and critical terms) are

1. James L. Harner, *Literary Research Guide: A Guide to Reference Sources for the Study of Literatures in English and Related Topics*, 5th ed. (2008).
2. Michael J. Marcuse, *A Reference Guide for English Studies* (1990).

And there are guides to these guides: reference librarians. If you do not know where to turn to find something, turn to the librarian. Many public, college, and university libraries now cluster and organize online reference resources and databases. You can explore for yourself, but, again, it can be very helpful, and can save you much time, if you seek out someone on the library's staff for guidance and advice.

THE BASICS

It is a good idea to have on your desk a reliable one-volume dictionary, such as *Encarta: World English Dictionary* (1999) or *The American Heritage Dictionary of the English Language*, 4th ed. (2000). Such a dictionary will give you word histories as well as definitions, and will provide information about classical myths and many historical events and figures.

Still other students log in to the online resources of their library's reference collection, with its range of dictionaries and encyclopedias, all of which can be accessed quickly during the paper writing and research process.

MOVING AHEAD: FINDING SOURCES FOR RESEARCH WORK

The more you gain experience as a student and writer in literature courses, the more you will want to know in-depth about reference and bibliographical works for your field. We have described a number of print and electronic sources in this chapter.

Not all of them, to be sure, will be relevant for your paper writing and research in a first-year course on literature and composition. But we hope you will see this material as a guide you can turn to when needed, whether for an assignment in a first-year course or in an intermediate or advanced course later on.

Feel free to jot down at the top or bottom of the page or in the margins the titles of other resources, in print or online, that you have found helpful when you worked on a project and that you want to remember.

And we will say again: speak with a member of your library's reference staff, who can tell you more about the print and online sources that are available to you.

WHAT DOES YOUR OWN INSTITUTION OFFER?

Many colleges and universities now offer as part of their resources for research a wide range of electronic materials and databases. At Wellesley College, for example, the library offers a detailed list of research resources, and there is another listing arranged according to department and interdisciplinary program. Some of these are open or free sites, available to anyone with a connection to the Internet. But others are by "subscription only," which means that only members of this academic community can access them.

Sign up for a library tutorial at your own school, and browse in and examine both the library's home page and the online catalog's options and directories.

One of the best research sites, to which many libraries subscribe, is the *FirstSearch* commercial database service. *FirstSearch* enables you to find books, articles, theses, films, computer software, and other types of material for just about any field, subject, or topic.

Make your "search" as focused as possible: Look for materials that bear on the topic that you are writing about, and, even more, that show a connection to the thesis that you are working to develop and demonstrate. Learn from what you find, but approach it critically: Is this source a good one? What are its strengths, and what are (or might be) its limitations? Keep in mind too that you engage in the process of selecting good sources in order to strengthen *your* topic and thesis. The quotations you give from the sources are there to support your ideas and insights. Above all, your reader is interested in what *you* have to say.

✍ A RULE FOR WRITERS

A good choice of secondary sources can help you to develop your analysis of a literary work, but remember that it is your point of view that counts. Use sources to present your own interpretation more effectively.

TAKING NOTES

Let us assume now that you have checked some bibliographies and that you have a fair number of references you must read to have a substantial knowledge of the evidence and the common interpretations of the evidence. Most researchers find it convenient, when examining bibliographies and the library catalog, to write down each reference on an index card—one title per card. On the card put the author's full name (last name first), the exact title of the book or of the article, and the name of the journal (with dates and pages). Titles of books and periodicals (publications issued periodically—for example, monthly or four times a year) are underlined; titles of articles and essays in books are put within quotation marks. It is also a good idea to put the library catalog number on the card to save time if you need to get the item for a second look.

Next, start reading or scanning the materials whose titles you have collected. Some of these items will prove irrelevant; others will prove valuable in themselves and also in the leads they give you to further references, which you should duly record on index cards. Notes—aside from these bibliographic notes—are best taken on larger index cards. Smaller cards do not provide enough space for summaries of useful material and for your thoughtful comments on these summaries. Be selective in taking notes.

Some students use note cards for taking notes during the process of research. Others write on separate sheets of a notebook, or on the sheets of a yellow legal pad. Still others take their notes using a computer, and then organize and rearrange this body of material by copying and pasting, moving the notes into a coherent order. (We advise you not to delete material that, when you reread your notes, strikes you as irrelevant. It *probably* is irrelevant, but, on the other hand, it may turn out to be valuable after all. Just put unwanted material into a file called "rejects," or some such thing, until you have completed the paper.)

Whichever method you prefer, keep in mind the following:

- **For everything you consult or read in detail, always name the source,** so that you know exactly from where you have taken a key point or a quotation.
- **Write summaries (abridgments), not paraphrases (restatements).**
- Quote **sparingly.** Remember that this is *your* paper; it will present your thesis, not the thesis and arguments and analyses of someone else. Quote directly only those passages that are particularly effective, or crucial, or memorable. In your finished paper these quotations will provide authority and emphasis.
- **Quote accurately.** After copying a quotation, check your transcription against the original, correct any misquotation, and then put a check mark after your quotation to indicate that it is accurate. Verify the page number also, and then put a check mark on your note after the page number. If a quotation runs from the bottom of, say, page 306 to the top of 307, on your note put a distinguishing mark (for instance, two parallel vertical lines after the last word of the first page), so that if you later use only part of the quotation, you will know the page on which it appeared.

    Use an ellipsis (three spaced periods) to indicate the omission of any words within a sentence. If the omitted words are at the end of the quoted sentence, put a period where you end the sentence, and then add three spaced periods to indicate the omission:

    > If the . . . words were at the end of the quoted sentence, put a period where you end. . . .

Use square brackets to indicate your additions to the quotation.
Here is an example:

Here is an [uninteresting] example.

- **Never copy a passage by changing an occasional word,**
  under the impression that you are thereby putting it into your
  own words. Notes of this sort may find their way into your paper,
  your reader will sense a style other than yours, and suspicions of
  plagiarism may follow. (For a detailed discussion of plagiarism,
  see pages 327–29, 364–71.)
- **Comment on your notes** as you do your work, and as you reflect later on what you have jotted down from the sources. Use a
  special mark—we recommend that you use double parentheses
  ((. . .)) or a different color pen to write, for example, "Jones
  seriously misreads the passage," or "Smith makes a good point
  but fails to see its implications." As you work, consider it your
  obligation to *think* about the material, evaluating it and using it as
  a stimulus to further thought.
- **In the upper corner of each note card write a brief key—**
  for example, "Swordplay in *Hamlet*"—so that later you can tell at
  a glance what is on the card.

INCORPORATING YOUR READING INTO YOUR THINKING: HOW TO USE AND SYNTHESIZE SOURCES

A much-quoted passage—at least by teachers of composition and
especially by teachers of courses in argument—is by Kenneth Burke
(1887–1993), a college drop-out who became one of America's most
important twentieth-century students of rhetoric. Burke wrote:

Imagine that you enter a parlor. You come late. When you arrive, others
have long preceded you, and they are engaged in a heated discussion,
a discussion too heated for them to pause and tell you exactly what it
is about. In fact, the discussion had already begun long before any of
them got there, so that no one present is qualified to retrace for you all
the steps that had gone before. You listen for a while, until you decide
that you have caught the tenor of the argument; then you put in your
oar. Someone answers; you answer him; another comes to your defense;

another aligns himself against you, to either the embarrassment or grati-
fication of your opponent, depending upon the quality of your ally's assistance. However, the discussion is interminable. The hour grows late,
you must depart. And you do depart, with the discussion still vigorously
in progress.

—*The Philosophy of Literary Form* (1941), 110–11

Why do we quote this passage? Because it is your turn to join the unending
conversation.

Notice that Burke says, in this metaphoric discussion of the life of a
thoughtful person, "You listen for a while, until you decide that you have
caught the tenor of the argument; then you put in your oar." There may
be times in your daily life when it is acceptable to make use of Twitter
and to shoot off 140 characters, but for serious matters you will want to
think about what you are saying before you give it to the world, and you
will want to convey more than 140 characters. (We admit that quite a lot
can be said in 140 characters, for instance the forceful words in *Brown v.
Board of Education of Topeka* that "Separate educational facilities are inherently unequal," or the anonymous insight that "There is no such thing
as a free lunch," but most of us lack the genius that will enable us to produce such compressed wisdom.)

When you use sources, you are joining the unending conversation.
During the process of reading, and immediately afterward, as well as
when you review your notes, you will want to listen, think, and say to
yourself something like

- "No, no, I see things very differently; it seems to me that . . ." or
- "Yes, of course, but on one large issue I think I differ," or
- "Yes, sure, I agree, but I would go further and add . . ." or
- "Yes, I agree with your conclusion, but I hold this conclusion for
  reasons very different from the ones that you offer."

During your college years, at least, and we think during your entire
life, you will be reading, or listening, and you will sometimes want to put
in your oar, to respond in writing, for example in a letter to the editor, or
in a memo at your place of employment. In the course of your response
you almost surely will have to summarize very briefly the idea or ideas
you are responding to, so that your readers will understand the context
of your remarks. These ideas may not come from a single source; you
may be responding to several sources, for instance to a report and also to
comments that the report evoked. In any case, you will state these ideas

briefly and fairly, and then set forth your thoughtful responses, thereby giving the reader a statement that you hope represents an advance in the argument, even if only a tiny one. That is, you will **synthesize** sources, combining existing material into something new, drawing nourishment from what has already been said (giving credit, of course) and converting it into something new, a view that you think is worth considering.

Consider this word **synthesis**. You probably are familiar with *photosynthesis*, the chemical process in green plants that produces carbohydrates from carbon dioxide and hydrogen. Synthesis, again, combines pre-existing elements and produces something new. In our use of the word *synthesis*, even a view that you utterly reject becomes a part of your new creation *because it helped to stimulate you to formulate your view*; without the idea that you rejected, you might not have developed the view that you now hold. Here are some words of Francis Bacon (1561–1626), Shakespeare's contemporary:

> Some books are to be tasted, others to be swallowed, and some few to be chewed and digested.

Your instructor will expect you to digest the readings—this does not mean you need to accept them, but only that you need to read them thoughtfully—and that, so to speak, you make them your own thoughts by refining them. Your readers will expect you to tell them *what you make out of the assigned readings*, which means that you will go beyond writing a summary and you will synthesize the material into your own contribution. *Your* view is what is wanted, and readers expect this view to be thoughtful, not mere summary and not mere tweeting.

✍ A RULE FOR WRITERS

In your final draft *you must give credit to all of the sources you use in your paper.* Let your reader know whether you are quoting (you will use quotation marks around all material directly quoted) or whether you are summarizing (you will explicitly say so) or whether you are paraphrasing (again, you will explicitly say so).

Experience has shown that, in the course of thinking about your reading, and in the process of introducing your reading into your own writing, certain long-established patterns—systems of organization, structures (sometimes called "templates")—will assist you to develop ideas. We made this point a moment ago (see page 323), but it is worth emphasizing. An example follows:

a. "Yes, I agree with your contention that _____,
b. but you fail to consider author X's point that _____.
c. It seems to me that when you consider this additional idea,
d. it is reasonable to conclude that _____."

Such a pattern ("Yes . . . but") is *not a* cookie-cutter that stifles thought, reducing the thought-process to a narrow formula. Rather, it is an aid to genuine thinking, a stimulus that will help you to improve your ideas and ultimately educate your readers.

DRAFTING YOUR PAPER

The difficult job of writing up your findings remains, but if you have taken good notes and have put useful headings on each note, you are well on your way.

- Read through the cards and sort them into packets of related material. Put aside all notes that you now see are irrelevant to your paper. (Do not destroy them, however; you may want them later.) Go through the notes again and again, sorting and resorting, putting together what belongs together.
- Probably you will find that you have to do a little additional research—somehow you are not quite clear about this or that—but after you have done this additional research, you should be able to arrange the packets into a reasonable and consistent sequence. You now have a kind of first draft, or at least a tentative organization for your paper.
- Beware of the compulsion to include every note card in your essay: that is, beware of telling the reader, "*A* says . . . ; *B* says . . . ; *C* says. . . ."
- You must have a point, a thesis. Make sure that you state it early, and that you keep it evident to your readers.
- Make sure also that the organization is evident to the reader. When you were doing your research, and even perhaps when you were arranging your notes, you were not entirely sure where you were going, but by now, with your notes arranged into what seems to you to be the right sequence, you think you know what

everything adds up to. Doubtless in the process of drafting, you will make important changes in your focus, but stay with the draft until you think it not only says what you want to say, but says it in what seems to you to be a reasonable order. The final version of the paper should be a finished piece of work, without the inconsistencies, detours, and occasional dead ends of an early draft. Your readers should feel that they are moving toward a conclusion (by means of your thoughtful evaluation of the evidence) rather than merely reading an anthology of commentary on the topic. And so we should get some such structure as "There are three common views on. . . . The first two are represented by A and B; the third, and by far the most reasonable, is C's view that . . . . A argues . . . but . . . . The second view, B's, is based on . . . but. . . . Although the third view, C's, is not conclusive, still. . . . Moreover, C's point can be strengthened when we consider a piece of evidence that she does not make use of. . . ."

- Tell the reader where you are going or, to put it a little differently, explain how the quotation fits into your argument.

Quotations and summaries, in short, are accompanied by judicious analyses of your own so that by the end of the paper your readers not only have read a neatly typed paper (see pages 309–14) and have gained an idea of what previous writers have said, but also they are persuaded that under your guidance they have seen the evidence, heard the arguments justly summarized, and reached a sound conclusion.

A bibliography or list of works consulted (see pages 330–40) is usually appended to a research paper so that readers may easily look further into the primary and secondary material if they wish; but if you have done your job well, readers will be content to leave the subject where you left it, grateful that you have set matters straight.

FOCUS ON PRIMARY SOURCES

Remember that your paper should highlight *primary* sources. It should be, above all, *your* paper, a paper in which you present a thesis that you have developed about the literary work or works that you have chosen to examine. By using secondary sources, you can enrich your analysis, as you place yourself in the midst of the scholarly community interested in this author or these authors. But keep a proper proportion between primary sources, which should receive the greater emphasis, and secondary sources, which should be used selectively.

To help make this come about, when you review your draft, mark with a red pen the quotations from and references to primary sources, and then with a blue pen do the same marking for secondary sources. If, when you scan the pages of your paper in progress, you see a lot more blue than red, you should change the emphasis, the proportion, to what it should be. Guard against the tendency to rely more than is proper on the secondary sources you have compiled. The point of view that really counts is your own.

> ✍ **A RULE FOR WRITERS**
>
> Your job is not to report what everyone says but to establish the truth or at least the probability of a thesis.

DOCUMENTATION

What to Document: Avoiding Plagiarism

Honesty requires that you acknowledge your indebtedness for material, not only when you quote directly from a work, but also when you appropriate an idea that is not common knowledge. Not to acknowledge such borrowing is plagiarism. If in doubt whether to give credit, give credit.

You ought, however, to develop a sense of what is considered **common knowledge.** Definitions in a dictionary can be considered common knowledge, so there is no need to say, "According to Webster, a novel is. . . ." (This is weak in three ways: It is unnecessary, uninteresting, and unclear; "Webster" appears in the titles of several dictionaries, some good and some bad.) Similarly, the date of first publication of *The Scarlet Letter* (1850) can be considered common knowledge. Few can give it when asked, but it can be found out from innumerable sources, and no one need get the credit for providing you with the date. The idea that Hamlet delays is also a matter of common knowledge. But if you are impressed by so-and-so's argument that Claudius has been much maligned, you should give credit to so-and-so.

Suppose that in the course of your research for a paper on Langston Hughes you happen to come across Arnold Rampersad's statement, in an essay in *Voices and Visions* (1987, ed. Helen Vendler), that

> Books alone could not save Hughes from loneliness, let alone give him the strength to be a writer. At least one other factor was essential in priming him for creative obsession. In the place in his heart, or psychology, vacated by his parents entered the black masses. (355)

This is an interesting idea, and in the last sentence the shift from heart to psychology is perhaps especially interesting. You certainly *cannot* say—implying that the idea and the words are your own—something like

> Hughes let enter into his heart, or his psychology—a place vacated by his parents—the black masses.

The writer is simply lifting Rampersad's ideas and making only tiny changes in the wording. But even a larger change in the wording is unacceptable unless Rampersad is given credit. Here is a restatement that is an example of plagiarism, even though the words differ from Rampersad's:

> Hughes took into himself ordinary black people, thus filling the gap created by his mother and father.

In this version, the writer presents Rampersad's idea as if it were the writer's own—and presents it less effectively than Rampersad. What to do? Give Rampersad credit, perhaps along these lines:

> As Arnold Rampersad has said, "in the place in his heart, or his psychology" where his parents had once been, Hughes now substituted ordinary black people. (355)

You can use another writer's ideas, and even some of the very words, but you must give credit, and you must use quotation marks when you quote.

✍ A RULE FOR WRITERS
Acknowledge your sources

1. if you quote directly and put the quoted words within quotation marks
2. if you summarize or paraphrase someone's material, even though you do not retain one word of your source
3. if you borrow a distinctive idea, even though the words and the concrete applications are your own.

✔ Checklist: Avoiding Plagiarism

❑ In taking notes, did you make certain to indicate when you were quoting directly, when you were paraphrasing, and when you were summarizing, and did you clearly give the source of any online material that you cut and pasted into your notes? (If not, you will have to retrieve your sources and check your notes against them.)

❏   Are all quotations enclosed within quotation marks and acknowledged?
❏   Are all changes within quotations indicated by square brackets [for additions] and an ellipsis mark (. . .) for omissions?
❏   If a passage in a source is paraphrased rather than quoted directly or summarized in the paper, is the paraphrase explicitly identified as a paraphrase, and is a reason given for offering a paraphrase rather than quoting directly (for instance, the original uses highly technical language, or the original is confusingly written).
❏   Are the sources for all borrowed ideas—not just borrowed words—acknowledged, and are these ideas set forth in your own words and with your own sentence structure?
❏   Does the list of sources include all the sources (online as well as print) that you have made use of?

Reminder: Material that is regarded as common knowledge, such as the date of Alice Walker's birth, is not cited because all sources give the same information—but if you are in doubt about whether something is or is not regarded as common knowledge, cite your source.

Note: You can test your understanding of plagiarism by taking the quiz on pages 364–69; answers are provided on pages 369–71.

How to Document: Internal Parenthetical Citations and a List of Works Cited (MLA Format)

Documentation tells your reader exactly what your sources are. At one time, the standard form of documentation was the footnote, which appeared at the bottom of the page where the work was cited and provided the title and author of the book from which a quotation was reprinted. More recently, however, the Modern Language Association has required that source information be provided in parenthetical citations *within* the text, linked to entries in a Works Cited list.

Internal Parenthetical Citations. On pages 312–13 we distinguish between embedded quotations (which are short, are run right into your own sentence, and are enclosed within quotation marks) and quotations that are set off on the page and are not enclosed within quotation marks (for example, three or more lines of poetry, five or more lines of typed prose).

   For an embedded quotation, put the page reference in parentheses immediately after the closing quotation mark, *without* any intervening punctuation. Then, after the parenthesis that follows the number, put the necessary punctuation (for instance, a comma or a period):

> Woolf says that in the struggling moth there was "something marvelous as well as pathetic" (180). She goes on to explain . . .

The period comes *after* the parenthetical citation. In the next example *no* punctuation comes after the first citation—because none is needed—and a comma comes *after* (not before or within) the second citation, because a comma is needed in the sentence:

> This is ironic because almost at the start of the story, in the second paragraph, Richards with the best of motives "hastened" (12) to bring his sad message; if he had at the start been "too late" (13), Mallard would have arrived at home first.

For a quotation that is not embedded within the text but is set off (by being indented ten spaces), put the parenthetical citation on the last line of the quotation, one space *after* the period that ends the quoted sentence.

Four additional points:

- The abbreviations *p., pg.,* and *pp.* are *not* used in citing pages.
- If you are referring to a poem, your instructor may tell you to use parenthetical citations of line numbers rather than of page numbers. But, again, your footnote will tell the reader that the poem can be found in this book, and on what page.
- If you are referring to a play with numbered lines, your instructor may prefer that in your parenthetical citations you give act, scene, and line, rather than page numbers. Use arabic (not roman) numerals, separating the act from the scene, and the scene from the line, by periods. A reference to Act 3, Scene 2, line 118 would be given as (3.2.118).

Parenthetical Citations and List of Works Cited Footnotes have fallen into disfavor. Parenthetical citations are now usually clarified not by means of a footnote but by means of a list, headed "Works Cited," given at the end of the essay. In this list you give alphabetically (last name first) the authors and titles that you have quoted or referred to in the essay.

Briefly, the idea is that the reader encounters an author's name and a parenthetical citation of pages. By checking the author's name in "Works

Cited," the reader can find the passage in the book. Suppose you are writing about Kate Chopin's "The Story of an Hour." We shall assume that you have already mentioned the author and the title of the story— that is, you have let the reader know the subject of the essay—and now you introduce a quotation from the story in a sentence such as this. (Notice the parenthetical citation of a page number immediately after the quotation.)

> True, Mrs. Mallard at first expresses grief when she hears the
> news, but soon (unknown to her friends) she finds joy in it. So,
> Richards's "sad message" (12), though sad in Richards's eyes, is in
> fact a happy message.

Turning to "Works Cited," the reader, knowing the quoted words are by Chopin, looks for Chopin and finds the following:

> Chopin, Kate. "The Story of an Hour." *A Short Guide to Writing about
> Literature*, 12th ed. By Sylvan Barnet and William E. Cain. New
> York: Longman, 20–22. Print.

Thus the essayist is informing the reader that the story quoted from is to be found on pages 20–22 of this book.

If you have not mentioned Chopin's name in some sort of lead-in, you will have to give her name within the parentheses so that the reader will know the author of the quoted words:

> What are we to make out of a story that ends by telling us that the
> leading character has died "of joy that kills" (Chopin 22)?

The closing quotation marks come immediately after the last word of the quotation; the citation and the final punctuation—in this case, the essayist's question mark—come *after* the closing quotation marks.

If you are comparing Chopin's story with Gilman's "The Yellow Wallpaper," in "Works Cited" you will give a similar entry for Gilman—her name, the title of the story, the book in which it appears, and the page numbers that the story occupies.

If you are referring to several works reprinted within one volume, instead of listing each item fully, it is acceptable in "Works Cited" to list each item by giving the author's name, the title of the work, then a period, a space, and the name of the author or anthologist, followed by the page numbers that the selection spans. Thus, a reference to Chopin's "The Story of an Hour" would be followed only by: Barnet 20–22. This form requires that the book itself also be cited, under the name of the first-listed author, thus:

> Barnet, Sylvan, and William E. Cain, *A Short Guide to Writing about Literature*, 12th ed. New York: Longman, 20–22, Print.

If you are writing a research paper, you will use many sources. Within the essay itself you will mention an author's name, quote or summarize from this author, and follow the quotation or summary with a parenthetical citation of the pages. In "Works Cited," you will give the full title, place of publication, and other bibliographic material.

Here are a few examples, all referring to an article by Joan Templeton, "The *Doll House* Backlash: Criticism, Feminism, and Ibsen." The article appeared in *PMLA* 104 (1989): 28–40, but this information is given only in "Works Cited," not within the text of the student's essay. If in the text of your essay you mention the author's name, the citation following a quotation (or a summary of a passage) is merely a page number in parentheses, followed by a period:

> In 1989 Joan Templeton argued that many critics, unhappy with recognizing Ibsen as a feminist, sought "to render Nora inconsequential" (29).

Or

> In 1989 Joan Templeton noted that many critics, unhappy with recognizing Ibsen as a feminist, have sought to make Nora trivial (29).

If you do not mention the name of the author in a lead-in, you will have to give the name within the parenthetical citation:

> Many critics, attempting to argue that Ibsen was not a feminist, have tried to make Nora trivial (Templeton 29).

Notice in all of these examples that the final period comes after the parenthetical citation.

If the quotation is longer than four lines and, therefore, is set off by being indented ten spaces from the left margin, end the quotation with the appropriate punctuation (period, question mark, or exclamation mark), hit the space bar once, and type (in parentheses) the page number. In this case, do not put a period after the citation.

If your list of works cited includes more than one work by an author, in your essay when you quote or refer to one or the other you will have to identify *which* work you are drawing from. You can provide the title in a lead-in:

> In "The *Doll House* Backlash: Criticism, Feminism, and Ibsen," Templeton says, "Nora's detractors have often been, from the first, her husband's defenders" (30).

Or you can provide the information in the parenthetical citation, giving a shortened version of the title—usually the first word, unless it is *A, An,* or *The,* in which case the second word usually will do, though certain titles may require still another word or two, as in this example:

> According to Templeton, "Nora's detractors have often been, from the first, her husband's defenders" ("*Doll House* Backlash" 30).

Forms of Citation in "Works Cited" In looking over the following samples of entries in "Works Cited," remember:

- The list of works cited appears at the end of the paper. It begins on a new page, and the page continues the numbering of the text.
- The list of works cited is arranged alphabetically by author (last name first).
- If a work is anonymous, list it under the first word of the title unless the first word is *A, An,* or *The,* in which case list it under the second word.
- If a work is by two authors, although the book is listed alphabetically under the first author's last name, the second author's name is given in the normal order, first name first.
- If you list two or more works by the same author, the author's name is not repeated but is represented by three hyphens followed by a period and a space.
- Each item begins flush left, but if an entry is longer than one line, subsequent lines in the entry are indented five spaces.

For details about almost every imaginable kind of citation, consult the *MLA Handbook for Writers of Research Papers,* 7th ed. (New York: Modern Language Association, 2009). We give here samples of the kinds of citations you are most likely to include in your list of works cited.

A Book by One Author

> Douglas, Ann. *The Feminization of American Culture.* New York: Knopf, 1977. Print.

Notice that the author's last name is given first, but otherwise the name is given as on the title page. Do not substitute initials for names written out on the title page.

Take the title from the title page, not from the cover or the spine, but disregard unusual typography—for instance, the use of only capital letters or the use of & for *and*. Italicize the title and subtitle. The place of publication is indicated by the name of the city alone. If the title page lists several cities, give only the first.

A Book by More than One Author

Gilbert, Sandra N., and Susan Gubar. *The Madwoman in the Attic: The Woman Writer and the Nineteenth-Century Literary Imagination.* New Haven: Yale UP, 1979. Print.

Notice that the book is listed under the last name of the first author (Gilbert) and that the second author's name is then given with first name (Susan) first. *If the book has more than three authors*, give the name of the first author only (last name first) and follow it with *et al.* (Latin for "and others").

A Book in Two or More Volumes

Cain, William E., ed. *American Literature.* 2 vols. New York: Pearson Longman, 2004. Print.

Pope, Alexander. *The Correspondence of Alexander Pope.* Ed. George Sherburn. 5 vols. Oxford: Clarendon, 1955. Print.

The total number of volumes is given, regardless of the number that you have used.

If you have used more than one volume, within your essay you will parenthetically indicate a reference to, for instance, page 30 of volume 3 thus: (3: 30). If you have used only one volume of a multivolume work— example, only volume 2 of McQuade's anthology—in your entry in "Works Cited" write Vol. 2 before the city of publication. In your parenthetical citation within the essay you will therefore cite only the page reference (without the volume number); the reader will (on consulting "Works Cited") understand that in this example the reference is in volume 2.

McPherson, James Alan. "Why I Like Country Music." *The Harper American Literature.* Ed. Donald McQuade et al. 2nd ed. Vol. 2. New York: Harper, 1994. 2304-15. Print.

This entry for McPherson specifies that only one selection ("Why I Like Country Music," found on pages 2304–2315 in volume 2) was used. If you use this sort of citation in "Works Cited," in the body of your essay a documentary reference to this work will be only to the page; the volume number will *not* be added.

A Book with a Separate Title in a Set of Volumes

Churchill, Winston. *The Age of Revolution*. New York: Dodd, 1957. Print. Vol. 3 of *A History of the English-Speaking Peoples*.

Jonson, Ben. *The Complete Masques*. Ed. Stephen Orgel. New Haven: Yale UP, 1969. Print. Vol. 4 of *The Yale Ben Jonson*.

A Revised Edition of a Book

Chaucer, Geoffrey. *The Riverside Chaucer*. Ed. Larry Benson. 3rd ed. Boston: Houghton, 1987. Print.

Ellmann, Richard. *James Joyce*. Rev. ed. New York: Oxford UP, 1982. Print.

A Reprint, Such as a Paperback Version of an Older Hardcover Book

Rourke, Constance. *American Humor*. 1931. Garden City: Doubleday, 1953. Print.

Notice that the entry cites the original date (1931) but indicates that the writer is using the Doubleday reprint of 1953.

An Edited Book

Keats, John. *The Letters of John Keats*. Ed. Hyder Edward Rollins. 2 vols. Cambridge: Harvard UP, 1958. Print.

An Anthology
You can list an anthology under the editor's name.

A Book with No Author
List by title of the book. Include such entries alphabetically. For example, the following entry might appear between entries of works written by Dobson, Martin and Ford, William.

Encyclopedia of the State of Massachusetts. Boston: Malden House, 1945. Print.

A Work in a Volume of Works by One Author

> Sontag, Susan. "The Aesthetics of Silence." *Styles of Radical Will.* By
> Sontag. New York: Farrar, 1969. 3-34. Print.

This entry indicates that Sontag's essay "The Aesthetics of Silence" appears in a book of hers titled *Styles of Radical Will.* Notice that the inclusive page numbers of the short work are cited, not the page numbers that you may happen to refer to.

A Work in an Anthology or Collection of Works by Several Authors

Begin with the author and the title of the work you are citing, not with the name of the anthologist or the title of the anthology. The entry ends with the pages occupied by the selection you are citing:

> Ng, Fae Myenne. "A Red Sweater." *Charlie Chan Is Dead: An Anthology
> of Contemporary Asian American Fiction.* Ed. Jessica Hagedorn.
> New York: Penguin, 1993. 358-68. Print.

Normally, you will give the title of the work you are citing (probably an essay, short story, or poem) in quotation marks. If you are referring to a book-length work (for instance, a novel or a full-length play), italicize it. If the work is translated, after the period that follows the title, write *Trans.* and give the name of the translator, followed by a period and the name of the anthology.

If the collection is a multivolume work and you are using only one volume, in "Works Cited" you will specify the volume, as in the example on page 334 of McPherson's essay.

Remember that the pages specified in the entry in your list of works cited are to the *entire selection,* not simply to the pages you refer to within your paper.

If you are referring to a *reprint of a scholarly article,* give details of the original publication:

> Mack, Maynard. "The World of Hamlet." *Yale Review* 41:4 (June 1952):
> 502-23. Rpt. in *Hamlet.* By William Shakespeare. Ed. Sylvan Barnet.
> New York: Penguin-Putnam, 1998. 265-87. Print.

Two or More Works in an Anthology

If you are referring to more than one work in an anthology, in order to avoid repeating all the information about the anthology in each entry in "Works Cited," for each work cited give the author and title of the work, then a period, a space, and the name of the anthologist, followed by the page numbers that the selection spans. Thus, a reference to Shakespeare's *Hamlet* would be followed only by

Barnet 265-87.

rather than by a full citation of Barnet's anthology. This form requires that the anthology itself also be listed, under Barnet.

Two or More Works by the Same Author

Notice that the works are given in alphabetical order (*Fables* precedes *Fools*) and that the author's name is not repeated but is represented by three hyphens followed by a period and a space. If the author is the translator or editor of a volume, the three hyphens are followed not by a period but by a comma, then a space, then the appropriate abbreviation (*trans.* or *ed.*), then the title:

Frye, Northrop. *Fables of Identity: Studies in Poetic Mythology.* New York: Harcourt, 1963. Print.
—. *Fools of Time: Studies in Shakespearean Tragedy.* Toronto: U of Toronto P, 1967. Print.

A Translated Book

Dostoyevsky, Fyodor. *Crime and Punishment.* Trans. Sidney Monas. New York: Signet, 1999. Print.

If you are discussing the translation itself, as opposed to the book, list the work under the translator's name. Then put a comma, a space, and "trans." After the period following "trans." skip a space, then give the title of the book, a period, a space, and then "By" and the author's name, first name first. Continue with information about the place of publication, publisher, date, and medium, as in any entry to a book.

An Introduction, Foreword, Afterword, or Other Editorial Apparatus

Pynchon, Thomas. Foreword. *1984.* By George Orwell. New York: New American Lib, 2003. Print.

Usually a book with an introduction or similar material is listed under the name of the author of the book rather than the name of the author of the editorial material (see the citation to Pope on page 334). But if you are referring to the editor's apparatus rather than to the work itself, use the form just given.

Words such as *preface, introduction, afterword,* and *conclusion* are capitalized in the entry but are neither enclosed within quotation marks nor underlined.

A Book Review

First, an example of a review that does not have a title:

> Vendler, Helen. Rev. of *Essays on Style*. Ed. Roger Fowler. *Essays in Criticism* 16 (1966): 457-63. Print.

If the review has a title, give the title after the period following the reviewer's name, before "Rev." If the review is unsigned, list it under the first word of the title, or the second word if the first word is *A, An,* or *The*. If an unsigned review has no title, begin the entry with "Rev. of" and alphabetize it under the title of the work being reviewed.

An Encyclopedia

The first example is for a signed article, the second for an unsigned article:

> Lang, Andrew. "Ballads." *Encyclopaedia Britannica*. 1910 ed. Print.
> "Metaphor." *The New Encyclopaedia Britannica: Micropaedia*. 15th ed. 2005. Print.

An Article in a Scholarly Journal

Some journals are paginated consecutively; that is, the pagination of the second issue picks up where the first issue left off. Other journals begin each issue with page 1. The forms of the citations in "Works Cited" differ slightly.

First, the citation of *a journal that uses continuous pagination:*

> Burbick, Joan. "Emily Dickinson and the Economics of Desire." *American Literature* 58 (1986): 361-78. Print.

This article appeared in volume 58, which was published in 1986. (Notice that the volume number is followed by a space, then by the year in parentheses, and then by a colon, a space, and the page numbers of the entire article.) Although each volume consists of four issues, you do *not* specify the issue number when the journal is paginated continuously.

For a *journal that paginates each issue separately* (quarterlies often begin each issue in the same year with page 1), give the issue number directly after the volume number and a period, with no spaces before or after the period:

Spillers, Hortense J. "Martin Luther King and the Style of the Black Sermon." *The Black Scholar* 3.1 (September 1971): 14-27. Print.

An Article in a Weekly, Biweekly, or Monthly Publication

Delbanco, Andrew. "Money and the Novel." *New Republic* 23 July 2007: 43-47. Print.

Notice that the volume number and the issue number are omitted for popular weeklies or monthlies such as *Time* and *Atlantic*.

An Article in a Newspaper

Because newspapers usually consist of several sections, a section number may precede the page number. The example indicates that an article begins on page 3 of section 2 of the late edition and is continued on a later page:

Wu, Jim. "Authors Praise New Forms." *New York Times* 8 Mar. 1996, late ed., sec. 2: 3+. Print.

You may also have occasion to cite something other than a printed source, for instance, a lecture. Here are the forms for the chief nonprint sources.

An Interview

Saretta, Howard. Personal interview. 3 Nov. 2007.

A Lecture

Heaney, Seamus. Lecture. Tufts University. 20 Sept. 2007.

A Television or Radio Program

60 Minutes. CBS. WGBH, Boston, 26 Aug. 2007. Television.

A Film, Videotape, or DVD

Modern Times. Dir. Charles Chaplin. United Artists, 1936. Film.

A Recording (Audio Tape, CD, or LP)

Frost, Robert. "The Road Not Taken." *Robert Frost Reads His Poetry*. Caedmon, TC 1060, 1956. LP.

A Performance

> *The Cherry Orchard.* By Anton Chekhov. Dir. Ron Daniels. Amer.
> Repertory Theatre, Cambridge, MA. 3 Feb. 1994. Performance.

Reminder: For the form of citations to electronic material, see pages 350–52.

SAMPLE ESSAY WITH DOCUMENTATION: "THE WOMEN IN *DEATH OF A SALESMAN*"

Some research papers focus on the relation of a work to its original context, for instance Elizabethan views of *Julius Caesar*, or Charlotte Perkins Gilman's representation of medical treatment for women. But there are other kinds of research papers. One kind is chiefly concerned with studying a critical problem, for instance, with deciding among a variety of interpretations of a literary work. A paper of this sort involves a certain amount of summarizing, but it is much more than a summary of those interpretations because it evaluates them and finally offers its own conclusions.

Two things motivated Ruth Katz, the author of the following paper, to choose the topic that she chose. The first was a classroom discussion, early in the semester, concerning the question of whether male authors typically represent females in certain ways. The second was a published essay that disparaged Linda, a character in Arthur Miller's *Death of a Salesman*.

Katz took notes on index cards, both from the play and from secondary sources, and she arranged and rearranged her notes as her topic and her thesis became clearer to her. Here we print the final version of her essay, prefaced with the rough outline that she prepared before she wrote her first draft.

Linda

   realistic   *Both? **Not** so foolish; knows how to calm*

   encourages Willy *him down*

   foolish? loving?

    prevented him from succeeding?

    doesn't understand W's needs? or nothing else to do?

    quote some critics knocking Linda

other women

5   the Woman

4   the two women in restaurant   (Forsythe first, then Letta)

3   Jenny

2   W's mother (compare with father?)

check to see exactly what the play says about her

1   Howard's wife (and daughter?)

6   discuss Linda last

titles?

Linda Loman

Women in Miller's Salesman

Gender in . . .   Male and female in Death . . .

Men and Women: Arthur M's View
Willy Loman's Women

Here is the final version of the essay.

Ruth Katz
Professor Wilde
English 10
21 December 2010

The Women in *Death of a Salesman*

Death of a Salesman is of course about a salesman, but it is also about the American dream of success. Somewhere in between the narrowest topic, the death of a salesman, and the largest topic, the examination of American values, is Miller's picture of the American family. This paper will study one member of the family, Willy's wife, Linda Loman, but before examining Miller's depiction of her, it will look at Miller's depiction of other women in the play in order to make clear Linda's distinctive traits. We will see that although her role in society is extremely limited, she is an admirable figure, fulfilling the roles of wife and mother with remarkable intelligence.

Much of the time, Linda is the only woman who is on stage but there are several other women in the play: "the Woman" (the unnamed woman in Willy's hotel room), Miss Forsythe and her friend Letta (the two women who join the brothers in the restaurant), Jenny (Charley's secretary), the various women that the brothers talk about, and the voices of Howard's daughter and wife. We also hear a little about Willy's mother.

We will look first at the least important (but not utterly unimportant) of these, the voices of Howard's daughter and wife on the wire recorder. Of Howard's seven-year-old daughter we know only that she can whistle "Roll Out the Barrel" and that according to Howard she "is crazy about me." The other woman in Howard's life is equally under his thumb. Here is the dialogue that tells us about her—and her relation to her husband.

> HOWARD'S VOICE. "Go on, say something." (*Pause*)
> "Well, you gonna talk?"
> HIS WIFE. "I can't think of anything."
> HOWARD'S VOICE. "Well, talk—it's turning."
> HIS WIFE (*shyly, beaten*). "Hello." (Silence.) "Oh, Howard, I can't talk into this . . ."
> HOWARD (*snapping the machine off*). That was my wife. (1419)

There is, in fact, a third woman in Howard's life, the maid. Howard says that if he can't be at home when the Jack Benny program comes on, he uses the wire recorder. He tells "the maid to turn the radio on when Jack Benny comes on, and this automatically goes on with the radio" (1419). In short, the women in Howard's world exist to serve (and to worship) him.

Another woman who seems to have existed only to serve men is Willy Loman's mother. On one occasion, in speaking with Ben, Willy remembers being on her lap, and Ben, on learning that his mother is dead, utters a platitudinous description of her, "Fine specimen of a lady, Mother" (1404), but that's as much as we learn of her. Willy is chiefly interested in learning about his father, who left the family and went to Alaska. Ben characterizes the father as "a very great and a very wild-hearted man" (1405), but the fact that the father left his family and apparently had no further communication with his wife and children seems to mean nothing to Ben. Presumably the mother struggled alone to bring up the boys, but her efforts are unmentioned. Curiously, some writers defend the father's desertion of his family. Lois Gordon says, "The first generation (Willy's father) has been forced, in order to make a living, to break up the family" (278), but nothing in the play supports this assertion that the father was "forced" to break up the family.

Willy, like Ben, assumes that men are heroic and women are nothing except servants and sex machines. For instance, Willy says to Ben, "Please tell about Dad. I want my boys to hear. I want them to know the kind of stock they spring from" (1405). As Kay Stanton, a feminist critic, says, Willy's words imply "an Edenic birth myth," a world "with all the Loman men springing directly from their father's side, with no commingling with a female" (69).

Another woman who, like Howard's maid and Willy's mother, apparently exists only to serve is Jenny, Charley's secretary. She is courteous, and she is treated courteously by Charley and by Charley's son, Bernard, but she has no identity other than that of a secretary. And, as a secretary—that is, as a nonentity in the eyes of at least some men—she can be addressed insensitively. Willy Loman makes off-color remarks to her:

> WILLY. . . . Jenny, Jenny, good to see you. How're ya? Workin'? Or still honest?
> JENNY. Fine. How've you been feeling?
> WILLY. Not much any more, Jenny. Ha, ha! (1426)

The first of these comments seems to suggest that a working woman is *not* honest—that is, is a prostitute or is engaged in some other sort of hanky-panky, as is the Woman, who in exchange for silk stockings and sex sends Willy directly into the buyer's office. The second of Willy's jokes, with its remark about not feeling much, also refers to sex. In short, though readers or viewers of the play see Jenny as a thoroughly respectable woman, they see her not so much as an individual but as a person engaged in routine work and as a person to whom Willy can speak crudely.

It is a little harder to be certain about the characters of Miss Forsythe and Letta, the two women in the scene in Stanley's

restaurant. For Happy, Miss Forsythe is "strudel," an object for
a man to consume, and for Stanley, she and her friend Letta are
"chippies," that is, prostitutes. But is it clear that they are prostitutes?
When Happy tells Miss Forsythe that he is in the business of
selling, he makes a dirty joke, saying, "You don't happen to sell,
do you?" (1431). She replies, "No, I don't sell," and if we take this
seriously and if we believe her, we can say that she is respectable
and is rightly putting Happy in his place. Further, her friend Letta
says, "I gotta get up very early tomorrow. I got jury duty" (1454),
which implies that she is a responsible citizen. Still, the girls do not
seem especially thoughtful. When Biff introduces Willy to the girls,
Letta says, "Isn't he cute? Sit down with us, Pop" (1438), and when
Willy breaks down in the restaurant, Miss Forsythe says, "Say, I
don't like that temper of his" (1438). Perhaps we can say this: It is
going too far—on the basis of what we see—to agree with Stanley
that the women are "chippies," or with Happy, who assumes that
every woman is available for sex, but Miss Forsythe and Letta do
not seem to be especially responsible or even interesting people.
That is, as Miller presents them, they are of little substance, simply
figures introduced into the play in order to show how badly Happy
and Biff behave.

The most important woman in the play, other than Linda,
is "the Woman," who for money or stockings and perhaps for
pleasure has sex with Willy, and who will use her influence as a
receptionist or secretary in the office to send Willy directly on to
the buyer, without his having to wait at the desk. But even though
the Woman gets something out of the relationship, she knows that
she is being used. When Biff appears in the hotel room, she asks
him, "Are you football or baseball?" Biff replies, "Football," and the
Woman, *"angry, humiliated,"* says, "That's me too" (1441). We can
admire her vigorous response, but, again, like the other women
whom we have discussed, she is not really an impressive figure.
We can say that, at best, in a society that assumes women are to be
exploited by men, she holds her own.

So far, then—though we have not yet talked about Linda—
the world of *Death of a Salesman* is not notable for its pictures of
impressive women. True, most of the males in the play—Willy, Biff,

Happy, Ben, and such lesser characters as Stanley and Howard—
are themselves pretty sorry specimens, but Bernard and Charley
are exceptionally decent and successful people, people who can
well serve as role models. Can any female character in the play
serve as a role model?

Linda has evoked strongly contrasting reactions from the
critics. Some of them judge her very severely. For instance, Lois
Gordon says that Linda "encourages Willy's dream, yet she will not
let him leave her for the New Continent, the only realm where the
dream can be fulfilled" (279). True, Linda urges Willy not to follow
Ben's advice of going to Alaska, but surely the spectator of the play
cannot believe that Willy is the sort of man who can follow in Ben's
footsteps and violently make a fortune. And, in fact, Ben is so vile
a person (as when he trips Biff, threatens Biff's eye with the point
of his umbrella, and says, "Never fight fair with a stranger, boy"
(1421), that we would not want Willy to take Ben's advice.

A second example of a harsh view of Linda is Brian Parker's
comment on "the essential stupidity of Linda's behavior. Surely it is
both stupid and immoral to encourage the man you love in
self-deceit and lies" (54). Parker also says that Linda's speech at
the end, when she says she cannot understand why Willy killed
himself, "is not only pathetic, it is also an explanation of the
loneliness of Willy Loman which threw him into other women's
arms" (54). Nothing in the play suggests that Linda was anything
other than a highly supportive wife. If Willy turned to other women,
surely it was not because Linda did not understand him.

Another example of the Linda-bashing school of commentary
comes from Guerin Bliquez, who speaks of "Linda's facility for
prodding Willy to his doom" (383). Bert Cardullo, in a recent essay,
goes even further, pointing to a basic flaw, a contradiction, in Miller's
conception of Linda as a character; she "is less a character than a
saint, on the one hand, or a co-dependent, on the other" (595).

The arguments against Linda are essentially that (1) she has
selfishly prevented Willy from going to Alaska, (2) she stupidly
encourages him in his self-deceptions, and (3) she is materialistic,
so that even at the end, in the Requiem, when she says she has
made the last payment on the house, she is talking about money.

But if we study the play we will see that all three of these charges are false. First, although Linda does indeed discourage Willy from taking Ben's advice and going to Alaska, she points out that there is no need for "everyone [to] conquer the world," and that Willy has "a beautiful job here" (1423), a job with excellent prospects. She may be mistaken in thinking that Willy has a good job—he may have misled her—but, given what seems to be the situation, her comment is entirely reasonable. So far as the second charge goes, that she encourages him in self-deception, there are two answers. First, on some matters she does not know that Willy has lied to her, and so her encouragement is reasonable and right. Second, on other matters she does know that Willy is not telling the truth, but she rightly thinks it is best not to let him know that she knows, since such a revelation would crush what little self-respect remains in him. Consider, for example, this portion of dialogue, near the end of the play, when Biff decides to leave for good: She goes to Willy and says, "I think that's the best way, dear. 'Cause there's no use drawing it out, you'll just never get along" (1446). Linda is not the most forceful person alive, or the brightest, but she is decent and she sees more clearly than do any of the other Lomans.

There is nothing in the play to suggest that Arthur Miller is a feminist or was ahead of his time in his view of the role of women. On the contrary, the play seems to give a prefeminist view, with women playing subordinate roles to men. The images of success of the best sort—not of Ben's ruthless sort—are Charley and Bernard, two males. Probably Miller, writing in the 1940s, could hardly conceive of a successful woman other than as a wife or mother. Notice, by the way, that Bernard—probably the most admirable male in the play—is not only an important lawyer but the father of two sons, apparently a sign of his complete success as a man. Still, Miller's picture of Linda is by no means condescending. Linda may not be a genius, but she is the brightest and the most realistic of the Lomans. Things turn out badly, but not because of Linda. The viewer leaves the theater with profound respect for her patience, her strength, her sense of decency, and, yes, her intelligence and her competence in dealing with incompetent men.

[New page]

Works Cited

Bliquez, Guerin. "Linda's Role in *Death of a Salesman*." *Modern Drama* 10 (1968): 383-86. Print.

Cardullo, Bert. "Death of a Salesman, Life of a Jew: Ethnicity, Business, and the Character of Willy Loman." *Southwest Review* 92:4 (2007): 583-596. Academic Search Complete. Web. 19 Oct. 2010.

Gordon, Lois. "*Death of a Salesman*: An Appreciation." *The Forties: Fiction, Poetry, Drama*. Ed. Warren French. Deland: Everett/ Edwards, 1969. 273-83. Print.

Miller, Arthur. *Death of a Salesman. An Introduction to Literature*, Ed. Sylvan Barnet, William Burto, and William E. Cain. 16th ed. New York: Longman, 2011. 1199-1267. Print.

Parker, Brian. "Point of View in Arthur Miller's *Death of a Salesman*." *University of Toronto Quarterly* 35 (1966): 144-47. Print.

Stanton, Kay. "Women and the American Dream of *Death of a Salesman*." *Feminist Readings of American Drama*. Ed. Judith Schlueter. Rutherford: Fairleigh Dickinson UP, 1989. 67-102. Print.

✔ Checklist: Reading the Draft of a Research Paper

❑ Is the tentative title informative and focused?

❑ Does the paper make a point, or does it just accumulate other people's ideas? (See pages 315, 322–24, 326–27.)

❑ Does it reveal the thesis early? (See page 305.)

❑ Are claims supported by evidence? (See pages 28, 49, 61, 93, 106.)

❑ Are all the *words* and *ideas* of the sources accurately attributed? (See pages 328–29.)

❑ Are quotations introduced adequately with signal phrases (such as "according to Ziff," or "Smith contents," or "Johnson points out" to indicate who is speaking? (See page 37.)

❑   Are all of the long quotations necessary, or can some of them be ef-
fectively summarized? (See page 321.)
❑   Are quotations discussed adequately? (See page 326.)
❑   Does the paper advance in orderly stages? Can your imagined reader
easily follow your thinking? (See Chapter 3.)
❑   Is the documentation in the correct form?

ELECTRONIC SOURCES

Encyclopedias: Print and Electronic Versions

Encyclopedias can give you the basics about a subject, but like all resources, they have limitations. An encyclopedia may not cover the subject
that you are researching or may not cover it in adequate depth. Knowledge
expands rapidly, and because it does, even a good encyclopedia lags somewhat behind current scholarship. A number of encyclopedias are now in
CD-ROM form, and the CD makes searches for information easier. Many
such encyclopedias are linked to the World Wide Web, where updated
information and links to reference and research resources are listed. It is
now even more common to find that encyclopedias and other reference
works are available online, through collections of reference resources organized by college, university, state, and local libraries. Be sure to check
with the librarians at your school; they can tell you about the kinds of
resources that are available. If your library offers a tutorial on the use of
electronic and Internet resources, we recommend that you sign up for
it. We take such tutorials ourselves with our students every year, and are
always surprised by the new resources we learn about.

It is helpful to have updated information and links, but only when
they are reliable. Remember to be a critical user of reference materials. Not everything is of equal value, and we must make good judgments
about the sources we consult—and whether or not we can depend on
them for reliable, accurate information.

The Internet and the Web

Because of the ease of using the Internet, with its access to electronic
mail (e-mail), newsgroups, mailing lists, and, especially, sites and links on
the Web, many students now make it their first—and, unfortunately, too
often their *only*—resource for research.

As we just noted, all of us must be *critical* users of the materials we find on the web. The web is up to date *and* out of date, helpful *and* disappointing. It can be a researcher's dream come true, but also a source of errors and a time-waster.

Keeping this point in mind, we recommend to students that for each Web site they consult, they should consult at least two print sources.

EVALUATING SOURCES ON THE INTERNET

For sources on the Web, as with print sources, you must evaluate what you have located and gauge how much or how little it will contribute to your literary analysis and argument. In the words of one reference librarian, Joan Stockard (formerly of Wellesley College), "The most serious mistake students make when they use the Internet for research is to assume everything is of equal (and acceptable) quality. They need to establish who wrote the material, the qualifications of the author to write on the topic, whether any bias is likely, how current the information is, and how other resources compare."

✔ Checklist: Using Web sites on the Internet

❑ Focus the topic of your research as precisely as you can before you embark on a Web search. Lots of surfing and browsing can sometimes turn up good material, but using the Web without a focus can prove distracting and unproductive. It takes you away from library research (where the results might be better) and from the actual planning and writing of the paper.

❑ Ask the following questions:
  • Does this site or page look like it can help me in my assignment?
  • Whose site or page is this?
  • Who is the intended audience?
  • What is the point of view? Are there signs of a specific slant or bias?
  • How good is the detail, depth, and quality of the material presented?
  • Is the site well-constructed and well-organized?
  • Is the text well-written?
  • Can the information be corroborated or supported by print sources?

- When was the site or page made available? Has it been recently revised or updated?
- Can the person, institution, company, or agency responsible for this site or page receive e-mail comments, questions, and criticisms?

WIKIPEDIA

Some instructors forbid students to use *Wikipedia* in research papers because its entries are not rigorously edited and may be inaccurate or misleading. This is true, but it also is true that many instructors and students do consult *Wikipedia*. Frequently it is the first listing result when we do a search for basic information about, or an overview of, a topic. Check with your instructor: What is his or her policy about *Wikipedia*? As a general rule, if you find a piece of information in a *Wikipedia* entry, verify it by using a second source, one that you know is reliable.

DOCUMENTATION: CITING A WEB SOURCE

For accuracy's sake, you will want to copy the URL from the location line of your browser and paste it into your draft list of works cited. However, your final Works Cited list should not include URLs, according to MLA guidelines, unless you think your readers would not be able to find the site without it.

✔ Checklist: Citing Internet Sources

Provide the following information:

- ❑ Author
- ❑ Title
- ❑ Publication information
- ❑ Title of archive or database
- ❑ Name of institution/organization that supports or is associated with the site
- ❑ Date (if given) when the site was posted; sometimes termed the "revision" or "modification" date
- ❑ The medium: Web.
- ❑ Date that you accessed this source

Many Web sites and pages, however, are not prepared according to the style and form in which you want to cite them. Sometimes the name of the author is unknown, and other information may be missing or hard to find. Nor can you be certain that the site will exist when your readers attempt to access it. These difficulties aside, perhaps the main point to remember is that a source on the Web is as much a source as is a book or article that you can track down and read in the library. If you have made use of it, you must acknowledge that you have done so and include the bibliographical information, as fully as you can, in your list of works cited for the paper.

Many college and university libraries offer, in their online resources, detailed descriptions of MLA formatting and style. This can be a valuable resource if you need to double-check something or are unsure about how to cite an online or a print source. Your instructor or reference librarian can tell you if this is the case at your school. You can also consult the excellent Web site maintained by the Purdue University Online Writing Lab (OWL): <http://owl.english.purdue.edu/>.

The Modern Language Association (MLA) recommends the following general conventions.

Publication and Access Dates For sources taken from the Internet, include the date the source was posted to the Internet or last updated or revised; give also the date the source was accessed.

Uniform Resource Locators Include a full and accurate URL only for a source that you believe will be hard to locate without using the URL. Enclose URLs in angle brackets (< >). When a URL continues from one line to the next, break it only after a slash. Do not add a hyphen.

When citing electronic sources, follow the formatting conventions illustrated by the following models.

An Online Scholarly Project or Database

> *The Walt Whitman Hypertext Archive.* Ed. Kenneth M. Price and Ed Folsom. College of William and Mary. 16 Mar. 1998. 3 Apr. Web. 1998.

1. Title of project or database
2. Name of editor of project
3. Sponsor of project
4. Date of publication
5. Medium
6. Date of access

A Short Work within a Scholarly Project

> Whitman, Walt. "Crossing Brooklyn Ferry." *The Walt Whitman Hypertext Archive.* Ed. Kenneth M. Price and Ed Folsom. College of William and Mary. 16 Mar. 1998. Web. 3 Apr. 1998.

An Online Book within a Scholarly Project

> Whitman, Walt. *Leaves of Grass.* Philadelphia: McKay, 1891-92. *The Walt Whitman Hypertext Archive.* Ed. Kenneth M. Price and Ed Folsom. College of William and Mary. 16 Mar. 1998. Web. 3 Apr. 1998.

1. Author's name
2. Title of the work
3. Name of the editor, compiler, or translator (if relevant)
4. Print publication information
5. Electronic publication information as in previous example

An Article in a Scholarly Journal

> Buincki, Martin T. "Walt Whitman and the Question of Copyright." *American Literacy History* 15:2 (Summer 2003): 248-275. Academic Search Complete. Web. 26 Aug. 2007.

1. Author's name
2. Title of the work or material in quotation marks
3. Name of periodical
4. Volume number, issue number, or other identifying number
5. Date of publication
6. Page numbers or number of paragraphs, pages, or other numbered sections (if any)
7. Name of database or Web site
8. Medium
9. Date of access

✏️ A RULE FOR WRITERS

Remember that when you use a source from an Internet Web site, you need to acknowledge and cite it, just as you do when you use a print source.

Appendix A

TWO STORIES

James Joyce
(1882–1941)

Araby

North Richmond Street, being blind,[1] was a quiet street except at the hour when the Christian Brothers' School set the boys free. An uninhabited house of two stories stood at the blind end, detached from its neighbors in a square ground. The other houses of the street, conscious of decent lives within them, gazed at one another with brown imperturbable faces.

The former tenant of our house, a priest, had died in the back drawing-room. Air, musty from having long been enclosed, hung in all the rooms, and the waste room behind the kitchen was littered with old useless papers. Among these I found a few papercovered books, the pages of which were curled and damp: *The Abbot,* by Walter Scott, *The Devout Communicant* and *The Memoirs of Vidocq.*[2] I liked the last best because its leaves were yellow. The wild garden behind the house contained a central apple-tree and a few straggling bushes under one of which I found the late tenant's rusty bicycle-pump. He had been a very charitable priest; in his will he had left all his money to institutions and the furniture of his house to his sister.

When the short days of winter came dusk fell before we had well eaten our dinners. When we met in the street the houses had grown sombre. The space of sky above us was the colour of everchanging violet and towards it the lamps of the street lifted their feeble lanterns. The cold air stung us and we played till our bodies glowed. Our shouts echoed in the silent street. The career of our play brought us through the dark muddy lanes behind the houses where we ran the gauntlet of

---

[1] **blind** a dead-end street.
[2] ***The Abbot*** is one of Scott's popular historical romances; ***The Devout Communicant*** is a Catholic religious manual; ***The Memoirs of Vidocq*** are the memoirs of the chief of the French detective force.

the rough tribes from the cottages, to the back doors of the dark dripping gardens where odours arose from the ashpits, to the dark odorous stables where a coachman smoothed and combed the horse or shook music from the buckled harness. When we returned to the street light from the kitchen windows had filled the areas. If my uncle was seen turning the corner we hid in the shadow until we had seen him safely housed. Or if Mangan's sister came out on the doorstep to call her brother in to his tea we watched her from our shadow peer up and down the street. We waited to see whether she would remain or go in and, if she remained, we left our shadow and walked up to Mangan's steps resignedly. She was waiting for us, her figure defined by the light from the half-opened door. Her brother always teased her before he obeyed and I stood by the railings looking at her. Her dress swung as she moved her body and the soft rope of her hair tossed from side to side.

Every morning I lay on the floor in the front parlour watching her door. The blind was pulled down to within an inch of the sash so that I could not be seen. When she came out on the doorstep my heart leaped. I ran to the hall, seized my books and followed her. I kept her brown figure always in my eye and, when we came near the point at which our ways diverged, I quickened my pace and passed her. This happened morning after morning. I had never spoken to her, except for a few casual words, and yet her name was like a summons to all my foolish blood.

Her image accompanied me even in places the most hostile to romance. On Saturday evenings when my aunt went marketing I had to go to carry some of the parcels. We walked through the flaring streets, jostled by drunken men and bargaining women, amid the curses of labourers, the shrill litanies of shop-boys who stood on guard by the barrels of pigs' cheeks, the nasal chanting of street-singers, who sang a *come-all-you* about O'Donovan Rossa,[3] or a ballad about the troubles in our native land. These noises converged in a single sensation of life for me: I imagined that I bore my chalice safely through a throng of foes. Her name sprang to my lips at moments in strange prayers and praises which I myself did not understand. My eyes were often full of tears (I could not tell why) and at times a flood from my heart seemed to pour itself out into my bosom. I thought little of the future. I did not know whether I would ever speak to her or not or, if I spoke to her, how I could tell her of my confused adoration. But my body was like a harp and her words and gestures were like fingers running upon the wires.

One evening I went into the back drawing-room in which the priest had died. It was a dark rainy evening and there was no sound in the house. Through one of the broken panes I heard the rain impinge upon the earth, the fine incessant needles of water playing in the sodden beds. Some distant lamp or lighted window gleamed below me. I was thankful that I could see so little. All my senses seemed

---

[3] **Jeremiah O'Donovan** (1831–1915), a popular Irish leader who was jailed by the British for advocating violent rebellion (his nickname was Dynamite Rossa). A **come-all-you** was a topical song that began "Come all you gallant Irishmen."

to desire to veil themselves and, feeling that I was about to slip from them, I pressed the palms of my hands together until they trembled, murmuring: *O love! O love!* many times.

At last she spoke to me. When she addressed the first words to me I was so confused that I did not know what to answer. She asked me was I going to Araby. I forget whether I answered yes or no. It would be a splendid bazaar, she said; she would love to go.

—And why can't you? I asked.

While she spoke she turned a silver bracelet round and round her wrist. She could not go, she said, because there would be a retreat that week in her convent. Her brother and two other boys were fighting for their caps and I was alone at the railings. She held one of the spikes, bowing her head towards me. The light from the lamp opposite our door caught the white curve of her neck, lit up her hair that rested there and, falling, lit up the hand upon the railing. It fell over one side of her dress and caught the white border of a petticoat, just visible as she stood at ease.

—It's well for you, she said.

—If I go, I said, I will bring you something.

What innumerable follies laid waste my waking and sleeping thoughts after that evening! I wished to annihilate the tedious intervening days. I chafed against the work of school. At night in my bedroom and by day in the classroom her image came between me and the page I strove to read. The syllables of the word *Araby* were called to me through the silence in which my soul luxuriated and cast an Eastern enchantment over me. I asked for leave to go to the bazaar on Saturday night. My aunt was surprised and hoped it was not some Freemason[4] affair. I answered few questions in class, I watched my master's face pass from amiability to sternness; he hoped I was not beginning to idle. I could not call my wandering thoughts together. I had hardly any patience with the serious work of life which, now that it stood between me and my desire, seemed to me child's play, ugly monotonous child's play.

On Saturday morning I reminded my uncle that I wished to go to the bazaar in the evening. He was fussing at the hallstand, looking for the hat-brush, and answered me curtly:

—Yes, boy, I know.

As he was in the hall I could not go into the front parlour and lie at the window. I left the house in bad humour and walked slowly towards the school. The air was pitilessly raw and already my heart misgave me.

When I came home to dinner my uncle had not yet been home. Still it was early. I sat staring at the clock for some time and, when its ticking began to irritate me, I left the room. I mounted the staircase and gained the upper part of the

---

[4] **Freemason** Irish Catholics viewed the Masons as their Protestant enemies.

house. The high cold empty gloomy rooms liberated me and I went from room to room singing. From the front window I saw my companions playing below in the street. Their cries reached me weakened and indistinct and, leaning my forehead against the cool glass, I looked over at the dark house where she lived. I may have stood there for an hour, seeing nothing but the brown-clad figure cast by my imagination, touched discreetly by the lamplight at the curved neck, at the hand upon the railings and at the border below the dress.

When I came downstairs again I found Mrs Mercer sitting at the fire. She was an old garrulous woman, a pawnbroker's widow, who collected used stamps for some pious purpose. I had to endure the gossip of the tea-table. The meal was prolonged beyond an hour and still my uncle did not come. Mrs Mercer stood up to go: she was sorry she couldn't wait any longer, but it was after eight o'clock and she did not like to be out late, as the night air was bad for her. When she had gone I began to walk up and down the room, clenching my fists. My aunt said:

—I'm afraid you may put off your bazaar for this night of Our Lord.

At nine o'clock I heard my uncle's latchkey in the halldoor. I heard him talking to himself and heard the hallstand rocking when it had received the weight of his overcoat. I could interpret these signs. When he was midway through his dinner I asked him to give me the money to go to the bazaar. He had forgotten.

—The people are in bed and after their first sleep now, he said.

I did not smile. My aunt said to him energetically:

—Can't you give him the money and let him go? You've kept him late enough as it is.

My uncle said he was very sorry he had forgotten. He said he believed in the old saying: *All work and no play makes Jack a dull boy.* He asked me where I was going and, when I had told him a second time he asked me did I know *The Arab's Farewell to His Steed.*[5] When I left the kitchen he was about to recite the opening lines of the piece to my aunt.

I held a florin tightly in my hand as I strode down Buckingham Street towards the station. The sight of the streets thronged with buyers and glaring with gas recalled to me the purpose of my journey. I took my seat in a third-class carriage of a deserted train. After an intolerable delay the train moved out of the station slowly. It crept onward among ruinous houses and over the twinkling river. At Westland Row Station a crowd of people pressed to the carriage doors; but the porters moved them back, saying that it was a special train for the bazaar. I remained alone in the bare carriage. In a few minutes the train drew up beside an improvised wooden platform. I passed out on to the road and saw by the lighted dial of a clock that it was ten minutes to ten. In front of me was a large building which displayed the magical name.

---

[5] *The Arab's Farewell* "The Arab to His Favorite Steed" was a popular sentimental poem by Caroline Norton (1808–77).

I could not find any sixpenny entrance and, fearing that the bazaar would be closed, I passed in quickly through a turnstile, handing a shilling to a weary-looking man. I found myself in a big hall girdled at half its height by a gallery. Nearly all the stalls were closed and the greater part of the hall was in darkness. I recognised a silence like that which pervades a church after a service. I walked into the center of the bazaar timidly. A few people were gathered about the stalls which were still open. Before a curtain, over which the words *Café Chantant* were written in coloured lamps, two men were counting money on a salver. I listened to the fall of the coins.

Remembering with difficulty why I had come I went over to one of the stalls and examined porcelain vases and flowered teasets. At the door of the stall a young lady was talking and laughing with two young gentlemen. I remarked their English accents and listened vaguely to their conversation.

—O, I never said such a thing!

—O, but you did!

—O, but I didn't!

—Didn't she say that?

—Yes! I heard her.

—O, there's a . . . fib!

Observing me the young lady came over and asked me did I wish to buy anything. The tone of her voice was not encouraging; she seemed to have spoken to me out of a sense of duty. I looked humbly at the great jars that stood like eastern guards at either side of the dark entrance to the stall and murmured:

—No, thank you.

The young lady changed the position of one of the vases and went back to the two young men. They began to talk of the same subject. Once or twice the young lady glanced at me over her shoulder.

I lingered before her stall, though I knew my stay was useless, to make my interest in her wares seem the more real. Then I turned away slowly and walked down the middle of the bazaar. I allowed the two pennies to fall against the six-pence in my pocket. I heard a voice call from one end of the gallery that the light was out. The upper part of the hall was now completely dark.

Gazing up into the darkness I saw myself as a creature driven and derided by vanity; and my eyes burned with anguish and anger.

Eudora Welty

(1909–2001)

A WORN PATH

It was December—a bright frozen day in the early morning. Far out in the country there was an old Negro woman with her head tied in a red rag, coming along a path through the pinewoods. Her name was Phoenix Jackson. She was very old and small and she walked slowly in the dark pine shadows, moving a little from side to side in her steps, with the balanced heaviness and lightness of a pendulum in a grandfather clock. She carried a thin, small cane made from an umbrella, and with this she kept tapping the frozen earth in front of her. This made a grave and persistent noise in the still air, that seemed meditative like the chirping of a solitary little bird.

She wore a dark striped dress reaching down to her shoe tops, and an equally long apron of bleached sugar sacks, with a full pocket: all neat and tidy, but every time she took a step she might have fallen over her shoelaces, which dragged from her unlaced shoes. She looked straight ahead. Her eyes were blue with age. Her skin had a pattern all its own of numberless branching wrinkles and as though a whole little tree stood in the middle of her forehead, but a golden color ran underneath, and the two knobs of her cheeks were illumined by a yellow burning under the dark. Under the red rag her hair came down on her neck in the frailest of ringlets, still black, and with an odor like copper.

Now and then there was a quivering in the thicket. Old Phoenix said, "Out of my way, all you foxes, owls, beetles, jack rabbits, coons and wild animals! . . . Keep out from under these feet, little bob-whites. . . . Keep the big wild hogs out of my path. Don't let none of those come running my direction. I got a long way." Under her small black-freckled hand her cane, limber as a buggy whip, would switch at the brush as if to rouse up any hiding things.

On she went. The woods were deep and still. The sun made the pine needles almost too bright to look at, up where the wind rocked. The cones dropped as light as feathers. Down in the hollow was the mourning dove—it was not too late for him.

The path ran up a hill. "Seem like there is chains about my feet, time I get this far," she said, in the voice of argument old people keep to use with themselves. "Something always take a hold of me on this hill—pleads I should stay."

After she got to the top she turned and gave a full, severe look behind her where she had come. "Up through pines," she said at length. "Now down through oaks."

Her eyes opened their widest, and she started down gently. But before she got to the bottom of the hill a bush caught her dress.

Her fingers were busy and intent, but her skirts were full and long, so that before she could pull them free in one place they were caught in another. It was not possible to allow the dress to tear. "I in the thorny bush," she said. "Thorns, you doing your appointed work. Never want to let folks pass, no sir. Old eyes thought you was a pretty little *green* bush."

Finally, trembling all over, she stood free, and after a moment dared to stoop for her cane.

"Sun so high!" she cried, leaning back and looking, while the thick tears went over her eyes. "The time getting all gone here."

At the foot of this hill was a place where a log was laid across the creek.

"Now comes the trial," said Phoenix.

Putting her right foot out, she mounted the log and shut her eyes. Lifting her skirt, leveling her cane fiercely before her, like a festival figure in some parade, she began to march across. Then she opened her eyes and she was safe on the other side.

"I wasn't as old as I thought," she said.

But she sat down to rest. She spread her skirts on the bank around her and folded her hands over her knees. Up above her was a tree in a pearly cloud of mistletoe. She did not dare to close her eyes, and when a little boy brought her a plate with a slice of marble-cake on it she spoke to him. "That would be acceptable," she said. But when she went to take it there was just her own hand in the air.

So she left that tree, and had to go through a barbed-wire fence. There she had to creep and crawl, spreading her knees and stretching her fingers like a baby trying to climb the steps. But she talked loudly to herself: she could not let her dress be torn now, so late in the day, and she could not pay for having her arm or her leg sawed off if she got caught fast where she was.

At last she was safe through the fence and risen up out in the clearing. Big dead trees, like black men with one arm, were standing in the purple stalks of the withered cotton field. There sat a buzzard.

"Who you watching?"

In the furrow she made her way along.

"Glad this not the season for bulls," she said, looking sideways, "and the good Lord made his snakes to curl up and sleep in the winter. A pleasure I don't see no two-headed snake coming around that tree, where it come once. It took a while to get by him, back in the summer."

She passed through the old cotton and went into a field of dead corn. It whispered and shook and was taller than her head. "Through the maze now," she said, for there was no path.

Then there was something tall, black, and skinny there, moving before her.

At first she took it for a man. It could have been a man dancing in the field. But she stood still and listened, and it did not make a sound. It was as silent as a ghost.

"Ghost," she said sharply, "who be you the ghost of? For I have heard of nary death close by."

But there was no answer—only the ragged dancing in the wind.

She shut her eyes, reached out her hand, and touched a sleeve. She found a coat and inside that an emptiness, cold as ice.

"You scarecrow," she said. Her face lighted. "I ought to be shut up for good," she said with laughter. "My senses is gone. I too old. I the oldest people I ever know. Dance, old scarecrow," she said, "while I dancing with you."

She kicked her foot over the furrow, and with mouth drawn down, shook her head once or twice in a little strutting way. Some husks blew down and whirled in streamers about her skirts.

Then she went on, parting her way from side to side with the cane, through the whispering field. At last she came to the end, to a wagon track where the silver grass blew between the red ruts. The quail were walking around like pullets, seeming all dainty and unseen.

"Walk pretty," she said. "This the easy place. This the easy going."

She followed the track, swaying through the quiet bare fields, through the little strings of trees silver in their dead leaves, past cabins silver from weather, with the doors and windows boarded shut, all like old women under a spell sitting there. "I walking in their sleep," she said, nodding her head vigorously.

In a ravine she went where a spring was silently flowing through a hollow log. Old Phoenix bent and drank. "Sweet-gum makes the water sweet," she said, and drank more. "Nobody know who made this well, for it was here when I was born."

The track crossed a swampy part where the moss hung as white as lace from every limb. "Sleep on, alligators, and blow your bubbles." Then the track went into the road.

Deep, deep the road went down between the high green-colored banks. Overhead the live-oaks met, and it was as dark as a cave.

A black dog with a lolling tongue came up out of the weeds by the ditch. She was meditating, and not ready, and when he came at her she only hit him a little with her cane. Over she went in the ditch, like a little puff of milkweed.

Down there, her senses drifted away. A dream visited her, and she reached her hand up, but nothing reached down and gave her a pull. So she lay there and presently went to talking. "Old woman," she said to herself, "that black dog come up out of the weeds to stall you off, and now there he sitting on his fine tail, smiling at you."

A white man finally came along and found her—a hunter, a young man, with his dog on a chain.

"Well, Granny!" he laughed. "What are you doing there?"

"Lying on my back like a June-bug waiting to be turned over, mister," she said, reaching up her hand.

He lifted her up, gave her a swing in the air, and set her down. "Anything broken, Granny?"

"No sir, them old dead weeds is springy enough," said Phoenix, when she had got her breath. "I thank you for your trouble."

"Where do you live, Granny?" he asked, while the two dogs were growling at each other.

"Away back yonder, sir, behind the ridge. You can't even see it from here."

"On your way home?"

"No sir, I going to town."

"Why, that's too far! That's as far as I walk when I come out myself, and I get something for my trouble." He patted the stuffed bag he carried, and there hung down a little closed claw. It was one of the bob-whites, with its beak hooked bitterly to show it was dead. "Now you go on home, Granny!"

"I bound to go to town, mister," said Phoenix. "The time come around."

He gave another laugh, filling the whole landscape. "I know you old colored people! Wouldn't miss going to town to see Santa Claus!"

But something held old Phoenix very still. The deep lines in her face went into a fierce and different radiation. Without warning, she had seen with her own eyes a flashing nickel fall out of the man's pocket onto the ground.

"How old are you, Granny?" he was saying.

"There is no telling, mister," she said, "no telling."

Then she gave a little cry and clapped her hands and said, "Git on away from here, dog! Look! Look at that dog!" She laughed as if in admiration. "He ain't scared of nobody. He a big black dog." She whispered, "Sic him!"

"Watch me get rid of that cur," said the man. "Sic him, Pete! Sic him!"

Phoenix heard the dogs fighting, and heard the man running and throwing sticks. She even heard a gunshot. But she was slowly bending forward by that time, further and further forward, the lids stretched down over her eyes, as if she were doing this in her sleep. Her chin was lowered almost to her knees. The yellow palm of her hand came out from the fold of her apron. Her fingers slid down and along the ground under the piece of money with the grace and care they would have in lifting an egg from under a setting hen. Then she slowly straightened up, she stood erect, and the nickel was in her apron pocket. A bird flew by. Her lips moved. "God watching me the whole time. I come to stealing."

The man came back, and his own dog panted about them. "Well, I scared him off that time," he said, and then he laughed and lifted his gun and pointed it at Phoenix.

She stood straight and faced him.

"Doesn't the gun scare you?" he said, still pointing it.

"No, sir, I seen plenty go off closer by, in my day, and for less than what I done," she said, holding utterly still.

He smiled, and shouldered the gun. "Well, Granny," he said, "you must be a hundred years old, and scared of nothing. I'd give you a dime if I had any money with me. But you take my advice and stay home, and nothing will happen to you."

"I bound to go on my way, mister," said Phoenix. She inclined her head in the red rag. Then they went in different directions, but she could hear the gun shooting again and again over the hill.

She walked on. The shadows hung from the oak trees to the road like curtains. Then she smelled wood-smoke, and smelled the river, and she saw a steeple and the cabins on their steep steps. Dozens of little black children whirled around her. There ahead was Natchez shining. Bells were ringing. She walked on.

In the paved city it was Christmas time. There were red and green electric lights strung and criss-crossed everywhere, and all turned on in the daytime. Old Phoenix would have been lost if she had not distrusted her eyesight and depended on her feet to know where to take her.

She paused quietly on the sidewalk where people were passing by. A lady came along in the crowd, carrying an armful of red-, green- and silver-wrapped presents; she gave off perfume like the red roses in hot summer, and Phoenix stopped her.

"Please, missy, will you lace up my shoe?" She held up her foot.

"What do you want, Grandma?"

"See my shoe," said Phoenix. "Do all right for out in the country, but wouln't look right to go in a big building."

"Stand still then, Grandma," said the lady. She put her packages down on the sidewalk beside her and laced and tied both shoes tightly.

"Can't lace 'em with a cane," said Phoenix. "Thank you, missy. I doesn't mind asking a nice lady to tie up my shoe, when I gets out on the street."

Moving slowly and from side to side, she went into the big building, and into a tower of steps, where she walked up and around and around until her feet knew to stop.

She entered a door, and there she saw nailed up on the wall the document that had been stamped with the gold seal and framed in the gold frame, which matched the dream that was hung up in her head.

"Here I be," she said. There was a fixed and ceremonial stiffness over her body.

"A charity case, I suppose," said an attendant who sat at the desk before her.

But Phoenix only looked above her head. There was sweat on her face, the wrinkles in her skin shone like a bright net.

"Speak up, Grandma," the woman said. "What's your name? We must have your history, you know. Have you been here before? What seems to be the trouble with you?"

Old Phoenix only gave a twitch to her face as if a fly were bothering her.

"Are you deaf?" cried the attendant.

But then the nurse came in.

"Oh, that's just old Aunt Phoenix," she said. "She doesn't come for herself— she has a little grandson. She makes these trips just as regular as clockwork. She lives away back off the Old Natchez Trace." She bent down. "Well, Aunt Phoenix, why don't you just take a seat? We won't keep you standing after your long trip." She pointed.

The old woman sat down, bolt upright in the chair.

"Now, how is the boy?" asked the nurse.

Old Phoenix did not speak.

"I said, how is the boy?"

But Phoenix only waited and stared straight ahead, her face very solemn and withdrawn into rigidity.

"Is his throat any better?" asked the nurse. "Aunt Phoenix, don't you hear me? Is your grandson's throat any better since the last time you came for the medicine?"

With her hands on her knees, the old woman waited, silent, erect and motionless, just as if she were in armor.

"You mustn't take up our time this way, Aunt Phoenix," the nurse said. "Tell us quickly about your grandson, and get it over. He isn't dead, is he?"

At last there came a flicker and then a flame of comprehension across her face, and she spoke.

"My grandson. It was my memory had left me. There I sat and forgot why I made my long trip."

"Forgot?" The nurse frowned. "After you came so far?"

Then Phoenix was like an old woman begging a dignified forgiveness for waking up frightened in the night. "I never did go to school, I was too old at the Surrender," she said in a soft voice. "I'm an old woman without an education. It was my memory fail me. My little grandson, he is just the same, and I forgot it in the coming."

"Throat never heals, does it?" said the nurse, speaking in a loud, sure voice to old Phoenix. By now she had a card with something written on it, a little list. "Yes. Swallowed lye. When was it?—January—two-three years ago—"

Phoenix spoke unasked now. "No, missy, he not dead, he just the same. Every little while his throat begin to close up again, and he not able to swallow. He not get his breath. He not able to help himself. So the time come around, and I go on another trip for the soothing medicine."

"All right. The doctor said as long as you came to get it, you could have it," said the nurse. "But it's an obstinate case."

"My little grandson, he sit up there in the house all wrapped up, waiting by himself," Phoenix went on. "We is the only two left in the world. He suffer and it don't seem to put him back at all. He got a sweet look. He going to last. He wear a little patch quilt and peep out holding his mouth open like a little bird. I remembers so plain now. I not going to forget him again, no, the whole enduring time. I could tell him from all the others in creation."

"All right." The nurse was trying to hush her now. She brought her a bottle of medicine. "Charity," she said, making a check mark in a book.

Old Phoenix held the bottle close to her eyes, and then carefully put it into her pocket.

"I thank you," she said.

"It's Christmas time, Grandma," said the attendant. "Could I give you a few pennies out of my purse?"

"Five pennies is a nickel," said Phoenix stiffly.

"Here's a nickel," said the attendant.

Phoenix rose carefully and held out her hand. She received the nickel and then fished the other nickel out of her pocket and laid it beside the new one. She stared at her palm closely, with her head on one side.

Then she gave a tap with her cane on the floor.

"This is what come to me to do," she said. "I going to the store and buy my child a little windmill they sells, made out of paper. He going to find it hard to believe there such a thing in the world. I'll march myself back where he waiting, holding it straight up in this hand."

She lifted her free hand, gave a little nod, turned around, and walked out of the doctor's office. Then her slow step began on the stairs, going down.

Appendix B

HOW MUCH DO YOU KNOW ABOUT CITING SOURCES? A QUIZ WITH ANSWERS[1]

Taking the quiz below will let you test yourself and will assist you in any discussion you have with your classmates about how to cite sources accurately and honestly.

QUIZ YOURSELF: HOW MUCH DO YOU KNOW ABOUT CITING SOURCES?

Section 1: Plagiarism and Academic Dishonesty

Which of the following examples describe violations of academic integrity? Check all the examples that are punishable under university rules.

_____ 1. You buy a term paper from a Web site and turn it in as your own work.

_____ 2. You ask a friend to write a paper for you.

_____ 3. You can't find the information you need, so you invent statistics, quotes, and sources that do not exist and cite them in your paper as if they were real.

_____ 4. Your professor requires you to use five sources, but you find one book written by one person that has all the information you need, so you cite that book as if it were information coming from other books and authors in order to make it look like you used five different sources.

---

[1]This quiz and the answers were written by Carmen Lowe, Director of the Tufts University Academic Resource Center. We are grateful to Ms. Lowe for permission to use her material.

_____ 5. Your history professor and your political science professor both assign a term paper. To save time, you write one paper that meets both requirements and hand it in to both professors.

_____ 6. You don't want to have too many quotes in your paper, so you do not put quotation marks around some sentences you copied from a source. You cite the source correctly at the end of the paragraph and in your bibliography.

_____ 7. You have copied a long passage from a book into your paper, and you changed some of the wording. You cite the source at the end of the passage and again in the bibliography.

_____ 8. While writing a long research paper, you come across an interesting hypothesis mentioned in a book, and you incorporate this hypothesis into your main argument. After you finish writing the paper, you can't remember where you initially found the hypothesis, so you don't bother to cite the source of your idea.

Section 2: Common Knowledge

Common knowledge is information that is widely known within a society or an intellectual community; therefore, if you include common knowledge in your paper, you do not need to cite where you found that information.

Answer _Yes_ or _No_ to the following questions:

_____ 1. In a high school class on American government, you learned about the checks-and-balances system of government which separates power into the judicial, executive, and legislative branches. Now, you are writing a paper for an introductory political science class and you mention the concept of checks-and-balances you learned in high school. Should you cite your old high school textbook?

_____ 2. In writing a paper about pop culture in the 1980s, you want to include the year that Reagan was shot but you cannot remember if it was 1980 or 1981, so you look up the correct date in an encyclopedia. Do you have to include that encyclopedia as a source for the date on which Reagan was shot?

_____ 3. You do most of your research online and find lots of interesting Web sites from which you quote several passages. After you write the first draft, you ask your older and more experienced roommate if he knows how to cite Web sites. He says that Web sites are in the public domain and constitute common knowledge, and therefore they do not need to be cited. Is this true?

_____ 4. In writing a research paper on astrophysics, you come across something called the Eridanus Effect several times. You have never heard of this effect nor discussed it in your class, but after reading about it in six different astrophysics journal articles, you have a pretty clear idea of what it is and its most common characteristics. Is the Eridanus Effect common knowledge within astrophysics?

_____ 5. Your older sister works for a nonprofit organization that runs adult literacy programs in factories and unemployment centers in several major cities. During winter break, she tells you about the success of one of the programs in St. Louis and the innovative curricula it has designed. Several weeks into spring semester, you remember your conversation as you are writing an economics term paper on empowerment zones and unemployment in the inner city. If you include a description of the program, do you need to cite a source, even if it is just your sister?

_____ 6. You are writing a paper on Shakespeare's *Hamlet*. Your textbook's introduction to the play mentions that Shakespeare was born in 1564 in Stratford-upon-Avon. You mention these facts in your paper's introduction. Do you need to cite the introduction to your textbook?

_____ 7. You are writing a paper on Shakespeare's *Hamlet*. A footnote in your textbook mentions that some literary historians now believe that Shakespeare himself played the ghost when the play was first performed. If you mention Shakespeare playing the ghost, do you need to cite this footnote in your textbook?

_____ 8. You are writing a paper on the assassination of Robert Kennedy. The three major biographies on him mention when he was killed and by whom. Do you have to cite all these biographies when you mention the date and murderer of RFK?

_____ 9. You are writing a paper on the assassination of Robert Kennedy. The most influential biography on him mentions a controversial conspiracy theory first put forward in the early 1970s by a journalist for the *Washington Post*. When you mention this conspiracy theory, should you cite the biography?

Section 3: Quoting, Paraphrasing, and Summarizing Texts

Read the following passage excerpted from an online edition of a foreign policy magazine. Determine whether any of the sample sentences that follow are improperly cited within the sentence or plagiarized.

> The illegal trade in drugs, arms, intellectual property, people, and money is booming. Like the war on terrorism, the fight to control these illicit markets pits governments against agile, stateless, and resourceful networks empowered by globalization. Governments will continue to lose these wars until they adopt new strategies to deal with a larger, unprecedented struggle that now shapes the world as much as confrontations between nation-states once did.
>
> —Moisés Naím, "The Five Wars of Globalization,"
> *Foreign Policy* Jan.-Feb. 2003.

Read the following passages and mark **OK** if the passage is fine. If the passage is plagiarized, improperly paraphrased, or otherwise cited inadequately, mark it **X**.

_____ 1. In his essay on "The Five Wars of Globalization," Moisés Naím argues that governments need to find new ways to handle the kinds of borderless illegal activity increasing under globalization.

_____ 2. In describing the "illegal trade in drugs, arms, intellectual property, people, and money" as "booming," Moisés Naím asserts that governments need to adopt new strategies to deal with this unprecedented struggle that now shapes the world (http://www.foreignpolicy.com).

_____ 3. Like the war on terror, the struggle to control illegal trade in drugs, arms, money, etc., pits governments against cunning, stateless, and enterprising networks empowered by globalization (Moises 2003).

_____ 4. Many experts believe that globalization is changing the face of foreign policy.

Read the following passage from a book on romance novels and soap operas, then read the citations of it that follow to determine whether any are plagiarized or improperly cited within the sentence.

> The complexity of women's responses to romances has not been sufficiently acknowledged. Instead of exploring the possibility that romances, while

serving to keep women in their place, may at the same time be concerned with real female problems, analysts of women's romances have generally seen the fantasy embodied in romantic fiction either as evidence of female "masochism" or as a simple reflection of the dominant masculine ideology. For instance, Germaine Greer, referring to the idealized males of women's popular novels, says, "This is the hero that women have chosen for themselves. The traits invented for him have been invented by women cherishing the chains of their bondage." But this places too much blame on women, and assumes a freedom of choice which is not often in evidence— not in their lives and therefore certainly not in their popular arts.

> —Tania Modleski, *Loving with a Vengeance: Mass-Produced Fantasies for Women* (1982), 37-38.

Read the following passages and mark **OK** if the passage is fine as is. If the passage is plagiarized in part or whole or is otherwise cited improperly, mark it **X**.

_____ 1. Tania Modleski claims that Germaine Greer oversimplifies why women read romance novels (38).

_____ 2. Modleski states that although romance novels may keep women in their place, they also address real female problems (37).

_____ 3. Feminist critics see the fantasy embodied in romance novels either as evidence of female "masochism" or as a simple reflection of male chauvinism (Modleski 37-38).

_____ 4. One feminist writer, Germaine Greer, says that the idealized male featured in women's popular romance novels "is the hero that women have chosen for themselves. The traits invented for him have been invented by women cherishing the chains of their bondage."(38).

_____ 5. Tania Modleski rejects the idea that the fantasies expressed in romance novels are merely a reflection of some innate masochism in women who, in the words of Germaine Greer, "cherish . . . the chains of their bondage" (37; Greer qtd. in Modleski, 38).

Section 4: Miscellaneous

_____ 1. **You read *Time* magazine every week and notice that the writers in the magazine never use footnotes or parenthetical citations. Why don't newswriters cite their sources?**
   a. Citing sources is required only of students, not professional writers.

    b. Professional publications are free to decide if they will require footnotes or citations of any kind.

    c. Newspapers and magazines have limited space on the page, so they cut off the citations or footnotes to make room for more copy.

_____ 2. **Plagiarism is a violation of which of the following laws:**

    a. Copyright.

    b. Intellectual property.

    c. Both (a) and (b) above.

    d. None of the above; it is not a legal issue and is not punishable by law because it pertains only to students.

_____ 3. **If you use a quote found in a book of quotes or from an online compilation of quotes, such as Bartlett's, how do you cite the quote?**

    a. You don't—quotes found in a collection of quotations (whether online or in a book) are considered well-known and in the public domain. Just include the name of the person to whom the quote is attributed. You can also add the date if it seems relevant.

    b. You should cite the original source of the quote followed by the bibliographic information from the quotation compilation, such as: Shakespeare, William. *A Midsummer Night's Dream.* Quoted in *Familiar Quotations: Being an Attempt to Trace to Their Sources Passages and Phrases in Common Use,* by John Bartlett (Boston: Little, Brown, 1886), 44.

    c. You should find the original source and cite that.

    d. All of the above: (a) is correct, and (b) and (c) are possible options if you want to be extra careful or if the quote is extremely important to your paper. Use your common sense in this situation.

ANSWER KEY TO PLAGIARISM QUIZ

The Plagiarism Quiz works best when the answers are discussed in class or one-on-one with a student and professor.

Section 1: Plagiarism and Academic Dishonesty

All eight incidents are forms of plagiarism or academic dishonesty. Many students are confused about the last four incidents, so please discuss them with your instructor if you need clarification.

Section 2: Common Knowledge

1. No; the basic facts about the checks-and-balances system are common knowledge and do not need to be cited.
2. No; even if you cannot remember the exact date of the assassination attempt on Reagan, it is common knowledge because the date is undisputed and can be found in a variety of sources.
3. No; writing on the Web is protected by copyright and must be cited, even if no author is listed.
4. Yes; it's common knowledge if it appears *undocumented* in five or more sources.
5. Yes; such a small program would not be widely known, so you should cite your sister as a source if you mention it. If you describe the program in more detail, it would make sense to research documents or newspaper descriptions and cite them rather than Big Sis.
6. No; the date and location of Shakespeare's birth is not in dispute and can be found in many sources, so it is common knowledge even if you did not know it.
7. Hmmm. This is a tricky situation. Since *some,* but not all, literary historians believe Shakespeare himself played the ghost, this is probably common knowledge among Shakespeare experts. You, however, are not a Shakespeare expert, so it would be wise to cite the footnote just to be safe. So, the answer is, Yes—cite it!
8. No; undisputed dates are common knowledge.
9. Yes; conspiracy theories are controversial, and the details of such controversies need to be cited.

Section 3: Quoting, Paraphrasing, and Summarizing Texts

Illegal Trade Passage:

1. OK; an example of summary. The sentence gives the author and the title. (Remember, the bibliography would provide more publication information.)
2. X; two things are wrong: some of the language is the same as the original, and the citation method is incorrect. Do not list the URL in your paper. The phrase "adopt new strategies to deal with this unprecedented struggle that now shapes the world" is too close to the source, in some places identical to it.

3. X; this paraphrase is too close to the original. The writer used a thesaurus to change key words, but the sentence structure is identical to the original. Plus, the author's last name (not first name) should appear in the parenthetical citation. (Also, using "etc" in the text is annoying!)
4. OK; This is common knowledge. The sentence is so general, it really has nothing to do with the passage from Moisés Naím, so there is no reason to cite him.

Romance Novel Passage:

1. OK; this summary is correct; the author's name appears in the sentence so it does not need to appear in the parenthetical citation.
2. X; although the source is documented properly, some of the language is too close to the source, especially the phrases "keep women in their place" and "real female problems." These phrases need to be put into quotation marks or rewritten.
3. X; most of this sentence is copied directly from the source; it needs to be rewritten or partially enclosed in quotes.
4. X; the quote is properly attributed to Greer, but the page number refers to Modleski's book. Also, the last word, bondage, should be followed by the quotation mark (not a period), a space, then the citation in parentheses and the period.
5. OK; this example shows how to properly cite one writer quoted within the work of another. Also note how the ellipsis indicates that something was deleted to make the quote flow better.

Section 4: Miscellaneous

1. (c)
2. (c)
3. (d)

Credits

Robert M. Adams: "Ibsen on the Contrary" in *Modern Drama*, ed. Anthony Caputi, New York: Norton, 1966.

W. H. Auden: *The Dyer's Hand and Other Essays*. New York: Random House, 1962.

Julia Bird: "14: a txt msg pom," *The Guardian*, May 3, 2001. Copyright Guardian News & Media Ltd 2001. Reprinted by permission.

William Blake: "The Sick Rose," 1794; "The Tyger," *Songs of Experience*, 1794.

Wayne Booth: *The Rhetoric of Fiction*, 2nd ed. Chicago: The University of Chicago Press, 1983.

Cleanth Brooks: "My Credo—The Formalist Critics," *The Kenyon Review 13:1*, (Winter 1951).

Gwendolyn Brooks: "We Real Cool" from *The Bean Eaters*. © 1960. Reprinted by consent of Brooks Permissions.

Kate Chopin: "Ripe Figs," 1893; "The Story of an Hour," 1894.

Joseph Conrad: *Heart of Darkness*, 1902.

Emily Dickinson: "Wild nights—wild nights!" Reprinted by permission of the publishers and the Trustees of Amherst College from *The Poems of Emily Dickinson*, Thomas H. Johnson, ed., Cambridge, Mass: The Belknap Press of Harvard University Press, Copyright © 1951, 1955, 1979, 1983 by the President and Fellows of Harvard College.

John Donne: "The Flea," 1633.

Elizabeth Drew: *The Novel: A Modern Guide to Fifteen English Masterpieces*. New York: Dell Publishing Co., 1963.

Francis Fergusson: *The Human Image in Dramatic Literature*. Garden City, NY: Doubleday, 1957.

Edward FitzGerald: "The Rubáiyát of Omar Khayyám," 1859.

E. M. Forster: *Aspects of the Novel*. London: Edward Arnold, 1927.

Robert Frost: "Stopping by Woods on a Snowy Evening" and "The Span of Life" from *The Poetry of Robert Frost*, edited by Edward Connery Lathem. Copyright 1936, 1951 by Robert Frost, copyright 1964 by Lesley Frost Ballantine, copyright 1923, 1969 by Henry Holt and Company. Reprinted by permission of Henry Holt and Company, LLC; "The Telephone," *Mountain Interval*, 1916.

Northrop Frye: *The Well-Tempered Critic*. Bloomington, IN: Indiana University Press, 1963.

Helen Gardner: *The Noble Moor*. London: Oxford University Press for The British Academy, 1956.

Martin Green: *Re-Appraisals: Some Commonsense Readings in American Literature*. New York: Norton, 1965.

Ernest Hemingway: "The Killers," *Scribner's Magazine*, 1927.

Robert Herrick: "Upon Julia's Clothes," 1648.

A. E. Housman: "Eight O'Clock," 1922.

Langston Hughes, "Ballad of the Landlord," "Harlem (2)" [A Dream Deferred], "Ruby Brown," and "The South" from *The Collected Poems of Langston Hughes* by Langston Hughes, edited by Arnold Rampersad with David Roessel, Associate Editor, copyright © 1994 by the Estate of Langston Hughes. Used by permission of Alfred A. Knopf, a division of Random House, Inc. (print), and by permission of Harold Ober Associates Incorporated (electronic).

James Joyce: "Araby," *Dubliners*, 1916.

Suzanne Juhasz: *Feminist Critics Read Emily Dickinson*. Bloomington, IN: Indiana University Press, 1983.

John Keats: "On first looking into Chapman's Homer," 1816.

Bernard Knox: "Sophocles' Oedipus," *Tragic Themes in Western Literature*, Cleanth Brooks, ed. New Haven, CT: Yale University Press, 1955.

D. H. Lawrence: *Lady Chatterley's Lover*, 1928.

Edna St. Vincent Millay: "I, being born a woman and distressed" from *Collected Poems*. Copyright 1923, 1951 by Edna St. Vincent Millay and Normal Millay Ellis. Reprinted by permission of Holly Peppe, Literary Executor, The Millay Society.

Pat Mora: "Immigrants" is reprinted by permission from the publisher of *Borders* by Pat Mora (© 1986 Arte Publico Press-University of Houston).

Richard G. Moulton: *Shakespeare as a Dramatic Artist*, 1893.

Kenneth Muir: *William Shakespeare: The Great Tragedies*. London: Longmans, Green, 1961.

"The Parable of the Prodigal Son." From the Gospel of Luke (15:11–32).

Alexander Pope: "Awake, My St. John," 1734.

From Revised Standard Version of the Bible, copyright 1952 [2nd edition, 1971] by the Division of Christian Education of the National Council of Churches of Christ in the United States of America. Used by permission. All rights reserved.

Adrienne Rich: From "When We Dead Awaken: Writing as Re-Vision," *College English* 34.1 (October 1972).

Christina Rossetti: "A Better Resurrection," 1862.

Richard B. Sewall: *The Vision of Tragedy*. New Haven: Yale University Press, 1959.

William Shakespeare: *Richard II*, 1595.

Mark Twain: *Adventures of Huckleberry Finn*, 1884.

Eudora Welty: "A Worn Path," from *A Curtain of Green and Other Stories*, copyright 1941 and renewed 1969 by Eudora Welty. Reprinted by permission of Harcourt, Inc.

Walt Whitman: "By Blue Ontario's Shore," 1881; "When I Heard the Learn'd Astronomer," 1865.

Edmund Wilson: *The Wound and the Bow*. New York: Oxford University Press, 1947.

William Wordsworth: "A Slumber Did My Spirit Seal," 1800.

W. B. Yeats: "The Balloon of the Mind," *The Wild Swans at Coole*, 1919; "The friends that have it I do wrong," *Collected Works in Verse and Prose*, Volume Two, 1908; "The Lake Isle of Innisfree," 1893.

Index of Authors, Titles, and First Lines of Poems

Adams, Robert M., 200
Anonymous
   The Judgment of Solomon, 52
Araby, 353–57
"A slumber did my spirit seal," 241
Auden, W. H., 187, 248, 292
Austen, Jane, 147

Ballad of the Landlord, 286
Balloon of the Mind, The, 245
Baudelaire, Charles, 108
Better Resurrection, A, 104
Bible
   Judgment of Solomon, 52
   The Prodigal Son, The, 55
Blake, William
   The Sick Rose, 236
   The Tyger, 68
Bodkin, Maud 115
Booth, Wayne, 147–48
Brontë, Emily, 140–41
Brooks, Gwendolyn
   We Real Cool, 60
Buffalo Bill 's, 277
Burke, Kenneth, 322
Byron, Lord, 304

Carroll, Lewis, 179, 292
Canetti, Elias, 184
Cather, Willa, 130
Carrillo, Tony
   F Minus, 183
Carlyle, Thomas, 101, 108
Carter, Angela, 89
Chopin, Kate
   Ripe Figs, 8, 141
      Student Essay on "Ripe Figs," 14
   The Story of an Hour, 20–22, 142

Student Essays on "The Story of
   an Hour," 39–41, 143–46
Conrad, Joseph, 155, 292
Cummings, E. E.
   Buffalo Bill 's, 277

Death on the Ridge Road, 181
Dickinson, Emily
   Wild Nights–Wild Nights!, 222
Didion, Joan, 292
Donne, John
   The Flea, 242
Drew, Elizabeth, 302

Eight O'Clock, 260
Eliot, T. S., 101, 257
Emerson, Ralph Waldo, 70, 315
Empson, William, 43

Fergusson, Francis, 201
Fetterley, Judith, 111
Fish, Stanley, 114
FitzGerald, Edward
   Rubáiyát of Omar Khayyám, 103
Flea, The, 242
F Minus, 183
*Friends that Have It I Do
      Wrong, The*, 73
Foes in '76, Friends in '85, 275
Forster, E. M, 184
Friedman, Norman, 306
Frost, Robert, 19, 82, 92, 221, 224,
   227, 281
   The Span of Life, 85
   *Stopping by Woods on a Snowy
      Evening*, 95
      Student Essay on "Stopping by Woods
         on a Snowy Evening," 96–97

Frost, Robert (*continued*)
  The Telephone, 227
Freytag, Gustav, 131
Frye, Northrop, 84, 294

Gardner, Helen, 295, 300
Glaspell, Susan
  Student Essay on *Trifles*, 210–13
Green, Martin, 295

"Hands, do what you're bid," 245
Harlem, 44
Hemingway, Ernest, 2
"He stood, and heard the steeple," 260
Herrick, Robert
  Upon Julia's Clothes, 237
    Student Essay on "Upon Julia's
      Clothes," 239–40
Housman, A. E.
  Eight O'Clock, 260
    Student Essay about "Eight
      O'Clock," 259–62
Hughes, Langston
  Ballad of the Landlord, 286
  Harlem, 44
    Student Essay on "Harlem,"
      48–49
  Ruby Brown, 285
  South, The, 283
    Student Essay on Hughes's
      poems, 287–89
Hurston, Zora Neale, 315

Ibsen, Henri
  A Doll's House, 208
  Hedda Gabler, 209
"I, being born a woman and
      distressed," 224
Immigrants, 92

Jackson, Shirley
  Student Essay on "The Lottery,"
    168–71
James, Henry, 132

Johnson, Samuel, 103
Joyce, James
  Araby, 353–57
    Foreshadowing in, 138
    Student Essay on "Araby," 152–54
Judgment of Solomon, The, 52
Juhasz, Suzanne, 121

Kafka, Franz, 83
Keats, John
  *On First Looking into Chapman's
    Homer*, 232
Knox, Bernard, 195
Kundera, Milan, 130

"Landlord, landlord," 286
Lawrence, D. H., 2, 105–06
Leonardo da Vinci, 267

"Mark but this flea, and
      mark in this," 242
Menander, 201
Millay, Edna, St. Vincent, "I, being
      born a woman and
      distressed," 234
Miller, Arthur
  Death of a Salesman, 209–10
    Student Essay on *Death of a
      Salesman*, 340–47
Mora, Pat
  Immigrants, 92
Morrison, Toni, 8
Moulton, Richard G., 201
"Much have I traveled in the
      realms of gold," 232
Muir, Kenneth, 206
Murasaki, Lady, 80
Murphy's Law, 108
"My life is like a broken bowl," 104

Nemerov, Howard, 56, 274
Notman, William
  Foes in '76, Friends in '85, 275

*On First Looking into Chapman's
    Homer,* 232
"O rose, thou art sick!" 236

Parable of the Prodigal Son, 55
Poirier, Richard, 304
Pound, Ezra, 80, 249
Pope, Alexander, 249
Prodigal Son, The, 55

Rampersad, Arnold, 327
Rich, Adrienne, 121
Richards, I. A., 101
Ripe Figs, 8
Rossetti, Christina,
    A Better Resurrection, 104
Ruskin, John, 89
Rubáiyát of Omar Khayyám, 103
Ruby Brown, 285

Salinger, J. D.
    Student Essay on *Catcher in the
        Rye,* 135–37
Sewall, Richard B., 306
Sexton, Anne
    The Starry Night, 270
        Student Essay on *The Starry
            Night,* 270–71
Shakespeare, William, 249–50
    As You Like It, 198
    Hamlet, 206
    Student Essay on *Hamlet,* 217–20
    Julius Caesar, 201–02
    Macbeth, 305
        Student Essay on *Macbeth,* 75–78
"When I do count the clock," 249–50
"She was young and beautiful," 285
Sick Rose, The, 236
Slumber Did My Spirit Seal, A, 241
South, The, 283
Span of Life, The, 85
Starry Night, The, 270

*Stopping by Woods on a Snowy
    Evening,* 95
Story of an Hour, The, 20–22
Styron, William, 2

Telephone, The, 227
"The friends that have it I do wrong," 73
"The lazy, laughing South," 283
"The old dog barks backward, without
    getting up," 85
"The town does not exist," 270
Twain, Mark, 149, 294
Tyger, The, 68
"Tyger! Tyger! burning bright," 68

Updike, John, 130
Upon Julia's Clothes, 237

Van Gogh, Vincent,
    The Starry Night, 269

Welty, Eudora, 156
    A Worn Path, 357–63
        Student Essay on "A Worn Path,"
            157–63
"What happens to a dream
    deferred" 44
"Whenas in silk my Julia goes," 237
*When I Heard the Learn'd
    Astronomer,* 256
"When I was just as far as I could
    walk," 227
Whitman, Walt
    *When I Heard the Learn'd
        Astronomer,* 256–57
"Whose woods these are I think I
    know, " 95
Wild Nights–Wild Nights!, 222
Wilde, Oscar, 108
Wilder, Thornton, 187
Williams, Tennessee
    Student Essay on *The Glass
        Menagerie,* 187–93

Wilson, Edmund, 302
Wood, Grant,
   Death on the Ridge Road, 181
Wordsworth, William
   A slumber did my spirit seal, 241
Worn Path, A, 357–63
"Wrap their babies in the American
   flag," 92

Yeats, William Butler, 105
   The Balloon of the Mind, 245
      Student Essay on "The Balloon of
      the Mind," 245–47
   *The friends that have it
      I do wrong*, 73

Index of Terms

accent, 248–50
action, 200–02
active voice, 35, 298–99
alliteration, 254
anagnorisis, 195
analysis, 51–55, 112
    vs. summary, 41
anapest, anapestic, 251
annotations, 11–12, 19, 45, 133, 138,
        237–38, 245–46
antecedent action, 203
antithesis, 255
apostrophe, 234, 314
archetype, 115–16
archetypal criticism, 115–16, 125
arguing a thesis, 29–31
argument, 29, 49, 66, 93
aside, 207
asking questions, 25–26, 284
assonance, 254,
assumptions, 109–10
atmosphere, 140–41
audience
    for essay, 3, 6, 13
    in a poem, 265

bibliography, 330–40
bibliographic guides, 316–20
biographical criticism, 118, 126
blank verse, 256
brackets, 311, 322
brainstorming, 22

caesura, 252
causation, 131
character, characterization, 53,
        131–32, 173–74, 206–07, 215
character, archetypal, 115

checklists
    basics, 7
    clarity, revising for, 34–35
    comedy, 199
    comparison, revising a, 59
    conciseness, 299
    draft, revised, 36–37
    drama, 214–16
    editing, 67
    explication, drafting, 50
    fiction 172–76
    film based on fiction, 176–78
    film based on drama, 216
    Internet sources, 350
    interpretation, 99
    paragraphs, 307–08
    peer review, 38
    plagiarism, avoiding, 328–29
    plot, 204
    poetry, 264–66
    research paper, draft of, 347–48
    theme, 163
    tragedy, 197
    web sites, using, 349–50
citations, parenthetic, 329–30
clarity, 34–35
climax, 201
closed couplet, 255
coherence, 301–04
comedy, 193, 197–99
common knowledge, 327–28
comparison, 56–59, 274–76
complex sentences, 300
complication, 130
conciseness, 297–99
concluding paragraphs, 37, 66–67, 98,
        171, 263, 305–07
concreteness, 294
conflict, 130, 201, 204, 214

connotation, 293
consistency building, 10
consonance, 254
content (meaning), 83–86
contrast. See comparison
convention, 207–08
conventional symbol, 236
costumes, 208
couplet, 255.
counterevidence, 28, 94,
crisis, 201
critical standards, 102–06
critical thinking, 3, 17–18, 27–29, 94–99
criticism, 101–27
    archetypal, 115–16, 125
    biographical, 118, 126
    deconstructive, 112–13
    evaluative, 62–63
    feminist, 110–12, 120–22, 127
    formalist, 110–12, 124
    gay, 122–23, 127
    gender, 119–23, 127
    historical, 116–17, 125
    lesbian, 122–23, 127
    Marxist, 117, 125–26
    myth, 115–16, 125
    New Criticism, 100–12, 124
    New Historicism, 117–18, 126
    psychological (psychoanalytic),
        124, 126
    reader response, 113–15, 127
    cultural context, 91
cultural studies, 86–87

dactyl (dactylic), 251
dash, 308
deconstruction, 112–13, 124–25
denotation, 293
dénouement, 130, 201
diction, 223–26, 265–66
dimeter, 252
discourses, 86–87
documentation, 322–52

draft, 31–38, 64–65
    checklist for revising, 36–37
    outlining, 31, 35–36
    research paper, 325–26
drama, 187–220
    writing a review of, 74–78
dramatic irony, 195n
dramatic point of view, 148

economy, 297–99
editing, 34, 67
effaced narrator, 148
electronic sources, 348–52
    documenting, 350–52
elegiac quatrain, 256
ellipsis, 311–12, 321
emphasis, 308
end rhyme, 254
end-stopped line, 252
English sonnet, 256
enjambment, 252
essay,
    choosing a title, 16, 41, 49, 65, 96,
        154, 171, 239, 309–10
    organization of, 205
evaluation, 101–07
    communicating, 62–63
evidence, 28, 49, 61, 93, 106, 133
exact rhyme, 253
examples, 294
exclamation marks, 308, 330
explication, 43–45, 244–48
exposition, 203–04
eye rhyme, 254

falling action, 201
feminine ending, 252
feminine rhyme, 254
feminist criticism, 120–22, 127
figurative language, 231–37
film
    based on fiction, 176–78
    based on drama, 216

first-person (participant) point of view, 149–51
first person, use of in essay, 63
focused free writing, 23–24
foil, 206–07
foot, metrical, 250
foreshadowing, 137–40, 204
form, 52–53, 80–88, 265
formalist criticism, 110–12, 124
format of essay, 309–14
free verse, 256
free writing, 23–24
Freytag's pyramid, 131

gaps, 10
gay criticism, 122–23, 127
gender criticism, 119–23, 127
gestures, 207–08
graphic fiction, 179–86

half-rhyme, 253
hamartia, 195–96
heptameter, 252
heroic couplet, 255
heroic quatrain, 256
hexameter, 252
highlighting, 11
historical criticism, 116–17, 125
hubris, hybris, 193–94
hyperbole, 244
hyphen, 308

"I," use of, 63
iamb, iambic, 251
image, imagery, 235–37
indeterminacy, 10, 112
innocent eye, 150
intention, 90
internal rhyme, 254
Internet, 348–49
interpretation, 89–100, 114
    checklist, 99
intrinsic criticism, 111

introductory paragraphs, 16, 41, 65–66, 98, 133, 171, 262, 304–05
irony, 194–95
    dramatic, 195n
    Sophoclean, 195
    unconscious, 150, 194–95
    verbal, 195n
Italian sonnet, 256
italics, 314

jargon, 294–95
journal, keeping a, 26–27, 46–47, 228–29, 245–46
judgments, 62–63

lead in (to quotations), 37
lesbian criticism, 122–23, 127
listing, 24–25
literacy, visual, 179
literature, nature of, 80–88
    as performance, 102
litotes, 244
logical structure, 242

manuscript form, 309–14
Marxist criticism, 117, 125–26,
masculine ending, 252
masculine rhyme, 254
mask, 221
meaning, 83–86, 89–100, 111, 114
metaphor, 231–32
meter, 250–52
metonymy, 233
MLA style, 329–43
monometer, 252
morality, 103–04
motivation, 131–32, 206–07
myth, 115
myth criticism, 115–16, 125

narrative structure, 241
narrator, 147–54. See also *point of view*
New Criticism, 110–12, 124

New Historicism, 117, 126
nonparticipant (third-person
        point of view), 147–49
nonverbal language, 215. See also
        visual literacy
notes, taking, 12–13, 133, 320–22

objective point of view, 148
octave, octet, 256
octosyllabic couplet, 255
off-rhyme, 253
omniscient narrator, 147–49
onomatopoeia, 254
open form, 258
organization
        of comparison, 57–58
        of explication, 47, 49
        of essay, 16, 61–62, 134, 155
outline, 5, 35–36
overstatement, 244

paradox, 244
paragraphs, 301–08
        coherence, 303–04
        concluding, 16, 37, 41, 49, 98,
            171, 263, 305–07
        introductory, 16, 41, 49, 65–66,
            98, 133, 171, 262, 304–05
        length of, 302
        unity in, 301–03
parallels, 299–300
paraphrase, 72–73, 82, 321
parenthetical citations, 329–30
participant (first-person) point
        of view, 149–51
passive voice, 35, 298–99
peer review, 6, 37–38
pentameter, 252
perfect rhyme, 253
performance, literature as, 102
peripeteia, 195
persona, 221
personification, 234

Petrarchan sonnet, 256
pictures, 179–96
        and poems, 267–80
        writing about, 273–74
plagiarism, 327–29, 364–71
plot, 130–32, 173, 201–05, 214
plot, archetypal, 115
poems, poetry, 221–80
point of view, 147–54, 174
polish, 33–34
possessive, 314
present tense, 41, 71
pre-writing, 19, 63–64
primary material, 316, 326–27
process, writing as a, 4–7
prologue, 203
prompts for writing, 134
pronouns, reference and
        agreement, 35
proofreading, 42
prose, 248
prosody, 248–62
proverbs, 81–82
psychological (psychoanalytic)
        criticism, 119, 126
punctuation with quotation marks,
        313–14, 330
purpose, 13–14
pyramidal structure, 131
pyrrhic, 251

quatrain, 256
queer theory, 122
questions, asking, 25–26, 284,
        on drama, 214–16
        on one's own essay, 36–37, 67,,
        on fiction, 172–76
        on film of literary work, 176–78,
        on poetry, 284
quotation marks, 310–12
        punctuation with, 313–14, 330
        vs. italics, 314
quotations

additions to, 311–12
citing, 329–30
evidence, 16, 311
leading into, 37, 311
long vs. short, 312–13, 332
omissions from, 311–12
punctuation with, 313–14, 330
use of, 16, 155, 310–11

reader (audience), 3, 4, 6, 13
reader-response criticism,
    113–15, 127
realism, 103–04
recognition, 195
reference of pronouns, 35
reference works, 316–20
    repetition, 295–97
repetitive structure, 241
research, 315–52
resolution, 130
responsive reading, 12–13,
    164–67, 264
reversal, 195
review, of a dramatic production,
    74–78
revision, 5–7, 34–35, 65–66
rhyme, 253
rhythm, 248–50, 253
rising action, 201
romantic comedy, 198
run-on line, 252

satiric comedy, 198
scansion, 248–53
secondary sources, 164–67, 316,
    326–27
selective omniscience, 147
sentences
    complex, 300
    topic, 302
sestet, 256
setting, 140–41, 175, 209
Shakespearean sonnet, 256

signal words, 304
simile, 231
soliloquy, 207
sonnet, 256
Sophoclean irony, 195
soundtrack, 177–78
sources, primary and secondary,
    164–67, 316, 326–27
    speaker, 221, 264–65
spondee, spondaic, 251
square brackets, 311, 322
standards, 101–07
stanza, 255–58
stress, 248–50
structure,
    logical, 242
    narrative, 241
    of poem, 237–43, 265
    pyramidal, 131
    repetitive, 241
style, 175, 292–308
subordination, 300–01
summary, 70–71, 171, 321
    vs. analysis, 41
suspense, 140
symbol, symbolism, 141–46, 177,
    235–37
synecdoche, 233–24
synthesis, 322–25

technical terms, 294–95
tense, present, 41
tercet, 256
tetrameter, 252
text, 86–87
theme, 155–63, 176, 199–201
thesis, 17, 29–31, 66, 305
thesis sentence, 30, 133
third person point of view, 147–49
title
    capitalization in, 310
    choosing a, 16, 41, 49, 65, 96, 154,
        171, 239, 309–10

in quotation marks, or underlined
(italicized), 314
significance of, 173
tone, 149, 223–26, 264–65
topic, 60–61. See also *thesis*
topic idea, 302
topic sentence, 302
tragedy, 193–97
tragic error (or flaw), 195–96
transitions, 303–04
trimeter, 252
triple rhyme, 254
triplet, 256
trochee, trochaic, 251
truth (in literature), 103–04

unconscious irony, 150
underlining, 314
understatement, 244

unity, in paragraphs, 301–03
unreliable narrator, 150
URL, 350

variation, 295–97
verbal irony, 195n, 244
vers libre, 256–57
verse, 255
verse paragraph, 256
versification, 250–63
visual literacy, 179
voice, 221

Web page, web site, 349–50
Wikipedia, 350
wordiness, 297–99
Works Cited, 330–40
World Wide Web, 348-50
writing process, 4-7